Lecture Notes in Artificial Intelligence   1202

Subseries of Lecture Notes in Computer Science
Edited by J. G. Carbonell and J. Siekmann

Lecture Notes in Computer Science

Edited by G. Goos, J. Hartmanis and J. van Leeuwen

Springer
Berlin
Heidelberg
New York
Barcelona
Budapest
Hong Kong
London
Milan
Paris
Santa Clara
Singapore
Tokyo

Peter Kandzia   Matthias Klusch (Eds.)

Cooperative Information Agents

First International Workshop, CIA'97
Kiel, Germany, February 26-28, 1997
Proceedings

 Springer

Series Editors
Jaime G. Carbonell, Carnegie Mellon University, Pittsburgh, PA, USA
Jörg Siekmann, University of Saarland, Saarbrücken, Germany

Volume Editors

Peter Kandzia
Matthias Klusch
Universität Kiel, Institut für Informatik und Praktische Mathematik
Olshausenstraße 40, D-24118 Kiel, Germany
E-mail: (pk/mkl)@informatik.uni-kiel.de

Cataloging-in-Publication Data applied for

Die Deutsche Bibliothek - CIP-Einheitsaufnahme

Cooperative information guide : first international workshop ; proceedings / CIA, '97,
Kiel, Germany, February 26 - 28, 1997. Peter Kandzia ; Matthias Klusch (ed.). - Berlin ;
Heidelberg ; New York ; Barcelona ; Budapest ; Hong Kong ; London ; Milan ; Paris ; Santa
Clara ; Singapore ; Tokyo : Springer, 1997
  (Lecture notes in computer science ; 1202 : Lecture notes in artificial intelligence)
  ISBN 3-540-62591-7

NE: Kandzia, Peter [Hrsg.]; CIA <1, 1997, Kiel>; GT

CR Subject Classification (1991): I.2, H.2, C.2.4, H.3.3, H.4.3

ISBN 3-540-62591-7 Springer-Verlag Berlin Heidelberg New York

© Springer-Verlag Berlin Heidelberg 1997
Printed in Germany

Typesetting: Camera ready by author
SPIN 10549535   06/3142 – 5 4 3 2 1 0   Printed on acid-free paper

Foreword

This volume contains the proceedings of the First International Workshop on Cooperative Information Agents, held in Kiel, February 26–28, 1997.

The call for papers included the motto 'Distributed Artificial Intelligence meets Databases' to point out the following idea: DAI deals with the design and implementation of so-called intelligent software agents. These agents are autonomous systems that cooperate in a distributed environment to achieve a goal of their own or certain global goals.

On the other hand there is a growing interest in multidatabase systems, i.e., collections of loosely coupled heterogeneous local databases with no unified schema for their integration. Major problems in the multidatabase area arise from, for example, the heterogeneity of the data and the autonomy of the local databases.

Combining multidatabase systems and DAI by extending each local database by an intelligent software agent is a promising way of tackling these problems. One of the main tasks of these *Cooperative Information Agents* is to search for relevant information in non-local databases while respecting the autonomy of the local systems. Appropriate methods for high-level communication and cooperation among such agents in a completely decentralized environment are needed.

The design of information agents requires expertise from several different research areas. Thus, the aim of this interdisciplinary workshop is to provide a forum for the presentation of ideas and for in-depth discussions of issues concerning the development of cooperative information agents.

The workshop features 7 invited lectures, and 15 contributed papers selected from 41 submissions. We regret that the invited contribution 'Ontologies are not the Panacea in Data Integration: A Common Coordinator to Mediate Context Construction' by Aris Ouksel could not be included in this volume as the paper did not arrive in time for the publisher's deadline.

The workshop is organized in cooperation with the research groups on

1. Distributed Artificial Intelligence (DAI),
2. Database Systems, and
3. Methods for Information Systems Development (EMISA)

of the German Society for Computer Science (GI).

We gratefully acknowledge financial support from the German Research Foundation (DFG), the German Society for Computer Science (GI), and the technical faculty of our university. Moreover, we would like to thank all members of the program committee and all external referees for their careful work in reviewing and selecting the contributions.

We hope that this workshop will promote mutually beneficial cooperation among all researchers in the area of cooperative information agents.

Kiel, January 1997   Peter Kandzia, Matthias Klusch

Program Committee

Luis Otavio Alvares	Universitade Federal do Rio Grande do Sul, Brasil
Wolfgang Benn	University of Chemnitz, Germany
Sonia Bergamaschi	University of Modena, Italy
Hans-Dieter Burkhard	Humboldt University Berlin, Germany
Misbah Deen	University of Keele, UK
Yves Demazeau	Leibniz/IMAG/CNRS, France
Frank Dignum	Eindhoven University, The Netherlands
Edmund Durfee	University of Michigan, USA
Tim Finin	University of Maryland, USA
Klaus Fischer	DFKI Saarbrücken, Germany
Joachim Hammer	Stanford University, USA
Peter Kandzia	University of Kiel, Germany
Larry Kerschberg	George Mason University, USA
Stefan Kirn	University of Ilmenau, Germany
Matthias Klusch	University of Kiel, Germany
Sarit Kraus	Bar Ilan University, Israel
Klaus Meyer-Wegener	University of Dresden, Germany
Jörg P. Müller	DFKI Saarbrücken, Germany
Aris Ouksel	University of Illinois, USA
Mike P. Papazoglou	University of Tilburg, The Netherlands
Jeffrey Rosenschein	Hebrew University, Israel
Tuomas Sandholm	University of Massachusetts at Amherst, USA
Onn Shehory	Carnegie Mellon University, USA
Antonio Si	Polytechnic University, Hong Kong
Gottfried Vossen	University of Münster, Germany
Gerd Wagner	University of Leipzig, Germany
Mike Wooldridge	Mitsubishi Electric Digital Library Group London, UK

Organization

Peter Kandzia and Matthias Klusch (University of Kiel, Germany)

External Reviewers

Domenico Beneventano	Stefano Lodi
Alastair Burt	Claudio Sartori
Margret Groß-Hardt	Rosa Maria Viccari
Somesh Jha	Gero Vierke
Ralf Kühnel	Maurizio Vincini
Antonio Carlos da Rocha Costa	Mathias Weske

Table of Contents

Invited Papers

Databases and Agent Technology

Agents for Database Search and Knowledge Discovery

Communication and Cooperation Among Information Agents

Agent-Based Access to Heterogeneous Information Sources

Issues in Agent-Based Software Engineering

Michael Wooldridge

Mitsubishi Electric Digital Library Group
18th Floor, Centre Point, 103 New Oxford Street
London WC1A 1EB, United Kingdom

mjw@dlib.com

Abstract. The technology of intelligent agents and multi-agent systems shows great potential for dealing with a range of difficult software engineering problems. But if this potential is to be realised, then serious attention must be given to *engineering* approaches to building agent systems. This purpose of this paper is to direct attention at these issues. It considers how we might specify, implement, and verify agent systems.

1 Introduction

Intelligent agents and agent-based computer systems represent an important, fundamentally new way of dealing with many important software application problems, for which mainstream computer science techniques offer no obvious solution. To date, most research on such systems has addressed rather abstract (though undoubtedly important) issues, such as the nature of cooperation. Little work has been directed at the *engineering* aspects of agent-based systems. The aim of this paper is to consider the problem of building agent-based systems as a *software engineering* enterprise. In so doing, the paper constructs a framework within which future work on agent-based software engineering may be placed. The paper begins by motivating and introducing the idea of agent-based systems, and then goes on to discuss the key software engineering issues of specification, refinement/implementation, and verification with respect to agent-based systems. We begin by briefly discussing the question of what a specification is, and go on to consider what an *agent-based* specification might look like. We then discuss some of the dimensions along which an agent-based specification framework might vary, with particular reference to the notion of agents as rational, mentalistic systems [36, 31]. We subsequently discuss the key issue of implementing or refining agent-based specifications into systems, and finally, we consider the verification of agent-based systems. Throughout the article, we take care both to illustrate the various issues with case studies, and to draw parallels with more mainstream software engineering research wherever possible. The article concludes with a discussion of future work directions. The emphasis of this paper is on *formal* methods for agent-based software engineering.

1.1 Agent-Based Systems

By an *agent-based system*, we mean one in which the key abstraction used is that of an *agent*. Agent-based systems may contain a single agent, (as in the case of user interface agents or software secretaries [23]), but arguably the greatest potential lies in the application of *multi*-agent systems [3]. By an *agent*, we mean a system that enjoys the following properties [41, pp116–118]:

- *autonomy*: agents encapsulate some state (that is not accessible to other agents), and make decisions about what to do based on this state, without the direct intervention of humans or others;
- *reactivity*: agents are *situated* in an environment, (which may be the physical world, a user via a graphical user interface, a collection of other agents, the INTERNET, or perhaps many of these combined), are able to *perceive* this environment (through the use of potentially imperfect sensors), and are able to respond in a timely fashion to changes that occur in it;
- *pro-activeness*: agents do not simply act in response to their environment, they are able to exhibit goal-directed behaviour by *taking the initiative*;
- *social ability*: agents interact with other agents (and possibly humans) via some kind of *agent-communication language* [12], and typically have the ability to engage in social activities (such as cooperative problem solving or negotiation) in order to achieve their goals.

1.2 Agents as Rational Systems

An obvious problem is how to conceptualize systems that are capable of 'rational' behaviour, of the type discussed above. One of the most successful solutions to this problem involves viewing agents as *intentional systems* [7], whose behaviour can be predicted and explained in terms of *attitudes* such as belief, desire, and intention [29]. This *intentional stance*, whereby the behaviour of a complex system is understood via the attribution of attitudes such as believing and desiring, is simply an *abstraction tool*. It is a convenient shorthand for talking about complex systems, which allows us to succinctly predict and explain their behaviour without having to understand how they actually work. Now, much of computer science is concerned with looking for good abstraction mechanisms, since these allow system developers to manage complexity with greater ease: witness procedural abstraction, abstract data types, and most recently, objects. So, why not use the intentional stance as an abstraction tool in computing — to explain, understand, and, crucially, *program* complex computer systems?

For many researchers in AI, this idea of programming computer systems in terms of 'mentalistic' notions such as belief, desire, and intention is the key component of agent-based computing. The concept was articulated most clearly by Yoav Shoham, in his *agent-oriented programming* (AOP) proposal [36]. There seem to be a number of arguments in favour of AOP. First, it offers us a familiar, non-technical way to talk about complex systems. We need no formal training to understand mentalistic talk: it is part of our everyday linguistic ability.

Secondly, AOP may be regarded as a kind of 'post-declarative' programming. In procedural programming, saying what a system should do involves stating precisely *how* to do it, by writing a detailed algorithm. Procedural programming is difficult because it is hard for people to think in terms of the detail required. In declarative programming (*à la* PROLOG), the aim is to reduce the emphasis on control aspects: we state a goal that we want the system to achieve, and let a built-in control mechanism (e.g., goal-directed refutation theorem proving) figure out what to do in order to achieve it. However, in order to successfully write efficient or large programs in a language like PROLOG, it is necessary for the programmer to have a detailed understanding of how the built-in control mechanism works. This conflicts with one of the main goals of declarative programming: to relieve the user of the need to deal with control issues. In AOP, the idea is that, as in declarative programming, we state our goals, and let the built-in control mechanism figure out what to do in order to achieve them. In this case, however, the control mechanism implements some model of rational agency (such as the Cohen-Levesque theory of intention [6], or the Rao-Georgeff BDI model [29]). Hopefully, this computational model corresponds to our own intuitive understanding of (say) beliefs and desires, and so we need no special training to use it. Ideally, as AOP programmers, we need not be too concerned with *how* an agent achieves its goals.

2 Specification

The software development process begins by establishing the client's requirements. When this process is complete, a *specification* is developed, which sets out the functionality of the new system. The purpose of this section is to consider what a specification for an agent-based system might look like. What are the requirements for an agent specification framework? What sort of properties must it be capable of representing? To answer this question, we return to the properties of agents, as discussed in the preceding section.

We observed above that agents are situated in an environment, and are able to perceive this environment through sensors of some kind. Agents thus have *information* about their environment. This leads to our first requirement: that the agent specification framework must be capable of representing both the state of the environment itself, and the information an agent has about the environment. It is worth making some comments about what properties this information might have. First, the information an agent has may be incorrect. The agent's sensors may be faulty, the information might be out of date, or the agent may have been deliberately or accidentally given false information. Secondly, the information an agent has is not directly available to other agents: agents do not share data structures, and do not have access to the private data structures of other agents (this is part of what we meant by autonomy). Third, the environment will contain other agents, each with their own information about the environment. Thus an agent may have information about the state of other agents: we may need to represent such 'nested' information. Note that it is common practice to refer to the information available to an agent as that agent's *beliefs*.

Now consider the notion of *reactivity*. Software systems may be broadly divided into two types: *functional* and *reactive* [27]. A functional system is one that simply takes some input, performs some computation over this input, and eventually produces some output. Such systems may be viewed as functions $f : I \rightarrow O$ from a set I of inputs to O of outputs. The classic example of such a system is a compiler, which can be viewed as a mapping from a set I of legal source programs to a set O of corresponding object or machine code programs. Although the internal complexity of the mapping may be great (e.g., in the case of a *really* complex programming language), it is nevertheless the case that functional programs are, in general, inherently simpler to specify, design, and implement than reactive systems. Because functional systems terminate, it is possible to use pre- and post-condition formalisms in order to reason about them [15]. In contrast, reactive systems do not terminate, but rather maintain an *ongoing interaction* with their environment. It is therefore not possible to use pre- and post-condition formalisms such as Hoare logic to reason about them. Instead, reactive systems must be specified in terms of their *ongoing behaviour*. The next requirement for our agent specification framework is that it must be capable of representing this inherently reactive nature of agents and multi-agent systems. Note that one of the most successful formalisms developed for specifying reactive systems is temporal logic. The idea is that when specifying a reactive system, one often wants to state requirements such as 'if a request is received, then a response is eventually sent'. Such requirements are easily and elegantly expressed in temporal logic.

The third aspect of agents as discussed above is *pro-activeness*, by which we mean that agents are able to exhibit goal-directed behaviour. (Note that we use the term 'goal' fairly loosely. We include such notions as commitments or obligations in our usage.) It does not follow that in order to exhibit goal-directed behaviour, an agent must explicitly generate and represent goals [22], although this is by far the most common approach. Our agent specification framework must be capable of representing these *conative* (goal-directed) aspects of agency.

Finally, our agents are able to *act*. Agents do not typically have *complete* control over their environment (our auto-pilot cannot control the weather), but they are generally able to *influence* their environment by performing actions, and may have reliable control over portions of it. We require some way of representing these actions within our specification framework. To summarize, an agent specification framework must be capable of capturing at least the following aspects of an agent-based system:

- the *beliefs* agents have;
- the *ongoing interaction* agents have with their environment;
- the *goals* that agent will try to achieve;
- the *actions* that agents perform and the effects of these actions.

What sort of specification framework is capable of representing such aspects of a system? The most successful approach appears to be the use of a *temporal modal logic* [4] (space restrictions prevent a detailed technical discussion on such logics — see, e.g., [41] for a detailed overview and extensive references). A typical temporal modal agent specification framework will contain:

- normal modal logic connectives for representing agent's beliefs;
- temporal logic connectives for representing the dynamics of the system — its ongoing behaviour;
- normal modal logic connectives for representing conatives (e.g., desires, intentions, obligations);
- some apparatus for representing the actions that agents perform.

Given these requirements, there are a great many dimensions along which an agent specification framework may vary. Some contemporary models are reviewed in [41].

Case Study: The Belief-Desire-Intention Model One of the most successful agent theories is the *belief-desire-intention* (BDI) model of Rao and Georgeff (see [29] for extensive references). The technical details of BDI are somewhat involved, and so here, we shall simply summarize the main concepts that underpin BDI models.

As the name suggests, the internal state of a BDI agent is comprised of three key data structures, which are intended to loosely correspond to beliefs, desires, and intentions. An agent's *beliefs* are intended to represent the information it has about the world, as we suggested above. Beliefs will typically be represented symbolically: in the Procedural Reasoning System (PRS) — the best-known BDI implementation — beliefs look very much like PROLOG facts [13]. An agent's *desires* may be thought of as the tasks allocated to it. An agent may not in fact be able to achieve all of its desires, and in humans, desires may even be inconsistent. An agent's *intentions* represent desires that it has committed to achieving. The intuition is that as agents will not, in general, be able to achieve *all* their desires, even if these desires *are* consistent, they must therefore fix upon some subset of available desires and commit resources to achieving them. Chosen desires are *intentions*. These intentions will then feedback into future decision making: for example, an agent should not in future adopt intentions that conflict with those it currently holds.

The BDI model of agency has been formalised by Rao and Georgeff in a family of *BDI logics* [30, 33]. These logics are extensions to the expressive branching time logic CTL* [8], which also contain normal modal connectives for representing beliefs, desires, and intentions. Most work on BDI logics has focussed on possible relationships between the three 'mental states' [30], and more recently, on developing proof methods for restricted forms of the logics [33].

2.1 Discussion

Specification languages for agent-based systems are an order of magnitude more complex than the comparatively simple temporal and modal languages that have become commonplace in mainstream computer science. Typically, they are temporal logics enriched by a family of additional modal connectives, for representing the 'mental state' of an agent. There are a number of problems with such languages, in addition their conceptual complexity. The most worrying of these is with respect to their semantics. While the temporal component of these logics tends to be rather standard, the semantics for the additional modal connectives are given in the normal modal logic tradition of *possible worlds* [4]. So, for example, an agent's beliefs in some state are characterised by a set of different states, each of which represents one possibility for how the world could actually be, given the information available to the agent. In much the same way, an agents desires in some state are characterised by a set of states that are consistent with the agents desires. Intentions are represented similarly. There are several advantages to the possible worlds model: it is well-studied and well-understood, and the associated mathematics (known as *correspondence theory*) is extremely elegant. These attractive features make possible worlds the semantics of choice for almost every researcher in formal agent theory. However, there are also a number of serious drawbacks to possible worlds semantics. First, possible worlds semantics imply that agents are logically perfect reasoners, (in that their deductive capabilities are sound and complete), and they have infinite resources available for reasoning. No real agent, artificial or otherwise, has these properties.

Secondly, possible worlds semantics are generally *ungrounded*. That is, there is usually no precise relationship between the abstract accessibility relations that are used to characterize an agents state, and any concrete computational model. As we shall see in later sections, this makes it is difficult to go from a formal specification of a system in terms of beliefs, desires, and so on, to a concrete computational system. Similarly, given a concrete computational system, there is generally no way to determine what the beliefs, desires, and intentions of that system are. If temporal modal logics of the type discussed above are to be taken seriously as *specification* languages, then this problem is significant.

3 Implementation

Specification is not the end of the story in software development. Once given a specification, we must implement a system that is correct with respect to this specification. The next issue we consider is this move from abstract specification to concrete computational model. There are at least three possibilities for achieving this transformation:

1. manually refine the specification into an executable form via some principled but informal refinement process (as is the norm in most current software development);
2. somehow directly execute or animate the abstract specification; or
3. somehow translate or compile the specification into a concrete computational form using an automatic translation technique.

In the sub-sections that follow, we shall investigate each of these possibilities in turn.

3.1 Refinement

At the time of writing, most software developers use structured but informal techniques to transform specifications into concrete implementations. Probably the most common techniques in widespread use are based on the idea of top-down refinement. In this approach, an abstract system specification is *refined* into a number of smaller, less abstract sub-system specifications, which together satisfy the original specification. If these sub-systems are still too abstract to be implemented directly, then they are also refined. The process recurses until the derived sub-systems are simple enough to be directly implemented. Throughout, we are obliged to demonstrate that each step represents a true refinement of the more abstract specification that preceded it. This demonstration may take the form of a formal proof, if our specification is presented in, say, Z [37] or VDM [17]. More usually, justification is by informal argument.

For functional systems, the refinement process is well understood, and comparatively straightforward. Refinement calculi exist, which enable the system developer to take a pre- and post-condition specification, and from it systematically derive an implementation through the use of proof rules [26]. Part of this reason for this comparative simplicity is that there is often an easily understandable relationship between the pre-

and post-conditions that characterize an operation and the program structures required to implement it.

For reactive systems, refinement is not so straightforward. This is because reactive systems must be specified in terms of their ongoing behaviour. In contrast to pre- and post-condition formalisms, it is not so easy to determine what program structures are required to realise such specifications. The refinement problem for agent-based systems, where specifications may be regarded as even more abstract than those for reactive systems, is harder still. As a consequence, researchers have only just begun to investigate the refinement of agent-based systems.

Case Study: A Methodology for BDI Agents In section 2, we noted that the belief-desire-intention (BDI) model is one of the most successful general frameworks for agency. In [20], Kinny *et al* propose a four-stage design methodology for systems of BDI agents. The methodology is closely linked to a specific realization of the BDI model: the PRS architecture [13]. The methodology may be summarized as follows:

1. Identify the relevant *roles* in the application domain, and on the basis of these, develop an *agent class hierarchy*. An example role might be weather monitor, whereby agent i is required to make agent j aware of the prevailing weather conditions every hour.

2. Identify the responsibilities associated with each role, the services required by and provided by the role, and then determine the *goals* associated with each service. With respect to the above example, the goals would be to find out the current weather, and to make agent j aware of this information.

3. For each goal, determine the plans that may be used to achieve it, and the context conditions under which each plan is appropriate. With respect to the above example, a plan for the goal of making agent j aware of the weather conditions might involve sending a message to j.

4. Determine the belief structure of the system — the information requirements for each plan and goal. With respect to the above example, we might propose a unary predicate $windspeed(x)$ to represent the fact that the current wind speed is x. A plan to determine the current weather conditions would need to be able to represent this information.

Note that the analysis process will be iterative, as in more traditional methodologies. The outcome will be a model that closely corresponds to the PRS agent architecture. As a result, the move from end-design to implementation using PRS is relatively simple.

Kinny *et al* illustrate their methodology by applying it to an implemented air traffic management system called OASIS. This system, currently being deployed at Sidney airport in Australia, is, by any measure, a large and difficult application. It is arguably the most significant agent application yet developed. That the agent approach has been successfully applied in this domain is encouraging; the use of the methodology even more so.

3.2 Directly Executing Agent Specifications

One major disadvantage with manual refinement methods is that they introduce the possibility of error. If no proofs are provided, to demonstrate that each refinement step is indeed a true refinement, then the correctness of the implementation process depends upon little more than the intuitions of the developer. This is clearly an undesirable state of affairs for applications in which correctness is a major issue. One possible way of circumventing this problem, that has been widely investigated in mainstream computer science, is to get rid of the refinement process altogether, and *directly execute* the specification.

It might seem that suggesting the direct execution of complex agent specification languages is naive. (It is exactly the kind of suggestion that detractors of symbolic AI hate.) One should be therefore be very careful about what claims or proposals one makes. However, in certain circumstances, the direct execution of agent specification languages *is* possible.

What does it mean, to execute a formula φ of logic L? It means generating a logical model, M, for φ, such that $M \models \varphi$ [10]. If this could done without interference from the environment — if the agent had complete control over its environment — then execution would reduce to constructive theorem proving, where we show that φ is satisfiable by building a model for φ. In reality of course, agents are *not* interference-free: they must iteratively construct a model in the presence of input from the environment. Execution can then be seen as a two-way iterative process:

- environment makes something true;
- agent responds by doing something, i.e., making something else true in the model;
- environment responds, making something else true;
- ...

Execution of logical languages and theorem proving are thus closely related. This tells us that the execution of sufficiently rich (quantified) languages is not possible (since any language equal in expressive power to first-order logic is undecidable).

A useful way to think about execution is as if the agent is *playing a game* against the environment. The specification represents the goal of the game: the agent must keep the goal satisfied, while the environment tries to prevent the agent doing so. The game is played by agent and environment taking it in turns to build a little more of the model. If the specification ever becomes false in the (partial) model, then the agent loses. In real reactive systems, the game is never over: the agent must continue to play forever. Of course, some specifications (logically inconsistent ones) cannot ever be satisfied. A *winning strategy* for building models from (satisfiable) agent specifications in the presence of arbitrary input from the environment is an execution algorithm for the logic.

Case Study: Concurrent METATEM Concurrent METATEM is a programming language for multi-agent systems, that is based on the idea of directly executing linear time temporal logic agent specifications [11, 9]. A Concurrent METATEM system contains a number of concurrently executing agents, each of which is programmed by giving it a temporal logic specification of the behaviour it is intended the agent should exhibit.

An agent specification has the form $\bigwedge_i P_i \Rightarrow F_i$, where P_i is a temporal logic formula referring only to the present or past, and F_i is a temporal logic formula referring to the present or future. The $P_i \Rightarrow F_i$ formulae are known as *rules*. The basic idea for executing such a specification may be summed up in the following slogan:

on the basis of the past *do* the future.

Thus each rule is continually matched against an internal, recorded *history*, and if a match is found, then the rule *fires*. If a rule fires, then any variables in the future time part are instantiated, and the future time part then becomes a *commitment* that the agent will subsequently attempt to satisfy. Satisfying a commitment typically means making some predicate true within the agent. Here is a simple example of a Concurrent METATEM agent definition:

$$\bullet ask(x) \Rightarrow \Diamond give(x)$$
$$(\neg ask(x) \; \mathcal{Z} \; (give(x) \wedge \neg ask(x))) \Rightarrow \neg give(x)$$
$$give(x) \wedge give(y) \Rightarrow (x = y)$$

The agent in this example is a controller for a resource that is infinitely renewable, but which may only be possessed by one agent at any given time. The controller must therefore enforce mutual exclusion. The predicate $ask(x)$ means that agent x has asked for the resource. The predicate $give(x)$ means that the resource controller has given the resource to agent x. The resource controller is assumed to be the only agent able to 'give' the resource. However, many agents may ask for the resource simultaneously. The three rules that define this agent's behaviour may be summarized as follows:

- Rule 1: if someone asks, then eventually give;
- Rule 2: don't give unless someone has asked since you last gave; and
- Rule 3: if you give to two people, then they must be the same person (i.e., don't give to more than one person at a time).

Note that Concurrent METATEM agents can communicate by asynchronous broadcast message passing, though the details are not important here.

3.3 Compiling Agent Specifications

An alternative to direct execution is *compilation*. In this scheme, we take our abstract specification, and transform it into a concrete computational model via some automatic synthesis process. The main perceived advantages of compilation over direct execution are in run-time efficiency. Direct execution of an agent specification, as in Concurrent METATEM, above, typically involves manipulating a symbolic representation of the specification at run time. This manipulation generally corresponds to reasoning of some form, which is computationally costly (and in many cases, simply impracticable for systems that must operate in anything like real time). In contrast, compilation approaches aim to reduce abstract symbolic specifications to a much simpler computational model, which requires no symbolic representation. The 'reasoning' work is thus done off-line, at compile-time; execution of the compiled system can then be done with little or no run-time symbolic reasoning. As a result, execution is much faster. The advantages of compilation over direct execution are thus those of compilation over interpretation in mainstream programming.

Compilation approaches usually depend upon the close relationship between models for temporal/modal logic (which are typically labeled graphs of some kind), and automata-like finite state machines. Crudely, the idea is to take a specification φ, and do a *constructive proof* of the implementability of φ, wherein we show that the specification is satisfiable by systematically attempting to build a model for it. If the construction process succeeds, then the specification is satisfiable, and we have a model to prove it. Otherwise, the specification is unsatisfiable. If we have a model, then we 'read off' the implementation from its corresponding model. In mainstream computer science, the compilation approach to automatic program synthesis has been investigated by a number of researchers. Perhaps the closest to our view is the work of Pnueli and Rosner [28] on the automatic synthesis of reactive systems from branching time temporal logic specifications. Similar automatic synthesis techniques have also been deployed to develop concurrent system skeletons from temporal logic specifications. Manna and Wolper present an algorithm that takes as input a linear time temporal logic specification of the *synchronization* part of a concurrent system, and generates as output a CSP program skeleton ([16]) that realizes the specification [25]. Very similar work is reported by Clarke and Emerson [5]: they synthesize synchronization skeletons from branching time temporal logic (CTL) specifications.

Case Study: Situated Automata Perhaps the best-known example of this approach to agent development is the *situated automata* paradigm of Rosenschein and Kaelbling [34, 19]. In this approach, an agent has two main components:

- a *perception* part, which is responsible for observing the environment, and updating the internal state of the agent; and
- an *action* part, which is responsible for deciding what action to perform, based on the internal state of the agent.

Rosenschein and Kaelbling developed two programs to support the development of the perception and action components of an agent respectively. The RULER program takes a declarative perception specification and compiles it down to a finite state machine. The specification is given in terms of a theory of knowledge. The semantics of knowledge in the declarative specification language are given in terms of possible worlds, in the way described above. Crucially, however, the possible worlds underlying this logic are given a precise computational interpretation, in terms of the states of a finite state machine. It is this precise relationship that permits the synthesis process to take place.

The action part of an agent in Rosenschein and Kaelbling's framework is specified in terms of *goal reduction rules*, which encode information about how to achieve goals. The GAPPS program takes as input a goal specification, and a set of goal reduction rules, and generates as output a set of *situation action rules*, which may be thought of as a lookup table, defining what the agent should do under various circumstances, in order to achieve the goal. The process of deciding what to do is then very simple in computational terms, involving no reasoning at all. (A similar technique, called *universal plans*, was developed by Schoppers [35].)

3.4 Discussion

Structured but informal refinement techniques are the mainstay of real-world software engineering. If agent-oriented techniques are ever to become widely used outside the academic community, then informal, structured methods for agent-based development will be essential. One possibility for such techniques is to use a standard specification technique, and use traditional refinement methods to transform the specification into an implementation. This approach has the advantage of being familiar to a much larger user-base than entirely new techniques, but suffers from the disadvantage of presenting the user with no features that make it particularly well-suited to agent specification. To use an obvious analogy, top-down stepwise refinement is a useful approach for designing systems in which the key programming abstraction is the procedure, but it has many well-documented features that make it quite unsuitable for developing object-oriented systems. It seems certain that there will be much more work on manual refinement techniques for agent-based systems in the immediate future, but exactly what form these techniques will take is not clear.

Now consider the possibility of directly executing agent specifications. A number of problems immediately suggest themselves. The first is that of finding a concrete computational interpretation for the agent specification language in question. To see what we mean by this, consider models for the agent specification language in Concurrent METATEM. These are very simple: essentially just linear discrete sequences of states. Temporal logic is (amongst other things) simply a language for expressing *constraints* that must hold between successive states. Execution in Concurrent METATEM is thus a process of generating constraints as past-time antecedents are satisfied, and then trying to build a next state that satisfies these constraints. Constraints are expressed in temporal logic, which implies that they may only be in certain, regular forms. Because of this, it is possible to devise an algorithm that is guaranteed to build a next state if it is possible to do so. Such an algorithm is described in [1].

The agent specification language upon which Concurrent METATEM is based thus has a concrete computational model, and a comparatively simple execution algorithm. Contrast this state of affairs with the kinds of temporal modal agent specification languages discussed in section 2, where we have not only a temporal dimension to the logic, but also modalities for referring to beliefs, desires, and so on. In general, these models have *ungrounded* semantics. That is, the semantic structures that underpin these logics (typically accessibility relations for each of the modal operators) have no concrete computational interpretation. As a result, it is not clear how such agent specification languages might be executed.

Another obvious problem is that execution techniques based on theorem proving are inherently limited when applied to sufficiently expressive (first-order) languages, as first-order logic is undecidable. However, complexity is a problem even in the propositional case — deciding classical propositional logic is NP-complete.

Turning to automatic synthesis, we find that the techniques described above have been developed primarily for propositional specification languages. If we attempt to extend these techniques to more expressive, first-order specification languages, then we again find ourselves coming up against the undecidability of quantified logic. Even in the propositional case, the theoretical complexity of theorem proving for modal and temporal logics is likely to limit the effectiveness of compilation techniques: given an agent specification of size 1000, a synthesis algorithm that runs in exponential time when used off-line is no more useful than an execution algorithm which runs in exponential time on-line.

Another problem with respect to synthesis techniques is that they typically result in finite-state, automata like machines, that are strictly less powerful than Turing machines. In particular, the systems generated by the processes outlined above cannot modify their behaviour at run-time. In short, they cannot learn. While for many applications, this is acceptable — even desirable — for equally many others, it is not. In expert assistant agents, of the type described in [23], learning is pretty much the *raison d'etre*. Attempts to address this issue are described in [18].

4 Verification

Once we have developed a concrete system, we need to show that this system is correct with respect to our original specification. This process is known as *verification*, and it is particularly important if we have introduced any informality into the development process. For example, any manual refinement, done without a formal proof of refinement correctness, creates the possibility of a faulty transformation from specification to implementation. Verification is the process of convincing ourselves that the transformation was sound. We can divide approaches to the verification of systems into two broad classes: (1) *axiomatic*; and (2) *semantic* (model checking). In the subsections that follow, we shall look at the way in which these two approaches have evidenced themselves in agent-based systems.

4.1 Axiomatic Approaches

Axiomatic approaches to program verification were the first to enter the mainstream of computer science, with the work of Hoare in the late 1960s [15]. Axiomatic verification requires that we can take our concrete program, and from this program systematically derive a logical theory that represents the behaviour of the program. Call this the program theory. If the program theory is expressed in the same logical language as the original specification, then verification reduces to a proof problem: show that the specification is a theorem of (equivalently, is a logical consequence of) the program theory.

The development of a program theory is made feasible by *axiomatizing* the programming language in which the system is implemented. For example, Hoare logic gives us more or less an axiom for every statement type in a simple PASCAL-like language. Once given the axiomatization, the program theory can be derived from the program text in a systematic way.

Perhaps the most relevant work from mainstream computer science is the specification and verification of reactive systems using temporal logic, in the way pioneered by Pnueli, Manna, and colleagues [24]. The idea is that the computations of reactive systems are infinite sequences, which correspond to models for linear temporal logic[1]. Temporal logic can be used both to develop a system specification, and to axiomatize a programming language. This axiomatization can then be used to systematically derive the theory of a program from the program text. Both the specification and the program theory will then be encoded in temporal logic, and verification hence becomes a proof problem in temporal logic.

Comparatively little work has been carried out within the agent-based systems community on axiomatizing multi-agent environments. We shall review just one approach.

Case Study: Axiomatizing two Multi-Agent Languages In [38], an axiomatic approach to the verification of multi-agent systems was proposed. Essentially, the idea was to use a temporal belief logic to axiomatize the properties of two multi-agent programming languages. Given such an axiomatization, a program theory representing the properties of the system could be systematically derived in the way indicated above.

A temporal belief logic was used for two reasons. First, a temporal component was required because, as we observed above, we need to capture the ongoing behaviour of a multi-agent system. A belief component was used because the agents we wish to verify are each symbolic AI systems in their own right. That is, each agent is a symbolic reasoning system, which includes a representation of its environment and desired behaviour. A belief component in the logic allows us to capture the symbolic representations present within each agent.

The two multi-agent programming languages that were axiomatized in the temporal belief logic were Shoham's AGENT0 [36], and Fisher's Concurrent METATEM(see above). The basic approach was as follows:

1. First, a simple abstract model was developed of symbolic AI agents. This model captures the fact that agents are symbolic reasoning systems, capable of communication. The model gives an account of how agents might change state, and what a computation of such a system might look like.
2. The histories traced out in the execution of such a system were used as the semantic basis for a temporal belief logic. This logic allows us to express properties of agents modelled at stage (1).
3. The temporal belief logic was used to axiomatize the properties of a multi-agent programming language. This axiomatization was then used to develop the program theory of a multi-agent system.
4. The proof theory of the temporal belief logic was used to verify properties of the system [40].

Note that this approach relies on the operation of agents being sufficiently simple that their properties can be axiomatized in the logic. It works for Shoham's AGENT0 and Fisher's Concurrent METATEM largely because these languages have a simple semantics, closely related to rule-based systems, which in turn have a simple logical semantics. For more complex agents, an axiomatization is not so straightforward. Also, cap-

---

[1] The set of all computations of a reactive system is a tree-like structure, corresponding to a model for branching time temporal logic [8].

turing the semantics of concurrent execution of agents is not easy (it is, of course, an area of ongoing research in computer science generally).

4.2 Semantic Approaches: Model Checking

Ultimately, axiomatic verification reduces to a proof problem. Axiomatic approaches to verification are thus inherently limited by the difficulty of this proof problem. Proofs are hard enough, even in classical logic; the addition of temporal and modal connectives to a logic makes the problem considerably harder. For this reason, more efficient approaches to verification have been sought. One particularly successful approach is that of *model checking*. As the name suggests, whereas axiomatic approaches generally rely on syntactic proof, model checking approaches are based on the semantics of the specification language.

The model checking problem, in abstract, is quite simple: given a formula φ of language L, and a model M for L, determine whether or not φ is valid in M, i.e., whether or not $M \models_L \varphi$. Model checking-based verification has been studied in connection with temporal logic [21]. The technique once again relies upon the close relationship between models for temporal logic and finite-state machines. Suppose that φ is the specification for some system, and π is a program that claims to implement φ. Then, to determine whether or not π truly implements φ, we proceed as follows:

- take π, and from it generate a model M_π that corresponds to π, in the sense that M_π encodes all the possible computations of π;
- determine whether or not $M_\pi \models \varphi$, i.e., whether the specification formula φ is valid in M_π; the program π satisfies the specification φ just in case the answer is 'yes'.

The main advantage of model checking over axiomatic verification is in complexity: model checking using the branching time temporal logic CTL ([5]) can be done in polynomial time.

Case Study: Model Checking BDI Systems In [32], Rao and Georgeff present an algorithm for model checking AOP systems. More precisely, they give an algorithm for taking a logical model for their (propositional) BDI agent specification language, and a formula of the language, and determining whether the formula is valid in the model. The technique is closely based on model checking algorithms for normal modal logics [14]. They show that despite the inclusion of three extra modalities, (for beliefs, desires, and intentions), into the CTL branching time framework, the algorithm is still quite efficient, running in polynomial time. So the second step of the two-stage model checking process described above can still be done efficiently. However, it is not clear how the first step might be realised for BDI logics. Where does the logical model characterizing an agent actually comes from — can it be derived from an arbitrary program π, as in mainstream computer science? To do this, we would need to take a program implemented in, say, PASCAL, and from it derive the belief, desire, and intention accessibility relations that are used to give a semantics to the BDI component of the logic. Because, as we noted earlier, there is no clear relationship between the BDI logic and the concrete computational models used to implement agents, it is not clear how such a model could be derived.

4.3 Discussion

Axiomatic approaches to the verification of multi-agent systems suffer from two main problems. First, the temporal verification of reactive systems relies upon a simple model of concurrency, where the actions that programs perform are assumed to be atomic. We cannot make this assumption when we move from programs to agents. The actions we think of agents as performing will generally be much more coarse grained. As a result, we need a more realistic model of concurrency. One possibility, investigated in [39], is to model agent execution cycles as intervals over the real numbers, in the style of the temporal logic of reals [2]. The second problem is the difficulty of the proof problem for agent specification languages. As we noted in section 2, the theoretical complexity of proof for many of these logics is quite daunting.

With respect to model-checking approaches, the main problem, as we indicated above, is again the issue of ungrounded semantics for agent specification languages. If we cannot take an arbitrary program and say, for this program, what its beliefs, desires, and intentions are, then it is not clear how we might verify that this program satisfied a specification expressed in terms of such constructs.

5 Conclusions

Agent-based systems are a promising development, not just for AI, but for computer science generally. If intelligent agent technology succeeds, then it will provide a solution to many important but difficult software problems. The challenge now before the intelligent agent community is to ensure that the techniques developed particularly over the past decade for building rational agents make a smooth transition from the research lab to the desk of the everyday computer worker. This is by no means easy, as the expert systems experience demonstrates. If the community is to succeed in this endeavour, then it will need to take very seriously the comment by Oren Etzioni, that opened this paper: agents are more a problem of computer science and software engineering than AI.

In this paper, we have set out a roadmap for work in agent-based software engineering. We have examined the fundamental problems of specification, implementation, and verification from the point of view of agent-based systems. Throughout, we have been careful to draw as many parallels as possible with more mainstream software engineering.

Acknowledgments

I would like to thank Michael Fisher for the (many) discussions we have had on software engineering for agent-based systems, and also Adam Kellett and Nick Jennings for their comments on this paper. This work was supported by the EPSRC under grant GR/K57282. The views expressed in this paper are those of the author, and are not necessarily those of Mitsubishi Electric.

References

1. H. Barringer, M. Fisher, D. Gabbay, G. Gough, and R. Owens. METATEM: A framework for programming in temporal logic. In *REX Workshop on Stepwise Refinement of Distributed Systems: Models, Formalisms, Correctness (LNCS Volume 430)*, pages 94–129. Springer-Verlag: Heidelberg, Germany, June 1989.

2. H. Barringer, R. Kuiper, and A. Pnueli. A really abstract concurrent model and its temporal logic. In *Proceedings of the Thirteenth ACM Symposium on the Principles of Programming Languages*, pages 173–183, 1986.

3. A. H. Bond and L. Gasser, editors. *Readings in Distributed Artificial Intelligence*. Morgan Kaufmann Publishers: San Mateo, CA, 1988.

4. B. Chellas. *Modal Logic: An Introduction*. Cambridge University Press: Cambridge, England, 1980.

5. E. M. Clarke and E. A. Emerson. Design and synthesis of synchronization skeletons using branching time temporal logic. In D. Kozen, editor, *Logics of Programs — Proceedings 1981 (LNCS Volume 131)*, pages 52–71. Springer-Verlag: Heidelberg, Germany, 1981.

6. P. R. Cohen and H. J. Levesque. Intention is choice with commitment. *Artificial Intelligence*, 42:213–261, 1990.

7. D. C. Dennett. *The Intentional Stance*. The MIT Press: Cambridge, MA, 1987.

8. E. A. Emerson and J. Y. Halpern. 'Sometimes' and 'not never' revisited: on branching time versus linear time temporal logic. *Journal of the ACM*, 33(1):151–178, 1986.

9. M. Fisher. A survey of Concurrent METATEM — the language and its applications. In D. M. Gabbay and H. J. Ohlbach, editors, *Temporal Logic — Proceedings of the First International Conference (LNAI Volume 827)*, pages 480–505. Springer-Verlag: Heidelberg, Germany, July 1994.

10. M. Fisher. Executable temporal logic. *The Knowledge Engineering Review*, 1996.

11. M. Fisher and M. Wooldridge. Executable temporal logic for distributed A.I. In *Proceedings of the Twelfth International Workshop on Distributed Artificial Intelligence (IWDAI-93)*, pages 131–142, Hidden Valley, PA, May 1993.

12. M. R. Genesereth and S. P. Ketchpel. Software agents. *Communications of the ACM*, 37(7):48–53, July 1994.

13. M. P. Georgeff and A. L. Lansky. Reactive reasoning and planning. In *Proceedings of the Sixth National Conference on Artificial Intelligence (AAAI-87)*, pages 677–682, Seattle, WA, 1987.

14. J. Y. Halpern and M. Y. Vardi. Model checking versus theorem proving: A manifesto. In V. Lifschitz, editor, *AI and Mathematical Theory of Computation — Papers in Honor of John McCarthy*. Academic Press, 1991.

15. C. A. R. Hoare. An axiomatic basis for computer programming. *Communications of the ACM*, 12(10):576–583, 1969.

16. C. A. R. Hoare. Communicating sequential processes. *Communications of the ACM*, 21:666–677, 1978.

17. C. B. Jones. *Systematic Software Development using VDM (second edition)*. Prentice Hall, 1990.

18. L. P. Kaelbling. *Learning in Embedded Systems*. The MIT Press: Cambridge, MA, 1993.

19. L. P. Kaelbling and S. J. Rosenschein. Action and planning in embedded agents. In P. Maes, editor, *Designing Autonomous Agents*, pages 35–48. The MIT Press: Cambridge, MA, 1990.

20. D. Kinny, M. Georgeff, and A. Rao. A methodology and modelling technique for systems of BDI agents. In W. Van de Velde and J. W. Perram, editors, *Agents Breaking Away: Proceedings of the Seventh European Workshop on Modelling Autonomous Agents in a Multi-Agent World, (LNAI Volume 1038)*, pages 56–71. Springer-Verlag: Heidelberg, Germany, 1996.

21. O. Lichtenstein and A. Pnueli. Checking that finite state concurrent programs satisfy their linear specification. In *Proceedings of the Eleventh ACM Symposium on the Principles of Programming Languages*, pages 97–107, 1984.

22. P. Maes. Situated agents can have goals. In P. Maes, editor, *Designing Autonomous Agents*, pages 49–70. The MIT Press: Cambridge, MA, 1990.

23. P. Maes. Agents that reduce work and information overload. *Communications of the ACM*, 37(7):31–40, July 1994.

24. Z. Manna and A. Pnueli. *Temporal Verification of Reactive Systems — Safety*. Springer-Verlag: Heidelberg, Germany, 1995.

25. Z. Manna and P. Wolper. Synthesis of communicating processes from temporal logic specifications. *ACM Transactions on Programming Languages and Systems*, 6(1):68–93, January 1984.

26. C. Morgan. *Programming from Specifications (second edition)*. Prentice Hall International: Hemel Hempstead, England, 1994.

27. A. Pnueli. Specification and development of reactive systems. In *Information Processing 86*. Elsevier Science Publishers B.V.: Amsterdam, The Netherlands, 1986.

28. A. Pnueli and R. Rosner. On the synthesis of a reactive module. In *Proceedings of the Sixteenth ACM Symposium on the Principles of Programming Languages (POPL)*, pages 179–190, January 1989.

29. A. S. Rao and M. Georgeff. BDI Agents: from theory to practice. In *Proceedings of the First International Conference on Multi-Agent Systems (ICMAS-95)*, pages 312–319, San Francisco, CA, June 1995.

30. A. S. Rao and M. P. Georgeff. Modeling rational agents within a BDI-architecture. In R. Fikes and E. Sandewall, editors, *Proceedings of Knowledge Representation and Reasoning (KR&R-91)*, pages 473–484. Morgan Kaufmann Publishers: San Mateo, CA, April 1991.

31. A. S. Rao and M. P. Georgeff. An abstract architecture for rational agents. In C. Rich, W. Swartout, and B. Nebel, editors, *Proceedings of Knowledge Representation and Reasoning (KR&R-92)*, pages 439–449, 1992.

32. A. S. Rao and M. P. Georgeff. A model-theoretic approach to the verification of situated reasoning systems. In *Proceedings of the Thirteenth International Joint Conference on Artificial Intelligence (IJCAI-93)*, pages 318–324, Chambéry, France, 1993.

33. A. S. Rao and M. P. Georgeff. Formal models and decision procedures for multi-agent systems. Technical Note 61, Australian AI Institute, Level 6, 171 La Trobe Street, Melbourne, Australia, June 1995.

34. S. Rosenschein and L. P. Kaelbling. The synthesis of digital machines with provable epistemic properties. In J. Y. Halpern, editor, *Proceedings of the 1986 Conference on Theoretical Aspects of Reasoning About Knowledge*, pages 83–98. Morgan Kaufmann Publishers: San Mateo, CA, 1986.

35. M. J. Schoppers. Universal plans for reactive robots in unpredictable environments. In *Proceedings of the Tenth International Joint Conference on Artificial Intelligence (IJCAI-87)*, pages 1039–1046, Milan, Italy, 1987.

36. Y. Shoham. Agent-oriented programming. *Artificial Intelligence*, 60(1):51–92, 1993.

37. M. Spivey. *The Z Notation (second edition)*. Prentice Hall International: Hemel Hempstead, England, 1992.

38. M. Wooldridge. *The Logical Modelling of Computational Multi-Agent Systems*. PhD thesis, Department of Computation, UMIST, Manchester, UK, October 1992. (Also available as Technical Report MMU–DOC–94–01, Department of Computing, Manchester Metropolitan University, Chester St., Manchester, UK).

39. M. Wooldridge. This is MYWORLD: The logic of an agent-oriented testbed for DAI. In M. Wooldridge and N. R. Jennings, editors, *Intelligent Agents: Theories, Architectures, and*

Languages (LNAI Volume 890), pages 160–178. Springer-Verlag: Heidelberg, Germany, January 1995.

40. M. Wooldridge and M. Fisher. A decision procedure for a temporal belief logic. In D. M. Gabbay and H. J. Ohlbach, editors, *Temporal Logic — Proceedings of the First International Conference (LNAI Volume 827)*, pages 317–331. Springer-Verlag: Heidelberg, Germany, July 1994.

41. M. Wooldridge and N. R. Jennings. Intelligent agents: Theory and practice. *The Knowledge Engineering Review*, 10(2):115–152, 1995.

A Database Perspective to a Cooperation Environment

S.M. Deen
DAKE Centre (Department of Computer Science)
University of Keele
Keele, Staffs, ST5 5BG
England
Email: deen@cs.keele.ac.uk

Abstract

This paper will present the author's view of a Cooperating Knowledge Based System (CKBS) as an applied multi-agent system with a database perspective, based on well-defined computer-science concepts, rather than AI concepts. Each agent will be seen as an autonomous (necessarily large-grain) system which implicitly cooperates with other agents to achieve a global goal in a potentially multi-user environment, where performance, reliability, concurrent usage, user-friendliness are particularly important.

In this model, each agent is capable of executing well-defined actions of one or possibly more skill types in a multi-layered architecture where inter-agent communications are carried out in a medium of what are called shadows, with distribution transparency. The architecture also supports user-defined cooperation strategies to be followed by the cooperating agents for specific tasks. The model provides a useful basis for real-world applications of a number of domains, such as agent-based manufacturing, distributed network traffic flow and distributed service ontology.

Keywords: Multi-agent Systems, Cooperating Knowledge Based Systems, Cooperating Agents, Cooperation Architecture.

1. Introduction

Multi-agent systems of Distributed Artificial Intelligent (DAI) are a well-established area of research, in which high-grain autonomous knowledge based systems called agents cooperate (or compete) in problem solving. The potential application domains include: Intelligent Manufacturing Systems, Travel Plans, Air-Traffic Control, Telecommunications Network Management, Distributed Decision Making, Distributed Office Procedures, Distributed Sensor Networks and Distributed Fault

Diagnostics. More recently, the database world has also became interested in these distributed application domains, partly as the natural extension of its activities in the area of distributed databases. This new area is referred to as the Cooperating Knowledge Based Systems (CKBSs), which provide a database perspective to multi-agent systems [1,2].

Traditional multi-agent researchers draw much of their inspiration from human social behaviour and formulate their models, primarily in terms of human behavioural concepts such as intention, desire, wish, commitment, oppose, propose, etc [30, 31]. Therefore, the objective in multi-agent research appears to be the simulation of human social behaviour, and to apply the resultant model in distributed problem solving. In contrast in a CKBS, the objective is to solve real-world problems, where the provision of performance, user-facilities and reliability are paramount. While ideas from both DAI and distributed databases are welcome in a CKBS, the simulation of human social behaviour is not attempted.

In terms of an architectural framework, the design characteristics of traditional multi-agent systems generally appear to be:

(i)   Each is an exclusive system, without any general architecture, except for the use of some general design features, such as blackboards or the Contract Net protocol.

(ii)   In the absence of a general model, each system is built typically from scratch.

This may be characterised as an individualistic approach, where each system is built to demonstrate the feasibility of some interesting ideas, and therefore the provision of a general architecture is less urgent. However if we were to develop systems for real-world applications, as the objective of CKBS is, then there is a need for a general architecture. Such an architecture should provide well-defined structures and components, permitting a foundation for application-independent development, thereby reducing the development time of specific application systems. It should also provide a framework for further systems-oriented research such as optimisation, reliability, concurrent usage etc. In addition a CKBS should ideally allow:

(1)   *User-defined strategies* that is high-level cooperation strategies that a user can specify differently for different tasks at different times as needed.

(2)   *Distribution transparency* which permits a user to view the multi-agent system as a mono-agent system, thus simplifying the specification of cooperation strategies.

(3)   *Ease of use* through a multi-level schema with user transparency, different levels for users with different expertise.

As implied earlier our architecture will be based on well-tried computer-science (particularly database) concepts, with a minimal injection of new concepts on the principle that if an old concept can be made to work, then do not invent a new one without a very sound justification. An earlier version of our ideas have been published in [38].

The remainder of this paper will proceed as follows: In section 2 we shall outline the cooperation environment used in our model, while in section 3, we shall introduce the main concepts. We devote section 4 to describe the schema and operational architecture, while in section 5 we demonstrate how cooperation strategies can be specified in a flexible manner with distribution transparency for task executions. A conclusion, with some general comments is given in section 6. We begin with a brief review of the state-of-the-art in multi-agent research.

Review of the State of the Art

Bond and Gasser [4] divide the field of distributed AI (DAI) into three research areas, namely (i) Parallel Processing (which we shall not consider here), (ii) Distributed Problem Solving (DPS) which includes Cooperative Distributed Problem Solving (CDPS), and (iii) Multi-agent Systems (MAS). In DPS the agents are typically low-grain sharing common facilities, while in MAS, the agents are meant to be a high-grain, autonomous and heterogeneous, as assumed in our presentation.

Much of the early research in DAI was focused on DPS, inspired by the Hearsay Speech Processing System [5], based on a blackboard architecture. Another distinguished prototype using the same approach is the DVMT system of Durfee *et al* [6-8]. The MACE system of Gasser *et al* [9] and AGORA of Bisiani *et al* [10] provide some development environments for DPS prototypes. Following the success of the blackboard approach, more general blackboard architectures have also been developed [11-13].

The blackboard architecture is not considered to be suitable for multi-agent systems, in which the contract-net protocol of Davis and Smith [14-15] is more appropriate. The air-traffic control models of Steeb *et al* and others [16-18] typify some MAS applications. Another application area with a number of publications is telecommunication network management [19-22]. The Actor Model of Agha *et al* [23] and the open system approach of Hewitt [24] offer some interesting ways of looking at multi-agent systems. In general however typical research activities in MAS include agent interactions, cooperation strategies, negotiation models, belief models, languages and so on, but not any general architectures where all these components fit together, no doubt due to the complexity and diversity of issues and requirements.

The exception to these are perhaps the EEC ESPRIT ARCHON [25] and IMAGINE [26] projects. The former has produced an application specific model (based on the requirements of power plants) and the latter attempted an application-independent model. The main problem faced by the IMAGINE model was the difficulty of translating the abstract social theories of human interactions into a comprehensive computer model (the author was a member of the IMAGINE consortium).

The DARPA proposal on DAI provides a Unix-based communication environment, and a Lisp based Knowledge Interchange Format, but no generic architecture [27-28]. More recently Schwuttke and Quan [29] have proposed an architecture for communications among agents for real-time diagnostics, which seem interesting. Some earlier work on a CKBS architecture by this author on manufacturing applications can be seen in [34, 35].

2. Cooperation Environment

In this section we shall clarify some background concepts, namely agents, cooperation and the role of a high-level language.

2.1 Agents

As stated earlier, we define an agent to be a knowledge based system, with a compulsory software component and an optional hardware component. A database can also be treated as an agent. Each agent is a dynamic system [37] with a controller, input, output and processor, the processor converting input into output, all under the control of the controller. Each agent is autonomous, to the extent its controller is independent of other agents. In a compound agent, which shows a master-slave relationship, the processor of the master agent controls the controller of the slave agents, thus the slaves have partial autonomy. In a peer relationship all agents are fully autonomous with respect to each other. A fully autonomous atomic agent does not have any master or slave. In the context of this paper, we shall assume all agents to be fully autonomous atomic agents (and hence displaying a peer relationship with respect to each other), since the extension of our model for the master-slave relationship is relatively trivial [35].

We shall assume each agent to be made up of two main parts, a head (which includes the controller) and a base, connected by a neck. The base, which can include hardware, is the body of the agent that performs its individual skills. In the context of a distributed databases, the base is equivalent to the nodal database system minus the nodal schema which in a CKBS resides in the head. The head has three components: (1) the operational environment in the upper head, (2) mappings between (1) and (3) in the middle head, and (3) the home model (equivalent to the nodal schema).

Although the heads of several agents could reside on the same computer, we shall generally assume the heads to be connected via a suitable communications network [34], transparent to the end-user. Agents can be heterogeneous, but the upper head (along with its system support facility) must conform to the requirements of the cooperation environment enabling inter-agent activities. In this paper, we shall treat the base largely as a black-box.

2.2 Cooperation

Cooperation is the ability of an agent to work with other agents to perform a task and as such it is a fundamental property of an agent. All our agents are *implicitly* cooperative, as they are so designed. In some tasks, agents may have to compete, but this competition takes place within a cooperation framework. We shall therefore use the term cooperation to include competition as well.

We define here a *basic cooperation block (BCB)* in which one agent acts as the *coordinator* and some other suitable agents as *cohorts*, each cohort executing a subtask. In general any *participant* (that is the coordinator or any cohort) of a BCB can be:

(i)   a stand-alone atomic agent

(ii)   a compound agent to execute a subtask with the help of its slaves.

(iii)   a coordinator of a lower-level BCB to execute a subtask with the help of some other autonomous agents.

(iv)   a participant in another autonomous BCB working concurrently on another task.

This relationship can be recursive. A multi-level cooperation hierarchy can be built up using BCBs. Each task is however specified by a user in a *user-agent*, which may act as the coordinator of the whole task, that is the coordinator of the initial (i.e. the first-level) BCB, if there are further cooperation levels. If the task requires a multi-level cooperation, then this initial BCB becomes the first level. We assume each basic cooperation block to be transparent (or apparently transparent) to other cooperation blocks and cooperation levels at any time. This transparency simplifies our model, as we need to consider only one basic cooperation block (more later).

The master-slave relationship displayed in a compound agent is *coercive* and permanent, whereas the cooperative relationship in a cooperation block is transitory, lasting only for the duration of the execution process of the task concerned. An autonomous agent can interact with other autonomous agents only through cooperation, of which there are two types: trivial and non-trivial [34]. A trivial cooperation between two agents involves a single *send* and a single *receive*, as in a retrieval command in a database. A non-trivial cooperation involves multiple exchanges (as in a 2PC of a distributed database update), generally with the following three (implicit if not explicit) stages:

Agreement:
    In this stage the agents concerned agree to perform a task, usually subject to some constraints and possibly preferences. This agreement itself could be arrived through a negotiation.

Interactions:
> The agents interact to achieve the joint goal in accordance with the agreement, and they may enter into further negotiations to achieve that goal, if necessary.

Termination:
> The process terminates, releasing the agents from further obligations.

We have proposed a three-stage coordination (3SC) protocol in [32] which embodies the above three stages, and provides a formalised framework for non-trivial cooperation. As stated in [32], a 3SC is a general protocol, which can be reduced to a 2SC in some applications. Any of the stages can recursively use further 3SC protocols implying lower-level BCBs.

Finally in the remainder of this paper, by cooperation, we shall imply non-trivial cooperation, except where indicated otherwise.

2.3 Cooperation Strategy

A strategy in a CKBS is a user-defined specification of how a task should be performed. It is assumed to be specified in a user-convenient language (high-level, graphical?) and can change from task to task and from time to time depending on the needs. Each relevant agent must be capable of executing its part of the strategy. A strategy can be specified in individual agents prescribing how to behave towards (i.e how to respond to) a request for an action from another agent, or even how to go about in executing the action (e.g. should it call another agent for assistance?).

A strategy at the coordinator specifies how to execute the task in cooperation with other agents. Query optimisation or 2-Phase Commit for distributed updates can be viewed as strategies in a database environment, although these strategies are normally pre-coded as part of the DBMS. In contrast, in a CKBS we want such strategies to be specified by the end-users. *The ability of an agent in a CKBS environment to execute different user-defined strategies gives the flexibility in our model.* Observe that an agent can take only those actions for which it has skills.

Example of a Strategy

Assume a user-agent (as coordinator) requests an Assembler agent (cohort) A-30 to schedule an operation.

- Allocate subtask S1 between 10 and 11 am. The prior Assembler is A-10 and the next Assembler is A-60. Negotiate with Tool agents for Tool TL33 at the cheapest price. We prefer a strong glue to screws for mounting.

- If it is not possible to allocate in that time slot, then allocate to the next free slot, and inform agents A-10 and A-60 and me about this change to the external relations E26, E12 and E63 respectively.

- If you need to use the services of some robot agents, then ensure they are acceptable to A-60 and that the transportation cost does not exceed 200 units. Our preferred delivery method is DM-45.

- If the allocation fails, send the status information to my external relation E21.

- If it is successful, then send a copy of the schedule to my external relation E24.

- Once the robots are chosen, send me a copy of this information to my external relation E21 for confirmation by me.

2.4 Distribution Transparency

We assume a task is executed within a cooperation strategy specified by the user. Since the different parts of that strategy have to be executed in different cohorts, how does the user specify it. The relevant questions are:

(i)   Does the user specify the different parts of the strategy in different cohorts?

(ii)   Is it possible to decompose a strategy into such sub-strategies cleanly and easily?

(iii) If the answer to both is yes, then how would the user identify the cohorts as these are determined dynamically during the execution time?

(iv)   If such a cohort can be identified how would the cohort, possibly participating in the executions of a number of tasks concurrently, manage and invoke these continually changing sub-strategies, different ones for different tasks at different times?

To resolve these issues, we advocate a concept called distribution transparency, in which a multi-agent system can be viewed as a mono-agent system. It gives an illusion that the coordinator is the only agent, and all the skills required are local. The user then specifies the cooperation strategy for this mono-agent for the execution of the requested task. A lower-level system-software identifies the remote agents dynamically, and despatch the sub-strategies to the relevant cohorts as parameters along with the subtask requests. A distribution transparency offers the following advantages to the end-users:

(1)   An apparent single agent to specify strategies

(2)   A strategy specification as a normal programme, without communication protocols.

(3)   Transparency from the details of 3SC protocol and message handling.

(4)   Transparency from the details of communication networks.

(5)   An integrated interoperable environment thorough that apparent single agent.

It is assumed that a high-level user-friendly language will be available to the end-users of that environment.

3. Foundation of Our Model

Within the cooperation framework described earlier, the major concepts used in our CKBS approach are:

• Skill Classes and Actions

• Shadows

• Inter-agent Activities

• Multi-layered Schemas

The first three items will be discussed below, and the last in section 4.

3.1 Skill Classes and Actions

We begin with the assumption that agents have skills, an execution of a skill being an *action*. Both skills and actions can display hierarchies, and each can be atomic. However the notion of action and its atomicity are perception-dependent. *Skills are what an agent offers to other agents.*

Each agent must have one or more skills at a suitable abstraction level. All agents having the same skill belong to the same skill class. Conversely an agent having multiple skills will belong to those skill classes. Associated with each skill class, there is a *n*-ary relation, called skill relation, where an attribute can be either atomic or composite. Each tuple there represents a requested or completed action, referred to as action tuple. We shall assume a skill relation to be conceptual entity resolved into a set of what we would call external relations. In the discussion below one external relation for each skill relation will be assumed. The skill (or equivalently external) relations, held at the upper head, are backed by home relations at the lower head for the exclusive use of this agent body, the mapping between the external and home relations being conducted through the middle head.

Status Indicators and Dependency Attributes

An action may have request types and each request progresses through a set of events. When a part of a request has been completed, an event has occurred. Each event is identified by a number, and the number of the last completed event is held in an indicator, referred to here as the status or event indicator. If an action is executed in several parallel streams, then there will be an indicator for events of each stream. At any time the execution status of a particular request can be found by examining the values of the status indicators. Additional internal status indicators can be defined to control internal activities, or to invoke appropriate procedures.

Some actions of this agent could be dependent on the outcome of some actions of other agents. We assume these indicator values will be sent by those other agents following the specification in the cooperation strategy, and will be held in attributes as part of the skill relation in this agent. These values can then be checked, say as preconditions before the relevant actions are executed.

Relations and Triggers

The description, to be referred to as *the scheme* of a skill relation or an external relation has two parts (i) attribute scheme: which gives the relation name along with the descriptions of its attributes, and (ii) the trigger scheme: which gives the descriptions of all its triggers. The general content of a skill relation is:

- Identity
    Agent-id, Requestor-id, Subtask-id

- Action details
    Operation, Operands, Times, Constraints
    Conditions, Dependency attributes, Status indicators, ...

- Cooperation Characteristics
    Parameters for lower-level cooperations, (if any)
    Parameters for special procedures
    Options, ...

- Triggers Specifications
    Parameters for Shadows,
    Status from other agents
    Parameters for Triggers,
    Parameters for messages from other agents

- Preferences
    Parameters and Variables

Some of the items listed above will be clearer later. The schemes for multiple triggers for a skill relation can be held in an associated special Trigger relation, such as:

Trig (Trig-name, Condition, Procname, Parameter-1 .. Parameter-n)

These triggers will be event-based. If and when the condition is satisfied the named procedure will be called. The condition may include not only the status indicator but also other attributes from the skill relation. All parameters in the condition and the named procedures must exist in the skill relation and its shadow (see below). The named procedure may activate appropriate lower-level actions including message transfers.

3.2 Shadows

Information on what skills are available at an agent is offered by what we call *shadows* of its skill relations. An *export shadow* Sb of skill relation Rb for skill class K of agent B is a scheme derived from the scheme Rb, possibly with added attributes. Any operation specified on the shadow Sb will always be forwarded for execution to its *source relation* Rb. A shadow of a source relation may be projected into a set of shadows if necessary.

If another agent A hold a copy of Sb, then this copy is an *import shadow* at agent A exported from agent B. A shadow Sb must include the scheme of all the relevant attributes and triggers in Rb that may have to be referenced or instantiated in a cooperation strategy at agent A for the skill K of agent B. Shadow Sb constitutes the knowledge of agent A on the skill K of agent B. Thus shadows act as templates of what inter-agent activities are feasible.

Import shadows at agent A received from different agents for the same skill K could be different, and if so, then it would be up to agent A to map these shadows into one common import shadow Sk for that skill for the convenience of operation at agent A. We shall assume shadows discussed below are identical for the same skill, irrespective of their source skill relations.

Agent A will generally hold import shadows for different skills from all of its acquaintances, such as agent B. The total collection of import shadows at agent A at any given time, constitutes the total knowledge this agent A has of the outside world at that time. We shall refer to it as the partial global knowledge of an agent, which is of course always partial, varying from time to time and from agent to agent.

3.3 Inter-agent Activities

In multi-agent research various proposals have been made, some inspired by the Speech-act Theory, for inter-agent communications. These involve communications primitives, such as propose, oppose, respond, refute, refuse etc. We take a different approach based on well-tried computer science concepts. We have only six request primitives which relate to actions:

> Retrieve - to get information from another agent
> Accept - to request an agent to carry out an action, .i.e to *insert* in
>   the request queue for that action

Modify - to modify parameters on the agreed action

Delete - to delete an agreed action

Commit - the final confirmation to go ahead with a particular version
    of the requested action

Abort - to abort the committed action.

Observe that the notion of Commit here is different from that used in the multi-agent scenario. Operations Modify and Delete will not work after a Commit has been issued. The first four primitives makes the acronym RAMD (or RIMD if we use the command Insert in place of Accept). If we consider agent A requesting agent B, with skill relation Rb and export shadow Sb, then the request-primitives will work as follows:

• Retrieve from Sb: Request for information from Rb at B.

• Insert in Sb: Request to B to carry out this action with the specification given.

• Modify Sb: Request to B to change the specification of the previously agreed action.

• Delete from Sb: Request to B to abandon this previously agreed action.

We can consider two kinds of Requests for an action by agent A to B as discussed below:

(1) Immediate execution: To execute an action immediately, such as to schedule, modify or delete a scheduled activity.

(2) Later execution: To execute a scheduled action at a later time in accordance with the schedule.

Immediate Execution

The scheduling of an action is itself an action with scheduling as the skill, complete with its skill relation and shadow for scheduling, say Rb and Sb respectively. Let us further assume that A has a relation for its requested schedules Ra with a shadow Sa. Then agent A holds Ra, import shadow Rb and export shadow Ra. Agent B holds Rb, export shadow Rb and import shadow Ra. Now a request from agent A to B for scheduling will proceed as follows:

The user of agent A will specify a cooperation strategy, which will include an Insert on Sb, with appropriate parameters. The lower-level software will recognise Sb to be a shadow and will despatch this request for an Insert to agent B, which will treat this as a Request for an action. Agent B will invoke its own procedures and will make its decision, which will be recorded in relation Rb as an action tuple tb. To communicate this decision to agent A, agent B will attempt to insert an appropriate subset of sub< tb > in Sa. The underlying system will send this subset to agent A and the sub< tb > will be inserted in Ra, assuming Ra and Rb to be union-compatible for that subset.

However, the return communication to agent A is not automatic, it has to be specified in the cooperation strategy of agent A. Within that strategy A can request for status reports from agent B on the various values of the status indicator, optionally with additional conditions. This will activate an appropriate trigger at B when the condition is satisfied. Note that the strategy at agent A must include the name of its export shadow Sa, since the partial global knowledge of agent B could include multiple import shadows from A and therefore B may not know which one is the right shadow for this purpose. The strategy at A may include additional measures to be taken on the various status values and the outcome of the requested action.

There could be choices in the schedule, the Commit will confirm the final choice, while Abort will discard a choice. The status indicator will display the various states of execution as it progresses. Finally a strategy specified at A will work at B only if B is capable of executing all its requirements. We may assume that every agent is capable of executing the requirements of any strategy associated with its skill. These requirements can be defined, although we have not done it here.

Later Executions

Agent B, which had scheduled an action (requested by A) at a later time, could become unable to fulfil that due to delays, breakdown or other causes. The original strategy of A should specify measures to be taken on such eventualities. Alternatively B can inform A (via some automatic trigger). Whether the scheduled action should commence automatically at the appropriate time, or whether it will require a further input (and possibly an additional strategy) from A nearer the time will also be the stated in the original strategy, i.e. part of the original agreement with B. The original strategy, or the additional strategy (if required), could specify measures to be taken under various status conditions, as the action progresses.

Agent A can receive information on the outcome of its requests to B in two ways: either by executing a retrieval command on the shadow Sb, or by invoking an appropriate trigger at the source skill relation Rb, provided the trigger exists at Rb; if a relevant trigger exists at Rb, then its shadow Sb must include it. To invoke the trigger, agent A must instantiate (at the time of making the request for insert) the relevant trigger parameters available through Sb.

Strategy Propagation

Consider again, agent A as the coordinator (at level 1) and its cohort agent B in turn acting as a coordinator of the next level where C is a cohort. A could be a Supervisor agent, B an Assembler agent and C a Tool agent. Assume also that a human user H specifies a cooperation strategy at A, as shown below:

$$\boxed{H} \to \boxed{A} \to \boxed{B} \to \boxed{C}$$

Observe that H can specify at A for B through shadow Sb only what B is capable of doing. Thus the strategy at A has to be described in terms of B's capability (as specified in Sb), irrespective of the internal features of B, or the existence of C as a lower-level of B. However, if B has a strategy for C, such that this strategy requires an input from A, then the necessary parameters should appear at Sb via Rb.

4. Schema and Operational Architecture

4.1 Schema and Knowledge

As indicated earlier an agent head will include:
- Self Knowledge (Public and Private)
- Acquaintances Knowledge (Import Shadows)
- Mappings
- Communications Facility
- Decision-Support Facility
- Software Support

We have used the term knowledge in the database perspective, in which case knowledge will consist of data, triggers and associated rules, but not programs or procedures. The self-knowledge will be skill relations, external relations, export shadows, internal relations, associated triggers and rules, and the required mappings. The following mappings will be called for:

Global Mappings
- Skill Relation <=> External Relation(s)
- External Relation(s) <=> Export Shadow(s)

Home Mappings
- External Relation(s) <=> Internal Relation(s)

Acquaintances (Acq) Mappings
- Common Import Shadows <=> Actual Import Shadows

An external relation, like an object in object-oriented programming, will have public and private attributes, leading to public and private knowledge; export shadows will include only the public knowledge. The private knowledge will be used for internal activities. Acquaintances knowledge will consists of common import shadows, actual import shadows and the mapping between the two. By *partial global knowledge* we shall imply acquaintances knowledge plus the public component of self-knowledge. The schema architecture is given in figure 1.

The Partial Global Schema holds skill relations, external relations, all shadows, and associated triggers and rules. Home Schema will include the internal relations, along with triggers and rules. The acquaintance schema at agent A from an acquaintance B is the collection of the export shadows of agent B known to A. It is assumed that a cooperation strategy will be written by a user in a convenient language, via an applicant-dependent user-friendly schema layer, shown in the diagram.

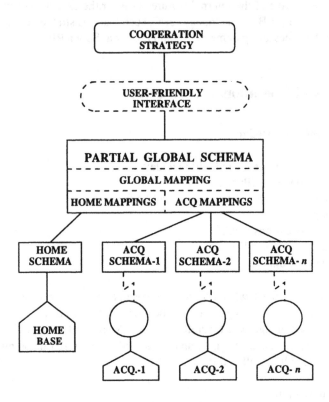

Figure 1: Schema Architecture

4.2 Operational Architecture

The operational scenario of a cohort responding to a request from a coordinator is shown in figure 2. Every agent requires acquaintances knowledge to communicate with the world outside. Once a request for an action is received, a cohort processes the request through its public knowledge, subject to any conditions that the request may include. The results are delivered to the coordinator via its relevant import shadow (acquaintances knowledge) of the coordinator. The action requested will have action states (to be displayed in status indicators), which will be executed with the help of the private knowledge and the processes of the agent base. The execution may invoke activators for actual actions, such "fill the glass with water".

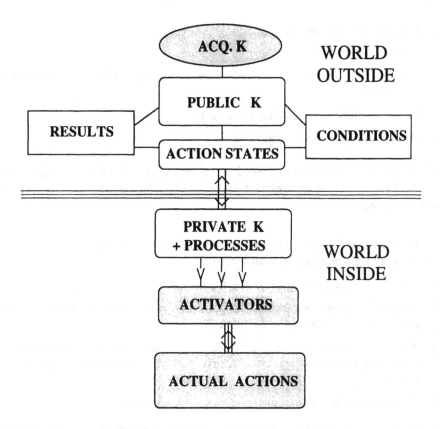

Figure 2: Operational Scenario at a Cohort

5. Strategy Specification

Having outlined our approach in the previous section, we shall demonstrate here how that approach can be used to define cooperation strategies flexibly, without being constrained by the limitation of precoded strategies. We shall specify a version of the Contract Net protocol as an illustration, using what we call COAL notation. However, we shall only code the main inter-agent communications to keep it simple. For this let us consider an example of scheduling of manufacturing operations (such as weld, glue, screw, cut, polish etc) for the assemblage of a product by a number of Assembler agents (cohorts). We shall refer to the user-agent that coordinates the assemblage of that product as the Parter agent. A traditional Contract Net protocol will usually proceed like this:

(1) The Parter invites tenders.

(2) The Assemblers bid.

(3) The Parter evaluates the bids, decides to accept some, and inform the bidders of the outcome.

(4) The successful bidders confirm agreements.

(5) The work is done and the protocol ends.

Since our strategies are not pre-defined, a user may code any suitable strategy at the Parter (subject to the capabilities of the Assemblers). We present below the steps in one such strategy:

(1) The Parter preselects suitable Assembler agents from the Directory agent. This step may yield more agents than needed.

(2) The Parter requests them to schedule the subtasks.

(3) The Parter receives the outcome (success/failure) of the requests, which is equivalent to bids/non-bids by the Assemblers.

(4) If more than one Assembler has agreed to perform the same subtask, the Parter decides which ones to accept and which ones to reject, and then it proceeds to step 5.

(5) Parter communicates Accept, and waits for confirmations.

(6) If all Assemblers confirm acceptance, which we assume they do, the rejection message is posted to the Assemblers rejected in step 4.

Observe that in Step 4 enough Assemblers may not have agreed, or in step 6 enough Assemblers may not have confirmed. These considerations will lead to additional processing not shown here.

Let us assume the Parter agent xp has an external relation PSR (with shadow Pshad) which holds tuples on the scheduled operations. PSR1 is a copy of PSR and has a shadow Pshad1. Each Assembler agent has an external relation ASR for scheduling, with shadow Ashad and a trigger Trig1 of the form:

Trig1 condition Proc-A (xparter#, xshad)

In Trig1 the Proc-A is a procedure which, if the condition is satisfied, copies the new tuples of ASR for Parter-id = xparter# to an export shadow xshad; i.e the tuples will be sent to the source relation of xshad. Therefore if xshad is set to Pshad1, PSR1 would be updated, but not PSR which would hold the original version. We also assume a Directory agent Directory with shadow Dshad. Now we follow the steps:

Step 1
The parter xp finds possible Assemblers as candidates from the Directory by

executing a retrieval operation, results to be stored at an appropriately defined temporary relation, say TRD(Ass#, Op#).

TRD:= ?[Ass#, Op#]
      Where Directory..Dshad [Op# = xop],
                PSR [Op# = xop]

Symbol ? means Retrieve, and symbol : Where. Directory..Dshad means relation Dshad of agent Directory. Each Dshad tuple that matches a PSR tuple on the value of Op# is selected. From each selected tuples two attributes Ass# and Op# are projected as the result to be stored in TRD. Variable xop acts like an example element of QBE. Thus the Ass# of all Assemblers capable of performing the operations listed in PSR will be copied to TRD.

Step 2

The parter xp requests the Assemblers for scheduling:

      Insert xag..Ashad [Parter# = xp, Op# = xop,
                        xtrig = Trig1, Condition = (Status = 14), Xshad = Pshad1
                        Time-out = to, Start-time = st, End-time = et, ...]
                Where TRD [Ass# = xag, Op# = xop]

Assume that the value of the status indicator becomes 14 when this action is completed. At that point the logic variable Condition becomes True. Variable xag holds the agent-id, and thus acts as the qualifier of relation Ashad above. We use the form:
    Agent-id..relationname.attributename.
for qualification. Since xag is Ass# in TRD, all the Assemblers in TRD will be selected for scheduling. Some other associated attributes, such as Time-out etc are also set.

Step 3

The outcome will be delivered to PSR1 via Pshad1 through Trig1 when the status indicator reaches Status = 14. So the success/failure can be determined from PSR1 after the Time-out = to.

Step 4

The parter will examine if Assemblers have been found for all subtasks. We assume they are found. Now, if any operation has more than one Assembler, Parter must decide which one to accept. Let us suppose the Parter copies the tuples for the accepted Assemblers from PSR1 to a temporary relation TSR1, and the rejected Assemblers from PSR1 to TSR2. The codes are not shown.

Step 5

The Parter will then communicate its final decision as a Commit to the accepted Assemblers:

Commit xag..Ashad [Parter# = xp, Op# = xop, Time-out = to,
xtrig = Trig1, Condition = (Status = 24), Xshad = Pshad1]
Where TSR1 [Ass# = xag, Op# = xop]

We assume Status = 24 implies the end of this action. The confirmation by the Assemblers, of acceptance, can be found from the new tuples in PSR1.

Step 6
Assuming all Assemblers have accepted, then the rejected Assemblers from TSR2 must be notified:

Delete xag..Ashad [Parter# = xp, Op# = xop]
Where TSR2 [Ass# = xag, Op# = xop]

We have demonstrated in this section how the idea of action tuples, external relations, shadows and triggers can be used to specify cooperation strategies at the coordinator agent. Strategies can naturally be specified for other agents as well, as needed.

If an Assembler acts as the coordinator for Tool agents, and if one of its strategies for Tools requires an input from the Parter, then this requirement must be expressed as a parameter in the appropriate shadow (via the action tuple at the source relation) of the Assembler exported to the Parter. A strategy can thus be propagated.

In the context of our model, strategies can be specified either for all instances of the same agent class or for only those agents of a class that are engaged in the execution of a task that needs these strategies. In the first case the strategies can be compiled before the execution-time, while in the other case the strategies have to be invoked dynamically during the execution of the task, when the particular agents involved in that task become known. Either is possible, and in either case a library facility can be used to hold the strategies.

6. Conclusion

As stated in the Introduction, CKBS is a relatively new area of research, which can benefit substantially from some generic model of cooperation, which at the moment does not exist. In this paper, we have blended ideas from the fields of both distributed databases and the multi-agent systems (of DAI), and have produced a model with a minimal deviation from the well-established database concepts. Our model cannot and is not meant to, simulate human behaviour in social context; we are instead aiming towards real-world applications where flexibility, performance, reliability, responsiveness, user-facilities and effective system-cycle are more important. We believe our model provides a foundation to develop these facilities, with the help of the following key features:

(i)   A scheme for the representation of actions, using n-tuples.

(ii)   A carrier or messenger in the form of shadows for inter-agent communication, distribution transparency.

(iii)   Four primitives: Retrieve, Insert, Modify, Delete (RIMD) to initiate inter-agent actions.

(iv)   Use of status indicators and triggers for the dynamic control and communications

(v)   Support for user-defined cooperation strategies for inter-agent activities.

The basis of our model is the association of one action tuple to each atomic action of an agent, with shadows and triggers for communications and a high-level language for flexible strategy specification. Classification of agents into action classes simplifies some of the handling. With this basis, we can abstract the requests for all agent actions to the four traditional database commands: retrieve, insert, modify and delete. Without such abstractions, it would be hard to define a generic model, which can be applied to all possible actions in transaction-oriented task execution.

During the development of our model, we have been guided by the following criteria, called the SENSE criteria:

SENSE criteria

(i)   *Simplicitly* : The model should be the simplest possible for the intended purpose. This is the Einstein's criteria of everything should be made as simple as possible - but not simpler.

(ii)   *Employability*: A model should be directly employable for the intended applications without requiring a huge amount of subjective interpretation. Some models are too abstract and too vague requiring so much interpretation that the model becomes worthless.

(iii) *Necessity*: All new concepts developed should be only those that were really necessary. A new concept should not be introduced when an old one is adequate without a very good justification, nor should it be built on the top of another unverified concept. This is an unwritten principle in Physics which seems to be very appropriate.

(iv) *Sufficiency*: The model developed and the concepts in it should be sufficient for the purpose - another unwritten principle of Physics.

(v)   *Extensibility*: The model should be extensible to cater for the needs of unforeseen requirements - typically for Computer Science.

We hope we have succeeded in meeting the SENSE criteria to some extent. We are aware that we need much further research in this area.

References

[1]   S.M. Deen: "Cooperating Agents - A Database Perspective", CKBS'90 - Proceedings of the International Working Conference on CKBS, Keele University, edited by S.M. Deen, published by Springer Verlag, pp 3-29, 1990.

[2]   M.N. Huhns: "A DAI Perspective on Cooperating Knowledge Based Systems", CKBS'94 - Proceedings of the Second International Working Conference on CKBS, Keele University, edited by S.M. Deen, published by the DAKE Centre, pp 3-11, June 1994.

[3]   IMS Programme: This is an international programme on Intelligent Manufacturing Systems (IMS), with the participation of major industries, some universities and research institutes from six regions: Australia, Japan, EFTA countries, EU countries, Canada and USA, partially funded by the Governments. It is intended as a ten year pre-competitive research programme, starting with a one-year feasibility phase to be completed early 1994, hopefully to be followed by the full programme after a suitable evaluation study. The programme has several themes or projects, one of which is the Holonic Manufacturing System (HMS) for high-variety low-volume manufacturing in a largely un-manned environment. A holon can be assumed be a CKBS agent. The author is a participant in this IMS/HMS project, which inspired some of the work presented here.

[4]   A. Bond and L. Gasser: "An Analysis of Problems and Research in DAI", Readings in Distributed Artificial Intelligence, edited by A. Bond and L. Gasser, chapter 1, pp 3-35, published by Morgan Kaufmann, 1988.

[5]   L.D. Erman and C.R. Lesser: "A Multi-level Organisation for Problem Solving Using Many Diverse Cooperating Sources of Knowledge", Proceedings of the International Joint Conference on Artificial Intelligence, pp 483-490, 1975.

[6]   E.H. Durfee et al: "Trends in Cooperative Distributed Problem Solving", IEEE TKDE (1:1), pp 63-83, March 1989.

[7]   V.R. Lesser, E.H. Durfee and D.D. Corkill: "Coherent Cooperation Amount Communicating Problem Solvers", Readings in Distributed Artificial Intelligence, edited by A. Bond and L. Gasser, chapter 4, pp 268-284, published by Morgan Kaufmann, 1988.

[8]   D.D. Corkill and V.R. Lesser: "The Use of Meta-level Control for Coordinating in a Distributed Problem Solving Network", Proceedings of the International Joint Conference on Artificial Intelligence, pp 758-756, 1983.

[9]   L. Gasser et al: "MACE: A Flexible test-bed for DAI", Distributed Artificial Intelligence, edited by M.N. Huhns, published by Pitman , pp 119-152, 1987.

[10]   R. Bisiani *et al*: "The Architecture of the AGORA Environment", Distributed Artificial Intelligence, edited by M.N. Huhns, published by Pitman, pp 99-118, 1987.

[11]   J.R. Ensor and J.D. Gable: "Transactional Blackboard", Blackboard Systems, edited by R. Englemore and T. Morgan, published by Addison-Wesley, pp 465-474, 1988.

[12]   B. Hayes-Roth and M. Hewett: "BB1: An Implementation of the Blackboard Control Architecture", Blackboard Systems, edited by R. Englemore and T. Morgan, published by Addison Wesley, pp 297-315, 1988. The same authors have another article on BB* in the same book on pp 543-560.

[13]   D.D. Corkill *et al*: "GBB: A Generic Blackboard Development System", Blackboard Systems, edited by R. Engelmore and T. Morgan, published by Addison-Wesley, pp 503-516, 1988.

[14]   R.G. Smith: "The Contract Net Protocol: High Level Communication and Distributed Problem Solver", Readings in Distributed Artificial Intelligence, edited by A. Bond and L. Gasser, published by Morgan Kaufmann, pp 357-366, 1988.

[15]   R. Davis and R.G. Smith: "Negotiation as a Metaphor for Distributed Problem Solving", Artificial Intelligence vol 20, pp 63-109, 1983.

[16]   R. Steeb *et al*: "Architecture for Distributed Air-Traffic Control", Readings in Distributed Artificial Intelligence, edited by A. Bond and L. Gasser, published by Morgan Kaufmann, pp 90-101, 1988.

[17]   S. Cammarata *et al*: "Strategies for Cooperation in Distributed Problem Solving", Readings in Distributed Artificial Intelligence, edited by A. Bond and L. Gasser, published by Morgan Kaufmann, pp 102-105, 1988.

[18]   N.V. Findler and R. Lo: "An Examination of Distributed Planning in the World of Air-Traffic Control", Readings in Distributed Artificial Intelligence, edited by A. Bond and L. Gasser, published by Morgan Kaufmann, pp 617-627, 1988.

[19]   R. Weihmayer *et al*: "Modes of Diversity: Issues in Cooperation Among Dissimilar Agents", Proceedings of the 10th International Workshop on DAI, MCC, Texas, edited by M.N. Huhns, October 1990.

[20]   M. Busuioc and D.G. Griffiths (British Telecom): "Cooperating Intelligent Agents for Service Management in Communications Networks", Proceedings of the 1993 CKBS-SIG Workshop, edited by S.M. Deen, published by the DAKE Centre, ISBN 0 9521789 1 5, pp 213-226, September 1993.

[21]   M. Walsh and S.M Deen: "A Study of Some Multi-Agent Application Design Strategies with a view to Enhancing Performance", Proceedings of the 1992 CKBS-SIG Workshop, edited by S.M. Deen, published by the DAKE Centre, ISBN 0 9521789 0 7, pp 75-88, September 1992.

[22]   M. Fletcher and S.M. Deen: "Design Considerations for Optimal Intelligent Network Routing", Proceedings of the 1992 CKBS-SIG Workshop, edited by S.M. Deen, published by the DAKE Centre, ISBN 0 9521789 0 7, pp 19-42, September 1992.

[23]   G. Agha and C. Hewitt "Concurrent Programming Using Actors: Exploiting Large Scale Parallelism", Readings in Distributed Artificial Intelligence, edited by A. Bond and L. Gasser, published by Morgan Kaufmann, pp 102-105, 1988.

[24]   C. Hewitt: "Towards Open Information Systems Semantics", Proceedings of the 10th International Workshop on DAI, edited by M.N. Huhns, MCC, Texas, October 1990.

[25]   N.R. Jennings: "The ARCHON Project and its Applications", Proceedings of the Second International Working Conference on CKBS, Keele University, edited by S.M. Deen, published by the DAKE Centre, pp 13-30, June 1994.

[26]   H. Haugeneder: "IMAGINE: A Framework for Building Multi-Agent Systems", Proceedings of the Second International Working Conference on CKBS, Keele University, edited by S.M. Deen, published by the DAKE Centre, pp 31-64, June 1994.

[27]   T.R. Gruber: "Ontolingua: A Mechanism to Support Portable Ontologies", version 3.0, Knowledge Systems Laboratory, Stanford University, June 1992,

[28]   M.R. Genesereth and R.E. Fikes: "Knowledge Interchange Format Reference Manual", version 3.0, Computer Science Department, Stanford University, June 1992.

[29]   M.M. Schwuttke and A.G. Quan: "Enhancing Performance of Cooperating Agents Real-time Diagnostic Systems", Proceedings of the 1993 International Joint Conference on Artificial Intelligence, pp 32-42, 1993.

[30]   A. Sehmi et al: "Support for Distributed Multi-Agent Systems", Proceedings of the Second International Working Conference on CKBS, Keele University, edited by S.M. Deen, published by the DAKE Centre, pp 357-376, June 1994.

[31]   M. Fisher et al: "Specifying and Executing Protocols for Cooperative Action", Proceedings of the Second International Working Conference on CKBS, Keele University, edited by S.M. Deen, published by the DAKE Centre, pp 295-306, June 1994.

[32]   S.M. Deen: "Systems Characteristics of Holons for Intelligent Manufacturing Systems" to be published by the IMS/HMS consortium, 1994. See reference [2].

[33]   S.M. Deen, "A General Framework for Coherence in CKBS", Journal of Intelligent Information Systems vol. 2, pp 83-107, published by Kluwer Academic Publishers, June 1993,

[34]   S.M. Deen: "Cooperation Issues in Holonic Manufacturing Systems", Pro-
         ceedings of the International Conference on Information Infrastructure Sys-
         tems for Manufacturing, University of Tokyo, held in Nov 1993, edited by
         H. Yoshikawa and J. Goosenaerts, published by Elsevier, pp 401-412, ISSN
         0926 5481.

[35]   S.M. Deen: "A Cooperation Framework for Holonic Interactions in Manu-
         facturing", CKBS'94, Proceedings of the Second International Working
         Conference on CKBS, Keele University, edited by S.M. Deen, published by
         the DAKE Centre, pp 103-124, June 1994, ISBN 0 9521789 2 3.

[36]   B.J. Banks et al: "Design and Implementation of DEAL", Data and Knowl-
         edge Base Integration, Edited by Deen and Thomas, published by Pitman
         (London), 1989, ISBN 0-273-08826-2, pp29-62.

[37]   S. M. Deen: "Systems Characteristics of Holon", DAKE Centre Technical
         Report DAKE/TR-93008, presented at the HMS project meeting (see [3]),
         Kobe 1993.

[38]   S. M. Deen: "An architectural Framework for CKBS Applications", IEEE
         Transactions on Knowledge and Data Engineering, Vol (8:4), Aug 1996, pp
         663-671.

Extraction of Informations
from Highly Heterogeneous Source of Textual Data⋆

Sonia Bergamaschi

Dipartimento di Scienze dell'Ingegneria
Universitá di Modena
CSITE-CNR Bologna
ITALY
sonia@dsi.unimo.it,sbergamaschi@deis.unibo.it

Abstract.
Extracting informations from multiple sources, highly heterogeneous, of textual data and integrating them in order to provide *true information* is a challenging research topic in the database area. In order to illustrate problems and solutions, one of the most interesting projects facing this problem, *TSIMMIS*, is presented. Furthermore, a *Description Logics* approach, able to provide interesting solutions both for data integration and data querying, is introduced.

1 Introduction

The availiability of large numbers of network informations sources (and the recent explosion of Internet) makes it possible to access to a very large amount of information sources all over the world. The increased amount of available informations has as a consequence the fact that, for a given query, the set of potentially interesting sites is very high but only very few sites are really relevant. Furthermore, informations are highly heterogeneous both in their structure and in their origin. In particular, not only data types are heterogeneus (textual data, images, sounds, etc.), but even the representation of a single data type can differ.

Even in the restricted domain of textual data, the problem of *organizing* data (often a huge amount) coming from multiple heterogeneous sources in *easily accessible structures*, in order to provide *true information*, is a challenging research topic for different research communities: database, artificial intelligence, information retrieval. Let us individuate two increasing complexity scenarios:

1. *known sources* – the sources of heterogeneous textual data are known;
2. *unknown sources* –the sources of *relevant* heterogeneous textual data must be individuated.

⋆ This research has been partially funded by the MURST 40 % Italian Project: '*Basi di dati Evolute: Modelli, metodi e sistemi*'.

The first scenario is, at present, heavily investigated in the database area, involving many research topics and application areas: decision support systems (DSS), integration of heterogeneous databases, datawarehouse. Decision makers need informations from multiple heterogeneous sources (including databases, file systems, knowledge bases, digital libraries, information retrieval systems, and electronic mail systems), but are usually unable to get and fuse them in a timely fashion due to the difficulties of accessing the different systems and to consistently integrate them. Significant contributions about the integration of well-structured conventional databases exist (e.g. [9, 21, 22, 24, 18]). Many projects have adopted OO models to facilitate integration [9, 13, 5] and, recently, systems for the integration of sources with minimal structure have appeared [17, 23, 4]. Futhermore, the DARPA Intelligent Integration of Information (I^3) research program is devoted to this problem. However, as a consequence of the rapid development of prototype implementations in this area, the initial outcome of this program appears to have been to produce a new set of systems. While they can perform certain advanced information integration tasks, they cannot easily communicate with each other. With a view to understanding and solving this problem, recently a workshop was held on this topic at the University of Maryland in April, 1996 [12].

The second, most complex scenario, is associated to the so-called *information discovery* problem. This problem arised mainly due to the *Internet* explosion. In this scenario we have, first, to face the problem of individuating among a huge amount of sources of heterogeneous textual data a *possibly low amount* of *relevant* sources and, then, to face, if necessary, the problem of scenario 1. Research efforts devoted to face this problem come from different research areas: information retrieval, artificial intelligence, database. This scenario is out of the scope of this paper as the amount of approaches and systems very recently proposed is as large as to require a paper on its own.

In this paper I will discuss problems and solutions of the extraction of informations from multiple sources, highly heterogeneous, of textual data and of their integration in order to provide *true information*. First, one of the most interesting projects facing this problem, *TSIMMIS*, is presented. Then, a *Description Logics (DL)* approach, able to provide interesting solutions both for data modelling and data querying, is introduced.

The outline of the paper is the following. Section 2 presents an overview of the *TSIMMIS* project, including the *OEM* data model and *MSL* language adopted in the project. Section 3 describes the architecture of a *TSIMMIS wrapper*, i.e., an extractor of informations from a textual source which convert data into the *OEM* data model. Section 4 describes *TSIMMIS* approach for generating *mediators* (a mediator is an integration and refinement tool of data coming from wrappers). Section 5 introduces *Description Logics*. Section 6 sketchs a *Description Logics* approach to the problems of data modelling and data querying in heterogeneous multiple sources of textual data.

Remarks all over the paper fix relevant choices for the design of I^3 systems.

2 The TSIMMIS project: an overview

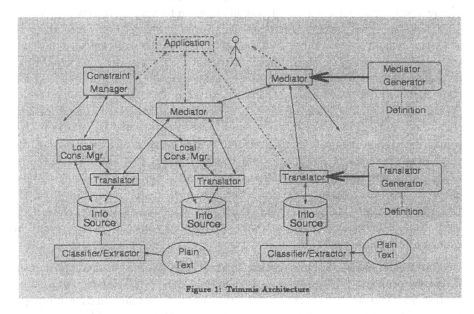

Figure 1: Tsimmis Architecture

Fig. 1. Tsimmis Architecture

Let us introduce the problems and the solutions recently proposed within scenario 1, by describing one of the most interesting projects: the **TSIMMIS** (The Stanford- IBM Manager of Multiple Information Sources) Data Integration Project, under development at the Department of Computer Science - University of Stanford (biblio references: http://db.stanford.edu). TSIMMIS is a joint project between Stanford and the IBM Almaden Research Center whose goal is the development of tools that facilitate the rapid integration of heterogeneous textual sources that may include both structured and unstructured data [1, 2].

The TSIMMIS data-integration system provides integrated access via an architecture that is common in many other projects: *wrappers/translators* [13, 25, 5] convert data into a common model; *Mediators* combine, integrates or refines the data from the wrappers. The wrappers also provide a common query language for extracting informations. Applications can access data directly through wrappers but they can also go through *mediators* [5, 29, 4].

In Figure 1, the TSIMMIS architecture is shown: above each source is a *translator (wrapper)* that logically converts the underlying data objects to a common information model; above the translators lie the *mediators*. The translator converts queries over information in the common model into requests that the source can execute and data extracted from the source into the common model. The common model is the *OEM (Object Exchange Model)*, a *tagged* model allowing simple nesting of objects. Furthermore, two query languages, *OEM-QL* and *MSL(Mediator Specification Language)*, for requesting *OEM* objects have been developed. *OEM-QL* is an SQL-like language, extended to deal with labels and object nesting and *MSL* is a high level language that allows the declarative specification of mediators. The possible bottlenecks of the above architecture are:

- an ad-hoc translator [2] must be developed for any information source;
- implementing a mediator can be complicated and time-consuming.

Thus, important goals of the project (and of any other project with the same aim) are:

1. **to provide translator generator** that can generate *OEM* translator based on a description of the conversion that need to take place for queries received and results returned (see *translator/generator* box in Figure 1);
2. **to automatically or semi-automatically generate mediators** from high level descriptions of the information processing they need to do (see *mediator/generator* box in Figure 1).

The solutions proposed in *TSIMMIS* for the above goals are described in Section 3 and 4.

2.1 The OEM model and the MSL language

Let us briefly introduce the *OEM* model [5]. It is a *self-describing model* [31] where each data item has an associated descriptive label and *without a strong typing system*. *OEM* is much simpler than conventional OO models: supports only *object nesting* and *object identity*, while other features, such as classes, methods and inheritance are not supported directly. An object description in *OEM* has the format:

```
<ob1: person, set,      {sub1,sub2,sub3,sub4,sub5}>
     <sub1: last_name,  str, 'Smith'>
     <sub2: first_name, str, 'John'>
     <sub3: role,       str, 'faculty'>
     <sub4: department, str, 'cs'>
     <sub5: telephone,  str, '32435465'>
```

Each *OEM* object has the following structure: an object-id, a label, a type, a value. A label is a variable-length string describing what the object represents. We have a top-level object (ob1) and five sub-objects(sub1 to sub5).

Remark 1 *A relevant feature of OEM is that objects sharing the same label do not follow a unique schema: for example an other object with the same label 'person' could have different sub-objects. This feature make the integration of data coming from heterogeneous sources with different schemas easier than in conventional OO data models.*

---

[2] translator and wrapper are synonimous in TSIMMIS.

Let us briefly introduce the *MSL* language [4] (a more detailed description is given in Section 4).

Remark 2 MSL *is a first-order logic language that allow the declarative specification of mediators; An* MSL *specification is a set of rules which define the mediator view of the data and a set of functions that are invoked to translate objects from one format to another. Each rule consists of a* head *and a* tail *separated by the symbol :-. The tail describes the pattern of the objects to be fetched from the source, while the head defines the pattern of the top-level integrated object supported by the mediator.*

3   The TSIMMIS wrapper generator

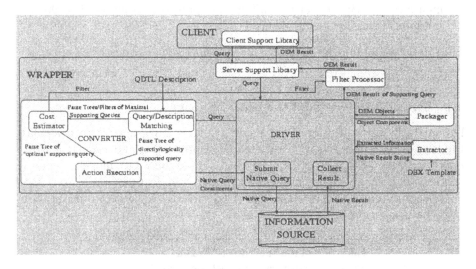

Fig. 2. TSIMMIS wrapper

TSIMMIS includes a toolkit, say *OEM Support Libraries*, to quickly implement wrappers, mediators and end-user interfaces. These libraries contain procedures that implement the exchange of *OEM* objects and queries between a server (either a translator or a mediator) and a client (either a mediator, an application or an interactive end-user) and procedures to translate queries into a suitable format.

The architecture of wrappers generated by using the toolkit is shown in Figure 2:

- the white rectangles are available in the toolkit: *CONVERTER, CLS (Client Support Library), SSL (Server Support Library), Filter Processor, Packager, Extractor;*

- The *CONVERTER* is the wrapper component which translates a query expressed in the *MSL* language into a sequence of operations executable by the information source. The translation is performed by using descriptions expressed in *QDTL (Query Description and Translation Language)*;
- *QDTL description* for the *CONVERTER* and *DEX template* for the *Extractor* must be specified;
- An architecture component, say the *DRIVER*, must be completely developed from scratch, for each wrapper, as it depends on the information source.

If we generate a wrapper exploiting the toolkit, it acts as a server in a client-server architecture (where the clients can be mediators or applications) in the following way:

- Clients use *CLS* to send queries and to receive *OEM* objects;
- by means of the *SSL*, the wrapper receives a query and send it to the *DRIVER* to be executed;
- the *DRIVER* invokes the *CONVERTER*, that, on the basis of the *QDTL description* , translates the query in a sequence of operations executable at the information source;
- the sequence of operations is sent to the *DRIVER* to be executed. The extracted data are passed by the *DRIVER* to the *Extractor*;
- by using the *DEX template*, the *Extractor* extracts the informations which will be translated into OEM objects by the *Packager*;
- if during the query conversion a filter has been generated, the *DRIVER* passes the filter and the *OEM* objects to the *Filter Processor*, then, by means of the *SSL*, the *OEM* objects are sent to the *CLIENT*.

3.1 CONVERTER and QDTL

To illustrate the *CONVERTER* functionalities and the *QDTL* syntax [3], let us refer to a university professors and students WHOIS information source. Let us suppose that this source allows only very simple retrieve operations, for example, the following:

1. retrieve persons with a given last_name: `>lookup -ln 'ss'`
2. retrieve persons with a given last_name and first_name: `>lookup -ln 'ss' -fn 'ff'`
3. retrieve all the records of the source : `>lookup`

The above operations are mapped into *QDTL* descriptions in order to make the *CONVERTER* able to decompose a *MSL* query into subqueries executable by the source. A *QDTL* description is composed by a set of templates with associated actions. The query templates for the three operations (no actions are specified for the moment) are:

---

[3] a full description of the *CONVERTER* and of *QDTL* is in [3]

D1:

```
(QT1.1) Query ::= *O :- <O person {< last_name $LN>}>
(QT1.2) Query ::= *O :- <O person {< last_name $LN>
                                   <first_name $FN>}>
(QT1.3) Query ::= *O :- <O person V>
```

Each query template is described after the ::= symbol and is a parameterized query. Identifiers preceded by the $ symbol represent the corresponding constants of an input *MSL* query. The variables in capital letters (V) correspond to variables of an input *MSL* query.

The *CONVERTER* includes an algorithm able to exploit each template to describe much more queries than the ones that could be executed directly using the template. The class of supported queries is thus:

- *Directly supported queries*: queries with a syntax analogous to the template;
- *Logical supported queries*: A query q is logically supported by a template t if q is *logically equivalent* to a query q' directly supported by t (two queries are logically equivalent if they give the same answer set in the same context);
- *Indirectly supported queries*: a query q is indirectly supported by a template t if q can be decomposed in a query q' directly supported by t and a *filter* that is applied on the results of q'.

Let us consider the query:

```
(Q6) *Q :- <Q person {<last_name 'Smith'> <role 'student'>}>
```

Q6 is not logically supported by any of the D1 templates, but the *CONVERTER* is able to detect that Q6 is subsumed by the query Q7 which is directly supported:

```
(Q7) *Q :- <Q person {<last_name 'Smith'>}>
```

Q7 contains all the informations necessary to determine Q6 answer set; to obtain Q6 answer set a filter, i.e. a new MSL query: *O :- <O person {<role 'student'>}> is generated which applied to Q7 answer set gives Q6 result.

More formally, with reference to indirectly supported queries, we define:

Query Subsumption: A query q is subsumed by a query q' if each object in the answer set of q is in the answer set of q'.

Query Equivalence: Two queries are logically equivalent if they give the same answer set in the same context.

Indirect Support: A query q is indirectly supported by a query q' if:
- q' subsumes q, and
- it exists a filter query that when applied to the answer set of q' gives the answer set of q.

Let us observe that, in general, for a given query q we can have more than one query able to support it. For example query Q6, besides Q7 is supported by the following Q11 query:

(Q11) O* :- <O person V>

which, in its turn, subsumes Q7.

Remark 3 .
The CONVERTER *should consider all the possible subsuming supporting queries in order to select the most efficient one. The lowest subsuming supporting query could be a good candidate.*

QDTL allows the use of non-terminal symbols to guarantee the support of more complex queries. Coming back to the example, we can have a combination of arguments (>lookup -fn 'hh' -ln 'iop', ecc.). An exaustive list of all the possible cases is impossible, thus non-terminal symbols that allow a concise expression of a set of queries have been introduced. For example, let us consider the *QDTL* description D4:

D4:
```
(QT4.1) Query    ::= *OP :- <OP person {_OptLN _OptFN _OptRole}>
(NT4.2) _OptLN   ::= <Last_name $LN>
(NT4.3) _OptLN   ::=
(NT4.4) _OptFN   ::= <first_name $FN>
(NT4.5) _OptFN   ::=
(NT4.6) _OptRole ::= <Role $R>
(NT4.7) _OptRole ::=
```

D4 describes all the queries that can be obtained by combining the three arguments. The non-terminal symbols are preceded by the character '_' ; each symbol has a description constituted by a set of non-terminal templates. For example, the symbol _OptRole is defined by NT4.6 and NT4.7 templates.

Direct Support: A query q is directly supported by a template t including non-terminal symbols if q is directy supported by one of the expansion of t.

An expansion is obtained by substituting each non-terminal symbol with its definition.

Actions in *QDTL* templates express the query in a format executable by the source. In the described Converter we use actions expressed in the C language. Let us refer to *D1* description to show some actions:

D2
```
(QT2.1) Query ::= *O :- <O person {<last_name $LN>}>
(AC2.1)               {printf (lookup_query, 'lookup -ln %s',$LN);}
(QT2.2) Query ::= *O :- <O person {<last_name $LN>
                                    <first_name $FN>}>
(AC2.2)               {printf (lookup_query, 'lookup -ln %s -fn %s ',
                           $LN,$FN);}
```

Furthermore, it is possible to associate non-terminal descriptions to actions:

```
(NT5.2) _OptLN ::= <last_name $LN>
(AC5.2)              {printf ($_OptLN, '-ln %s', $LN);}
```

3.2 Extractor, DEX templates and Filter Processor

A query result is often expressed in a unstructured format. The *Extractor* component uses the *DEX* templates to analyze and structure data received from the sources. *DEX* templates contain the description of the data received from a source and informations about the fields to be extracted. After the extraction of the needed informations from the source output, they are converted by the *Packager* into a set of *OEM* objects. Then, this set of objects is filtered in the *Filter Processor*. The filter to be applied to the set of objects is a *MSL* query built by the *Converter* during the translation activity of the input query into executable commands. The *Filter Processor* applies this query to the set of retrieved objects and send the subset thus obtained to the *Client*.

4 The TSIMMIS mediator generator

The **MedMaker** system [4] is the *TSIMMIS* component developed for declaratively specifying mediators. It is targeted for integration of sources with unstructured or semi-structured data and/or sources with changing schemas. MedMaker provides the high level language *MSL* that allows the declarative specification of mediators.

At run time, when the mediator receives a request for information, the *Mediator Specification Interpreter (MSI)* collects and integrates the necessary informations from the sources, according to the specification. The process is analogous to expanding a view against a conventional relational database and *MSL* can be seen as a view definition language that is targeted to the *OEM* data model and the functionality needed for integrating heterogeneous sources.

4.1 The Mediator Specification Language MSL: an example

Let us introduce an example to illustrate *MSL*. We have two input sources: a relational database with two tables
```
employee(first_name,last_name,title,report_to)
student(first_name,last_name,year)
```

and a university system 'WHOIS' with informations on students and professors. For the first source, a wrapper called **'CS'** exports the informations (some of which are shown in Figure 3), as *OEM* objects; the second source uses a wrapper called **'whois'** (some objects are shown in Figure 4).

We want to develop a mediator, called **'MED'** with objects integrating all the informations about a person, say 'Chung', of the department 'cs', coming

```
<&e1, employee, set,        {&f1,&l1,&t1, &rep1}>
    <&f1,      first_name, string,  'Joe'>
    <&l1,      last_name,  string,  'Chung'>
    <&t1,      title,      string,  'professor'>
    <&rep1,    reports_to, string,  'John Hennessy'>

<&e2, employee, set,        {&f2,&l2,&t2}>
    <&f2,      first_name, string,  'John'>
    <&l2,      last_name,  string,  'Hennessy'>
    <&t2,      title,      string,  'chairman'>
..............etc.

<&s3, student,  set,        {&f3,&l3,&y3}>
    <&f3,      first_name, string,  'Pierre'>
    <&l3,      last_name,  string,  'Huyn'>
    <&y3,      year,       integer, 3>
```

Fig. 3. CS objects in OEM

from the two wrappers. Given the objects of Figure 3 and 4, **MED** must be able
to combine them to obtain the object of Figure 5.

Let us introduce the rules, expressed in in MSL, which define the mediator MED:

```
(MS1) Rules:
<cs_person {<name N> <rel R> Rest1 Rest2}>
        :- <person {<name N> <dept 'cs'> <relation R> | Rest1}>
           @whois
           AND decomp(N, LN, FN)
           AND <R {<first_name FN> <last_name LN> | Rest2}>@cs
External:
decomp(string,string,string)(bound,free,free) impl by name_to_lnfn
decomp(string,string,string)(free,bound,bound) impl by lnfn_to_name.
```

Remark 4

```
<&p1, person,  set,     {&n1, &d1, &rel1, &elem1}>
    <&n1,     name,     string, 'Joe Chung'>
    <&d1,     dept,     string, 'cs'>
    <&rel1,   relation, string, 'employee'>
    <&elem1,  e_mail,   string, 'chung@cs'>
..............etc.
```

Fig. 4. whois objects in OEM

```
<&cp1, cs_person, set,      {&mn1, &mrel1, &t1, &rep1, &elm1}>
      <&mn1,     name,       string, 'Joe Chung'>
      <&mrel1,   relation,   string, 'employee'>
      <&t1,      title,      string, 'professor'>
      <&rep1,    reports_to, string, 'John Hennesy'>
      <&elem1,   e_mail,     string, 'chung@cs'>
```

Fig. 5. object exported by MED

The 'creation process' of a mediator object is a pattern matching process: first the object extracted by the wrapper satisfying the tail are collected and their component are linked to the variables, then the bindings are used to create objects expressed in the head.

With reference to the example, we want to search the objects of the sources 'cs' and 'WHOIS' which links to the tail expressed in rule 'MS1' (i e. top-level person object of 'whois' with sub-object name, dept='cs' and relation; top-level person object of 'cs' with FN and LN obtained from the corresponding N of whois (&e1 satisfy the model).

The decomp function executes the string transformations in order to obtain first_name and last_name of a person. When the objects satisfying the tail pattern have been obtained, the rule head is used to build the virtual object which is the union of data coming from the wrappers (&cp1 is the result of the union of &p1 e &e1).

MSL has other querying functionalities to facilitate integration of heterogeneous sources: expressing only variables in the value fields it is possible to obtain informations about the structure of an information source (e.g. after a schema changing). MSL allows 'wildcard' to search objects at any nesting level without specifying the whole path as it would be necessary with conventional OO languages.

4.2   Architecture and implementation of MSI

The Mediator Specification Interpreter *(MSI)* is the component of *MedMaker* which process a query on the basis of the rules expressed with *MSL*. It is composed of three modules: *VE&AO (View Expander and Algebraic Optimizer)*; *cost-based optimizer; datamerge engine. VE&AO* reads a query and, on the basis of the *MSL* specification, discovers what objects have to be obtained from a source and determines the conditions that the obtained objects must satisfy; gives a result called *logical datamerge program* which is passed to the second module *cost-based optimizer*. The optimizer develops an access plane to retrieve and combine objects, i.e. , what requests to submit to the sources; the order of requests submissions; how to combine the results to obtain the requested objects.

The access plane is passed to the third component, *datamerge engine*, which executes it and gives the results. Let us consider an example of the *MSI* query processing.

Suppose that a client want to retrieve informations about 'Joe Chung'; the query expressed in *MSL* is the following:

```
(Q1) JC :- JC :< cs_person {<name 'Joe Chung'>}> @MED
```

The object pattern in the tail of the query Q1 is matched against the structure of the objects hold in *MED*. **View expansion** - having as input the query Q1 and the *MSL* rules, *VE&AO* substitutes the query tail with the pattern of the objects in the sources, obtaining the datamerge rule R2:

```
(R2) <cs_person {<name 'Joe Chung'> <rel R> Rest1 Rest2}>
            :- <person {<name 'Joe Chung'> <dept 'cs'>
                        <relation R> | Rest1}>@whois
        AND decomp( 'Joe Chung', LN, FN)
        AND <R {<first_name FN> <last_name LN> |
                Rest2 }>@cs.
```

The rule obtained in this way has a head representing the query and a tail, obtained from *MS1* rule, indicating how to select the objects from the wrappers. **Execution plan** - when the *MSI* knows what objects have to be fetched from the sources, the *cost-based optimizer* build the *physical datamerge program*, that specify what query should be sent to the sources. A possible efficient plan to process query Q1 is the following:

1. Bindings for variables R   and Rest1 are obtained from the source by **whois** execution of the following query:

```
<bind_for_whois {<bind_for_r R> < bind_for_Rest1 Rest1>}>
        :- <person {<name 'Joe Chung'> < dept 'cs' >
                    < relation R> | Rest1 }>@whois
```

2. Bindings for variables LN and FN are obtained from one of the two decomp functions: decomp (name_to_lnfn)
3. Each bind of R is combined with a value obtained at step 2. and the query is submitted to **CS** to obtain the values of the variable Rest2.
4. the objects satisfying the head of rule R2 can be generated (e.g. &cp1 should be an object built following these steps)[4].

5 Description Logics: overview

Description Logics languages - *DLs* [4], derived from the KL-ONE model [69], have been proposed in the 80's in the Artificial Intelligence research area. DLs

---

[4] *DLs* are also known as *Concept Languages* or *Terminological Logics*.

are fragments of first order logic: they enable *concepts* to be expressed, that can be viewed as logical formulas built using unary and binary predicates, and contain one free variable (to be filled with instances of the concept). They bear similarities with Complex object data models (*CODMs*), recently proposed in the database area [34, 35, 36, 39, 48, 61, 62]. CODMs are concerned with only the structural aspects of object-oriented data models proposed for Object-Oriented Databases (*OODBs*) [38, 59, 14] and represent well-known notions such as types, complex values, classes, objects with identity and inheritance. DLs too are concerned with only structural aspects; concepts roughly correspond to database classes and are organized in inheritance taxonomies. An additional feature of DLs with respect to CODMs is that concepts are differentiated in *primitive* and *defined*: a primitive concept description represents necessary conditions (thus corresponding to the usual database class semantics); a defined concept description represents necessary and sufficient conditions (thus corresponding to a database view semantics).

Remark 5 *By exploiting defined concepts semantics of DLs, and, given a type as set semantics to concept descriptions, it is possible to provide reasoning techniques: to compute* subsumption *relations among concepts(i.e. "isa" relationships implied by concepts descriptions) and to detect* incoherent *(i.e. always empty) concepts.*

The research on DLs has provided reasoning techniques to determine incoherence and subsumption of concepts and has assessed the complexity of these inferences for a variety of *acyclic* , i.e. not allowing recursive descriptions, DLs (see e.g.[56]).

DLs reasoning techniques are profitable for database design activities, as will be briefly argued in the following. In fact, if we map a database schema including only classes (no view) into one of the DLs supported by a system, we are able to automatically detect incoherent classes. A more active role can be performed with the introduction of views.

Remark 6 *By means of DLs reasoning techiques, a view, can be automatically* classified *(i.e., its right place in an already existing taxonomy can be found) by determining the set of its most specific subsumer views (subsumers) and the set of its most generalized specialization views (subsumees).*

Thus, besides a passive consistency check, *minimality* of the schema with respect to inheritance can easily be computed. [49] reports a fundamental work in a database environment, where well-known conceptual data models have been mapped in a suitable DL and polynomial subsumption and coherence algorithms are given.

The expressiveness of CODMs gave rise to new problems for this mapping, as many of their features were not supported by implemented DLs. For instance, most of the CODMs introduces a clear cut distinction between values and objects with identity and, thus, between object classes and value types. This distinction was not present in DLs. Further, CODMs often support additional type constructors, such as set and sequence. Mostly important, CODMs support the representation and management of *cyclic classes*, i.e., classes which directly or indirectly refer to themselves, are allowed.

Recently, a description logics (odl = *Object Description Logics*) [5] overcoming the above problems, and a theoretical framework for database design based on subsumption computation and coherence detection has been proposed in [48].

Remark 7 *The* odl *description logics represents the structural part of OODB data models (and of the standard data model ODM of ODMG93 [14]) and incorporates: value-types, complex values, classes, objects with identity, and inheritance.*

The main extension of odl, with respect to CODMs, is the capability of expressing *base* and *virtual* classes. Base classes correspond to ordinary classes used in database systems and virtual classes (corresponding to defined concepts semantics) are similar to database *views* [6]. Cyclic classes (base and virtual) are allowed and a *greatest-fixedpoint* semantics has been adopted for cyclic virtual classes.

Note that the interpretation of tuples in odl implies an *open world semantics for tuple* types similar to the one adopted by Cardelli [26].

For instance, if we have the following assignments of values to objects:

$$
\delta: \begin{cases}
o_1 & \mapsto [\text{a: "}xyz\text{", b: } 5] \\
o_2 & \mapsto \langle true, false \rangle \\
& \vdots \\
o_{128} & \mapsto \{o_1, o_2\} \\
& \vdots
\end{cases}
$$

Adopting an *open world semantics for tuple*, it follows that

$$
o_1 \in \mathcal{I}\Big[\triangle[\text{a: String}]\Big], \qquad o_1 \in \mathcal{I}\Big[\triangle[\text{a: String, b : Int}]\Big],
$$
$$
o_2 \in \mathcal{I}[\triangle\langle \text{Bool}\rangle], \qquad o_{128} \in \mathcal{I}[\{\triangle\top_C\}].
$$

Remark 8 *The adoption of an open world semantics for tuple types in* odl *permits an alternative formulation of the OEM feature expressed in Remark 1: objects of a class share a common minimal structure, but could have further additional properties.*

Remark 9 *Coherence checking and subsumption computation are effective for query optimization. A query has the semantics of a virtual class, as it expresses a set of necessary and sufficient conditions. If we restrict the query language to the subset of queries expressible with the schema description language we can perform incoherence detection and subsumption computation for queries.*

The choice of restricting the query language in order to have DDL=DML has been made in the some works on query optimization based on acyclic DLs such as CANDIDE [45], CLASSIC [51], BACK [66] and [52].

---

[5] not to be confused with the homonymous ODL language of ODMG93 [14].

[6] Views in OODB have been called virtual classes by Abiteboul and Bonner [33].

Remark 10 *Coherence checking and subsumption computation can be classified as* semantic query optimization *techniques [60, 55, 68], as they perform a transformation of a query into a semantically equivalent one, that minimizes query execution costs.*

- *if the query is detected as incoherent a null answer can immediately be returned without accessing the database;*
- *if the query is coherent, it can be temporarily classified in the schema with respect to views. As a result, either an* equivalent *view or the set of* immediate subsumers *and* immediate subsumees *is returned. In the former case, the answer set is simply the set of all objects that are instances of the view equivalent to the query; in the latter case, the union of the sets of instances of immediate subsumee views are included in the answer set and only objects that are instances of the immediate subsumer view, but not instances of the immediate subsumee views, have to be checked against the query condition.*

Usually, in database environment, query languages are more expressive than schema description languages. This holds for Relational Databases and, more recently, for OODBs, see for example the proposed standard *OQL* language [14].

Remark 11 *In the context of extraction and integration of textual heterogeneous data sources, provided that a highly expressive OO schema description language is available, we can adopt as query language the same language* [7]

As a matter of fact *recursive* [8] views and queries are relevant for OODB query languages. For instance, object-oriented recursive queries are important in engineering DBs [54]. Unfortunately, while many works have been developed in deductive relational databases [57, 37], very few proposals have been presented for OODB query languages. Recently, significant contributions in this environment have been presented. In [50] a form of recursion was introduced which corresponds to the notion of linear recursive queries; in [32] the effectiveness of incoherence detection and subsumption computation for semantic optimization of cyclic views and queries, expressed in odl[48], is shown by adopting different styles of semantics: *greatest fixed-point, least fixed-point,* and *descriptive semantics.*

A system, implementing algorithms for incoherence detection and subsumption computation in odl has been developed. It is composed of two modules: the odldesigner prototype [41] and the DBott prototype. odldesigner was first developed in Sicstus Prolog at CIOC-CNR, Bologna, as part of the *logidata* project [41] and implements DLs reasoning techniques for advanced database management systems handling complex objects data models. It is an active tool which supports automatic building of type taxonomies for complex object database systems, preserving coherence and minimality with respect to inheritance. It implements the theoretical framework of [48].

---

[7] the choice of a simple query language (a significant restriction of OQL) has been also recently made at the I^3 workshop on mediators language standards [12].

[8] In the following cyclic and recursive will be used as synonymous.

The actual version of `odldesigner` has been developed (in C language) at the Department of Engineering Sciences of the University of Modena and provides an ODL (ODMG93) standard interface to input a schema description. Furthermore, it includes an extension of `odl`, called `ocdl`, allowing to express *quantified path types* and *integrity constraints* rules. The former extension has been introduced to deal easily and powerfully with nested structures. Paths, which are essentially sequences of attributes, represent the central ingredient of OODB query languages to navigate through the aggregation hierarchies of classes and types of a schema. In particular, *quantified* paths to navigate through set types are provided. The allowed quantifications are existential and universal and they can appear more than once in the same path. Integrity constraints rules, *if then rules*, whose antecedent and consequent are ODL *virtual* types (i.e. a type description expresses a set of sufficient and necessary conditions) allows the declarative formulation of a relevant set of integrity constraints.

`DBott` prototype was developed at the Department of Engineering Sciences of the University of Modena to perform semantic optimization of OODB queries [42, 43]. It has been developed in C and provides an OQL(ODMG93) standard interface. A demo of `DBott` is available on Internet at the following address: (http://sparc20.dsi.unimo.it/).

6 A Semantic approach for Mediators: ocdl Description Logics

The *TSIMMIS OEM + MSL* approach towards *mediators* development is 'structural':

- OEM [5] , in fact, is a *self-describing model* [31] where each data item has an associated descriptive label and *without a strong typing system*;
- *semantic informations are effectively encoded in the MSL rules* that do the integration.

There are many projects following the 'structural approach' [10, 16, 11]. Let us introduce some fundamental arguments in favour of the 'structural approach' (considering *TSIMMIS* as a target system):

1. the power, along with the flexibility, generality and coinciseness of OEM and MSL make the 'structural' approach a good candidate for the integration of widely heterogeneous and semistructured information sources;
2. MSL and OEM can be seen as a form of first-order logic: rules are supported allowing the sharing of definitions of terms among components;
3. the schema-less nature of OEM objects is particularly useful when a client does not know in advance the labels or structure of OEM objects.
   - In traditional data models, a client must be aware of the schema in order to pose a query. With this approach, a client can discover the structure of the information as queries are posed.

– A conventional OO language breaks down in such a case, unless one defines an object class for every possible type of irregular object.

Many other projects follow a 'semantic' approach [19, 20]. This approach can be characterized as follows:

– for each source, meta-data, i.e. conceptual schema, must be available;
– semantic informations are encoded in the schema;
– a common data model as the basis for describing sharable informations must be available;
– partial or total schema unification is performed.

Let us introduce some fundamental arguments in favour of a 'semantic approach' adopting conventional OO data models:

1. in most research areas (programming languages, databases and artificial intelligence) conventional OO models with strong type systems and including: classes, aggregation and inheritance hierarchies to model structural intensional knowledge and, often, methods to model behavioural knowledge are at present adopted;
2. a relevant effort has been devoted to develop OO standards: CORBA [15] for object exchanging among heterogeneous systems; ODMG93 (including ODM model and ODL language for schema description; OQL language as query language) for object oriented databases [14];
3. the schema nature of conventional OO models together with classification aggregation and generalization abstract modelling primitives allows to organize extensional knowledge;
4. the adoption of a *type as a set* semantics for a schema permits to check consistency of instances with respect to their descriptions;
5. semantic informations encoded into a schema permit to efficiently extract informations.

By coupling a system based on description logics (`odldesigner` + `DBott`), a 'semantic approach' and some interesting features of *TSIMMIS* it is possible to devise a powerful I^3 system that conforms to the ODMG93 standard:

1. the standard ODM model and ODL language as common data model and common data language are adopted both for sources and mediators;
2. the ODL language is extended to represent rules in analogy with *MSL*;
3. the ODL language is extended to represent QDTL;
4. a *minimal core language* which is a restriction of the object oriented query language OQL such that it will accept queries for relational databases is adopted[9];
5. a system based on description logics (`odldesigner` + `DBott`) with interfaces for the above languages is adopted;
6. `ocdl` is extended to support QDTL translation.

---

[9] this choice is also suggested in the proposal for a standard in mediator languages [12]

A mediator can be generated with the above system by introducing the following knowledge:

- describe the schemata of the sources to be integrated and the mediator schema in the ODL language;
- describe query templates in the *minimal core language*;
- describe the mediator rules.

Having (odldesigner + DBott) available, the knowledge expressed in the standard languages above is automatically translated into ocdl classes and virtual classes and the the the ocdl incoherence detection and subsumption algorithms can be exploited in the following way:

- to perform data integration by exploiting mediator rules;
- to execute a query by determining the most efficient one among the supported subsuming query.

Two final remarks: as observed in Remark 8, the adoption of an open world semantics overcomes the problems of conventional OO data models above mentioned; for sources supporting OODBMS or RDBMS, query templates are not necessary and DBott can be used as a powerful query optimizer for OQL queries.

References

1. Chawathe S., H. Garcia Molina, J. Hammer, K.Ireland, Y. Papakostantinou, J.Ullman, and J. Widom. The TSIMMIS Project: Integration of Heterogeneous Information Sources. In *Proceedings of IPSJ Conference*, pages. 7–18, Tokyo, Japan, October 1994. (Also available via anonymous FTP from host db.stanford.edu, file /pub/chawathe/1994/tsimmis-overview.ps.).
2. H. Garcia-Molina et al. The TSIMMIS approach to mediation: Data models and languages. In *Proceedings of 1995 NGITS workshop*. (ftp://db.stanford.edu/pub/garcia/1995/tisimmis-models-languages.ps.).
3. Y. Papakonstantinou, H. Garcia-Molina, J. Ulman and Ashish Gupta. A query Translation scheme for rapid implementation of wrappers. avaible at ftp://db.stanford.edu/pub/papakonstantinou/1995/querytran-extended.ps.
4. Y. Papakonstantinou, H. Garcia-Molina, J. Ulman, "MedMaker: A mediation system based on declarative specification", avaible at ftp://db.stanford.edu/pub/papakonstantinou/1995/medmaker.ps.
5. Y. Papakonstantinou, H. Garcia-Molina and J. Widom. Object Exchange Across Heterogeneous Information Sources. In Proceedings of IEEE International Conference on Data Engineering, pages. 251–260, Taipei, Taiwan, March 1995. (Also available via anonymous FTP from host db.stanford.edu file /pub/papakonstantinou/1994/object-exchange-heterogeneous-is.ps.)
6. H. Garcia-Molina, J. Hammer, K. Ireland, Y. Papakonstantinou, J. Ullman, and Jennifer Widom. Integrating and Accessing Heterogeneous Information Sources in TSIMMIS. In *Proceedings of the AAAI Symposium on Information Gathering*, pages. 61–64, Stanford, California, March 1995. (Also available via anonymous FTP from host db.stanford.edu, file /pub/garcia/1995/tsimmis-abstract-aaai.ps.)

7. A. Rajaraman, Y. Sagiv, and J. Ullman. Answering Queries Using Templates with Binding Patterns. In *Proceedings of the 14th ACM PODS*, pages. 105–112, San Jose, California, May 1995. (Also available via anonymous FTP from host db.stanford.edu, file /pub/rajarman/1994/limited-opsets.ps).

8. D. Quass, A. Rajaraman, Y. Sagiv, J. Ullman, and J. Widom. Querying Semistructured Heterogeneous Information. In *International Conference on Deductive and Object-Oriented Databases*, 1995. (Also available via anonymous FTP from host db.stanford.edu, file /pub/quass/1994/querying-full.ps)

9. R. Ahmed et al. The Pegasus heterogeneous multidatabase system. *IEEE Computer*, 24:19-27, 1991.

10. E. Bertino.. Integration of heterogeneous data repositories by using object-oriented views. In *Proc. Intl Workshop on Interoperability in Multidatabase Systems*, pages 22-29, Kyoto, Japan,1991.

11. Y.J. Breibart et al. Database integration in a distributed heterogeneous database system. In *Proc. 2nd Intl IEEE Conf. on Data Engineering*, Los Angeles, CA, February 1986.

12. P. Bunemann, L. Raschid, J. Ulman. Mediator Languages - a Proposal for a standard.
Report of an I3/POB working group held at the University of Maryland, April 1996 (available as ftp://ftp.umiacs.umd.edu/pub/ONRrept/medmodel96.ps).

13. M.J. Carey et al. Towards heterogeneous multimedia information systems: the Garlic approach. Technical Report RJ 9911, IBM Almaden Research Center, 1994.

14. R. G. G. Cattel, et al. *The Object Database Standard - ODGM93. Release 1.2*. Morgan Kaufmann,1996.

15. Object Request Broker Task Force. The Common Object Request Broker: Architecture and Specification, December 1993. Revision 1.2, Draft 29.

16. U. Dayal and H. Hwuang. View definition and generalization for databse integration in a multidatabase system. In *Proc. IEEE Workshop on Object-Oriented DBMS*, Asilomar, CA, September 1986.

17. M. Freedman. WILLOW: Technical overview. Available by anonymous ftp from ftp.cac.washington.edu as the file willow/Tech-Report.ps, September 1994.

18. A. Gupta. *Integration of Information Systems: Bridging heterogeneous Databases* IEEE Press, 1989.

19. J. Hammer and D. McLeod. An approach to resolving semantic heterogeneity in a federation of autonomous, heterogeneous database systems. *Intl Journal of Intelligent and Cooperative Information Systems*, 2: 51-83, 1993.

20. M. Huhns et al. Enterprise information modeling and model integration in Carnot. Technical Report Carnot128-92, MCC,1992.

21. W. Kim et al. On resolving schematic heterogeneity in multidatabase systems. *Distributed and Parallel Databases*, 1:251-279, 1993.

22. W. Litwin, L. Mark, and N. Roussopoulos. Interoperability of multiple autonomous databases. *ACM Computing Surveys*, 22:267-293, 1990.

23. K. Shoens et al. The RUFUS system: Information organization for semistructured data. newblock In *Proc. VLDB Conference*, Dublin, Ireland, 1993.

24. G. Thomas et al. Heterogeneous distributed database systems for production use. *ACM Computing Surveys*, 22: 237-266,1990.

25. J.C. Franchitti and R. King. Amalgame: a tool for creating interoperating persistent, heterogeneous components. In *Advanced Database Systems*

26. L. A. Cardelli. Semantics of multiple inheritance. In *Semantics of Data Types*, pages 51–67. Springer-Verlag, Berlin, Heidelberg, New York, 1984.

27. D. Calvanese, G. De Giacomo and M. Lenzerini. Structured Objects: Modeling and Reasoning. In *Proceedings of International Conference on Deductive and Object-Oriented Databases*, 1995.

28. G. De Giacomo and M. Lenzerini. PDL based framework for reasoning about actions. In *Proceedings of the AI*IA '95*, LNAI 992, pages 103–114, Spriger Verlag 1995.

29. G. Wiederhold. Mediators in the architecture of future information systems. *IEEE Computer*, 25:38-49,1992.

30. W.A. Woods and J.G. Schmolze. The KL-ONE family. In F.W. Lehmann, editor, *Semantic Networks in Artificial Intelligence*, pages 133-178, Pergamon Press 1992.

31. L. Mark and N. Roussopoulos. Information interchange between self-describing databases. *IEEE Data Engineering*, 10:46-52,1987.

32. D. Beneventano and S. Bergamaschi. Incoherence and Subsumption for cyclic queries and views in Object Oriented Databases. In *DKE*, january, 1997.

33. S. Abiteboul and A. Bonner. Objects and views. In *SIGMOD*, pages 238–247. ACM Press, 1991.

34. S. Abiteboul and S. Grumbach. Col: a logic-based language for complex objects. In S. Ceri, J.W. Schmidt, and M. Missikoff, editors, *EDBT '88 - Lecture Notes in Computer Science N.303*, pages 271–293. Springer-Verlag, 1988.

35. S. Abiteboul and R. Hull. IFO: A formal semantic database model. *ACM Transactions on Database Systems*, 12(4):525–565, 1987.

36. S. Abiteboul and P. Kanellakis. Object identity as a query language primitive. In *SIGMOD*, pages 159–173. ACM Press, 1989.

37. R. Agrawal. Alpha: An extension of relational algebra to express a class of recursive queries. *IEEE Transactions on Software Enginering*, 14(7), July 1988.

38. M. Atkinson et al. The object-oriented database system manifesto. In *1nd Int. Conf. on Deductive and Object-Oriented Databases*. Springer-Verlag, 1989.

39. P. Atzeni, editor. *LOGIDATA+: Deductive Databases with Complex Objects*. Springer-Verlag: LNCS n. 701, Heidelberg - Germany, 1993.

40. F. Baader. Terminological cycles in KL-ONE-based knowledge representation languages. In *8th National Conference of the American Association for Artificial Intelligence*, volume 2, pages 621–626, Boston, Mass., USA, 1990.

41. J. P. Ballerini, S. Bergamaschi, and C. Sartori. The ODL-DESIGNER prototype. In P. Atzeni, editor, *LOGIDATA+: Deductive Databases with complex objects*. Springer-Verlag, 1993.

42. D. Beneventano, S. Bergamaschi and C. Sartori. Using Subsumption for Semantic query optimization in OODB. *International Workshop on Description Logics*, DFKI Technical Report D-94-10.

43. D. Beneventano, S. Bergamaschi, S. Lodi, and C. Sartori. Using subsumption in semantic query optimization. In A. Napoli, editor, *IJCAI Workshop on Object-Based Representation Systems*, Chambery - France, August 1993.

44. G. Di Battista and M. Lenzerini. Deductive entity relationship modeling. *IEEE Trans. on Knowledge and Data Engineering*, 5(3):439–450, June 1993.

45. H.W. Beck, S.K. Gala, and S.B. Navathe. Classification as a query processing technique in the CANDIDE data model. In *5th Int. Conf. on Data Engineering*, pages 572–581, Los Angeles, CA, 1989.

46. C. Beeri. Formal models for object-oriented databases. In W. Kim, J.M. Nicolas, and S. Nishio, editors, *Deductive and Object-Oriented Databases*, page 405:430. Elsevier Science Publisher, B.V. - North-Holland, 1990.

47. D. Beneventano and S. Bergamaschi. Subsumption for complex object data models. In J. Biskup and R. Hull, editors, *4th Int. Conf. on Database Theory - Berlin*, pages 357–375, Heidelberg, Germany, October 1992. Springer-Verlag.

48. S. Bergamaschi and B. Nebel. Acquisition and validation of complex object database schemata supporting multiple inheritance. *Applied Intelligence: The International Journal of Artificial Intelligence, Neural Networks and Complex Problem Solving Technologies*, 1993.

49. S. Bergamaschi and C. Sartori. On taxonomic reasoning in conceptual design. *ACM Transactions on Database Systems*, 17(3):385–422, September 1992.

50. E. Bertino, M. Negri, G. Pelagatti, and L. Sbattella. Object-oriented query languages: The notion and the issues. *IEEE Trans. Knowl. and Data Engineering*, 4(3):223–236, June 1992.

51. A. Borgida, R.J. Brachman, D.L. McGuinness, and L.A. Resnick. CLASSIC: A structural data model for objects. In *SIGMOD*, pages 58–67, Portland, Oregon, 1989.

52. M. Buchheit, M. A. Jeusfeld, W. Nutt, and M. Staudt. Subsumption between queries to object-oriented database. In *EDBT*, pages 348–353, 1994.

53. L. Cardelli. A semantics of multiple inheritance. In *Semantics of Data Types - Lecture Notes in Computer Science N. 173*, pages 51–67. Springer-Verlag, 1984.

54. R.G.G. Cattell and J. Skeen. Object operations benchmark. *ACM Transactions on Database Systems*, 17(1), 1990.

55. U. S. Chakravarthy, J. Grant, and J. Minker. Logic-based approach to semantic query optimization. *ACM Transactions on Database Systems*, 15(2):162–207, June 1990.

56. F.M. Donini, M. Lenzerini, D. Nardi, and W. Nutt. The complexity of concept languages. In J. Allen, R. Fikes, and E. Sandewall, editors, *KR '91 - 2nd Int. Conf on Principles of Knowledge Representation and Reasoning*, pages 151–162, Cambridge - MA, April 1991. Morgan Kauffmann Publishers, Inc.

57. H. Gallaire, J. Minker, and J.M. Nicholas. Logic and databases: a deductive approach. *ACM Computing Surveys*, 16(2), 1984.

58. M. Kifer, W. Kim, and Y. Sagiv. Querying object-oriented databases. In *SIGMOD '92*, pages 393–402. ACM, June 1992.

59. W. Kim and F. Lochovsky, editors. *Object-Oriented Concepts, Databases, and Applications*. Addison-Wesley, Reading (Mass.), 1989.

60. J. J. King. Quist: a system for semantic query optimization in relational databases. In *7th Int. Conf. on Very Large Databases*, pages 510–517, 1981.

61. C. Lecluse and P. Richard. Modelling complex structures in object-oriented databases. In *Symp. on Principles of Database Systems*, pages 362–369, Philadelphia, PA, 1989.

62. C. Lécluse and P. Richard. The O_2 data model. In *Int. Conf. On Very Large Data Bases*, pages 411–422, Amsterdam, 1989.

63. J.W. Lloyd. *Logic Programming*. Springer-Verlag, Berlin, 1987.

64. B. Nebel. Terminological reasoning is inherently intractable. *Artificial Intelligence*, 43(2), 1990.

65. B. Nebel. Terminological cycles: Semantics and computational properties. In J.F. Sowa, editor, *Principles of Semantic Networks*, chapter 11, pages 331–362. Morgan Kaufmann Publishers, Inc., 1991.

66. B. Nebel and C. Peltason. Terminological reasoning and information management. Technical Report 85, Tech. Univ, Berlino, October 1990.

67. D.A. Schmidt. *Denotational Semantics: A Methodology for Language Development.* Allyn and Bacon, Boston, 1986.
68. S. Shenoy and M. Ozsoyoglu. Design and implementation of a semantic query optimizer. *IEEE Trans. Knowl. and Data Engineering*, 1(3):344–361, September 1989.
69. W.A. Woods and J.G. Schmolze. The kl-one family. In F.W. Lehman, editor, *Semantic Networks in Artificial Intelligence*, pages 133–178. Pergamon Press, 1992. Pubblished as a Special issue of *Computers & Mathematics with Applications*, Volume 23, Number 2-9.

Cases, Information, and Agents

Hans-Dieter Burkhard

Inst. of Informatics
Humboldt University Berlin
10099 Berlin, Germany
e-mail: hdb@informatik.hu-berlin.de

Abstract. Case Retrieval Nets (CRNs) have been developed for the fast and flexible retrieval of previous cases ("experiences") from large case bases. They permit the ranking of stored information according to their similarity to a query.

As an effective flexible information gathering technique they are appropriate for building information agents working over inhomogeneous data bases, too.

CRNs allow the addition and/or removal of information and indexes even at runtime, which makes them potentially useful for the adaptation and self-organization of information agents in changing environments.

1 Introduction

Agents are used for information gathering in large data collections. Complex agents need data management for their beliefs, their goals, their capabilities. Agents ought to be capable of learning. Learning may be realized by acting according to previous experiences. Previous experiences may be described by cases, as in Case Based Reasoning.

To make use of cases, they have to be stored in a data base, the case base. But the retrieval should not be performed by exact matching, *similarity* and *relevance* establish the signposts to potentially useful previous experiences. Thus, a very flexible information retrieval is necessary to make use of case bases.

Having good flexible retrieval techniques for cases, the same techniques can be used by information gathering agents to get a better and more flexible access to large data collections. Ranking of information according to the strength of matching is necessary to prevent from information overflow. In Case Based Reasoning, ranking of cases is essentially as well, – in order to decide which of previous experiences should guide the actual problem solution. Considering *similarity of indexes* and *relevance of indexes for* cases leads to better results.

Complex agents have to decide according to conflicting desires, appropriate plans, utility of next actions [16]. Again, ranking techniques are needed to measure the appropriateness of desires, plans, actions etc. for a given situation (e.g. for the matching between pre- and postconditions of an action/plan and the actual beliefs and intentions).

In our work on case based reasoning we have developed a very flexible and effective case retrieval technique – the *Case Retrieval Nets (CRNs)* [2], [3], [12],

[13] – which are successfully used in different applications of case based reasoning. We also use the CRN techniques in different applications for information gathering. CRNs allow a fast and flexible retrieval by a spreading activation process, implementing the following idea:

1. A query leads to an initial activation of some nodes in the net, namely the IE-nodes representing *Information Entities (IEs)* addressed by that query.
2. Further IE-nodes are activated by activation propagation via so-called *similarity arcs*.
3. Case-nodes are activated from the IE-nodes via so-called *relevance arcs*.
4. The ranking of cases is given by the strength of activation at the case nodes.

The spreading activation process implements to some extend the idea from psychology of

Reminding as reconstruction

(cf. e.g. [1], [7]). But differently from the Dynamic Memory approach [17], [7], the retrieval process in CRNs is performed "bottom-up" rather than "top-down", and activations of different strength give additional means for expressing "power of reminding". The similarity propagation is related to processing in Semantic Networks, but CRNs are structured under the viewpint of "episodes" (cf. Section 2), have different weights for propagations, and have a final "collection step" at the cases by relevance propagation. The propagation process is to some extend similar to the processing in Neural Networks, but interpretation and usage are different. Nevertheless, improvements of CRNs using learning techniques from Neural Networks are possible and recently under investigation.

The paper is organized as follows: A short introduction to Case Based Reasoning is given in the following Section 2. Special emphasis is put on case retrieval techniques. Sections 3 explains the basic ideas of CRNs, and Section 4 gives a formal description of the basic CRN model with the spreading activation process. Some possible extensions are discussed in Section 5. The last Section 6 outlines some features of the model and some further possible applications as in the field of flexible information access and agent architectures.

2 Basic ideas of Case Based Reasoning (CBR)

Several points have been identified in the introduction, which allow the usage of CBR techniques, especially the retrieval techniques, for information gathering and for the design of intelligent agents, respectively. A short description of CBR is given in the following.

Human problem solving is guided to a great extend by experience. Concrete episodes are called cases.

Generalization leads to "vertical" hierarchical structures: a concept describes on a "higher level" a set of related individuals of a "lower level". Cases may be seen as an "orthogonal" structuring, which combines individuals from different concepts only because of their combination in an episode. The underlying hypothesis of CBR is the repetition of events under similar circumstances. This leads to the ability of future directed behaviour without deeper domain knowledge, guided only by experience: A successful solution may be tried again in a similar problem situation (as well as an unsuccessful trial should be avoided in the future).

The formulation of rules depends on a deeper domain knowledge, or on a larger number of similar episodes (cases) justifying an induction. The reliability of a single case may be not high, but a case can give first hints in the absence of justified rules. Especially for the treatment of the "unexpected situations", a case base of *exceptional cases* is useful to maintain the situations not covered by the rules. Such information is useful even for experts (which do not need support for the regular problem treatment).

Thus, the aim of CBR is the guidance of problem solving by reminding of helpful cases. A case base is necessary to store cases. Given a new problem, a set of helpful cases has to be found from the case base, and the found information (e.g. the solutions and their results) from the past must be adapted for the actual situation. After application in the reality, a new episode has occurred which can be stored as a new case in the case base. In this way, CBR provides a simple and effective design for a learning system.

A central part of the CBR technique is the retrieval of "useful cases". As problem situations usually do not coincide in all aspects, CBR needs the possibility to retrieve *similar cases*, where *similarity* is meant to imply *usefulness* (at least to some extend ...). Since there is often no way to pre-define what usefulness means for the retrieval (and how it can be checked during the retrieval), a related notion of similarity has to express which episode (case) is to be remembered for which situation (query). This remark is necessary, since similarity can be defined in very different and even contrary ways:

> *Any two things which are from one point of view similar may be dissimilar from another point of view.* (POPPER)
> *An essay is like a fish.* (TVERSKY)

The aim of retrieval in CBR is the presentation of the most similar cases for a given query. That means, that a ranking of the cases in the case base has to be performed during the retrieval process. If similarity is not totally equivalent with usefulness (see above), then an additional step for critics of the retrieved most similar cases is necessary to exclude the not useful cases from the retrieved ones.

First requirements for the retrieval method may be

Efficiency : Fast access to the most similar cases.
Completeness : Find all the most similar cases.
Correctness : Find only the most similar cases.

A trade-off may exist between efficiency on the one hand side, and completeness/correctness on the other hand side.

The correctness requirement may be suspended to some extend: If an additional step for critics is used according to differences between similarity and usefulness, it also serves for rejecting incorrect results of retrieval.

The completeness requirement has to be modified in some applications: Not the most similar cases may be the only interesting ones – especially if they all lead to nearly identical solutions. It might be more useful to obtain a collection of (may be less similar) cases which give information about different alternatives.

Further requirements for the retrieval method may concern

Efficiency of updating :
Fast (e.g. incremental) update of the case base for new cases.
Flexibility of similarity assessment :
Change of similarity at runtime (according to special preferences of a user).
Case dependent similarity :
Certain aspects may be very important for one case, but unimportant for another one.

Different retrieval methods have been proposed in the literature. The simplest one, the so-called "linear search", performs the comparison of a query with each case from the case base. It is suitable for small case bases. It is also useful in combination with a raw retrieval method which selects at first a certain set from the case base, and the final ranking is performed by linear search for this set in a reasonable time.

Different approaches use decision trees. An extension of the well-known k-d-trees was worked out in [18], it uses a special technique to solve the problem of similar cases "behind the border" of a boundary plane. The Dynamic Memory is also related to decision trees. A special problem of all decision tree methods is the treatment of unknown values: It requires the search in different subtrees.

A comparison of different methods can be found in [18], [5], and concerning CRN related techniques in [12].

3 Basic ideas of *Case Retrieval Nets*

The most fundamental item in CRNs are so-called *Information Entities* (IEs). They may represent any basic knowledge item, such as a particular attribute-value-pair, or a key word. The IEs play the role of indexes. They are defined under the view point of "relevant parts of cases to be used in reminding". They are integrated into the CRN as far as they appear in the cases of the case base, or in expected queries, respectively. The special treatment of attributes with large domains (e.g. numerical ones) was discussed in [2].

For the retrieval, the cases are simply considered as *sets of IEs*. The case base is a net with nodes for the IEs and additional nodes ("case descriptors") denoting the particular cases. The case descriptors may point to additional information (e.g. to a complete textual description of an episode).

IE nodes may be connected by *similarity arcs*, and a case node is reachable from its constituting IE nodes via *relevance arcs*. Given this structure, case retrieval is performed by

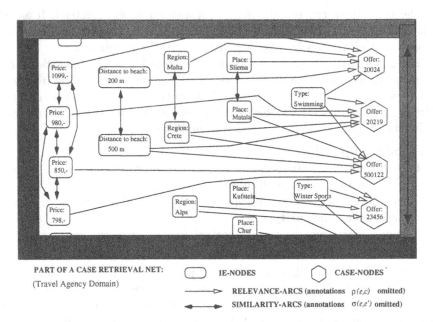

PART OF A CASE RETRIEVAL NET: ⬭ IE-NODES ⬡ CASE-NODES

(Travel Agency Domain)

————▷ RELEVANCE-ARCS (annotations $\rho(e,c)$ omitted)

◀———▶ SIMILARITY-ARCS (annotations $\sigma(e,e')$ omitted)

Fig. 1. Example of a CRN in the TRAVEL AGENCY domain.

- *activating* the IEs given in the query case,
- *propagating* this activation according to similarity through the net of IEs, and
- *collecting* the achieved activation to the associated case nodes.

Different degrees of similarity and relevance may be expressed by arcs weights.

The idea is illustrated for the TRAVEL AGENCY domain in Figure 1: A case is a special travel offer, denoted by a case descriptor, e.g. `<Offer 20219>`. It consists of a set of corresponding IEs giving the specification of that offer, in case of `<Offer 20219>` the IE nodes `<Type:Swimming>`, `<Price:980,->`, `<Place:Matala>`, `<Region:Crete>`, `<Distance to beach:500 m>` are connected with that case node. Asking for an offer in region Crete for swimming and not to far from the beach, the IE nodes `<Type:Swimming>`, `<Distance to beach:200 m>` and `<Region:Crete>` are initially activated. By similarity, the IE nodes `<Region:Malta>` and `<Distance to beach:500 m>` will be activated in the next step, but the amount of activation may depend on arc weights. Finally, the three offers `<Offer 20024>`, `<Offer 20219>`, `<Offer 500122>` will each get some activation. These final case node activations are computed from the incoming activations of IE nodes, which again may be weighted according to the relevance of an IE for case selection. The highest activated cases are proposed to the customer. Here the conflict arises whether the customer accepts a greater distance to the beach for being in Crete or if she changes to Malta. Special preferences may be expressed by initial weights, similarity weights and relevance weights, respectively. A first list of proposals might include both alternatives. Then, if the customer decides for Crete, an appropriate tuning of net parameters can prune all other offers in the future.

The example in its simple form already points out some features of the retrieval mechanism:

- It can handle *partially specified queries* without loss of efficiency (most case retrieval techniques have problems with partial descriptions).
- Case retrieval is seen as a kind of *case completion*, i.e. whatever part of a case will be given as a description, the retrieval algorithm will deliver the remaining part and thus complete the case. In contrast to, for example, classification tasks here is no distinction between a *description* of a problem and a *solution*. This is in some sense similar to queries to a database where arbitrary parts of the database record may be specified to obtain other parts — however, there is nothing like a *primary key* to support efficiency for only special indexes..
- It can be tuned to express different similarities/relevances at run time (by simply changing related arc weights, while other techniques need a new compilation step).
- Cases can (but need not) be described by attribute vectors. Thereby, the cases may be related to different attributes (e.g., for Winter Sports, the <Distance to beach> is not relevant).
- Insertion of new cases (even with new attributes) can be performed incrementally by injecting related nodes and arcs.

4   A formal model of *Case Retrieval Nets*

A formal description of *Case Retrieval Nets* in a basic version is given in the following. It can serve as a base for more extended models, and it allows a detailled investigation of the approach.

Definition 1

An Information Entity *(IE) is an atomic knowledge item in the domain, i.e. an IE represents the lowest granularity of knowledge representation, such as a particular attribute-value-pair. (Later on, in extended versions, IEs themselves may be structured, e.g. composed from "lower level" IEs).*   □

Definition 2

A case *consists of a set of IEs. It is denoted by a unique case descriptor.* □

Definition 3

A Basic Case Retrieval Net (BCRN) *is given by* $N = [E, C, \sigma, \rho, \Pi]$ *with*

E *is the finite set of* information entities (IE) *("IE nodes"),*

C is the finite set of case descriptors *("case nodes"),*
σ *is the* similarity function

$$\sigma : E \times E \rightarrow \mathcal{R}$$

which describes the similarity $\sigma(e', e'')$ between IEs e', e'',
ρ *is the* relevance function

$$\rho : E \times C \rightarrow \mathcal{R}$$

which describes the relevance $\rho(e, c)$ of the IE e for the case c.
Π *is the set of* propagation functions π_n *for each node $n \in E \cup C$ with*

$$\pi_n : \mathcal{R}^E \rightarrow \mathcal{R}. \qquad \square$$

The graphical description (cf. Figure 1) is given by a graph with nodes $E \cup C$ and directed arcs between them. The arc from $e' \in E$ to $e'' \in E$ is labelled by $\sigma(e', e'')$, the arc from $e \in E$ to $c \in C$ is labelled by $\rho(e, c)$. Arcs are omitted if they are labelled by zero. The functions π_n are annotations to the nodes n.

An IE e belongs to a case c if $\rho(e, c) \neq 0$. Its relevance for a case c is given by the value of $\rho(e, c)$ expressing the importance for remembering the case c if the IE e is in the actual "scope of attention". Similarity between IEs e', e'' is measured by $\sigma(e', e'')$. The functions π_n are used to compute the new activation of node n depending on the incoming activations (a simple setting may use the sum of inputs as π_n, – see below).

The *"state"* of a BCRN is defined by the activation of the nodes:

Definition 4

An activation *of a BCRN $N = [E, C, \sigma, \rho, \Pi]$ is a function*

$$\alpha : E \cup C \rightarrow \mathcal{R}. \qquad \square$$

In the graphical notation, an activation α can be represented as a (temporary) annotation to the nodes $n \in E \cup C$. Informally, the activation α describes a *scope of attention*: All activated IEs e ($\alpha(e) \neq 0$) play a role in the process of reminding. The value $\alpha(e)$ of the IE e expresses the importance of that IE for the actual problem. The influence of an IE to the result of the case retrieval depends on its actual importance $\alpha(e)$ and its relevances $\rho(e, c)$ for the cases c (where π_c might express further preferences). Negative values can be used as an indicator for the rejection of cases containing that IE.

The dynamics of the retrieval process are described as *"state transitions"*, i.e. as changing activations. Formally, the propagation process for the basic model is given by the next definition.

Definition 5

Consider a $BCRN$ $N = [E, C, \sigma, \rho, \Pi]$ with $E = \{e_1, ..., e_s\}$ and let be $\alpha_t : E \cup C \to \mathcal{R}$ the activation at time t.
The activation of IE nodes $e \in E$ at time $t + 1$ is given by

$$\alpha_{t+1}(e) = \pi_e(\sigma(e_1, e) \cdot \alpha_t(e_1), ..., \sigma(e_s, e) \cdot \alpha_t(e_s)),$$

and the activation of case nodes $c \in C$ at time $t + 1$ is given by

$$\alpha_{t+1}(c) = \pi_c(\rho(e_1, c) \cdot \alpha_t(e_1), ..., \rho(e_s, c) \cdot \alpha_t(e_s)). \qquad \square$$

Given an initial activation α_0, then by Definition 5 it is well-defined how the activation α of each node $n \in C \cup E$ has to be computed at any later time point. If we regard similarity and relevance, then the earliest time point to consider the ranking of cases (according to their resulting activations) is after two propagation steps. Hence for the basic model, the propagation process is a three-step process (as in the introduction):

Step 1 – Query :
According to the query, the *primary scope of attention* is given by α_0 which is determined for all IE nodes as follows:

$$\alpha_{query}(e) = \begin{cases} 1 & : \quad \text{for IE nodes } e \text{ of the new problem} \\ 0 & : \quad else \end{cases}$$

For more subtle queries, α_0 might assign different weights to special IE nodes, and some *context* may be set as an initial activation for further nodes.

Step 2 – Similarity propagation between IE nodes :
The activation α_0 is propagated to all IE nodes $e \in E$ leading to an *extended scope of attention*:

$$\alpha_1(e) = \pi_e(\sigma(e_1, e) \cdot \alpha_0(e_1), ..., \sigma(e_s, e) \cdot \alpha_0(e_s)),$$

Step 3 – Relevance propagation from IE nodes to case nodes :
The result of step 2 is propagated to the case nodes $c \in C$:

$$\alpha_2(c) = \pi_c(\rho(e_1, c) \cdot \alpha_1(e_1), ..., \rho(e_s, c) \cdot \alpha_1(e_s)).$$

In this computation model all similarity computation has to be performed in Step 2 in a direct manner between adjacent IE nodes.

More subtle computations (including e.g. concepts, micro features, rules) may use *several steps* (e.g. from a "simple IE" to a more general "concept IE", then to another "concept IE" by "firing a rule", and back again to certain "simple IEs", which then leads to the activation of cases – cf. Section (5)). All these steps can be implemented as activation passing, but some care is necessary to prevent from unwanted effects (circular activation, asynchronous propagation etc.). On the other hand side, computations over longer time intervals may be considered as "any time" computations: If the first activations arriving at the case nodes are sufficient to solve the problem, then the process of reminding may stop. Otherwise, some reminder from more far regions may come to account by further activation steps.

For the 3-Step activation process we obtain the final activation $\alpha_N(c)$ at the case nodes c by combining the formulae from above:

$$\alpha_N(c) = \pi_c(\ \rho(e_1, c) \cdot \pi_{e_1}(\sigma(e_1, e_1) \cdot \alpha_{query}(e_1), ..., \sigma(e_s, e_1) \cdot \alpha_{query}(e_s)\ )$$
$$, ...,$$
$$\rho(e_s, c) \cdot \pi_{e_s}(\sigma(e_1, e_s) \cdot \alpha_{query}(e_1), ..., \sigma(e_s, e_s) \cdot \alpha_{query}(e_s)\ )).$$

Thus we can summarize the concept of case retrieval in the basic model of CRN:

> Consider a BCRN $N = [E, C, \sigma, \rho, \Pi]$ and the activation functions α_t as defined in Definitions 4 and 5. The result of the case retrieval for a given query activation α_0 is the *preference ordering* of cases according to decreasing activations $\alpha_N(c)$ of case nodes $c \in C$. $\qquad\square$

As already discussed in Section 2, the further processing in a case based system can exploit the ranking of cases in different ways. Some further steps may also use the derived state of the BCRN.

We call the highest activated cases (according to α_N) the *answer cases* of the retrieval. Usually, not all IE nodes e of the answer cases have already been in the extended scope of attention after the similarity activation step ($\alpha_1(e) = 0$, computed in Step 2). Such an IE node e was a constituent part of an answer case c, but it was not addressed by the query: That means it was not known for the actual problem. Hence it is a candidate for the completion of the actual case, and we call such IEs the *completion candidates*. A completion candidate could be a proposal for the solution of the actual problem.

It is crucial here to remind that an IE may be any relevant index for a case, especially the "solution parts" of the cases can be integrated as IEs into a CRN (then they could be used in a query, too). Many CBR systems cannot integrate the solution parts in such a way because the have problems with unknown values.

As far as all answer cases provide similar completion candidates of a certain aspect, we have a high evidence that the actual problem would behave in a similar way for that aspect. On the other hand side, if there are dissimilar completion candidates, then our actual problem needs further investigation. If for example there are different solutions possible in a diagnosis problem, then we have to test further symptoms. By comparing the answer cases with different solutions, we may find the symptoms which are correlated to the different diagnostics. These symptoms can be found by further propagation steps back from the answer cases to the IEs in the CRN (cf. [14]).

But not all applications must try to find a single solution. In the travel agency example the assistance system should even better make a set of different proposals (which even should be dissimilar to some extend) and let the final choice to the costumer.

The section is closed with a consideration of some standard techniques as an application field for CRN.

Case based systems as well as classification systems often use a fixed set of features/attributes $a_1, ..., a_k$ with values in $W_1, ..., W_k$ (such that the problems are described as feature vectors $[x_1, ..., x_n] \in W_1 \times ... \times W_k$, – e.g. as vectors of symptom values). Similarities between such vectors may be computed as the weighted sum of attribute similarities ("composite similarities"):

Definition 6

A similarity function

$$sim : \quad (W_1 \times ... \times W_k) \quad \times \quad (W_1 \times ... \times W_k) \quad \to \quad \mathcal{R},$$

is called composite *if it is combined by a function $\phi : \mathcal{R}^k \to \mathcal{R}$ from feature similarity functions $\sigma_i : W_i \times W_i \to \mathcal{R}$ such that*

$$sim([x_1, ..., x_n], [y_1, ..., y_n]) = \phi(\sigma_1(x_1, y_1), ..., \sigma_k(x_k, y_k)). \quad \Box$$

The weighted sum of the feature similarities may serve as an example of a composite similarity function:

$$sim([x_1, ..., x_n], [y_1, ..., y_n]) = \sum_{i=1,...,k} g_i \cdot \sigma_i(x_i, y_i).$$

Composite similarities can be easily implemented by special BCRNs [2, 13]. We consider the case where the functions π_n (collecting propagations in the nodes n) are specified as the sum of incoming (weighted) activations. Then we obtain for the steps from above:

$$\text{Step 2:} \quad \alpha(e) = \sum_{e'} \sigma(e', e) \cdot \alpha_{query}(e')$$

$$\text{Step 3:} \quad \alpha(c) = \sum_{e} \rho(e, c) \cdot \alpha(e)$$

And the resulting activation in the case nodes for a query α_{query} is given by

$$\alpha_N(c) = \sum_{e} \rho(e, c) \cdot \sum_{e'} \sigma(e', e) \cdot \alpha_{query}(e').$$

But while in the formula for the weighted sum from above the weights g_i are constant values, the relevances $\rho(e, c)$ in the net permit individual weights of incoming arcs for each case c.

5 Extensions

(B)CRNs offer the possibility of extensions in various ways, some of them will be shortly discussed in this section.

Extensions are possible for the structuring of the net (especially allowing for different kinds of IEs) and for the computation process, respectively. Extensions of the structure usually lead to a more subtle computation process as already mentioned in the last section.

But special computation processes may also result from effectiveness considerations. The so-called "Lazy propagation" [11] propagates similarity activations in a first step along only those similarity arcs with high weights $\sigma(e, e')$. It then follows an estimation process, and further possible propagations are performed only if they have the potential to change the final ranking of cases. This procedure is complete and correct in the sense of Section 2 (the ranking is the same as in the simple computation process of BCRN).

In a similar setting, again the most promising similarity propagations are performed first. Only if they don't lead to satisfactory cases, then further propagations are performed for lower similarity weights. This process may lead to a different ranking. It can be seen as a kind of any-time computation (and it is easy to imagine that it can be sufficient in the travel agency example).

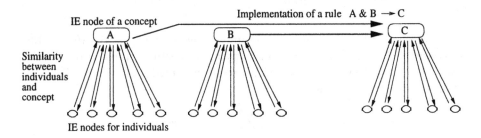

Fig. 2. Concepts and rules in a CRN.

Cases represent special forms of knowledge, where individuals of different kind (belonging to different concepts) are combined because of their common occurrence in an episode. As already mentioned in Section 2, they are considered as "orthogonal" structuring in comparison with "hierarchical" structures leading to concepts. The flat structure of BCRN do not use concepts.

Nevertheless, concepts and rules can be integrated in the net formalism as well (cf. Figure 2). We can save memory by a concept node (as a special kind of an IE node) Caribbean which is connected to n IE nodes of n Caribbean places by $2n$ arcs (in both directions). Then after an initial activation of a *single* Caribbean place (e.g. the IE node for Jamaica), the activation is first propagated to the concept node Caribbean and then activated to *all* IE nodes of Caribbean places. This saves space (for arcs), because in the simple setting of BCRN, all

Caribbean places had to be connected by n^2 similarity arcs. But note that two steps are needed for the similarity propagation via the concept nodes.

By concept nodes we can introduce hierarchical structures into CRNs. This can be done for "is–a–" and "has–part–"relations as well (cf. [14] for an application in technical diagnosis).

Then on the "higher level" of concepts we can again perform "horizontal" propagations between concept nodes, e.g. a rule of the form

The summer in the Caribbean belongs to the rainy season.

can be implemented by related connections from concept nodes **summer** and **Caribbean** to the concept node **rainy season** (where an appropriate setting of the function π_e at the **rainy season**–node can implement the conjunction of the preconditions of that rule).

If the IE node of a concept is connected to all the related IE nodes of the individuals by similarity arcs of equal weight, then the membership to the concept is considered as having equal importance for all the individuals. In a more general approach, the membership is considered with different strength (such that e.g. **Jamaica** belongs with strength 100 to the concept **Caribbean**, while **Venezuela** belongs to it only with strength 80). This idea corresponds to the notion of a *fuzzy set*, and it is implemented in the CRN model by different similarity weights $\sigma(e, e')$ between the nodes of the individuals and the nodes of the concept. *Fuzzy rules* can then be implemented, too.

On the other hand side, IEs on the "lower level" may themselves be specified by so-called micro-features [12]. A place like Crete is characterized by features like beaches, mountains, Ancient Culture, Mediterranean Sea etc., and an activation of Crete reminds the presence of that features. Some of that features may also remind e.g. for Malta. Instead of a direct similarity arc between the nodes **Crete** and **Malta**, the similarity might be computed (using several computation steps) by a spreading activation process using the related micro-feature nodes (note that such a part of a net is again similar to a BCRN "on a lower level").

A problem still under consideration concerns the question, how far it is possible to simulate such computations over more steps (as needed with concepts/rules or micro-features) by simple one-step propagations (i.e. if a more complicated CRN can be "compiled" down to a simple BCRN). The question is related to the training of frequently performed human actions (like car driving), which starts with rule-guided clumsy behaviour and which is replaced after sufficient experience by direct reactions. Related insights could be useful for the design of adapting agents.

6 Discussion

The CRNs are useful as an effective and flexible retrieval method for case based reasoning (cf. the remarks at the end of Section 3). The main idea is the "bottom-up" case reconstruction ("case completion") as a process of reminding in the scope of activated IEs. Each part of a case may be used to retrieve other parts and no *a priori* distinction between a *problem description* and a *solution* is necessary.

The efficiency has been shown by several experiments [10], [12] on Pentium PC and SPARC-20 with retrieval times comparable to that of commercial data base systems for case bases with up to 35 000 cases.

As for data base systems, the access is possible for any set of specified attributes, while methods based on decision trees have problems with unknown values. Moreover, CRNs do not distinguish special primary keys.

It is not necessary (but possible) to consider a fixed set of attributes for the case descriptions. A case is any set of IEs (Definition (2)). It is possible to add new IEs (and to consider new attributes as well) by incremental addition of further nodes and arcs to the net.

The net structure allows for parallel processing in a straight forward way (not tested up to now), and it offers the possibility of bridging to subsymbolic inferences (Neural Networks) using related net structures.

Besides Neural Networks, related models are Semantic Networks, Dynamic Memory, Associative Memory, Discrimination Networks. A comparison with recent developments can be found in [12].

As a retrieval technique, CRNs can be used in various applications for answering partially specified questions, even for only vague specified values. We have implemented and tested applications in

- technical diagnosis [6], [14], [15], using the ideas of case completion described in Section 4, and hierarchically structured IEs as discussed in the previous section,
- assistant systems for travel agencies as in the example CRN of Section 2, [8],
- price assessment for real estates [9], using the information usually given in the newspaper offers – with the need to deal with different sets of attributes and missing values,
- help desk applications based on natural language queries.

Assistant systems for medical domains are under development [4]. Related systems are to be implemented as information gathering agents.

CRN techniques are useful in the design of information gathering agents because of the flexible structuring of information items and the incremental update. The techniques which are useful for the help desk applications apply as well. These techniques can be used for a comfortable interface to the agents, too.

The "bottom-up" reconstruction of information is useful for the activation of knowledge and/or capabilities. The next actions of an agent can be chosen w.r.t. utility [16]. Thus, the internal reasoning for determining the ranking of actual goals, actions, behaviours, capabilities etc. in the scope of actual information (belief) and intentions might be more effectively performed by CRN techniques than by rules. Some rankings can be interpreted as the strength of motivation [19]. These ideas are still under investigation at present time.

The possibility of incremental updates in CRNs is useful for agents with adaptation and learning by experiences – which leads us back to the roots in CBR.

7 Summary

Information gathering is a non-trivial task in a world of information overflow. Techniques are needed which are flexible and adaptable to the user's needs without great effort. Especially the *ranking* of information under more than only statistical view points is important. CRNs perform a ranking according to the relevance of indexes while considering even the mutual reference between indexes.

The technique of CRNs was developed for the retrieval of cases (experiences from the past) in Case Based Reasoning. The ideas of CRNs in their recent stage of development have been presented in this article, together with a discussion of potential applications in the area of information gathering and in the area of agent oriented techniques.

Acknowledgments. A great part in the development of the theory and the main work in the implementation of CRNs was done by Mario Lenz. The author wants to thank for this work and for all our discussions. Thanks for many fruitful discussions are also due to the colleagues in the field.

References

1. R. Bartlett. *Remembering: A study in experimental and social psychology.* Cambridge University Press, London, 1932.
2. H.-D. Burkhard. Case retrieval nets. Techn. report, Humboldt University, Berlin, 1995.
3. H.D. Burkhard and M. Lenz. Case retrieval nets: Basic ideas and extensions. In *4th German Workshop on CBR*, eds., H.D. Burkhard and M.Lenz, pp. 103–110. Humboldt University Berlin, (1996).
4. H.D. Burkhard, G. Lindemann, S.A. Loening, and J. Neymeyer. Remembering the Unexpected Cases – CBR for Experts in Urology. Proc. ECAI-96-WS "Intelligent Data Analysis in Medicine and Pharmacology (IDAMAP-96)" , 11-14.
5. K. Goos. Preselection strategies for case based classification. In B.Nebel, and Dreschler-Fischer,L., eds.: KI-94: Advances in Case-Based Reasoning. Springer, 1994.
6. G. Kamp, P. Pirk, and H.D. Burkhard. FALLDATEN: Case-based Reasoning for the Diagnosis of Technical Devices. KI-96: Advances in Artificial Intelligence. (Proc. 20th Annual German Conference on AI.) LNAI 1137, pp. 149-161 (1996).
7. J. L. Kolodner. *Case-Based Reasoning.* Morgan Kaufmann, San Mateo, 1993.
8. M. Lenz. Case-based reasoning for holiday planning. In W. Schertler, B. Schmid, A. M. Tjoa, and H. Werthner, editors, *Information and Communications Technologies in Tourism*, pages 126–132. Springer Verlag, 1994.
9. M. Lenz, H. Ladewig. Fallbasierte Unterstützung bei der Immobilienbewertung. Wirtschaftsinformatik 38(1), Schwerpunktheft "Fallbasierte Entscheidungsunterstützung", 1996.
10. M. Lenz. Case Retrieval Nets applied to large case bases. In H.-D. Burkhard, B. Bartsch-Spörl, D. Janetzko, and S. Weß, editors, *4th German Workshop on CBR — System Development and Evaluation*, Berlin, 1996. Humboldt University.

11. M. Lenz and H.D. Burkhard. 'Lazy propagation in case retrieval nets'. In *12th ECAI 1996*, ed., W. Wahlster, pp. 127–131. John Wiley & Sons, (1996).
12. M. Lenz and H.D. Burkhard. Case Retrieval Nets: Basic Ideas and Extensions. KI-96: Advances in Artificial Intelligence. (Proc. 20th Annual German Conference on AI.) LNAI 1137, pp. 227-239 (1996).
13. M. Lenz and H.-D. Burkhard. Case retrieval nets: Foundations, properties, implementation, and results. Techn. report, Humboldt University, Berlin, 1996.
14. M. Lenz, H.D. Burkhard, and S. Brückner. Applying Case Retrieval Nets to Diagnostic Tasks in Technical Domains. I. Smith, B. Faltings (Eds.): Advances in Case-Based Reasoning. Proc. of the Third European Workshop EWCBR-96. Lecture Notes in Artificial Intelligence, 1168, Springer, pp. 219–233 (1996).
15. M. Lenz, E. Auriol, H.D. Burkhard, M. Manago, and P. Pirk. CBR for Diagnosis and Decision Support. AI Communications 9 (1996) 1-9.
16. A. S. Rao and M. P. Georgeff. Modeling agents within a BDI-architecture. *Proc. of the First Int. Conf. on Multi-Agent Systems (ICMAS-95))*, ed., V. Lesser, pp. 312-319. MIT-Press, (1995).
17. R. Schank. *Dynamic memory: A theory of learning in computers and people.* Cambridge Unv. Press, New York, 1982.
18. S. Weß. *Fallbasiertes Problemlösen in wissensbasierten Systemen zur Entscheidungsunterstützung und Diagnostik.* PhD thesis, Universität Kaiserslautern, 1995.
19. D. Wieczorek. ELIAS – Ein persönLicher Internet ASsistent. Diploma thesis, Humboldt University Berlin (in preparation).

Knowledge Rovers: Cooperative Intelligent Agent Support for Enterprise Information Architectures

Larry Kerschberg

Center for Information Systems Integration and Evolution
Department or Information and Software Systems Engineering
MSN 4A4, George Mason University, Fairfax, VA 22032-4444
email: kersch@gmu.edu

Abstract. The paper presents an information architecture consisting of the information interface, management and gathering layers. Intelligent active services are discussed for each layer, access scenarios are presented, and the role of knowledge rovers is discussed. Knowledge rovers represent a *family* of cooperating intelligent agents that may be configured to support enterprise tasks, scenarios, and decision-makers. These rovers play specific roles within an enterprise information architecture, supporting users, maintaining active views, mediating between users and heterogeneous data sources, refining data into knowledge, and roaming the Global Information Infrastructure seeking, locating, negotiating for and retrieving data and knowledge specific to their mission.

Keywords: Knowledge Rovers, Active Services, Active Databases, Cooperative Intelligent Agents, Information Architectures.

1 Introduction

Some dozen years ago, I saw the need to promote the integration and interchange of research in AI, Logic Programming, Information Retrieval and Databases, calling it *Expert Database Systems* [31-34]. Since then, we have made substantial progress in learning how to make Database Management Systems more active and knowledgeable, while at the same time facilitating access to large databases by Expert Systems and other knowledge-based systems.

Recently, research has focused on the Intelligent Integration of Information (I*3) [73]. Here the problem is to *access* diverse data residing in multiple, autonomous, heterogeneous databases, and to *integrate* or *fuse* that data into coherent information that can be used by decision makers. To make the problem even more interesting:

1) data may by multimedia (video, images, text, and sound);

2) sources may store the data in diverse formats (flat files, network, relational-, or object-oriented databases);

3) data *semantics* data may conflict across multiple sources;

4) the data may have diverse temporal and spatial granularities;

5) much of the *interesting* and *valuable* data may reside outside the enterprise, in the open-source literature accessible via subscription services or on the World Wide Web (WWW)[3]; and

6) the data may be of uncertain quality, and the reliability of the source may be questionable.

The I*3 research has been sponsored primarily by DARPA, the Defense Advanced Research Project Agency, and our group at George Mason University (GMU) has been funded under this program, and more recently by the DARPA Advanced Logistics Program. The work reported in this paper reflects our research in I*3 in which we proposed a *federated* approach to providing I*3 *services* to support information integration needs. These points will be elaborated later in the paper. We have extended these notions further by incorporating cooperating agents into our work in the Advanced Logistics Program.

It is becoming increasingly apparent that one cannot expect to solve I*3 and other large-scale system problems with a monolithic and integrated solution. Rather, the system should be composed of smaller components, with each component having the requisite knowledge to perform its tasks within the larger problem-solving framework. Thus, the topic of Cooperative Intelligent Agents for this symposium is very timely in helping us to address, discuss and understand the issues in building next-generation *intelligent information systems*.

2 Enterprise Data and Information Requirements

In this section we address enterprise data and information requirements with emphasis on I*3 tasks. These requirements are general and apply to most enterprises that have legacy systems and also access information on the Internet. We discuss the notions of data pull and data push requirements, review important concepts of intelligent agents as they pertain to data and information architectures, and introduce the notion of active services that will be implemented through a family of configurable and cooperating agents.

2.1 Data Pull and Data Push Requirements

In our research in architectures for large-scale systems [27, 35, 42], inspired primarily by our participation in an Independent Architecture Study of NASA's Earth Observing System Data and Information System (EOSDIS), we have identified two types of data requirements and their associated scenarios: Data Pull and Data Push.

Data Pull denotes a user-initiated information request, for example, in accessing data from EOSDIS archives, or in creating a logistics plan and then accessing multiple databases to instantiate that plan with actual data.

Data Push corresponds to the continual updating of databases used by the enterprise. These updates are under the control of the organizations that designed, built, control, and maintain the databases. The organizations have *autonomy* over and *responsibility* for the data, ensure its quality, and share the data within a federation of information systems [35, 36, 39, 56, 62].

Thus, a system must support both data pull and data push, while providing reasonable service to all users. The approach proposed in this paper is a family of intelligent agents, called *knowledge rovers*, which provide services, such as, access, query formulation, facilitation, brokerage, mediation, integration, wrapping, etc., that enable the modern enterprise to realize its information management needs, while serving its users in a timely, efficient and cost-effective manner.

2.2 Intelligent Agents for the Enterprise

Bird [5] has proposed an agent taxonomy based on two client/server classes. They are *Mobile Agents* (Clients) for Content, Communications and Messaging Services and Static Agents (Servers).

We add third type of agent, *Active View* Agents, which support active objects and views. Active view agents may act on behalf of users in *materializing* objects based on real-time events and conditions, as well as pre-defined rules provided by either users or other agents.

Bird notes that distributed intelligent systems share many of the same characteristics of multidatabase systems [62], in particular, distribution, heterogeneity, and autonomy. Knowledge and data may be *distributed* among various experts, knowledge bases and databases, respectively. Problem-solving should be a cooperative endeavor [15, 30]. Multiple copies of knowledge and data, possibly in differing formats, must be maintained by the system.

There are several facets to the *heterogeneity* of information in systems [5]: syntactic, control and semantic.

1) *Syntactic heterogeneity* refers to the myriad of knowledge representation formats [28], data definition formats to represent both knowledge and data.

2) *Control heterogeneity* arises from the many reasoning mechanisms for intelligent systems including induction, deduction, analogy, case-based reasoning, etc. [6, 15, 18, 22, 23, 30, 63, 64].

3) *Semantic heterogeneity* [10, 20, 30, 69, 70, 78, 79] arises from disagreement on the meaning, interpretation and intended use of related knowledge and data.

A third characteristic of intelligent systems is that of *autonomy*. There are several aspects to autonomy; in the control structure of an agent, in the extent to which an agent shares information with other agents [22, 24], the manner in which an agent associates with other agents, and structural autonomy in the way an agent fits into an organization of agents for problem-solving [13, 21, 29, 36-39, 41, 55, 63].

2.3 Enterprise Information Architecture

Bowman et al [7, 8] describe a three-layer architecture for scalable Internet resource discovery, proposed by the Internet Research Task Group. Table 1 denotes the three-layer architecture which provides access to heterogeneous repositories, including those on the WWW.

Table 1: Internet Three Layer Information Architecture

Information Layer	Layer Service
Information Interface Layer	Users perceive the available information at this layer and may query and browse the data. This layer must support scalable organizing, browsing and search.
Information Management Layer	Responsible for the replication, distribution, and caching of information.
Information Gathering Layer	Responsible for the collecting and correlating the information from many incomplete, inconsistent, and heterogeneous repositories.

Figure 1 depicts GMU approach to the three-layer architecture for the application domain of logistics; the architecture is general enough to apply to most enterprises. The information architecture incorporates the three information layers consisting of:

1) *Information interface layer* where users access the system, formulate queries, collaborate in problem-solving activities, initiate pull scenarios and receive information from push scenarios. Users have access to their local databases and work through local views. We assume that collaboration mechanisms and tools exist at this layer;

2) *Information management layer* where objects, mediated active views, and information in an Information Repository are integrated, managed, replicated, updated. This layer mediates between the information interface layer and the information gathering layer, allowing users to perceive an *integrated information space*, when in reality, data resides in multiple heterogeneous databases and information sources. A mediated view of data is provided at this layer and user views are materialized from the mediated view.

The Real-Time Information Processing and Filtering process constantly monitors the system for events of importance to enterprise activities, and informs users, the mediated view, and the Information Repository should these events occur.

The Information Repository contains meta-data and knowledge associated with enterprise resources. It is provided information by the Data/Knowledge Refinement, Fusion and Certification process, and constantly updates the repository. Here data from diverse, heterogeneous inter-networked information sources are mined, scrubbed, refined and evolved to produce high-quality information.

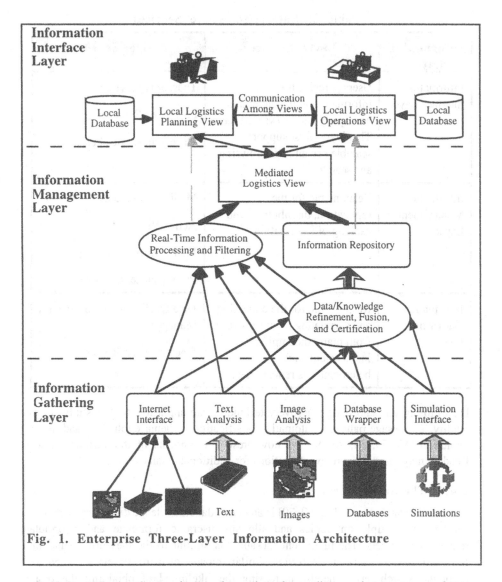

Fig. 1. Enterprise Three-Layer Information Architecture

3) *Information gathering layer* where data from diverse, heterogeneous inter-networked information sources are accessed. Special rovers are used to perform the mediated access to local as well as internet resources.

2.4 Enterprise Active Services

Table 2 presents a collection of active services for the enterprise. These services reflect our I*3 research, particularly in mediated data access through brokerage, facilitation and wrapping services. The GMU research group has developed a federated service architecture that provides Federation Interface Managers (FIMs) as active wrappers for information sources, an intelligent thesaurus [69, 70], temporal mediation services [4, 66-68], active views [1, 57-61], and inconsistency management services [45-52].

Table 2: Enterprise Active Services

Information Layer	Layer Service	Active Services
Information Interface Layer	Users perceive the available information at this layer and may query and browse the data. This layer must support scalable organizing, browsing and search.	Thesaurus Services Federation Services Place your service here![1]
Information Management Layer	Responsible for the replication, distribution, and caching of information.	Mediation Services Active Views I*3 Services Place your service here!
Information Gathering Layer	Responsible for the collecting and correlating the information from many incomplete, inconsistent, and heterogeneous repositories.	Data Quality and Inconsistency Management Place your service here!

Data mining and knowledge discovery techniques are applicable to the study of data quality, user usage patterns, automatic classification, schema evolution, and system evolution [43, 53, 54, 76-79]. We now present a synopsis of the various services. Readers may consult the relevant citations for additional details.

2.4.1 Thesaurus Services

The *intelligent thesaurus* [35, 69, 70] is an *active* data/knowledge dictionary capable of supporting multiple ontologies and allowing users to formulate and reformulate requests for objects. The intelligent thesaurus is similar to the thesaurus found in a library; it assists users in identifying similar, broader or narrower terms related to a particular search term, thereby increasing the likelihood of obtaining the desired information from the information repository. In addition, active rules may be associated with object types as well as their attributes and functions.

2.4.2 Federation Services

At GMU we have developed an I*3 federated distributed client/server architecture [25] in which the constituent systems maintain authority and autonomy over their data

---

[1] This is an invitation to classify your services within the framework. Ideally they should be modular, serve a specific need, and be composable with other services.

which at the same time sharing certain information with the federation. Client software and/or server software is provided to members so that they can interface existing information systems with the federation. This was proposed in our Independent Architecture Study for the EOSDIS system [26, 35, 42], and some form of federation is planned for EOSDIS.

A Federation Interface Manager (FIM) is associated with each information system joining the federation. It is specialized into client and server FIMs. Each Client-Federation Interface Manager (FIM) consists of three subsystems, a Client Router, Client-to-Federal Translation Services, and Federal-to-Client Translation Services. The translation services map local data objects to the DPSC representation and vice-versa. The Client-FIM 1) accepts local transactions (including query requests) from local clients in the format used by the local information system, and 2) the router determines whether the transaction is for a local server or a remote server of the federation. If the destination is a valid server, the request is passed to the Client-to-Federal Translation Services so the request may be translated to standard federal transaction format prior to routing it to the appropriate server.

The Server-FIM consists of Federal-to-Server Translation Services, Server-to-Federation Translation Services, and the Server Router. When a transaction arrives at a destination, the Federal-to-Server Translation Services translates the federal transaction into the local transaction format of the server. After translation the transaction is sent to the server router. The router receives all transactions, both locally and remotely generated, and logs them. Transactions are then queued for processing. Once the server has processed the transaction, the server router sends the response, if necessary, to the Server-to-Federal Translation Services, for server to DPSC translation, and then routes the response to the appropriate Client-FIM, where the response is translated into the local format.

2.4.3 Mediation Services

Mediation refers to a broad class of services associated with I*3 [72-75]. At GMU we have focused on the mediation of temporal data of differing granularity. This is of particular importance in the context of multidimensional databases and data warehousing applications, where historical data is integrated and analyzed for patterns and interesting properties.

A *temporal mediator* [4, 67, 68] consists of three components: 1) a repository of *windowing functions* and *conversion functions*, 2) a time unit thesaurus, and 3) a query interpreter. There are two types of windowing functions: the first associates time points to sets of object instances, and the other associates object instances to sets of time points. A conversion function transforms information in terms of one time unit into that in terms of some other time unit. The time unit thesaurus stores the knowledge about time units (e.g., names of time units and relationships among them). The time-unit thesaurus stores concepts such as the seasons, fiscal year definitions, and calendars, and effects translation of these time units into others.

Users pose queries using the windowing functions and desired time units using a temporal relational algebra. To answer such a user query, the query interpreter first employs the windowing functions together with the time unit thesaurus to access the temporal data from the underlying databases and then uses the time unit thesaurus to select suitable conversion functions which convert the responses to the desired time units. Thus, a temporal mediator provides a simple, yet powerful, interface that supports multiple temporal representations in a federated environment. Temporal mediators may also be used to compare historical databases such as those needed for auditing and data warehousing purposes.

2.4.4 Active Views

Active views are motivated by the need to mediate between users and the plethora of enterprise data and information being generated. Active views can be used to define complex objects, events and conditions of interest.

Thus, active views mitigate the need for users to constantly issue queries to verify the existence of certain events or condition in the enterprise, or to be bombarded constantly with irrelevant information. The active view automates this task by compiling user object specifications into rules monitored by active databases [11, 16, 17, 71], or polling queries issued against traditional enterprise database systems. These rules can also be given rovers that comb the WWW seeking relevant information. Active views also provide active caching [1, 59] of materialized views so as to support subscription services, notification services, and to update user profiles. Further, materialized views can be updated automatically. Active views are discussed in more detail later in this paper.

2.4.5 Data Quality and Inconsistency Management

In any environment of multiple information resources one would expect that sources would overlap in providing similar but inconsistent data. Inconsistencies are detected during the process of integration, and *harmonization agents* are engaged to resolve them. The concept of the harmonization agent is incorporated in the Multiplex [46, 49] proof-of-concept system which considers the reliability and quality of the conflicting information sources, and resolves conflicts in a way that increases the overall value of the information[52].

3 Knowledge Rover Architecture

The concept of Knowledge Rovers serves as a metaphor for the family of cooperating intelligent agents that support the information architecture. The notion of a rover is that it can be configured automatically with appropriate knowledge bases (ontologies), task-specific information, negotiation and communication protocols for its mission into cyberspace. Figure 2 superimposes the various agents in the Knowledge Rover Family onto Figure 1, and roles are described below:

3.1 Knowledge Rover Types

Executive Agent — is a *coordinator* for a group of agents. It is informed of significant events. A significant event can lead to the activation of new agents. For example, if the enterprise is notified of disaster-relief request, then the executive agent would coordinate with other agents in implementing the relief scenario.

User Agents — acts on behalf of a user, and is responsible for assisting users: 1) in browsing catalogs and information holdings such as the information repository, 2) in the intelligent formulation of queries, and 3) in the planning of tasks within a mission-specific scenario such as provisioning logistic support for a disaster relief effort.

Real-time Agents — are mission-specific, defined and configured to process incoming data, and update the appropriate database or notify the appropriate users. The real-time agents are autonomous, communicate with each other using a pre-defined protocol.

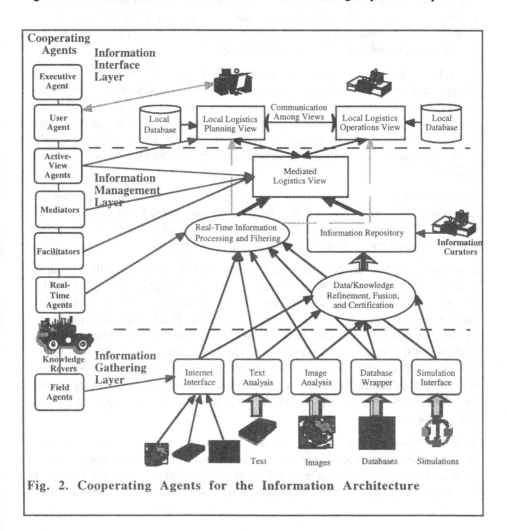

Fig. 2. Cooperating Agents for the Information Architecture

Real-time agents are responsible for monitoring the external environment, interacting with other systems, or acting on inputs from users. When an event is detected by a real-time agent, it is signaled to the relevant agents.

Facilitation Agents — provide intelligent dictionary and object location services. For example a facilitation agent [24] might accept a request from the Executive Agent to find all *external* providers of 'antibiotics,' and it might respond with the pharmaceutical producers and suppliers for the region in question. Other agents such as *knowledge rovers* (defined below) could then arrange for the items to be requisitioned, retrieved, and paid for. A knowledge rover could also post a request for bids, accept responses, make contracts, and provision the requested items.

Mediation Agents — are configured to assist in the integration of information from multiple data and information sources, having diverse data formats, different meanings, differing time units, and providing differing levels of information quality. Mediators [72, 73] are configured to accept queries from the Executive, translate the queries into the query language of the appropriate database system, accept the retrieved result, integrate it with results from other sources, and return the information to the Executive for presentation to the User Interface Agent.

Active View Agents — are created to monitor real-time events from the environment or from databases, and to use these events to initiate actions that will result in the update and synchronization of objects in the Data Warehouse and also in local views maintained at user workstations. These agents are configured to perform very specialized monitoring tasks and have a collection of rules and actions that can be executed in response to events and conditions that occur in the environment or in the databases.

Information Curators — are responsible for the quality of information the Information Repository. They assist in evolving the data and knowledge bases associated with enterprise information resources. They work with knowledge rovers to incorporate newly discovered resources into the information repositories.

Knowledge Rovers — are instructed carry out specific tasks on behalf of the executive, such as to identify which vendors have a specific item on hand. This would involve obtaining information from several vendors. The knowledge rover dispatches *field agents* to specific sites to get the relevant information. If the knowledge rover gets similar information from more than one source, it may ask a *mediator* such as Multiplex [49] to resolve the inconsistency. The knowledge rover reports back to the Executive Agent. The rovers are also responsible for Internet resource discovery. These new information sources and their data are analyzed to determine the adequacy, quality and reliability of retrieved information and whether it should be incorporated into the information repository.

Field Agents — are *specialized* rovers that have expertise in a certain domain, for example, pharmaceuticals, and knowledge about domain-specific information holdings at one or more sites. For example, a field agent could be tasked to monitor all aspects of a single item, say an 'antibiotic' produced by several manufactures and distributed by several vendors. They negotiate with the local systems through their *wrapper*, or Federation Interface Manager, retrieve appropriate data, and forward it to the appropriate requesting agent.

3.2 Scenarios for Knowledge Rover Family

This section presents examples of *push* and *pull* scenarios showing how the agent community would cooperate in providing information to logistics users. A pull scenario is one initiated by the user. A user agent acts on behalf of the user. We include in our pull scenario, access to commercial services available on the Internet [9, 14, 40, 65].

A push scenario is a pre-defined scenario, or pattern, in which incoming data is processed in real-time by real-time agents and passed onto active view agents to update the mediated and local logistics views shown in Figure 2. A push scenario defines a configuration of cooperating agents, the data to be collected in real-time from the external environment, the events to be monitored, and to whom they should be communicated.

3.2.1 Pull Scenario

In a pull scenario, the user would initiate a query or propose a set of tasks to be handled by the executive agent. For example, suppose the user notices that a convoy of ships suddenly has a *new* but unidentified object nearby. He works with the user agent to formulate a query [2, 4, 12, 19, 44, 69, 78, 79] which has both temporal and spatial conditions; the English version of the query might be as follows:

> Determine the identity and type of any objects X that are or have been near Convoy Y (using either radar or satellite imagery or contact reports or a combination of the three) during the last two hours. The search for information should be within 5 degrees latitude and longitude from the present position of X in the convoy.

Suppose the fleet is in the Equatorial Pacific and the ship in question is also in that area. Further suppose the Local Logistics View has an object representing the convoy and another representing the unknown vessel. The User Agent would translate the user's query into an object-relational query based on the object specifications supplied by the local logistics view agent, the thesaurus, and the Information Repository.

The query might have the form:

> FIND identity(X), type(X) FOR X NEAR Convoy Y
> WHERE TIME INTERVAL BETWEEN (NOW — Two Hours)
> AND REGION IS BETWEEN (-5 and +5 Degrees Latitude
> AND 120 and 130 Degrees West Longitude)

The following is a possible scenario involving the cooperation of several agents in processing the query:

1) The User Agent assists the user in formulating the query, most probably by means of a graphical user interface that allows the specification of geographical

queries involving latitude and longitude specifications and with pop-up menus for the specification of temporal constraints.

2) The query is then handed over to the Executive who is responsible for decomposing it into subqueries for the appropriate agents to handle. The executive consults the Local Logistics View agent responsible for the objects specified in the query to determine which underlying databases containing the desired information.

3) The LLV agent, in turn, consults with the Mediated Logistics View Agents, and one or more facilitators, to determine which databases should be queried.

4) The LLV sends the Executive a list of databases to be queried, and also suggests consulting with Jane's Ships Encyclopedia on the Internet [9] for identification of the object in question.

5) After consulting the Military Satellite Imagery Field Agent, the LLV notes that there was a forty-five minute gap in military imagery over the Equatorial Pacific during the time period in question, and suggests going out to the Internet for commercially-available imagery. The Field Agent suggests using the GENIE Satellite Imagery Broker operated by Lockheed [40, 65].

6) The Executive configures a Knowledge Rover to negotiate with the GENIE broker to determine the availability, appropriateness and cost of the images. Also several lower-resolution quick-look samples are requested to determine if the object in question appears in some of the images.

7) The appropriate images are ordered, paid for, and retrieved using electronic commerce services provided by the Internet, and the knowledge rover asks a translator mediator to translate the images into the appropriate format, and an image understanding field agent begins the object classification and identification process.

8) Concurrent with steps 6 and 7, the executive tasks a field agent capable of understanding messages to review contact reports for the time-period in question. The executive also asks a field agent to review radar screens for the moment the object might have appeared on the radar screens.

The various agents complete their tasks and report back to the executive, who then asks several mediators to integrate the information from these multiple sources into a coherent object-oriented multimedia presentation which the user can review. The user or an agent can ascertain the moment the ship was first spotted on the radar or images.

3.2.2 Push Scenario

For a push scenario, the following agents would be involved: Executive, Real-time, Active View, MLV and LLV, Facilitation, Mediation, Knowledge Rovers, and possibly User Agents.

Consider the following scenario:

1) A real-time agent is processing incoming radar images. It signals an event when a certain object is detected.

2) The object-detected event is communicated to the relevant agents such as:

- Active view agents, which are responsible for updating the views in the mediated and local logistics views,
- User agents, who have specifically requested to be notified of this event,
- An executive agent, as this event necessitates the coordination of other agents to act upon this event.

3) The executive agent selects a knowledge rover to initiate a search to identify the object, or if known, to confirm it.

4) The knowledge rover combs local and Internet sites for relevant information about this object, identifies the object, and then sends a message to the executive agent identifying the object.

5) The executive agent compares this result with that from the real-time agent, confirming the identity of the object, and sends a message to user agent informing it of the confirmation.

Once this event and the associated information were accepted by the user, the executive agent would communicate with the MLV agent and the Information Curator to incorporate the event and associated information into the information repository.

3.3 Active Views

The active view concept is based on the notion of *quasi-views* as described in [58-61], and was motivated by the concept of quasi-copies introduced in [1]. An active view represents a complex object of interest to the decision maker, and this object may be materialized [57] from data in multiple heterogeneous databases.

It is assumed that the decision-maker is not interested in every single update to a the Local Logistics Views (LLV), the Mediated Logistics View (MLV), the Information Repository, or the constituent databases. Rather, he wants to be notified *only when* certain *threshold events or conditions* warrant an updated situation assessment. With an active view the decision-maker can specify those variations of interest, based on the following types of *consistency* conditions: 1) the version of an update, 2) the time between refresh, 3) the percent deviation from an initial value, 4) attribute-value conditions, 5) refresh when an attribute value is a member of a list of values, and 6) general relational operations among attribute values.

These are termed staleness conditions, because the decision-maker or other agents are interested in updating cached objects in their views when they become stale as per the view specification.

Note that the concept of active view is very powerful precisely because there are intelligent agents working on behalf of objects and views to ensure that the information is up-to-date, synchronized and correct. The LLV's agent interacts with the MLV agent to ensure the active view is properly updated based on the specified rules and conditions.

The Active View agent provides a *mediation service* between the user and the constituent databases. Note that once a collection of active views have been defined, they can be "reused" by various decision-makers; they may also be generalized or specialized by changing certain conditions in the view specification.

Figure 3 illustrates a specification, in an extended version of SQL, for an active view class called *FriendlyTrack*, which provides position and other information on military ships and planes from selected friendly countries. FriendlyTrack has attributes ID, Velocity, Location, Home-port, Image, Flag, and Force-magnitude, and it has one superclass, InterestingEntity.

The "select always" statement means that an instance of FriendlyTrack should be created whenever there is an instance of Track with Flag equal to either "US", "UK", or "DE". Had "always" been omitted, the active view would contain only those instance of Track satisfying the predicate at active view initialization time; the server would not continue to monitor for new Track instances meeting the predicate.

create active view FriendlyTrack
        (ID, Velocity, Location, Home-port, Image, Flag, Force-magnitude)
        under InterestingEntity **as**
        select always ID, Speed, List(Latitude, Longitude),
                Name(Home-facility), Image, Flag
                from Track
                where Flag in ("US", "UK", "DE")
    with   **staleness-conditions**
            percent Speed 50,
            version 5,
            any change to Image,
            user-defined-delta
                    > (delta (Latitude, Longitude), 20))
                    with delta-function Distance-using-lat-long
    with **hints**
            refresh-strategy eager **except** Image

Fig. 3. Example Active View Specification

Following the keyword "always" is a list of derivations of attributes of FriendlyTrack. These derivations are illustrated in Figure 4. ID, Image, and Flag are derived trivially from Track.ID, Track.Image, and Track.Flag respectively. Location is derived by applying the function *list* to the arguments Track.Latitude and Track.Longitude. The derivation of Home-port illustrates the resolution of structural heterogeneity; it is derived by applying the *name* function to the value of Track.Home-Facility, whose domain consists of instances of the class Facility. More complex forms of heterogeneity could be resolved similarly using arbitrary functions (nested as required) in derivations. No derivation is specified for the attribute force-magnitude, because it is a non-persistent attribute meaningful only within the application program.

The *staleness conditions* describe the conditions under which the active view no longer meets the user's specified coherency requirements. This occurs when Track.Speed varies by more than 50 percent from the value of Velocity for a corresponding active copy, whenever a cached instance of Track is updated 5 or more times since the last refresh, or whenever Track.Image is updated.

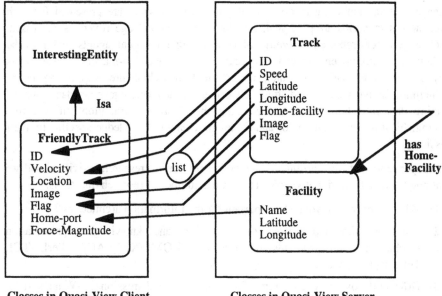

Classes in Quasi-View Client   **Classes in Quasi-View Server**

Fig. 4. Attribute Derivation for FriendlyTrack Example.

The last staleness condition is a *user-defined-delta*, used to describe data changes in the server that cause quasi-copies to become stale when those conditions depend upon changes to multiple attributes or to non-atomic or non-numeric attributes. The example illustrates how a user-defined-delta can track the magnitude of changes in Location, which is represented as a pair of complex attributes. The interpretation of the last staleness condition is this: an active copy becomes stale when the change in <Latitude, Longitude> exceeds 20, where the delta is measured by invoking the function Distance-using-lat-long with the arguments Latitude, Longitude, Cached-value-for-Latitude, and Cached-value-for-Longitude.

One implementation hint is specified in Figure 3: that the refresh strategy is "eager except Image." This indicates that quasi-copies should be refreshed as soon as they become stale, except for the attribute Image, which is refreshed only when it is accessed.

An implementation of the active view concept is part of the Mediator for Approximate Consistency (MAC) [61] which has been implemented in Common Lisp and ITASCA object-oriented database system. There are a number of research issues that need to be addressed to enhance the MAC: 1) address scaleup issues for the system to handle large collections of active views defined on multiple databases, and 2) extend the active view concepts to incorporate issues related to object replication, synchronization and survivability.

4 Conclusions and Future Research

This paper has an information architecture consisting of the information interface, management and gathering layers. Intelligent active services are presented for each layer, access scenarios are presented, and the role of knowledge rovers is discussed. Knowledge rovers represent a *family* of cooperating intelligent agents that may be configured to support enterprise tasks, scenarios, and decision-makers. These rovers play specific roles within an enterprise information architecture, supporting users, maintaining active views, mediating between users and heterogeneous data sources, refining data into knowledge, and roaming the Global Information Infrastructure seeking, locating, negotiating for and retrieving data and knowledge specific to their mission.

This paper represents the current architectural *vision* for our research activities, and we continue to work toward that vision. There are a number of research questions:

1) What other rovers would be important for the information architecture?

2) What are the appropriate communication and knowledge representation mechanisms and protocols for rovers? KQML/KIF, ACL, Perl, TCl, Telescript, Java, etc.?

3) How will rovers be configured for their tasks and missions? What sort of knowledge representation will permit the tailoring of rover knowledge for specific missions?

4) What types of active services are important to users and the enterprise, and how should the rovers support these services?

5) How can enterprise workflow requirements be specified so that rover can enable such workflow?

6) How can rovers learn, adapt and evolve to user patterns and preferences as well as enterprise data usage? How can knowledge be refined from the Information Repository so as to evolve the quality of enterprise information resources?

7) How can networks of active views be specified, coordinated, monitored, and certified to provide accepted levels of performance?

5 Acknowledgments

I would like to acknowledge discussions and joint work with my co-Principal Investigators on the Knowledge Rover and I*3 research projects: Hassan Gomaa, Sushil Jajodia and Ami Motro. My doctoral students, past and present, through joint collaborations, have also influenced this work: Dr. Len Seligman, Dr. Doyle Weishar, Professor Jong Pil Yoon, Mr. Wiput Phijaisanit, Ms. Sonali Banerjee, Mr. Samuel Varas, Ms. Willa Pickering, and Mr. Anthony Scime.

This research was sponsored by DARPA grants N0060-96-D-3202 for Knowledge Rovers and N00014-92-J-4038, administered by the Office of Naval Research, for the I*3 research.

6 References

[1]   R. Alonso, D. Barbara, and H. Garcia-Molina, "Data Caching Issues in an Information Retrieval System," *ACM Transactions on Database Systems*, vol. 15, 1990.

[2]   Y. Arens, C. A. Knowblock, and W.-M. Shen, "Query Reformulation for Dynamic Information Integration," *Journal of Intelligent Information Systems*, vol. 6, 2/3, pp. 99-130, 1996.

[3]   T. Berners-Lee, R. Cailliau, A. Loutonen, H. F. Nielsen, and A. Secret, "The World-Wide Web," *Communications of the ACM*, vol. 37, pp. 76—82, 1994.

[4]   C. Bettini, X. S. Wang, E. Bertino, and S. Jajodia, "Semantic Assumptions and Query Evaluation in Temporal Databases," ACM SIGMOD International Conference on Management of Data, San Jose, CA, 1995.

[5]   S. D. Bird, "Toward a taxonomy of multi-agent systems," *International Journal of Man-Machine Studies*, vol. 39, pp. 689-704, 1993.

[6]   A. Bond and L. Gasser, "Readings in Distributed Artificial Intelligence," . San Mateo, CA: Morgan Kaufmann Publishers, Inc., 1988.

[7]   C. M. Bowman, P. B. Danzig, D. R. Hardy, U. Manber, M. F. Schwartz, and D. P. Wessels, "Harvest: A Scalable, Customizable Discovery and Access System," University of Colorado, Boulder, Technical Report CU-CS-732-94, March 1995.

[8]   C. M. Bowman, P. B. Danzig, U. Manber, and M. F. Schwartz, "Scalable Internet Resource Discovery: Research Problems and Approaches," *Communications of the ACM*, vol. 37, pp. 98—107, 1994.

[9]   BTG and Janes, *Jane's Electronic Information System*: http://www.btg.com/janes/, 1996.

[10] S. Ceri and J. Widom, "Managing Semantic Heterogeneity with Production Rules and Persistent Queues," IBM Research Laboratory, San Jose, CA, Technical Report RJ9064 (80754), October 1992.

[11] S. Chakravarthy and J. Widom, "Foreword to Special Issue on Active Database Systems," *Journal of Intelligent Information Systems*, vol. 7, pp. 64, 1996.

[12] W. W. Chu, H. Yang, K. Chiang, M. Minock, G. Chow, and C. Larson, "CoBase: A Scalable and Extensible Cooperative Information System," *Journal of Intelligent Information Systems*, vol. 6, 2/3, pp. 223-259, June, 1996.

[13] M. Cutkosky, R. Englemore, R. Fikes, M. Genesereth, T. Gruber, W. S. Mark, J. Tenenbaum, and J. Weber, "PACT: An Experiment in Integrating Concurrent Engineering Systems," In *IEEE Computer*, vol. 26, 1993, pp. 28-37.

[14] S. Dao and B. Perry, "Information Mediation in Cyberspace: Scalable Methods for Declarative Information Networks," *Journal of Intelligent Information Systems*, vol. 6, 2/3, pp. 131-150, 1996.

[15] R. Davis and R. Smith, "Negotiation as a Metaphor for Distributed Problem Solving," *Artificial Intelligence*, vol. 20, pp. 63-109, 1983.

[16] U. Dayal, B. Blaustein, A. Buchmann, U. Chakravarthy, R. L. M. Hsu, D. McCarthy, A. Rosenthal, S. Sarin, M. J. Carey, M. Livny, and R. Jauhari, "The HiPAC Project: Combining Active Databases and Timing Constraints," *ACM SIGMOD Record*, vol. 17, pp. 51-70, 1988.

[17] U. Dayal, A. P. Buchmann, and D. R. McCarthy, "Rules Are Objects Too: A Knowledge Model For An Active, Object-Oriented Database System," Proc. of 2nd Int'l Workshop on Object-Oriented Database Systems, Bad Munster am Stein-Ebernberg, Germany, 1988.

[18] R. Engelmore and T. Morgan, "Blackboard Systems," In *The Insight Series in Artificial Intelligence*, T. Morgan, Ed.: Addison-Wesley Publishing Company, 1988, pp. 602.

[19] C. Faloutsos, R. Barber, M. Flickner, J. L. Hafner, W. Niblack, D. Petovic, and W. Equitz, "Efficient and Effective Querying by Image Content," *Journal of Intelligent Information Systems*, vol. 3, pp. 231-262, 1994.

[20] A. Farquhar, R. Fikes, W. Pratt, and J. Rice, "Collaborative Ontology Construction for Information Integration," Knowledge Systems Lab, Computer Science Department, Stanford University, Palo Alto, CA, KSL-95-63, August 1995.

[21] T. Finin, "CIKM '94 Workshop on Intelligent Information Agents," , T. Finin, Ed. Baltimore, MD, 1994.

[22] R. Fritzen, T. Finin, D. McKay, and R. McEntire, "KQML — A Language and Protocol for Knowledge and Information Exchange," International Distributed Artificial Intelligence Workshop, Seattle, WA, 1994.

[23] L. Gasser and M. N. Huhns, "Distributed Artificial Intelligence," In *Research Notes in Artificial Intelligence*, vol. II. London and San Mateo: Pitman; Morgan Kaufmann Publishers, Inc., 1989, pp. 519.

[24] M. Genesereth and S. P. Ketchpel, "Software Agents," *Communications of the ACM*, vol. 37, pp. 48-53, 1994.

[25] H. Gomaa and G. K. Farrukh, "An Approach for Configuring Distributed Applications from Reusable Architectures," IEEE International Conference on Engineering of Complex Computer Systems, Montreal, Canada, 1996.

[26] H. Gomaa, D. Menascé, and L. Kerschberg, "A Software Architectural Design Method for Large-Scale Distributed Information Systems," *Journal of Distributed Systems Engineering*, vol. September, 1996.

[27] H. Gomaa, D. A. Menascé, and L. Kerschberg, "A Software Architectural Design Method for Large-Scale Distributed Data Intensive Information Systems," *Journal of Distributed Systems Engineering*, To appear.

[28] T. Gruber, "A Translation Approach to Portable Ontology Specifications," *Knowledge Acquisition*, vol. 5, pp. 199-220, 1993.

[29] R. V. Guha and D. B. Lenat, "Enabling Agents to Work Together," *Communications of the ACM*, vol. 37, pp. 126-142, 1994.

[30] C. Hewitt, "Open Information Systems Semantics for Distributed Artificial Intelligence," *Artificial Intelligence*, vol. 47, pp. 79-106, 1991.

[31] L. Kerschberg, "Expert Database Systems: Proceedings from the First International Workshop," . Menlo Park, CA: Benjamin/Cummings, 1986, pp. 701.

[32] L. Kerschberg, "Expert Database Systems: Proceedings from the First International Conference," . Menlo Park, CA: Benjamin/Cummings, 1987, pp. 501.

[33] L. Kerschberg, "Expert Database Systems: Proceedings from the Second International Conference," . Redwood City, CA: Benjamin/Cummings, 1988, pp. 777.

[34] L. Kerschberg, "Expert Database Systems: Knowledge/Data Management Environments for Intelligent Information Systems," *Information Systems*, vol. 15, pp. 151-160, 1990.

[35] L. Kerschberg, H. Gomaa, D. A. Menascé, and J. P. Yoon, "Data and Information Architectures for Large-Scale Distributed Data Intensive Information Systems," Proc. of the Eighth IEEE International Conference on Scientific and Statistical Database Management, Stockholm, Sweden, 1996.

[36] M. Klusch, "Using a Cooperative Agent System FCSI for a Context-Based Recognition of Interdatabase Dependencies," Workshop on Intelligent Information Agents, CKIM Conference, Gaithersburg, MD, 1994.

[37] M. Klusch, "Utilitarian Coalition Formation Between Information Agents," In *Cooperative Knowledge Processing*, S. Kirn and G. O'Hare, Eds. London: Springer-Verlag, 1996.

[38] M. Klusch and O. Shehory, "Coalition Formation Among Rational Information Agents," Seventh European Workshop on Modelling Autonomous Agents in a Multi-Agent World (MAAMAW-96), Eindhoven, Netherlands, 1996.

[39] M. Klusch and O. Shehory, "A Polynomial Kernel-Oriented Coalition Algorithm for Rational Information Agents," Second International Conference on Multi-Agent Systems, Kyoto, Japan, 1996.

[40] D. Kuokka and L. Harada, "Integrating Information via Matchmaking," *Journal of Intelligent Information Systems*, vol. 6, 2/3, pp. 261-279, 1996.

[41] P. Maes, "Designing Autonomous Agents: Theory and Practice from Biology to Engineering and Back," In *Special Issues of Robotics and Autonomous Systems*. Cambridge, MA, London, England: The MIT Press, 1990, pp. 194.

[42] D. A. Menascé, H. Gomaa, and L. Kerschberg, "A Performance-Oriented Design Methodology for Large-Scale Distributed Data Intensive Information Systems," First IEEE International Conference on Engineering of Complex Computer Systems, Southern Florida, USA, 1995.

[43] R. S. Michalski, L. Kerschberg, K. Kaufman, and J. Ribeiro, "Mining for Knowledge in Databases: The INLEN Architecture, Initial Implementation and First Results," *Journal of Intelligent Information Systems*, vol. 1, pp. 85-113, 1992.

[44] A. Motro, "FLEX: A Tolerant and Cooperative User Interface to Databases," *IEEE Transactions on Knowledge and Data Engineering*, vol. 2, pp. 231-246, 1990.

[45] A. Motro, "Accommodating Imprecision in Database Systems: Issues and Solutions," In *Multidatabase Systems: An Advanced Solution to Global Information Sharing*, A. R. Hurson, M. W. Bright, and S. Pakzad, Eds.: IEEE Computer Society Press, 1993, pp. 381-386.

[46] A. Motro, "A Formal Framework for Integrating Inconsistent Answers from Multiple Information Sources," Department of Information and Software Systems Engineering, George Mason University, Fairfax, VA, Technical Report ISSE-TR-93-106, October 1993.

[47] A. Motro, "Intensional Answers to Database Queries," *IEEE Transactions on Knowledge and Data Engineering*, vol. 6, pp. 444-454, 1994.

[48] A. Motro, "Management of Uncertainty in Database Systems," In *Modern Database Systems: The Object Model, Interoperability and Beyond*, W. Kim, Ed.: Addison-Wesley Publishing Company/ACM Press, 1994.

[49] A. Motro, "Multiplex: A Formal Model for Multidatabases and Its Implementation," ISSE Department, George Mason University, Fairfax, VA, Technical Report ISSE-TR-95-10, 1995.

[50] A. Motro, "Responding with Knowledge," In *Advances in Databases and Artificial Intelligence, Vol. 1: The Landscape of Intelligence in Database and Information Systems*, vol. 1, L. Delcambre and F. Petry, Eds.: JAI Press, 1995.

[51] A. Motro, D. Marks, and S. Jajodia, "Aggregation in Relational Databases: Controlled Disclosure of Sensitive Information," European Symposium on Research in Computer Security, 1994.

[52] A. Motro and P. Smets, "Uncertainty Management in Information Systems: from Needs to Solutions," . Norwall, MA: Kluwer Academic Publishers, 1996, pp. 480.

[53] G. Piatetsky-Shapiro and W. J. Frawley, "Knowledge Discovery in Databases," . Menlo Park, CA: AAAI Press/MIT Press, 1991.

[54] J. Ribeiro, K. Kaufman, and L. Kerschberg, "Knowledge Discovery in Multiple Databases," ISMM International Conference on Intelligent Information Management Systems, Washington D.C., 1995.

[55] D. Riecken, "M: An Architecture of Integrated Agents," *Communications of the ACM*, vol. 37, pp. 106-116, 1994.

[56] M. Rusinkiewicz and others, "OMNIBASE: Design and Implementation of a Multidatabase System," *Newsletter of the Computer Society of the IEEE Technical Committee on Distributed Processing*, vol. 10, pp. 20--28, 1988.

[57] A. Segev and J. Park, "Updating Distributed Materialized Views," *IEEE Transactions on Knowledge and Data Engineering*, vol. 1, pp. 173-184, 1989.

[58] L. Seligman, "A Mediated Approach to Consistency Management Among Distributed, Heterogeneous Information Systems," In *Information and Software Systems Engineering*. Fairfax: George Mason University, 1994.

[59] L. Seligman and L. Kerschberg, "An Active Database Approach to Consistency Management in Heterogeneous Data- and Knowledge-based Systems," *International Journal of Cooperative and Intelligent Systems*, vol. 2, 1993.

[60] L. Seligman and L. Kerschberg, "Knowledge-base/Database Consistency in a Federated Multidatabase Environment," IEEE RIDE — Interoperability in Multidatabase Systems, Vienna, Austria, 1993.

[61] L. Seligman and L. Kerschberg, "Federated Knowledge and Database Systems: A New Architecture for Integrating of AI and Database Systems," In *Advances in Databases and Artificial Intelligence, Vol. 1: The Landscape of Intelligence in Database and Information Systems*, vol. 1, L. Delcambre and F. Petry, Eds.: JAI Press, 1995.

[62] A. Sheth and J. Larson, "Federated Database Systems for Managing Distributed, Heterogeneous, and Autonomous Databases," *ACM Computing Surveys*, vol. 22, pp. 183-236, 1990.

[63] M. Tambe, W. L. Johnson, R. M. Jones, F. Koss, J. E. Laird, P. S. Rosenbloom, and K. Schwamb, "Intelligent Agents for Interactive Simulation Experiments," In *AI Magazine*, vol. 16, 1995, pp. 15-39.

[64] M. Tambe and P. S. Rosenbloom, "Event Tracking in a Dynamic Multi-Agent Environment," USC — Information Sciences Institute, Technical Report ISI-RR-393, September 11, 1994.

[65] C. Toomey and others, "Software Agents for Dissemination of Remote Terrestrial Sensing Data," i-SAIRAS 94, Pasadena, CA, 1994.

[66] X. S. Wang, C. Bettini, A. Brodsky, and S. Jajodia, "Logical design for temporal databases with multiple granularities," *ACM Trans.on Database Systems*, To appear.

[67] X. S. Wang, S. Jajodia, and V. S. Subrahmanian, "Temporal Modules: An Approach Toward Federated Temporal Databases," ACM SIGMOD International Conference on Management of Data, Washington, D.C., 1993.

[68] X. S. Wang, S. Jajodia, and V. S. Subrahmanian, "Temporal Modules: An Approach toward Federated Temporal Databases," *Information Sciences*, vol. 82, pp. 103-128, 1995.

[69] D. Weishar, "A Knowledge-Based Architecture for Query Formulation and Processing in Federated Heterogeneous Databases," In *Information and Software Systems Engineering*. Fairfax, VA: George Mason University, 1993, pp. 230.

[70] D. Weishar and L. Kerschberg, "Data/Knowledge Packets as a Means of Supporting Semantic Heterogeneity in Multidatabase Systems," In *ACM SIGMOD Record*, 1991.

[71] J. Widom and S. Ceri, "Active Database Systems: Triggers and Rules for Advanced Database Processing," : Morgan Kaufmann Publishers, Inc., 1995.

[72] G. Wiederhold, "The Roles of Artificial Intelligence in Information Systems," *Journal of Intelligent Information Systems*, vol. 1, pp. 35-56, 1992.

[73] G. Wiederhold, "Foreword to Special Issue on the Intelligent Integration of Information," *Journal of Intelligent Information Systems*, vol. 6, 2/3, pp. 93-97, 1996.

[74] G. Wiederhold, S. Jajodia, and W. Litwin, "Dealing with Granularity of Time in Temporal Databases," In *Lecture Notes in Computer Science*, vol. 498, R. Anderson and others, Eds.: Springer-Verlag, 1991, pp. 124-140.

[75] G. Wiederhold, S. Jajodia, and W. Litwin, "Integrating Temporal Data in a Heterogeneous Environment," In *Temporal Databases: Theory, Design, and Implementation*, A. U. Tansel, S. Jajodia, and others, Eds.: Benjamin/Cummings, 1993, pp. 563-579.

[76] J. P. Yoon and L. Kerschberg, "A Framework for Constraint Management in Object-Oriented Databases," International Conference on Information and Knowledge Management, Baltimore, MD, 1992.

[77] J. P. Yoon and L. Kerschberg, "A Framework for Knowledge Discovery and Evolution in Databases," *IEEE Transactions on Knowledge and Data Engineering*, 1993.

[78] J. P. Yoon and L. Kerschberg, "Semantic Query Reformulation in Object-Oriented Systems," In *International Conference on Deductive and Object-Oriented Databases*, vol. 760. Phoenix, AZ: Springer-Verlag, 1993.

[79] J. P. Yoon and L. Kerschberg, "Semantic Update Optimization in Active Databases," Proceedings IFIP WG2.6 Working Conference on Database Semantics (DS-6), Atlanta, 1995.

The CORBA Specification for Cooperation in Heterogeneous Information Systems

Gottfried Vossen

Universität Münster, Institut für Informatik, Grevenerstraße 91, D-48159 Münster, Germany

Abstract. CORBA (Common Object Request Broker Architecture) is an interoperability standard for middleware in distributed object management systems which has resulted from the efforts of one of the largest computer industry consortia ever formed (the *Object Management Group*). CORBA defines client/server middleware in which objects are uniformly used for letting existing applications discover each other, interoperate, and interact with each other. Through a variety of predefined object services, CORBA additionally allows to create and delete objects, access them by name, make them transactional or secure, and store them persistently in a vastly arbitrary external storage system. In this paper, the core components of CORBA, which are collectively called the *Object Management Architecture*, are described in some detail. It is indicated how CORBA can be employed for developing distributed information systems.

1 Introduction

Recent developments in the areas of information processing and information systems have concentrated on the use of the object-oriented paradigm. Reasons for this include the fact that objects are well-manageable and well-organizable units of information, can be employed for both information sharing and hiding, and can help in building distributed information systems even involving heterogeneous hard- or software components. However, for such components to properly and efficiently interact, well-defined platforms are needed which shield applications from the details of underlying operating and communication systems, and which are agreed upon by the various vendors contributing to this scenario. CORBA (*Common Object Request Broker Architecture*) is such a platform [16]. In this paper, we survey the major features of CORBA, indicate their motivation, and discuss ways of exploiting them.

In brief, CORBA [25] is an interoperability standard for middleware in distributed object management systems which has resulted from the efforts of an industry consortium called the *Object Management Group* (OMG), which has over 650 member companies. CORBA defines client/server middleware [21] in which objects are uniformly used for letting existing applications discover each other, interoperate, and interact with each other; they do so by looking at specifications delivered in an independent language (the *Interface Definition Language* or IDL). Through a variety of predefined object services, CORBA additionally allows to create and delete objects, access them by name, make them transactional or secure, and store them persistently in an arbitrary external storage system. The core components of CORBA, which are collectively called the *Object Management Architecture* (OMA) [17], include the *Object Request Broker* (ORB), the *Common Object Services*, the *Common Facilities*, and *Application Objects*. Market-wise, CORBA implementations (more precisely: products which are "CORBA compliant") are beginning to emerge, and numerous developments in the area of information systems are beginning to rely on them. Thus, CORBA can be considered an important line of development which has good chances to become standard software on network-usable platforms in the near to middle future.

This survey paper is organized as follows: In Section 2, we motivate standards like CORBA by briefly looking into the area of distributed object management. In Section 3 we discuss the major OMA components, and in Section 4 we present the main features of CORBA. Section 5 looks at sample exploitations of CORBA in the area of information systems. Section 6 gives some conclusions.

2 Distributed Object Management

The paradigm of *object-orientation* [3, 4, 9, 11, 26] has essentially penetrated several major areas in computer science, including programming languages, software engineering, database management systems [29], and artificial intelligence. The common expectation today is that object-oriented systems are able to run on vastly any type of computer, under the control of an object-oriented operating system, and be coupled with object-oriented programming languages, user interfaces, or database systems. Their development can be done in a piece-wise fashion, resulting in components that can easily be plugged together to form larger components; moreover, such systems are no longer restricted to single locations. Indeed, using a variety of mechanisms (including names, message queues, or object identifiers), object-based systems are commonly assumed to be distributed in nature.

Essentially this vision of component software is the basis of *Distributed Object Management* (DOM), which is considered a promising concept to achieve the two major goals of

- *interoperability*, i.e., the ability of different pieces of software to collaborate in a heterogeneous and distributed hardware environment, and
- adequate *integration* of newly developed and existing legacy systems.

DOM can support this in two ways: First, the data structures and the functionality of such systems are represented as encapsulated objects which communicate by sending messages to well-defined interfaces; second, transparent access to (server) objects is made possible for (client) applications (i.e., without knowing the exact location, the internal representation or the access language used). Legacy systems are integrated by putting a *wrapper* around them, which makes

Fig. 1. The client/server concept.

them look like objects. As a result, all resources available in a network are presented to the user as a collection of generally accessible objects which can be combined appropriately for specific applications. A *Distributed Object Management System* (DOMS) comprises an arbitrary number of distributed nodes which run application programs, database systems or simple objects (the available resources), and a collection of clients, which can also be application programs, software tools or simple objects (which issue requests that are served by the resources). Thus, it is clear that the DOM view is an appropriate basis for the future development of information systems.

For distributed systems in general, and for DOMS in particular, the *client/server* paradigm [21], originally developed as a simple paradigm for software architecture models, is now generally accepted (cf. Figure 1). Clients typically talk to servers in terms of request/reply pairs exchanged via some *middleware* or distribution platform which supports the interaction and interoperability between applications running on different (and eventually heterogeneous) systems, by shielding from the underlying operating and communication systems. The idea is that applications access middleware functionality via an appropriate interface, and the middleware isolates these applications from the details of the lower system levels. Middleware can be categorized into *general* middleware, which comprises functionality such as a directory service, a security service, cooperation like RPC, or clock synchronization, and *server-specific* middleware which accounts for server applications such as databases, online transaction processing, groupware, or the Internet. Specific examples of server-specific middleware include

- ODBC (Open DataBase Connectivity, by Microsoft), DRDA (Distributed Relational Database Architecture, by IBM), and the SAG/CLI (SQL Access Group/Call-Level Interface) for databases,
- TUXEDO and ENCINA for transaction processing monitors,
- Lotus Notes for Groupware,
- the HTTP protocol for the Internet, and
- CORBA as discussed below for distributed object systems.

For detailed information the reader should consult [21].

CORBA and related developments (such as Microsoft's OLE) have the general goal of coupling middleware functionality for distributed systems with the object-oriented paradigm. Essentially, a major goal of the OMG has been to define a broker, the ORB, as a uniform interface between the hard- and software components of different manufacturers. The ORB later became a central component of CORBA which describes the architecture of heterogeneous and interoperable systems at the interface and service levels. The main feature of CORBA is that it combines the idea of trading and brokering services to clients in a platform-independent way with the paradigm of object-orientation. As a result, the whole world consists of objects which ask each other for services by sending around messages, and by communicating with a brokering device.

Given this, a DOMS can be build from distributed object managers mediating between clients and resources by referring to a CORBA (or other) middleware layer. The broker component available at that layer can pass service requests to servers and later return results to the clients. Thus, not every object needs to know what service can be accessed in another object or which type of functionality is to be expected. Instead, clients can now turn to the mediator if they want to learn which object in the system supplies a particular service.

3 The Object Management Architecture

According to what was stated in the previous section, the OMG is standardizing DOM architectures and services. Its recommendations are based on an object model, used to support the integration of distributed applications. The general framework of the OMG activities is set by the *Object Management Architecture* (OMA). This architecture defines a reference model which identifies and characterizes the components, interfaces and protocols which together form a distributed object architecture. The OMA consists of four essential components, shown in some detail in Figure 2:

1. *Application Objects*: The OMA actually aims at applications which are interoperable, portable, and reusable. Therefore, application objects are specific to the individual end-user applications, and represent business objects or application programs operating on such objects.
2. *Object Request Broker* (ORB): This is the central component mediating between the distributed objects, passing on method calls to the appropriate target objects, and returning the results back to the caller. Architecture and function of the broker, which is sometimes also called the "CORBA object bus," are laid down in the CORBA specifications. We will say more about the broker in Section 4.
3. *Common Object Services*: These services support the communication between distributed objects, and essentially define the system-level object frameworks which extend the broker.
4. *Common Facilities*: They form a collection of objects for general purposes (e.g., error handling or printing) which are required by many applications. The Common Facilities are divided into horizontal and vertical facilities (which is not shown in Figure 2) and can be used directly by business objects.

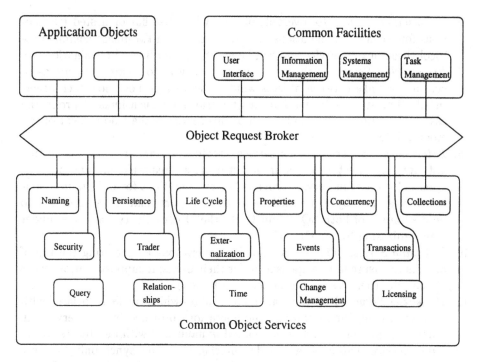

Fig. 2. Object Management Architecture (OMA).

We now take a closer look at the CORBA object services, which are system-level services with interfaces specified in a specifically designed language called the *Interface Definition Language* (IDL) [23]. These services can be used to create components, name them and introduce them to the environment; in particular, they allow the handling of objects that would normally be restricted to appear in a database. At the time of this writing (fall of 1996), the OMG has defined the following 13 object services:

1. *Life Cycle Service*: This service defines operations for creating, copying, moving, and deleting components on the bus.
2. *Persistence Service*: This service provides a uniform interface for storing objects persistently on a variety of storage servers (such as object-oriented databases, relational database or file systems).
3. *Naming Service*: This service allows objects to locate other objects by name; objects can be bound to existing network directories or naming contexts (such as OSF DCE or Sun NIS).
4. *Event Service*: Objects can register or unregister their interest in specific events through this service. It defines an object called event channel which collects and distributes events among objects.
5. *Concurrency Control Service*: This service provides a lock manager able to obtain locks on behalf of transactions or threads.

6. *Transaction Service*: Recoverable objects which use flat or nested transactions for concurrent operations are provided with a two-phase commit protocol through this service and can hence enjoy coordinated termination.
7. *Relationship Service*: This service provides a way to create dynamic associations or links between objects which otherwise do not know each other. In addition, it provides mechanisms for traversing such links to group the associated objects. One application of this service is the enforcement of referential integrity.
8. *Externalization Service*: This service provides a standard way for getting data into an object or out of an object using a stream-like mechanism.
9. *Query Service*: This service provides query operations for objects in a similar way as do object-oriented databases. In particular, it is supposed to be a superset of both SQL3 and OQL, the Object Query Language under standardization by the ODMG.
10. *Licensing Service*: This service provides operations for metering the use of objects to ensure fair compensation for their usage; it supports various ways of charging (per session, per node, per site etc.).
11. *Properties Service*: Properties are named values which can be associated with objects or components through the operations provided by this service. In particular, properties can be associated dynamically with an objects state.
12. *Time Service*: This service provides interfaces for time synchronization in a distributed object environment as well as operations for defining and managing time-triggered events.
13. *Security Service*: Finally, this service provides a framework for distributed object security, including authentication, access control lists, confidentiality, or the management of credentials delegation between objects.

A corresponding illustration of the OMA specifications which even includes services that still need to be specified (Trader Service, Change Management Service, Collections Service) is shown in Figure 2.

In a business OMA application, the application objects would include features such as invoicing, acceptance of orders or repair work, which will typically take the form of encapsulated business objects. These objects may even represent encapsulated legacy systems which resemble objects only from outside. The common facilities could include databases or information systems which are managed and accessed by company-wide data servers. The object services needed in this scenario handle, for example, database interactions (queries, transactions, etc.), various management functions and general functionalities such as name services or registration. A detailed example is discussed in [2].

In the context of the OMA, the broker is regarded as a kind of connection bus for the exchange of messages which may even span several systems. As mentioned earlier, the basic idea behind the ORB is the mediation between service user and service provider. The provider of a service informs the ORB about the type of service being offered as well as the corresponding invocation interface. A client acting as a caller of an object service communicates indirectly, i.e., via the broker, with a server object which may perform the desired service. A request consists

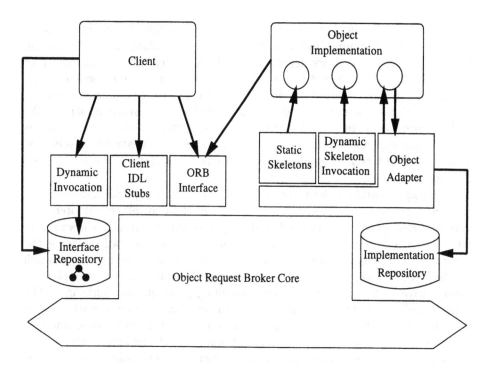

Fig. 3. Overview of CORBA.

of an operation, a target object and (possibly) parameters as well as an optional context for the request. The task of the ORB is to find the object implementation which corresponds to the indicated target object, to call this implementation, to hand over the request for processing and to eventually return the results.

4 CORBA

The Common Object Request Broker Architecture (CORBA) [25] acts as central DOM architecture of the OMG putting into concrete terms the synthesis, functionality, and the interfaces of a broker. Figure 3 gives an overview of CORBA.

The emphasis of this specification is on the *interfaces* which are offered by an ORB, and this is both good and bad: On the one hand, it allows for a high flexibility, since everything can be attached to a broker that comes with an appropriate interface specification. However, as has been found out in various projects which have tried to build upon CORBA, what exactly has to be specified is vage at times, so attaching service providers or users is not always easy.

The CORBA interfaces are distinguished into *call interfaces*, allowing client objects to send calls to a server object, and the *ORB interface*, allowing server and clients to access the infrastructure functions of the ORB. Call interfaces can be divided into static and dynamic ones. Prior to executing the client program, static interfaces create a *stub* (a fixed component of the program) from the interface description and statically bind it to the program. Dynamic interfaces allow the dynamic composition and invocation of calls. Both the static and the dynamic client interfaces are described in IDL. A service call reaches the server object via the specific object adapter and the corresponding IDL skeleton. The caller will not know whether the desired object is placed locally or on a remote node. Again, there are static and dynamic skeletons: The static or server IDL stubs provide static interfaces to each service exported by the server, whereas the dynamic skeleton interface provides a run-time mechanism for servers that need to handle incoming method calls addressed to objects without compiled IDL stubs.

The *Implementation Repository* is a database containing information on implementations of server objects which can be used by an object adapter. The *Interface Repository* contains the IDL descriptions of the currently known server interfaces which may be used for the definition of new applications or for the construction of dynamic request (by clients). IDL defines object interfaces which are determined independently of an object's implementation (where implementations have to be provided in a corresponding programming language). The definition of an interface is made up of a number of method or operation signatures together with a possibly empty set of type declarations which define new types for the use within the declaration. A signature of this kind consists of an operation name, a set of input parameters, a result and exceptions which can be triggered by the operation.

CORBA has currently reached its version 2.0 [18, 20, 21, 19]. The original CORBA 1.1 was concerned with creating portable object applications only, and left the ORB implementation to vendors. CORBA 2.0 has brought along interoperability, by specifying a so-called *Internet Inter-ORB Protocol* (IIOP). In essence, IIOP is the well-known TCP/IP protocol, enhanced by specific message exchanges which serve as a common backbone protocol.

We finally mention that platforms for cooperating objects or CORBA implementations (more precisely: CORBA-"compliant" brokers) are already commercially available; these include DEC's ObjectBroker, IBM's Distributed System Object Model (DSOM), HP's ORBplus, IONA's Orbix, Sun's NEO and JOE, Expertsoft's PowerBroker, or PostModern's BlackWidow. At this very moment, however, it is still difficult to obtain a broker which fully supports CORBA 2.0; this situation is expected to change soon.

5 Using CORBA in Information Systems

Before looking briefly into CORBA exploitations, we should mention that the OMG does *not* provide a genuine object model as part of their specifications which would have to be supported by all parties who try to be compliant (see [23] for details on what the OMG calls their model). Instead, the idea is to use just the IDL for specifying the core of object properties, and to augment that with application-dependent "components" which together deliver a *profile*. For

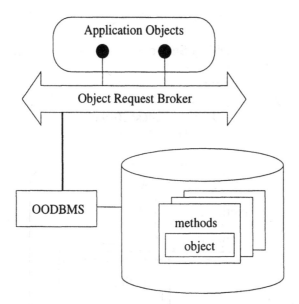

Fig. 4. Database access via CORBA.

example, the ODMG-93 specifications, tailored towards object-oriented databases, form such a profile; details can be found in [1, 4, 5].

5.1 General considerations

With respect to the development of future distributed and heterogeneous information systems, CORBA and the OMA can be exploited in a variety of ways.
We now sketch two of these, where we start, for the sake of simplicity, by looking
at databases capable of handling objects.

An *object-oriented database system* [11, 14, 9, 15], i.e., a database system with
full structural and behavioral object-oriented capabilities, can straightforwardly
be attached to a CORBA implementation: An ORB is employed to manage ac-
cesses to objects stored in the database; hence, applications get access to the
database via the broker, and actually they even have access to all databases
connected to the broker. This is illustrated in Figure 4 for the case of a single
database system. Using the appropriate CORBA services, it is furthermore possible to access multiple databases within a single application, which opens new
possibilities to build multidatabase systems [3].

The entirety of all objects within a distributed object architecture can itself be regarded as an object database, provided that relevant services with a
database-like functionality are available. Since the Common Object Services of
CORBA as described above already bring along several parts of such a functionality, this approach is realistic. From this point of view CORBA is no longer
merely a communication mechanism, but assumes the role of an internal implementation tool, as illustrated in Figure 5.

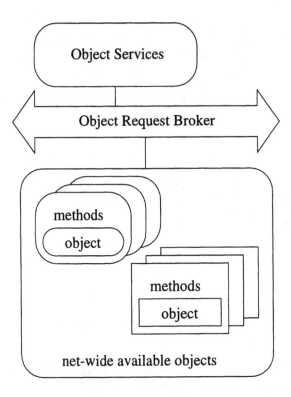

Fig. 5. CORBA as a database system.

It turns out that exactly this seems to be among the visions of the OMG, since the Persistence Service of CORBA, also called the *Persistent Object Service* (POS) [23], could suffice for creating a simple, yet flexible heterogeneous system for storing data persistently. Essentially, POS allows objects to persist beyond the lifetime of the application which create the objects or beyond the clients which use them. POS renders it possible to save the state of an object in a persistent store and retrieve or restore it from there when needed. The idea is to support a variety of storage services, including SQL database systems, object-oriented database systems, document filing systems or simple file systems. This approach is illustrated in Figure 6.

Under POS, client applications can access objects whose state is stored persistently. Every *Persistent Object* (PO) has a unique identifier which describes the location of that object within a storage component. An object can be made persistent by having it inherit the behavior from the PO class via IDL. The *Persistent Object Manager* (POM), an implementation-independent interface for operations dealing with persistence, shields the objects from a particular *Persistent Data Service* (PDS), which provides an interface to a particular storage-system implementation. A PDS moves data between objects and storage devices. It is required that all PDSs implement an IDL-specific POM interface; in addition, they may support implementation-dependent protocols, including the *Dynamic Data Object* (DDO) for relational databases, *ODMG-93* for object-oriented da-

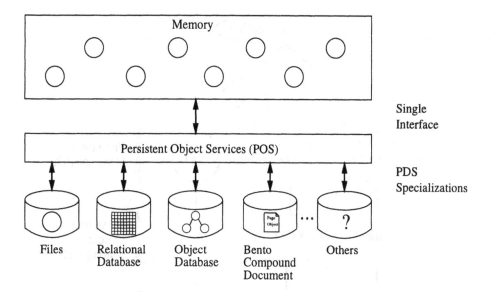

Fig. 6. The POS uniform storage interface.

tabases, and the *Direct Attribute* (DA) for other types of stores. The POM can route object calls to the appropriate PDS by looking at information in the given ID. Finally, data stores are implementations holding the persistent data of an object independent of the address space keeping the object. These architectural component considerations are summarized in Figure 7, where the Datastore-CLI denotes an API-like interface to SQL databases combining ODBC and the *Integrated Database Application Programming Interface* (IDAPI) [26].

Further details can be found in [21, 20, 11]. It should be mentioned that the OMG specifications are pretty vage on POS yet, a problem discussed in some detail in [10].

5.2 Sample realizations

We conclude this section by mentioning that numerous other ways of exploiting CORBA in the context of new types of information systems are currently under experimentation, where it is often the case that CORBA serves as an implementation vehicle, but is not as visible or as explicit as in the approaches described above. One of these directions is the area of *workflow management*, which aims at specifying, verifying, controlling, executing, and managing the activities and processes in business applications. A sample system development exploiting CORBA technology is the Mentor project [32], in which a CORBA-compliant broker is used to integrate external applications into a workflow execution environment. Details can be found in [31]. In terms of the OMG, the goal in workflow management is the creation of *business objects*, i.e., application-level components which can be used in unpredictable combinations; see [20] for details.

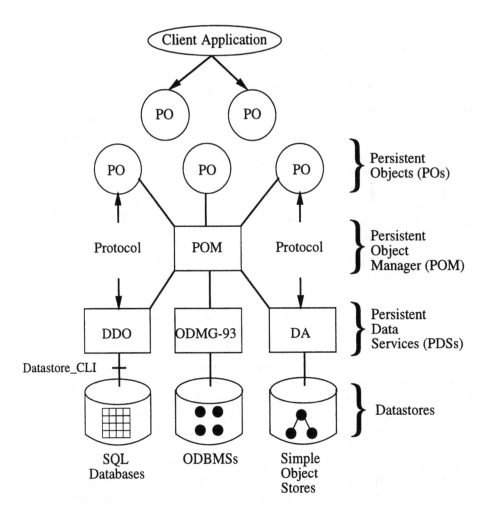

Fig. 7. POS components.

In [12], the notion of an *alliance* is introduced as a construct for regulating the collective behavior of a set of cooperating objects in such a way that individual objects have ample freedom to respond to other objects, and that a variety of unexpected situations can be handled. Specifically, alliances are used for representing the specification of workflow execution control, and it is demonstrated how alliances can be integrated into DOM systems. To this end, various implementation alternatives based on CORBA are discussed. [13] describes the architecture of a federated environmental information system which uses CORBA for providing a homogeneous view of the sources from which geographic and other information or data is drawn. Particular attention is paid in this architecture to the automatic detection of critical situations as they arise in environmental measurements and their impact on data sources; to this end, event-condition-action (ECA) rules as used in active databases are implemented by exploiting CORBA functionality.

Further projects making use of CORBA technology for building new types of systems include a project on the electronic provision of pricing and product information to customers by DEC, see [7], the Sunrise Project at Los Alamos National Laboratory [27], or the COMA Project on distributed parallel processing at Indiana University [6].

6 Conclusions

What we have tried to convey in this short survey is that the OMA and CORBA can serve well as a basis for the development of distributed object systems and of DOM architectures which incorporate database or, more generally, data storage systems and hence provide information system functionality and technology. Numerous projects are now underway to construct new systems, and integrate old ones, based on the CORBA platform. Moreover, methodologies are emerging which can be exploited well in a CORBA environment; examples are methods for migrating legacy systems [2] or for transitioning to open systems [24].

It should be mentioned, however, that CORBA is not the only player in the field. Indeed, competing developments include *compound documents, component objects, agents*, and *coordinators*. A major competitor, concept-wise, is the integration of application objects into so-called *compound documents* where a "document" consists of a set of objects. Essentially, a compound document can be considered as an integration framework for visual components, which provides protocols that let the component managing a document communicate with the components that own objects within the document. Two representatives of this category are (the CORBA compatible) OpenDoc by Apple, IBM and others, which is now used by the OMG as the basis of their compound documents specification, and OLE (Object Linking and Embedding) by Microsoft, which is not CORBA compatible, but which is included in the Windows95 and Windows NT 4 operating systems (and hence essentially for free). If components are carved out of existing applications, a typical scenario could see compound documents on the client side, and CORBA on the server side. OLE is itself built on top of an ORB called the *Distributed Component Object Model* (DCOM); together, OLE and DCOM will provide the basis for Microsoft's future distributed computing environment. Different from OpenDoc, OLE is a complete environment for components, with a set of common services that allow these components to collaborate intelligently. Details can be found in [21].

Since there is considerable competition between commercial CORBA implementations and other (and even free) platforms for component software, the near future will certainly bring a decision on which approach will survive. Independent of who will make it in the long run, these approaches seem to play a similar role as did, for example, the well-known ISO-OSI 7-layer reference architecture some 10 years ago: They provide necessary standardization, and good implementations deliver helpful platforms for building even world-wide information systems. On the other hand, it seems that *conceptually*, i.e., from a more theoretical point of view, there are no new models, abstraction concepts, or methodologies behind, or underneath, middleware constructions like CORBA. What is new, but not CORBA-specific, is the view that computing "worlds" can be perceived as populations of interacting objects, and that software will soon be more and more component-based so that plugging the right things together will vastly suffice for building big applications. CORBA, then, is just an implementation vehicle, and it is even one not everybody is happy to employ [30].

We finally mention that, as is common practice nowadays, numerous information is available online (on the Web) on the subject of this short survey; to get started, the reader is encouraged to look at [19, 8, 22].

References

1. Bancilhon F., Ferran G.: The ODMG Standard for Object Databases. In Proc. 4th International Conference on Database Systems for Advanced Applications (1995), 273–283
2. Brodie M.L., Stonebraker M.: *Migrating Legacy Systems Gateways, Interfaces & The Incremental Approach.* San Francisco, CA: Morgan Kaufmann (1995)
3. Bukhres O.A., Elmagarmid A.K., Eds.: *Object-Oriented Multidatabase Systems.* Englewood Cliffs, NJ: Prentice Hall (1996)
4. Cattell R.G.G.: *Object Data Management — Object-Oriented and Extended Relational Database Systems*, revised edition. Reading, MA: Addison-Wesley (1994)
5. Cattell R.G.G., Ed.: *The Object Database Standard: ODMG-93*, Release 1.2. San Francisco, CA: Morgan Kaufmann (1996)
6. COMA Project at Indiana University, see
   `http://www.cs.indiana.edu/hyplan/kksiazek/writeup.html`
7. Hastings E.E., Kumar D.H.: Providing Customers Information Using the WEB and CORBA — Integrating Transactions, Objects, and the Web. available from `http://www.ncsa.uiuc.edu/SDG/IT94/Proceedings/DDay/hastings/hastings.html`
8. Keahey K.: A Brief Tutorial on CORBA. available at
   `http://www.cs.indiana.edu/hyplan/kksiazek/tuto.html`
9. Kim W., Ed.: *Modern Database Systems — The Object Model, Interoperability, and Beyond.* Reading, MA: Addison-Wesley (1995)
10. Kleindienst J., Plasil F., Tume P.: Lessons Learned from Implementing the CORBA Persistent Object Service. In Proc. OOPSLA '96 Conference, ACM SIGPLAN Notices 31 (10) 1996, 150–167
11. Lausen G., Vossen G.: *Models and Languages of Object-Oriented Databases.* Reading, MA: Addison-Wesley (1997), to appear
12. Lockemann P.C., Walter H.D.: Object-Oriented Protocol Hierarchies for Distributed Workflow Systems. Theory and Practice of Object Systems 1 (1995), 281–300
13. Lockemann P.C., Kölsch U., Koschel A., Nikolai R., Kramer R., Walter H.D.: Object Orientation: Escape from Large-Scale Chaos? In Proc. 2nd STIA Conference (1996), Technical University of Ilmenau, Germany, 1–15

14. Loomis M.E.S.: *Object Databases — The Essentials.* Reading, MA: Addison-Wesley (1995)
15. Manola F.: *An Evaluation of Object-Oriented DBMS Developments,* 1994 Edition. Technical Report TR-0263-08-94- 165. Waltham, MA: GTE Laboratories (1994)
16. Object Management Group: *The Common Object Request Broker: Architecture and Specification.* OMG Document Number 91.12.1, Revision 1.1 (1991)
17. Object Management Group: *Object Management Architecture Guide.* OMG Document Number 92.11.1, Revision 2.0 (1992)
18. Object Management Group: *The Common Object Request Broker: Architecture and Specification.* Version 2.0, (1995)
19. Object Management Group: Public Documents List, see http://www.omg.org/public-doclist.html
20. Orfali R., Harkey D., Edwards J.: *The Essential Distributed Objects Survival Guide.* New York: John Wiley & Sons, Inc. (1996)
21. Orfali R., Harkey D., Edwards J.: *The Essential Client/Server Survival Guide,* 2nd edition. New York: John Wiley & Sons, Inc. (1996)
22. Schmidt D.: Distributed Object Computing with CORBA. see http://www.cs.wustl.edu/ schmidt/corba.html
23. Sessions R.: *Object Persistence — Beyond Object-Oriented Databases.* Upper Saddle River, NJ: Prentice Hall PTR (1996)
24. Shaffer S.L., Simon A.R.: *Transitioning to Open Systems.* San Francisco, CA: Morgan Kaufmann (1996)
25. Siegel J., Ed.: *CORBA Fundamentals and Programming.* New York: John Wiley & Sons (1996)
26. Simon A.R.: *Strategic Database Technology: Management for the Year 2000.* San Francisco, CA: Morgan Kaufmann (1995)
27. Sunrise Project at Los Alamos, see http://www.acl.lanl.gov/sunrise/
28. Von Bültzingsloewen G., Koschel A., Kramer R.: Active Information Delivery in a CORBA-based Distributed Information System. In Proc. 1st IFCIS International Conference on Cooperative Information Systems (1996), 218–227
29. Vossen G.: Databases and Database Management. In Coffman E.G., Lenstra J.K., Rinnooy Kan A.H.G. (eds.): *Handbooks in Operations Research and Management Science,* Vol. 3: *Computing.* Amsterdam: North-Holland (1992) 133–193
30. Wallace E., Wallnau K.C.: A Situated Evaluation of the Object Management Group's (OMG) Object Management Architecture (OMA). In Proc. OOPSLA '96 Conference, ACM SIGPLAN Notices 31 (10) 1996, 168–178
31. Wodtke D.:L *Modellbildung und Architektur von verteilten Workflow-Management-Systemen.* Ph.D. Dissertation, Universität des Saarlandes, Germany (1996)
32. Wodtke D., Weissenfels J., Weikum G., Kotz Dittrich A.: The Mentor Project: Steps Towards Enterprise-Wide Workflow Management. In Proc. 12th IEEE International Conference on Data Engineering (1996), 556–565

Enriching Active Databases with Agent Technology

Johan van den Akker
Arno Siebes

CWI
P.O.Box 94079, 1090 GB Amsterdam, The Netherlands
e-mail: {vdakker,arno}@cwi.nl

Abstract. Intelligent agents are software components with a largely autonomous behaviour, that are fitted out with a considerable degree of artificial intelligence. They are a promising paradigm to serve as a foundation for future computing environments in general, and information systems in particular. At the same time database research has seen the rise of active databases, database systems that add autonomous behaviour to a database. In this paper, we investigate the addition of notions from intelligent agents to an active database. We explain why active databases already implement weak agency, and look into the benefits stronger agency can bring to an active database. It turns out that these are mainly found in the increased flexibility facilitated by the reasoning abilities strong agency implies. For example, an agent can have multiple strategies to maintain a constraint instead of a one fixed strategy defined by triggers.

1 Introduction

The ongoing miniaturisation of computers is leading us to a world, where computers are omnipresent. This phenomenon has become widely known under the name *ubiquitous computing*. Although this development is still in its early stages, there is already some consensus on the software architecture for ubiquitous computing. This consensus considers *intelligent agents* the most promising paradigm for future information systems. In this paradigm, software consists of a number of entities collaborating towards a common goal, functioning autonomously with little intervention. Hence it is reasonable to expect that, in future computing environments, information systems will be based on a large number of cooperating agents.

At the same time, research in databases, the traditional foundation of an information system, has addressed the inclusion of additional modelling notions in databases. This has lead, among other things, to active databases, i.e. databases that include production rules. This allows databases to react autonomously to certain situations in the database.

Since databases are the current foundation and agents a future foundation of information systems, the question rises how information systems might evolve from databases to agents. Since active databases are the first step in this evolution, we examine the role agent technology can play in an active database. The possibility of integrating agents in active databases was earlier mentioned in [4], which compared active databases and agent systems. Its main focus, however, was on the similarity of concepts in both areas, whereas we look into the opportunities agent technology offers active databases.

In this paper, we first identify the "level of agency" in a state-of-the-art active database model. Then, we present our view on the benefits the addition of further features of agent technology can bring to active databases.

2 Active databases

An active database [12] is a database that exhibits autonomous behaviour. That is, it executes actions without explicit intervention from a user. This behaviour is modelled by production rules, usually specified by an event-condition-action triple. If the event occurs and the condition is satisfied, the action of a rule is executed.

Originally, rules were introduced in databases in order to deal with constraints more flexibly, but rules have found much wider use. In fact, large parts of an application can often be specified by rules. The use of active databases has been classified by Kappel and Schrefl in [7]. They categorise applications of rules as follows:

1. maintaining static integrity constraints
2. maintaining derived data and materialised views
3. maintaining dynamic integrity constraints
4. database access authorisation
5. work step ordering
6. representing permissions to act
7. representing obligations to act

Of these seven, the first four are implementations of DBMS functionality. The fifth is relatively specific to certain applications, esp. workflow management applications. It can be regarded as a special case of the third application. The last two applications are forms of *business rules*. Business rules are a specification of company policy, or a description of the behaviour of a company. Simple examples are rules in an inventory application, that reorder an item if the stock falls below a certain level. More advanced business rules describes the competence of persons in the organisation. These business rules are the rules used to specify application functionality.

For the discussion in the remainder of the paper, we now introduce a state-of-the-art active database model developed at CWI, named DEGAS[1]. Here, we will

---

[1] DEGAS stands for Dynamic Entities Get Autonomous Status

only give an impression necessary for the discussion in this paper. For a full introduction the reader is referred to [1].

The core of DEGAS is formed by autonomous objects. Object autonomy means that an object is as independent as possible, both in its behaviour and its specification. Thus, an autonomous object encapsulates its complete behaviour. Its structure is given by attributes. The behaviour of a DEGAS object consists of *potential* behaviour, specified by methods and lifecycles, and *actual* behaviour, specified by rules. Methods specify the actions an object can execute, while an object's lifecycle specifies the possible execution sequences of its actions. Rules specify actual actions of the object in specified situations. They are given in the Event-Condition-Action format [6] commonly accepted in active databases.

An example of a DEGAS object is given in Figure 1. This object models an investor, who uses information from his newspaper to take decisions about his share portfolio. The syntax of attributes and methods is straightforward. The attributes specify the information stored by the investor, such as his name and birth data, the identity of his shares and his newspaper, and the currently perceived "reasonable" price for his shares. The methods specify the possible actions of the investor. He has methods to sell his shares and methods to deal with good and bad news about his shares.

Lifecycles are defined using process algebra [3] extended with guard conditions. In process algebraic terms, the process executed by the object must be a trace of the process specified by the lifecycle. For a further discussion of lifecycles in DEGAS, the reader is referred to [2]. In this example, the lifecycle regulates two things, sequence and access to methods. The first lifecycle specifies that a tryToSell action must always be followed by a Sell action or a cancelSupply action. The latter action withdraws an offer to sell shares that did not succeed. The two other lines in the lifecycle specification restrict access to the goodNews and badNews actions to the subscribed newspaper.

The event specification of a rule is also a process algebraic expression. The condition can be any condition on the object, while the action is a method call, either on the object itself, or to another object. After each method execution, the rule set of an object is checked against the object's history. If the specified event did occur and the rule's condition is satisfied, the action is executed. For each event, a variable is bound to the time the event occurred. This timestamp can be used in the condition to refer to historical values of the object's attributes. For example, the first rule of the investor object specifies that he tries to buy additional shares, if good news breaks twice within a week.

Interaction between objects takes place through message passing. In addition, objects can engage in relations. Relations allows objects to share and exchange information on a more permanent basis. More on the subject of relations between objects in DEGAS can be found in [1].

Object Investor
Attributes
   name : string
   birthday : time
   birthplace : string
   share : Oid
   subscription : Oid
   transactionPrice : real
Methods
   tryToSell(company:string, number:integer, minPrice:real) = {
     SupplyClass.initiateShareholder(company,number,minPrice)
   }
   Sell(buyer,price) = {
     share.transferOwnership(buyer,price)
     Supply.drop
   }
   cancelSupply = {
     Supply.drop
   }
   goodNews(company : string) = {
     transactionPrice = subscription.priceAdvice(company)
   }
   badNews(company : string) = {
     transactionPrice = subscription.priceAdvice(company)
   }
Lifecycles
   (tryToSell;(Sell+cancelSupply))*
   ([sender==subscription]goodNews*)
   ([sender==subscription]badNews*)
Rules
   On goodNews(company)(t_1);goodNews(company)(t_2)
     if $t_2 - t_1 \leq 7$ days
     do tryToBuy(company,transactionPrice)
   On badNews(company)(t_1);badNews(company)(t_2)
     if $(t_2 - t_1) \leq 7$ days && transactionPrice$(t_2) \leq$ transactionPrice(t_1)
     do tryToSell(transactionPrice)
   On goodNews(t_1);badNews(t_2)
     if $t_2 - t_1 \leq 7$ days && transactionPrice$(t_1) ==$ max(transactionPrice, t_1, t_2)
     do tryToSell(transactionPrice)
EndObject

Fig. 1. An investor modelled in DEGAS

3 Agency in Active Databases

In the previous section, we saw a state-of-the-art active database model based on objects with considerable autonomy. Hence, we could say that these objects are simple agents. In this section, we identify the level of agency offered by active databases in general, and DEGAS in particular.

Research on agents generally distinguishes *weak* and *strong* agency. A software system is said to have weak agency, if it possesses the following four properties [13]:

- autonomy
- social ability
- reactivity
- pro-activeness

Object *autonomy* is one of the base assumptions in DEGAS. Each DEGAS object is itself a process. Furthermore, its dependence on other objects is as small as possible through complete encapsulation and minimal assumptions about the behaviour of other objects. Hence, the criterion of autonomy is satisfied by DEGAS objects. *Social ability* means that agents interact with other agents in the system through an agent communication language. DEGAS objects pass messages to other objects and engage in relations with them. DEGAS objects *react* to their environment by answering messages. Furthermore, rules also specify reactions to situation that occur in the DEGAS database. *Pro-activeness* means that agents can take the initiative to achieve certain goals. Although goals are not explicit in a DEGAS object, active rules are instrumental to achieving a goal.

There is less consensus over stronger levels of agency. In general, strong agency is concerned with mentalistic notions. For the discussion in this paper, we take the four dimensions formulated by Shoham [9]:

- knowledge
- belief
- intention
- obligation

These notions are not explicitly supported by DEGAS objects. Although rules can be used to express obligations, they are not formulated as such. An obligation of an agent is specified by a goal that must be achieved. Instead an ECA rule is just an instruction to execute a certain action in a specified situation, although this action will be instrumental in fulfilling the obligation.

Likewise intention is only implicitly present, and as far as it is present, not arrived at by the DEGAS object itself. We could say, that a rule to maintain a database constraint expresses the intention to maintain that constraint. Intention and instrument to realise this intention, however, are fixed to each other. If intention is an independent notion to an agent, it first derives its intention and then reasons about the actions to realise it.

Knowledge and belief are unknown notions in an active database. Although a lot of information is stored, the way to process these data is fixed by the methods and rules specified. Furthermore, a database usually lacks the ability to reason with and about the information it contains in a general way.

4 Extending the Level of Agency in an Active Database

In the previous section, we saw that DEGAS supports weak agency. In addition, limited representation of obligation and intention are present. In this section, we look at the potential results of extending the level of agency in an active database, taking DEGAS as a starting point. In particular, we consider the benefits of stronger agency for general database functionality.

Stronger agency is introduced in an active database by extending the capabilities of the objects in the database. While DEGAS currently is a database of autonomous objects, we would then have a database of agents. The agents in such a database[2] each manage a part of real world data, like an object represents a piece of data. This means that an agent contains a piece of data, and additionally possesses a number of goals it has to achieve or maintain. Furthermore, a data agent will have a number of obligations. In part, these will exist to facilitate DBMS functionality, e.g., an obligation to answer queries. Another part of the obligations will be to other agents, caused by relations between agents.

The key advantage of the promotion of autonomous objects to agents lies in the reasoning ability of agents. This allows a more abstract specification of the database, both in application modelling and in implementing database functionality. Triggers implement a tight binding between goals and means, so that an object has only one means achieve a specific goal. By formulating goals and means separately, more flexible solutions are possible for a lot of information systems functionality.

A prime example of the additional flexibility provided by separate goals and means is given by constraints. In Section 2, we mentioned that triggers were originally devised to deal with constraints more flexibly. The improvement triggers offered over existing mechanisms was, that we could use different strategies to maintain different constraints, instead of a single strategy for all constraints. Strong agency, by separating goals and means, gives us additional flexibility by allowing multiple strategies to maintain a single constraint. The agent can then infer which strategy is optimal in the current situation. In addition, the presence of general problem-solving strategies in the database obviates the need for specialised compilers, e.g., to produce rules to maintain constraints [5].

---

[2] or would we have to call it a data management society?

As an example consider the limit on the negative balance of a bank account. A limit of 2000 in the red is specified by the constraint:

$balance \geq -2000$

Suppose now that a requested payment violates this constraint. In this situation, we have a number of strategies to enforce this constraint, of which we mention four:

1. Refuse the payment
2. Transfer funds from a savings account
3. Sell some shares
4. Arrange a temporary loan

If we were to use triggers, we can specify only one action to enforce the limit on this account. With its enhanced reasoning capabilities, an agent can choose the best strategy to enforce this constraint, given its other goals, such as the quality of its relation with the customer, income in the near future etc.

Another advantage of stronger agency over triggers, is found in the problem of deciding termination of trigger sets. In general, we can decide termination only for very simple trigger languages [10]. Such languages, however, are too simple for most applications. Hence, we must find another way of dealing with this problem than deciding it in advance or imposing conservative pre-conditions on trigger sets. Stronger agency can help counter the problem of non-termination in two ways. First, the separation of multiple means to achieve the goal of a trigger, allows an agent to choose another means to achieve its goal, if the means originally chosen has undesirable side-effects. Second, not every possible execution of a non-terminating trigger set is non-terminating. This means, that the agents can cooperate to avoid the non-terminating execution sequence of their triggered actions.

As an example, consider the trigger activation graph given in Figure 2. In this graph the nodes are database states and the edges are trigger executions. For example, in database state c trigger $t3$ is triggered, whose execution brings the database in state e. The trigger set in this graph is non-terminating, since there exists a cycle of triggers $t2$ and $t1$ in this activation graph, which keeps the database shuttling between database states b and c. We can easily see, however, that there is also a terminating execution sequence for this trigger set, viz., the sequence $t1; t3; t2; t1$ that leads to the stable state f.

The advantages given above of strong agency over the weak agency in an active database also apply to dynamic database constraints. In DEGAS, the dynamic constraints of an autonomous object are given by the lifecycles. This lifecycle is fixed. Hence, a message that does not fit in the lifecycle is rejected outright. If an autonomous object had higher level reasoning facilities, it would be possible to negotiate a deal with the sending agent. For example, the receiving object might

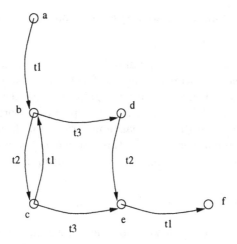

Fig. 2. A trigger activation graph

give an indication of the time when it will be able to execute the requested action. The sending object can then decide, depending on its other goals and obligations, whether it can wait or take another course to achieve its goal.

If negotiations between agents are to take place between different agents in the databases, we need, besides a language to conduct the negotiations in, a measure of the value of the different propositions being negotiated. This implies the use of a monetary model. The use of such a model is experimented in a somewhat different context by Stonebraker in the Mariposa system [11]. Here, the allocation of data storage and query processing in a distributed database is managed through a bidding system. The fixed bidding protocol in Mariposa, however, leads to undesirable effects in the allocation of data. In fact, it turns out that the richest site will end up with all the data, which means that it only gets richer by consequently under-bidding the other sites for query processing. Clearly, more sophisticated bidding and negotiation protocols are needed, which leaves the components (agents) in the database more room for manoeuvring to avoid undesired outcomes. For example, in the example of the richest site taking all data, the other sites might temporarily adopt a "dumping" strategy, i.e. working at a loss in order to gain back work and data.

The examples given of agents working out solutions for databases problems by negotiating between themselves, can only work under certain assumptions about their intentions. As research in game theory has shown [8], it is difficult to come up with strategies without undesirable outcomes, if not all players are cooperative. Therefore, agent research often assumes, as Shoham does [9], the veracity and benevolence of agents towards each other. This assumption cannot be held if agents in our information system must interact with agents owned by other people or organisations. Hence, agent research must find a solution for dealing with uncooperative, lying and malevolent agents in order to be able to form the foundation of an information system, or an information infrastructure in general.

Further potential of agent technology in databases is found on the architectural side. If agent technology matures enough to form the basis of a database management system, this will implicate a large gain in flexibility of a DBMS. The different components of a DBMS, such as query optimiser, storage manager, etc., can each be an agent with its own goals and strategies. Besides the increased flexibility of the individual components, this also means increased freedom for a systems designer to choose the components constituting his DBMS.

5 Conclusions

In this paper, we discussed the autonomous behaviour that active databases add to traditional databases. We saw that DEGAS, a state-of-the-art active database model, implements weak agency, since DEGAS objects interact with each other, react to their environment, and autonomously pursue their defined goals. These functions, however, are limited by their fixed, pre-programmed character.

The extension of autonomous DEGAS objects to stronger agents with general purpose reasoning abilities greatly increases the adaptability and flexibility of an active database system. The improvements originate in the ability to adapt strategies to the actual situation, and the ability of agents to cooperate with each other. Hence, the incorporation of agent technology in databases opens up new perspective in tackling long-standing database issues. Increased coupling and inter-operation of information systems, however, also poses some new challenges for agent technology in order to deal with lying or malicious agents from outside.

References

1. Johan van den Akker and Arno Siebes. DEGAS: Capturing dynamics in objects. In P. Constantopoulos, J. Mylopoulos, and Y. Vassiliou, editors, *Advanced Informations Systems Engineering - Proc. of CAiSE'96*, pages 82-98, Heraklion, Crete, Greece, May 1996. Springer. LNCS 1080.
2. Johan van den Akker and Arno Siebes. Object histories as a foundation for an active OODB. In R. Wagner and H. Thoma, editors, *Proceedings of the 7th International Workshop on Database and Expert Systems Applications (DEXA'96)*, pages 2-8, Zürich, Switzerland, 1996. IEEE Computer Society.
3. J.C.M. Baeten and W.P. Weijland. *Process Algebra*. Number 18 in Cambridge Tracts in Theoretical Computer Science. Cambridge University Press, Cambridge, UK, 1990.
4. James Bailey et al. Active databases and agent systems - a comparison. In Timos Sellis, editor, *Proc. of the 2nd Intl. Workshop on Rules in Databases (RIDS'95)*, pages 342-356, Athens, Greece, 1995. Springer. LNCS 985.
5. Stefano Ceri and Jennifer Widom. Deriving production rules for constraint maintenance. In D. MacLeod, R. Sacks-Davis, and H. Schek, editors, *Proceedings of the 16th International Conference on Very Large Data Bases*, pages 566-577, 1990.

6. U. Dayal et al. The HiPAC project: Combining active databases and timing constraints. *SIGMOD Record*, 17(1):51–70, March 1988.

7. Gerti Kappel and Michael Schrefl. Modeling object behavior: To use methods or rules or both? In R. Wagner and H. Thoma, editors, *Proceedings of the 7th International Conference on Database and Expert Systems Applications (DEXA'96)*, pages 584-602. Springer, 1996. LNCS 1134.

8. Jeffrey S. Rosenschein and Gilad Zlotkin. Designing conventions for automated negotiation. *AI Magazine*, 15(3):29-46, 1994.

9. Yoav Shoham. Agent-oriented programming. *Artificial Intelligence*, 60:51-92, 1993.

10. A.P.J.M. Siebes, J.F.P. van den Akker, and M.H. van der Voort. (un)decidability results for trigger design theories. Technical Report CS-R9556, CWI, Amsterdam, The Netherlands, 1995. Available through WWW (http://www.cwi.nl/~vdakker/).

11. Michael Stonebraker et al. Mariposa: A wide-area distributed database system. *VLDB Journal*, 5(1):48-63, 1996.

12. Jennifer Widom and Stefano Ceri. *Active Database Systems: Triggers and Rules for Advanced Database Processing*. Morgan Kaufmann, San Francisco, CA, USA, 1995.

13. Michael Wooldridge and Nicholas R. Jenning. Intelligent agents: theory and practice. *The Knowledge Engineering Review*, 10(2):115-152, 1995.

Result Sharing Among Agents Using Reactive Rules

M. Berndtsson[1] and S. Chakravarthy[2] and B. Lings[3]

[1] Department of Computer Science, University of Skövde. Box 408, 541 38 Skövde,
Sweden
email: spiff@ida.his.se

[2] Database Systems Research and Development Center, Computer and Information
Science and Engineering Department,University of Florida, Gainesville FL 32611
email: sharma@cise.ufl.edu

[3] Department of Computer Science, University of Exeter, Exeter EX4 4PT, U.K.
email: brian@dcs.exeter.ac.uk

Abstract. This paper critically analyse the use of active databases as
an enabling technology for *result sharing* as defined in the DAI literature. In particular, we demostrate how ECA (Event-Condition-Action)
rules can be used for supporting result shared cooperation. Further, we
demonstrate how composite events as defined within active databases can
help a problem solving agent to precisely specify when to take responsive
action to multiple result notifications.

Keywords: Active databases, result sharing, cooperative problem solving.

1   Introduction

In its full generality, cooperative problem solving (CPS) is a complex activity
requiring harmonious and dynamic interaction between heterogeneous agents.
It incorporates high level activities related to sequencing, decision making and
collaboration, and lower-level activities such as inferencing, algorithmic computation, coordination, and data/knowledge storage. By definition, a problem in
this category cannot be solved without cooperation among the problem solving
agents (PSAs) although each agent is autonomous and capable of sophisticated
problem solving. The objective of cooperative problem solving is to minimize
the use of human agents and maximize the use of computer agents to solve a
problem belonging to this category.

In [20] a distinction is made between two types of cooperation: task shared
and result shared. Briefly, task-shared cooperation means that nodes share the
computational load between them (it is assumed that each node has domain
specific knowledge). This is in contrast to result-shared cooperation where nodes
assist each other by sharing partial results.

1.1   Two Related Views of Cooperation

The AI and database research communities can be said to view this problem at
different levels of abstraction.

Database approaches to cooperation can be characterized as *bottom-up*, wherein existing solutions to simpler problems are extended to more complex ones in an incremental manner. For example, going from centralized databases to the distributed case adds a coordination component. Further, heterogeneous/federated databases not only add the coordination component but semantic issues of integration as well. Distributed database researchers have developed techniques for processing queries as well as transactions over a distributed environment whilst guaranteeing certain properties (such as atomicity, durability).

Distributed Artificial Intelligence (DAI) approaches can be termed *top-down* and seem to take a more ambitious view, addressing the most general (and difficult) problem, or issues related to the most general problem. The emphasis in this approach seems to be on new techniques that will lead to solutions to difficult/most general problems and usually prototype systems are developed to test the feasibility of the results.

It is likely that integration of the results obtained from these communities will enable the delivery of resilient systems. In particular, these systems need to encompass:

- *distributed, heterogeneous environments*, since PSAs are most likely to be distributed and to be working with heterogeneous environments/tools
- *coordinated behavior*, since PSAs need to react to other PSAs' activities
- *collaborative behaviour*, since each interaction between PSAs will have a special semantic content and intention
- *access to current and relevant information*, since PSAs need to be able to monitor evolving states, typical of many industrial applications

We believe that active database technology can contribute much in the support of DAI solutions for each of these requirements, but that such complex application domains also pose interesting questions for designers of active database systems. Initial work [4] concentrated on supporting protocols for *task sharing*, an aspect which is well covered in the literature [21, 2, 16].

In this paper we critically analyse the use of active databases as an enabling technology for *result sharing* as defined in the DAI literature.

2 Active Databases

Active databases can be seen as an approach to the efficient support of automatic situation monitoring and reactive behaviour expressed through event-condition-action (ECA) rules. The semantics of ECA rules are: when an event E occurs, evaluate condition C, and if condition C is satisfied, then execute action A.

The use of ECA rules rather than standard production rules (CA) is important for the applications under consideration. A clear distinction between events and conditions is presented in [9]:

- Different roles: the event specifies when to check, whereas a condition specifies what to check.

- External events: it is easier to model reactions to external signals if events are explicit.
- Finer control for database state transitions: asymmetric responses to database state transitions are not easy to model without explicit events.
- Execution semantics: condition evaluation can, for example, be deferred to a later point in time, e.g. end of transaction.
- Optimization: evaluate conditions when a specific event occurs, not always.

Events can be classified into: i) primitive events and ii) composite events. Primitive events refer to elementary occurrences which are predefined in the system, such as transaction events, method events, and database events. A composite event is a set of primitive events or composite events related by defined event operators such as disjunction, conjunction, and sequence.

Simple forms of active rules (triggers, ECA rules, alerters etc) are currently provided by most commercial relational database systems. This is in contrast to commercially available object-oriented database systems which do not yet support active rules. However, extensive work on active object-oriented databases (AOODBMS) has been carried out in recent years [13, 1, 12, 3, 6]. This area of research can be seen as an enabling technology for supporting applications in heterogeneous information systems. Examples of applications in this category are advanced workflow management systems, real-time plant control systems, and process-centred software development environments [8].

The interested reader is referred to [22, 8] for a general introduction to active databases.

3 The Chosen Problem

In this paper we consider distribution and collaboration as they relate to certain aspects of *result sharing*. Research on result sharing has not been as exhaustive as it has been on task sharing, so is less well reported.

We next summarize proposals elaborated in the research literature and then position our work with respect to these.

3.1 Producers and Consumers of Result Notifications

Essentially, result shared cooperative problem solving is based on distributing notifications of results between producers and consumers. Thus, these notifications can broadly be categorised into

- result notifications to known consumers
- result notifications to unknown consumers

The limitation of the first approach is that the consumers have to know exactly to which producer they should subscribe. It is not always the case that a consumer knows where to locate the producer of a result in a distributed environment. Similarly, the producer does not always know where to locate the consumers of a result. For example, the consumer may not yet have been added to the number of known agents in the network. Hence, the second approach provides support for the situations in which the consumers and producers do not know about each other's existence. Thus, result notifications to unknown consumers will be routed through a broker, a match-maker, or stored in shared memory for future use.

Both approaches rely on the use of subscription and notification mechanisms. These range from simple ones such as defined within active databases [1, 3], to more complex techniques such as content-based routing as defined within multi-agent based approaches for result sharing [17, 18].

Support for the more advanced techniques require that a number of open issues and extensions are addressed [18]. For the purpose of this paper we briefly highlight some of the relevant issues:

- generality of advertisements and request. For example, one could introduce a SQL construct such as the *where* clause to prune the number of result notifications and subscriptions.
- error recovery. One of the issues in this category is concerned with how/if the transaction model as defined within the database community should be introduced to support error recovery for agent protocols.
- scalability. As the number of agents increases several issues such as consistency, efficiency, conciseness and accuracy need to be addressed.
- persistent requests. Requests for results (and information) need to be supported beyond one-time requests.

3.2 Sharing of Information

In the literature the notions of *result sharing* and *information sharing* are used interchangeably. As the DAI community has not dealt with the notion of transactions and committed data, it is felt that a clear separation of the notions *result sharing* and *information sharing* is needed when considering database systems. Hence, in our work we make the following categorizations:

- sharing of committed information (result sharing). The information obtained will not change subsequently (cannot issue a cancel).
- sharing of uncommitted information (information sharing). The information may change subsequently (a cancel can be issued).
- sharing meta-data. This information is associated with the meta-data of an agent (capabilities).

Given the above categorization, information sharing can be seen as the more general case of result sharing.

3.3 Distributed and Federated Aspects

Distributed and federated aspects are inherent when dealing with CPS in general. When CPS activities, such as result sharing, take place within a single application then it does not cause any major problems in terms of interactions between the agents, since all agents are within the same address space. However, when agents are not within the same address space there is a need for an information channel such as RPC, CORBA, or email. The information channel will make it possible for an agent to exchange messages with other agents which are located outside the current address space. For example, agents need to: react to changes done by other agents, and be able to propagate appropriate local information to other agents (both on demand and on a non-demand basis) in a timely and efficient manner.

The information channel is viewed as a means for transportation of information and not as an approach to supporting complex interactions at a higher level. Thus, a specific language or protocol for knowledge and information sharing needs to be provided, such as KQML [11, 19].

3.4 Multiple Responses from Multiple Agents

It is noted in [14] that,

> For DAI systems which use result sharing, the user may be confronted with a number of different agent responses to the same demand. This could be extremely confusing, unless the DAI system facilitated her interactions with a mechanism to view and understand the different results obtained for the same problem.

We postulate that the use of composite events as defined within active databases can help the user to specify, view and understand multiple results for the same problem.

3.5 Research Goals

In this paper we present our approach for supporting result sharing based on an active database paradigm. We focus on:

- use of ECA rules for result sharing. The results are sent as event parameters, which can be passed on to the condition and action part of the ECA rules.
- use of composite events and event contexts for reacting to multiple result notifications. This will aid us in precisely specifying when to take responsive action to multiple result notifications.

We limit our current work to considering sharing of committed results. Sharing of uncommitted results (requiring a refined transaction model), and federated and distributed aspects (requiring a redefined event specification language) are part of ongoing work.

4 Use of ECA Rules for Result Sharing

Event parameters in active databases are usually passed on to the condition and/or action part of a rule and so are available for providing context information.

There is no real consensus in the active object-oriented database community on which set of event attributes is minimal. In Sentinel [1] the minimal set consists solely of the identification of the object (oid) for which a primitive event is applicable. Additional event attributes for supporting method events in Sentinel are: class, method, actual parameters and time stamp. A similar approach has been taken in SAMOS [12] which distinguishes between:

- environment parameters. For example, time stamp (when was the event raised), transaction id (in which transaction did the event occur) and user id (which user caused the event).
- parameters which depend on the type of an event. For example, method events have in addition the identification of the object (oid) and the parameters of the invoked method.

If ECA rules are to be used for supporting result sharing, then the only way they can transmit information is by the aid of event parameters. According to the categorization made in SAMOS, we propose that results in result shared CPS are to be sent as event parameters which depend on the type of the event. Below we outline how this can be realized.

One of the most widely used subscription techniques within active object-oriented databases is to subscribe ECA rules to specific events [3]. The semantics of this approach are:

> When an event has been generated by an object check only those rules which have subscribed to the generated event.

This approach is appealing since it reduces unnecessary triggering of rules compared with other approaches such as rules indexed by classes. In our work on supporting result sharing by using ECA rules, we see the need to constrain the behaviour of the above subscription technique. This is a consequence of the semantics of result sharing. In the current (non-constrained) version it is possible to subscribe to events which are generated either *before* or *after* the completion of a task/operation. Clearly, the *before* option is not appropriate for supporting result shared CPS, since the result will not be available until the task/operation has been completed. Thus, the semantics of the result shared CPS subscription mechanism are as follows.

> A consumer of a result can subscribe to results generated by a producer, by subscribing to an event that indicates the completion of the operation that produces them.

The subscription process can roughly be divided into the following steps:

1. A consumer locates the set of producers that can provide the requested results, either directly or by the aid of a matchmaker.
2. Having identified the producers of the results, a formal subscription will take place. The subscription includes a *consumer-id* which is a unique identifier of the consumer, and an *operation-id* which is a unique identifier of the operation that produces the results.

    SUBSCRIBE consumer-id TO RESULTS OF operation-id
3. Results will be sent to the consuming agent until it unsubscribes.

The semantics of the keywords *TO RESULTS OF*, implies that a consumer has subscribed to an event that is raised after the completion of the operation that produces them. For example,

SUBSCRIBE Agent 4 TO RESULTS OF (Agent 1: calculate-answer(x,y))

In the above subscription *Agent 4* has subscribed to the results of the task *calculate-answer(x,y)*. A potential control flow based on ECA rules can be encoded as follows:

1. SUBSCRIBE Agent 4 TO RESULTS OF (Agent 1: calculate-answer(x,y)
2. execute calculate-answer(10,10):return-value
3. raise event(event-id, return-value, ..)
4. trigger rules which have subscribed to event-id

This scenario highlights an important aspect which is currently not supported within current active databases. In order to be able to notify the consumer about the result, the return-value of the operation needs to be sent as an event parameter. In current active databases it is possible to send the input parameters of the method, e.g. (x,y), as event parameters. We see the need to extend this to also be able to send the return values of an operation as event parameters.

5 The Power of Composite Events

In most situations it is useful to react to result notifications from more than one source. Currently, we have not seen any robust way of handling multiple responses from multiple agents in the literature on result sharing. Thus, we propose the use of composite events, as defined within active databases, as an alternative to current DAI based approaches.

We apply the usage of composite events to concurrent engineering as it encompasses result shared interaction.

5.1 Example

Concurrent Engineering (CE) is a departure from the earlier approach that can be termed as *islands of automation*. The need for a shift to CE is due to the fact that it allows companies to develop products much more quickly and with higher quality than with traditional *sequential* methods. CE relies on forming a full-time multidisciplinary task group for each new project and the use of disciplined techniques [15]. A task group typically consists of people and computer based tools from different areas such as product design, manufacturing, marketing, purchasing, and finance.

Although each group member is capable of performing sophisticated activities on its own, it needs to be informed about recent design changes made by other group members, in a timely and efficient manner. Similarly, each member needs to route its own design changes to potentially interested group members.

Consider a CE scenario where a designer is developing a new product. The designer needs to be informed about changes in available stock sizes for those parts that are part of the new product. Similarly, he/she needs to be informed about any changes in stock-cost options (the sub parts cannot be too expensive). Whenever the designer receives a request from the chief designer concerning a meeting about the new product, the designer needs to present the current status of the new product and also be able to present any related important changes to, for example, stock-cost options.

The above scenario could be modeled in an active database context as follows. Four agents will be created: Agent 1 (inventory agent), Agent 2 (purchasing agent), Agent 3 (chief designer), and Agent 4 (the designer). Agent 4 will subscribe to events that are generated by the other agents (Figure 1). The events indicate the following:

- *E1*, change in available stock sizes for sub parts involved in the new product.
- *E2*, change in stock-cost options, i.e. new prices.
- *E3*, request for group meeting in the chief designer's office.

Having subscribed to the above events, the designer (Agent 4) can then take responsive action (preparations for meeting) based upon the results that are received when at least one result has been obtained from all three agents, with the result from Agent 3 (E3) being the last one.

In our scenario, the events are signaled to the designer as illustrated in Figure 2, (example borrowed from [7]).

We adopt the notation E $(e^1, e^2, ...e^n)$ to represent an event E, where e^1 and e^2 denote the first occurrence and second occurrence of E, respectively. Given the above semantics for when Agent 4 should take responsive action, the following issues need to be addressed:

- when should the triggered action be executed?
- assuming that each event e1, e2, and e3, by means of event parameters, carry results that will influence the work done by Agent 4, then which set of event parameters will be involved when the triggered action is executed?

In current approaches for result sharing it is not obvious how the above scenario would be supported. Most approaches would try to encode the semantics by using condition-action (CA) rules. This will imply that control knowledge needs to be incorporated in rule specification. For example, in order to reflect

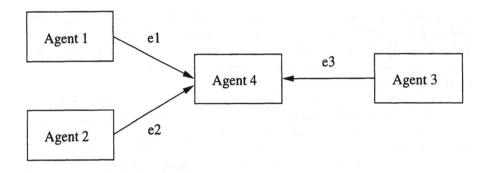

Fig. 1. Agent 4 receives notifications from other agents

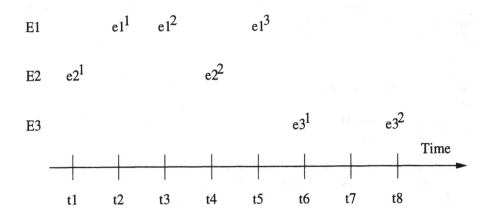

Fig. 2. Event time line

the desired ordering between rule actions, rules need to be arranged in a strict sequential thread. This also implies that condition specifications need to be repeated in several rules.

Even though primitive events are introduced, there are complex events that cannot be provided by using multiple rules based on primitive events [7]. Importantly, we believe that event consumption modes can only be properly supported if composite events are used. Thus, it is not possible to provide a range of event contexts for CA rules which most CPS-based systems for result sharing are currently using.

Composite events are used to model complex situations which cannot be expressed by a single primitive event. Thus, a composite event can be viewed as an abstraction of other events. Using a composite event (CE-1), the previous scenario would be modeled as:

CE-1: ((E1(parameters) and E2(parameters)) sequence E3(parameters))

Reconsider the scenario in Figure 1, the ordering of event occurrences in Figure 2, and the above composite event CE-1.

- In the *recent* context, only the most recent occurrence of the initiator for any event that has started the detection of a composite event will be used. All other event occurrences will be deleted once the composite event has been detected. Thus, the first occurrence of CE-1 and the triggered action will be based upon the following event occurrences along with their event parameters:$< e2^2, e1^3, e3^1 >$.

- In the *chronicle* context the oldest occurrence of each component event will be used. Thus, the first occurrence of CE-1 and the triggered action will be based upon the following event occurrences along with their event parameters: $< e2^1, e1^1, e3^1 >$. The second occurrence of CE-1 will include: $< e1^2, e2^2, e3^2 >$.

- In the *continuous* context each initiating event occurrence is a candidate for starting the detection of CE-1. Thus, the four first occurrences of CE-1 will be as follows: $< e2^1, e1^1, e3^1 >$, $< e1^1, e2^2, e3^1 >$, $< e1^2, e2^2, e3^1 >$, and $< e2^2, e1^3, e3^1 >$.

- In the *cumulative* context all initiators are combined into one event detection. Thus, the first (only) occurrence of CE-1 will include the following: $< e2^1, e1^1, e1^2, e2^2, e1^3, e3^1 >$.

To the best of our knowledge, neither composite events nor event contexts are supported within current approaches for result sharing.

6 Implementation Status

We have implemented an active database prototype, ACOOD [5], which is built as a reactive layer on top of ONTOS DB^{TM}.

Currently result sharing is supported by the aid of event parameters, and specification/detection of multiple responses from multiple producers of results by using composite events. The limitation is that the consumers and producers cannot be located at separate address spaces.

In order to overcome the above limitation we are working on extending the approach to a distributed, heterogeneous environment. As a proof of principle prototype, we have taken a composite event detector module, named CEDE [10], and distributed event signaling using CORBA as the distribution layer. Basically, each agent has a CORBA *client* process to allow it to subscribe to remote events, and a CORBA *server* process to receive remote event signals.

7 Conclusions

In this paper we have considered the domain of result sharing as defined within DAI literature. This has allowed us to posit how active databases might be used as a supporting technology for result sharing among agents.

We have made a clear separation of the notions *result sharing* and *information sharing* when considering database systems: i) sharing of committed information (result sharing), ii) sharing of uncommitted information (information sharing), and iii) sharing meta-data.

We have shown that results can be sent as event parameters of ECA rules. A refined subscription mechanism for supporting result sharing in active databases has been proposed.

We have demonstrated the applicability of using composite events as defined within active databases for supporting responses from multiple agents. Composite events provide the user with well established mechanisms for specification, and understanding of multiple results from multiple agents.

7.1 Future work

There are a number of open issues which need more research if active databases are to be considered as platforms for result sharing among agents.

- Context based subscription is useful when a consumer wants to subscribe to a specific result generated by an operation. This is in contrast to subscribing to any results generated by an operation. Context based subscriptions in active databases are usually modeled in rule conditions. Thus, if results are sent as event parameters then for each specialization of the event parameters (e.g. $p(x)$), a corresponding rule condition needs to be modeled. Preliminary results indicate that this approach leads to increased rule triggering and problems with respect to event consumption modes and modularity.
- Distributed and federated aspects are of importance when considering real world applications. With regard to active databases, the event language needs to support specification of global and local events. Furthermore, a careful integration with existing standards and protocols such as CORBA and KQML are required.

References

1. E. Anwar, L. Maugis, and S Chakravarthy. A new perspective on rule support for object-oriented databases. In *Proceedings of the International Conference on Management of Data*, pages 99–108, May 1993.
2. M. Barbuceanu and M.S. Fox. Capturing and Modelling Coordination Knowledge for Multi-Agent Systems. *International Journal of Cooperative Information Systems*, 5(2–3):275–314, 1996.
3. M. Berndtsson. Reactive Object-Oriented Databases and CIM. In *Proceedings of the 5th International Conference on Database and Expert System Applications*, Lecture Notes in Computer Science, pages 769–778. Springer-Verlag, September 1994.
4. M. Berndtsson, S. Chakravarthy, and B. Lings. Coordination Among Agents Using Reactive Rules. Technical Report HS-IDA-TR-96-011, Department of Computer Science, University of Skövde, 1996.

5. M. Berndtsson and B. Lings. On Developing Reactive Object-Oriented Databases. *IEEE Quarterly Bulletin on Data Engineering, Special Issue on Active Databases*, 15(1-4):31–34, December 1992.

6. A. Buchmann, J. Zimmermann, J. Blakelyand, and D. Wells. Building an integrated active oodbms: Requirements, architecture, and design decisions. In *Proc. of IEEE Data Engineering*, 1995.

7. S. Chakravarthy and D. Mishra. Snoop: An Expressive Event Specification Language For Active Databases. Technical Report UF-CIS Technical Report TR-93-007, University of Florida, 1993.

8. The ACT-NET Consortium. The Active Database Management System Manifesto: A Rulebase of ADBMS Features. *ACM Sigmod Record*, 25(3), September 1996.

9. U. Dayal. Ten Years of Activity in Active Database Systems: What Have We Accomplished? In *Proceedings of the 1st International Workshop on Active and Real-Time Database Systems (ARTDB-95)*, Workshops in Computing, pages 3–22. Springer-Verlag, 1995.

10. J. Eriksson. CEDE: Composite Event Detector in an Active Object-Oriented Database. Master's thesis, University of Skövde, 1993.

11. T. Finin, R. Fritzson, D. McKay, and R. McEntire. Kqml - an information and knowledge exchange protocol. In Kazuhiro Fuchi and Toshio Yokoi, editors, *Knowledge Building and Knowledge Sharing*. Ohmsha and IOS Press, 1994.

12. S. Gatziu and K. Dittrich. Events in an active object oriented database system. In *Proceedings of the 1st Workshop of Rules in Database Systems*, pages 23–29, 1993.

13. N. Gehani, H. V. Jagadish, and O Smueli. Event specification in an active object-oriented database. In *Proc. of the ACM SIGMOD International Conference on Management of Data*, pages 81–90, 1992.

14. L.E. Hall. user design issues for distributed artificial intelligence. In G.M.P. O'Hare and N.R. Jennings, editors, *Foundations of Distributed Artificial Intelligence*, chapter 21, pages 543–556. Wiley-Interscience, 1996.

15. John R. Hartley, editor. *Concurrent Engineering: Shortening Lead Times, Raising Quality, and Lowering Costs*. Productivity Press, 1992.

16. N. R. Jennings. The ARCHON System and its Applications. In *Proceedings of the CKBS-SIG Workshop on Cooperating Knowledge Based Systems*, pages 13–30, 1994.

17. D. R. Kuokka, J. C. Weber, and et al. Shade: Knowledge-Based Technology for the Re-Engineering problem. Technical report, Lockhead Palo Alto Research Laboratories, 1993. Annual Report.

18. D.R. Kuokka and L.T. Harada. Issues and extensions for information matchmaking protocols. *International Journal of Cooperative Information Systems*, 5(2–3):251–274, 1996.

19. Y. Labrou and T. Finin. A semantics approach for kqml – a general purpose communication language for software agents. In *Proceedings of the Third International Conference on Information and Knowledge Management (CIKM'94)*, 1994.

20. R. G. Smith and R. Davis. Frameworks for cooperation in distributed problem solving. *IEEE Transactions on Systems, Man, and Cybernetics*, 1981.

21. R.G. Smith. The Contract Net Protocol: High Level Communication and Control in a Distributed Problem Solver. *IEEE Transactions on Systems, Man, and Cybernetics*, SMC-10(12), December 1980.

22. J. Widom and S. Ceri, editors. *Active Database Systems: Triggers and Rules for Advanced Database Processing*. Morgan Kufmann Publisher, 1995.

Metadatabase Meets Distributed AI

Gilbert Babin, Zakaria Maamar and Brahim Chaib-draa

{babin,maamar,chaib}@ift.ulaval.ca
Département d'informatique, Université Laval
Ste-Foy, Québec, Canada, G1K 7P4

Abstract. Heterogeneous Distributed Database Management Systems (HDDBMS) involve the interoperability of data sources. One approach to achieve this type of integration is to build interfaces between the different databases being integrated. This approach holds, for a particular case, at a specific point in time. In this case however, the database structures need to be adapted. Such adaptation is not advisable since the local systems are usually important for their organizations. Therefore, an integration model that assures flexibility and scalability must be based on some knowledge of the underlying model of the different local databases. One solution is the use of the metadata concept, as a means to describe the logical and physical data characteristics. The metadata concept leads to the development of a Metadatabase system, which is viewed as a knowledge base about the local systems. The Metadatabase work at Rensselaer Polytechnic Institute (Troy, New- York) [11] and Université Laval (Ste-Foy, Québec) [2] has focused on creating such an integration environment and on defining its principal components. These solutions have been developed outside the context of Distributed Artificial Intelligence (DAI) and would certainly benefit from the results in that field of research. In this paper, we explain how the Metadatabase approach can be mapped into or associated with DAI concepts, and how it could benefit from techniques and theories pertaining to the DAI field.

1 Introduction

The computer network domain and the globalization of economy have forced the enterprises to adopt a distributed structure which, in turn, implies a distribution of resources of those enterprises, particularly their information systems. In this case, it becomes more and more important to provide enterprises with integration tools to consolidate the information available throughout the distributed databases. The integration concept is supported by an interoperability process which means the ability of two or more distributed database systems to mutually exchange information, independently of their constraints of distribution and heterogeneity, in order to work together to execute well-defined and delimited tasks jointly. Notice that the integration approaches traditionally proposed assume the interoperability at the application level (i.e. between local systems) via a global schema or a common manipulation language [6,18]. On one hand, designing a global schema implies the combination of different kinds of domains in one model which is generally difficult to obtain and to maintain. On the other hand, finding a common language is not easy because each system has its own standards and needs. One original solution to the integration problem that assures flexibility and scalability is the use of the *metadata* concept. This concept lead to the development of a Metadatabase system, that is, a knowledge base about the logical and physical data characteristics of local systems.

The Metadatabase work at Rensselaer Polytechnic Institute (Troy, New-York) [11] and Université Laval (Ste-Foy, Québec) [2] has focused on creating an integration environment and on defining its principal components, producing a Metadatabase-supported, Rule-Oriented concurrent systems solution to the enterprise information integration and management problem. These solutions have been developed outside the context of Distributed Artificial Intelligence (DAI) and would certainly benefit from the results in that field of research, like using the software agents as modules for the problem resolution [14] and the multiples techniques (interaction, cooperation, negotiation, etc.) as principles for the behavior specification [15].

In this paper, we explain how the Metadatabase approach can be mapped into or associated with DAI concepts, and how it could benefit from techniques and theories pertaining to the DAI field. Section 2, which follows, describes in more details the Metadatabase approach and the internal functions of ROPE shells. In Section 3, we give an overview of the Distributed Artificial Intelligence (DAI) field and its application to the distributed Knowledge Based-Systems (KBS). Section 4 investigates the use of DAI to improve the Metadatabase integration approach. We conclude the paper in Section 5.

2   The Metadatabase Approach

Rensselaer's Metadatabase approach [3,4,12,13] was developed to integrate information systems, more specifically manufacturing systems. Manufacturing systems are heterogeneous and distributed by nature. To produce finished goods, many systems must cooperate. These systems might include an Order Processing System, used to record customers' orders, a Process Planning System, determining the steps to follow to obtain finished goods, and a Shop Floor Control System, dealing with process planning, job assignment, production status, etc. These systems are highly specialized, in the sense that only certain systems can perform specific tasks; for instance, only certain machines can drill a hole into a sheet of metal, for instance. These systems are also autonomous; each one manages its own database, which makes data consistency an issue. The problem then is how to coordinate the tasks performed by each of these systems and integrate the information stored in their local databases.

2.1 The Concurrent Architecture

The Metadatabase approach uses a concurrent architecture (Fig. 1) containing: (1) a central knowledge base and (2) distributed rule processors. The central knowledge base, called a Metadatabase, contains a description of the different (manufacturing) systems and the knowledge describing how they are integrated and semantically interrelated. This knowledge includes (1) database integrity rules, enforcing consistency across the distributed databases, and (2) business rules, automating information flows across these systems.

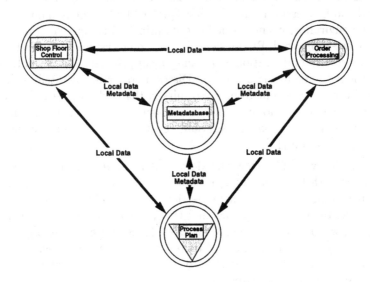

Fig. 1. The Metadatabase Concurrent Architecture

For each of the (manufacturing) systems, we define a rule processor. The rule processor's role is twofold. First, it encapsulates the system, ensuring that the system remains autonomous and independent, while making the system's capabilities available to other systems. Hence, although the shells are identical in structure, they differ in their capabilities, since each one has access to the special capabilities of the system it encapsulates. Second, it enables integration by providing knowledge processing capabilities to the system it encapsulates.

The Metadatabase and the rule processors form an integrated cell. The Metadatabase manages the knowledge, providing a global coherent view of the whole system, and distributes it to the local rule processors, hence achieving operational integration. In a Wide-Area Network (WAN), we can rely on a number of such integrated cells to provide a more robust framework (Fig. 2).

2.2 The Rule-Oriented Programming Environment

The ROPE (Rule-Oriented Programming Environment) [1] was developed as one implementation of the Metadatabase concurrent architecture. It creates a

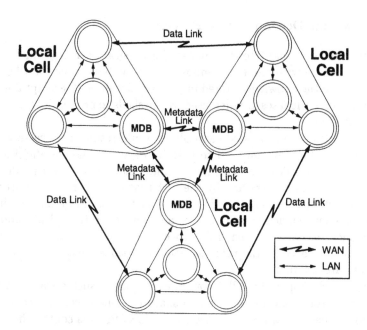

Fig. 2. Distributed Metadatabase Architecture

distributed rule processing environment, where fact bases and inference engines are distributed. The collaboration of rule processors is minimized by utilizing most of the information contained in the Metadatabase.

The ROPE approach defines the shell technology needed for the concurrent architecture evolution. Specifically, it defines: (1) how rules are stored in the local shells, (2) how rules are processed, distributed, and managed, (3) how the shell interacts with its corresponding system, (4) how the different shells interact with each other, and finally (5) how the shells are structured. The main advantage of the ROPE approach is that shells are invisible to the users. They are able to control the external behaviors of the local systems, without user intervention.

The ROPE shells have the following functions (See [1] for more details):

1. Global Query Processing: a global query is a data retrieval query that needs the participation of one or many local systems from the integration environment.
2. Global Update Processing: a global update processing represents a set of transactions (insertion, deletion or modification) that act on the data of the local systems. As a result, every local behavior change that has an impact (as updating data which pertain to another local system) on the behavior of the integration environment, has to be immediately transmitted to the rest of the appropriate systems.
3. Adaptability and Flexibility: the adaptability of the concurrent architecture refers to the ability of shells to change their behavior. This change is based on the knowledge stored in the Metadatabase.

2.3 Knowledge Decomposition Process

The Metadatabase is used to decompose the integration rules and to supply the shells' rulebase with these decomposed rules, at build-time, or whenever a change occurs in the knowledge stored in the Metadatabase (for adaptability and flexibility). These rulebases are then used by the shells to perform the integration tasks, at run-time.

If all the rules were processed centrally, it would result in processing bottlenecks. To avoid this problem, and to take into account the specificities of the different shells, the rules are decomposed and distributed. The rule decomposition process is also constrained by the fact that the different rule processors (shells) have different capabilities. This is in fact the case in manufacturing systems, where a single machine can perform a specific operation (drill, sand, etc.). It also implies that the different rule processors must collaborate to a certain extent in order to execute the rule; i.e., specific actions must be executed from the appropriate location.

The approach proposed in [2] decomposes the rule in such a way that (1) the different rule processors do not need to share the rule execution control, and (2) there is no need for a central process controller. Process control, however, is passed sequentially from one rule processor to the other, using a simple message protocol. A rule is decomposed into subrules; these subrules are then distributed to the shells. The decomposition algorithm uses the fact that a rule can be broken down into five stages of execution: (1) rule triggering, (2) data retrieval, (3) condition evaluation and actions execution, (4) result storage, and (5) rule chaining. The idea is to serialize the execution of the rule using these five stages and to assure that the condition and actions of each subrule produced are localized in the same rule processor.

Once the rule is triggered, a global query is launched by the shell where the triggering event occurred. This global query was preprocessed by the Metadatabase, prior to rule distribution. The result from the global query is a fact table that will be used by the rule processors. Each subrule will be executed in sequence at the appropriate shell, using that fact base. When every subrule is executed, the data contained in the fact base will be used to update the (distributed) databases from which the data was retrieved. Rule chaining occurs then, all possibly chained rules being launched in parallel. The decomposition process will minimize the total number of subrules to reduce the network load and the total execution time.

3 An Overview of DAI

Generally, the DAI field aims to construct systems of intelligent entities that interact productively with one another. More precisely, DAI is concerned with studying a broad range of issues related to the distribution and coordination of knowledge and actions in environments involving multiple entities. These entities, called *agents*, can be viewed collectively as a society. The agents work together to achieve their own goals, as well as the goals of the society considered as a whole.

A major distinction in the DAI field is between research in distributed problem solving (DPS), and research in multiagent systems (MAS) [7]. Early DPS work concentrated on applying the power of networked systems to a problem exemplified by the three–phase nomenclature. In the first phase, the problem is decomposed into subproblems. The decomposition process may involve a hierarchy of partitionings. The second phase involves solution of the kernel subproblems by agents that communicate and cooperate as necessary. Finally, the subproblems' results are integrated to produce an overall solution. DPS work also addressed the robustness available from multiple sources of expertise, multiple views and multiple capabilities. Generally, multiple views referred to distributed applications (air-traffic control, urban-traffic control, etc.). In summary, in all of DPS work, the emphasis was on the *problem* and how to get multiple intelligent entities (programmed computers) to work together to solve it in a efficient manner.

In MAS, the agents are autonomous, potentially preexisting, and typically heterogeneous. Research here is concerned with coordinating intelligent behaviors among a collection of autonomous agents, that is, how these agents can coordinate their knowledge, goals, skills, and plans jointly to take action and to solve problems. In this type of environment, the agents may be working toward a single global goal, or toward separate individuals goals that interact. Like solvers in DPS, agents in MAS might share knowledge about tasks and partial works. Conversely, to the DPS approach however, they must also reason about the process of coordination among the agents. Coordination is central to multiagent systems: without it, any benefits of interaction vanish and the behavior of the group of agents can become chaotic.

4 Towards an Approach Based on DAI for Interoperability

DAI and distributed database systems (DDBS) concentrate on different objectives and hence use different techniques for achieving their purposes. Thus, DAI concentrates on DPS and on interaction between autonomous intelligent agents whereas DDBS basically deals with the problem of management and integration of a collection of distributed data. However, from both a conceptual as well as a functional point of view, there are some similarities between our Metadatabase model and DAI approach.

4.1 The Metadatabase architecture is a Distributed Problem Solving System

The DPS approach suggests that a certain category of problems can be resolved by distributing them on a collection of nodes. This suggestion is motivated by the following points: the problems have a distributed and heterogeneous nature, the network imposes a distributed vision and software engineering is oriented towards a design based on autonomous and interactive entities, i.e. software agents. These elements are supported by the Metadatabase technology. Each ROPE shell has the required knowledge to function locally. But, in order to accomplish a global operation, all the ROPE shells need to cooperate with each other. This kind of operation generally implies the management of knowledge disparities, access privileges, distributed sources, resource conflict, etc. The DAI principles used in these situations seem adequate.

4.2 The Metadatabase Architecture is a Multiagent System

The primary objective of the Metadatabase architecture is to build a cooperative environment. As mentioned in Section 1, the Metadatabase allows a set of distributed and heterogeneous local systems to interact, without changing their internal structure or behavior. It should be noted that application systems need not be modified to interoperate. The ROPE shells support all the operations from and to the different systems. Combining a local system with its representative ROPE shell gives an integrated component. The same approach can be found in [5]. The author considers a Cooperative KBS as a collection of autonomous KBS, referred to as agents, which are able to interact with each other. The same idea is found in the Metadatabase approach, in which the ROPE shell can be seen as a reactive agent. Data and rules are contained in the local system and the ROPE shell, respectively. Rules (integrity and business) determine the accomplishment of (1) the consistency across systems, (2) the reliability of the overall environment, and (3) the integration of sub-solutions. Furthermore, each shell has specific capabilities which are the actions that it can perform within the local system. These capabilities are unique, since we assumed, for sake of simplicity, that every local system has unique functions (e.g., no two machines can perform a drilling operation).

It is also possible to consider the Metadatabase architecture as a multiagent system. Each shell-application pair has specific functionalities that describe how to support its responsibilities, how to interact with the external world and particularly how to cooperate to support the work of other pairs. These functionalities are globally controlled by the Metadatabase (Fig 1). The management mechanisms of the central knowledge can be compared to a coordination protocol which controls the distributed knowledge, manages the knowledge of the domain application via the metadata, supports *ad hoc* requests, etc.

The coordination aspect in a multiagent system implies two elements [8]: mechanisms needed to establish reliable communication with the right agent, and mutual and useful understanding of the communication contents. For such problems, some authors suggest the introduction of an additional kind of agents, communication facilitators [9] and communication mediators[17], respectively. Such facilitators and mediators communicate among themselves using well-defined protocols which are independent from the language or languages which the agent uses to exchange knowledge; see [10] for other examples. The different functionalities being associated to these new kind of agents are included in the

Metadatabase architecture. The communication aspect is handled by the ROPE shell, since it uses its own knowledge to know how to interact with another local system via its associated ROPE shell. In addition, the semantic problem of the exchanged knowledge can be supported by the content of the Metadatabase schema. It uses the metadata concept to have a extensive description of the local information characteristics (as, formats, structures, values, etc.). Furthermore, the Metadatabase (and the ROPE shells) uses a special type of rules (equivalence rules) to ensure a coherent transformation of knowledge during the interaction between local systems.

4.3 Improving the Metadatabase Approach Using DAI Concepts

In their current state, the shells only react to events occurring in their local environment: changes in the local databases, reception of a message, etc. In fact, inter-shell communications are at their simplest expression: a shell receives execution orders from other shells. Furthermore, the relative order in which these execution commands are performed is predetermined during the rule decomposition process. It is clear that, since only a specific shell has a specific capability, only that shell can perform that specific operation. In that context, using negotiation techniques is useless and even cumbersome.

However, this assumption does not reflect the reality of manufacturing systems. Often times, a same functionality will be performed by multiple instances of the same machine. In this perspective, the decomposition process could determine the subrules needed, but not the processor which will execute it. In that new context, a shell must be able to select one or many processors that will be able to execute the next subrule, most likely based on the workload of the different shells having the appropriate capabilities. We can now see how negotiation and inter-agent cooperation techniques could be used to improve the functionalities of the shell. For this type of approach to be feasible, the shells must have a minimal notion of self-knowledge. For instance, they should be able to answer the following questions:

- What are my functional capabilities (types of functions I can accomplish)?
- What is my current workload?
- What are my processing capabilities (amount of work I can accomplish)?
- etc.

In this case, shells can be considered as autonomous cognitive agents that have the capacity to coordinate their activities through contracts to accomplish specific tasks [16]. A shell, acting as *manager*, decomposes rules into subrules to be accomplished by other *potential contractor* shells. For each subrule the manager announces a task to the other shells. These shells receive and evaluate the announcement, and those with appropriate resources, workload and capabilities reply to the manager with *bids* that indicate their ability to achieve the announced task. The manager evaluates the bids it has received and awards the task to the most suitable shell, called the contractor. Finally, manager and contractor exchange information together during the accomplishment of the task.

The cooperation between Metadatabase model and DAI approach brings to us many issues for our future work, particularly the following aspects:

- Enabling local shells to represent and reason about locally stored data and knowledge as well as information regarding other agents;
- Forming coalition of shells (or cells) according to shared characteristics, such as domain of expertise;
- Enabling local cells to negotiate and interact efficiently;
- Reconciling the disparate views (by the negotiation) between shells and between local cells.

5   Conclusion

In this paper, we presented the Metadatabase approach as a solution to the problem of systems integration in heterogeneous and distributed environments, more specifically for manufacturing systems. We also showed how the Metadatabase approach can be assimilated to a Distributed Artificial Intelligence (DAI) system. Finally, we proposed ways to improve the Metadatabase approach using the DAI perspective.

Acknowledgments

Part of this research was funded by the Natural Sciences and Engineering Research Council of Canada (grants #OGP0155899 and #OGP0121634), by Université Laval (Startup grant), and by Samsung Electronics Co.

References

1. G. Babin. *Adaptiveness in Information Systems Integration.* PhD thesis, Decision Sciences and Engineering Systems, Rensselaer Polytechnic Institute, Troy, N.Y., August 1993.
2. G. Babin and C. Hsu. Decomposition of knowledge for concurrent processing. *IEEE Transactions on Knowledge and Data Engineering*, 1995. Forthcoming.
3. M. Bouziane. *Metadata Modeling and Management.* PhD thesis, Computer Sciences, Rensselaer Polytechnic Institute, Troy, N.Y., June 1991.
4. W. Cheung. *The Model-Assisted Global Query System.* PhD thesis, Computer Sciences, Rensselaer Polytechnic Institute, Troy, N.Y., November 1991.
5. S.M. Deen. A general framework for coherence in ckbs. *Intelligent Information Systems*, 1(3), 1 Septembre 1992.
6. D.M. Dilts and W. Hua. Using knowledge-based technology to integrate cim databases. *IEEE Expert*, 3(2):237–245, 1991.
7. E. Durfee and J. S. Rosenschein. Distributed problem solving and multi-agent systems: comparisons and examples. In *Proc. of 13th Int. DAI Workshop*, Seattle, USA, 1994.
8. T. Finin, R. Fritzson, and D. McKay. A language and protocol to support intelligent agent interoperability. has appeared in the Proceedings of the CE & CALS Washington '92 Conference, june 1992.

9. M.R. Genesereth. An agent-based approach to software interoperability. In *Proceedings of the DARPA Sotware Technology Conference*, 1992.

10. M.R. Genesereth and A.P. Ketchpel. Software agents. *Communication of the ACM*, 37(7):48–53, July 1994.

11. C. Hsu. *Enterprise Integration and Modeling — the Metadatabase Approach*. Kluwer Academic Publisher, Boston, Mass., USA, 1996.

12. C. Hsu, G. Babin, M. Bouziane, W. Cheung, L. Rattner, and L. Yee. Metadatabase modeling for enterprise information integration. *Journal of Systems Integration*, 2(1):5–39, January 1992.

13. C. Hsu, M. Bouziane, L. Rattner, and L. Yee. Information resources management in heterogeneous, distributed environments: A metadatabase approach. *IEEE Transactions on Software Engineering*, 17(6):604–625, June 1991.

14. S.-N. Hyacinth. Software agents: An overview. *Knowledge Engineering Review*, 11(3):1–40, Sept 1996.

15. B. Moulin and B. Chaib-Draa. An overview of distributed artificial intelligence. In *Foundations of Distributed Artificial Intelligence*, chapter Formulative Readings, pages 3–55. G.M.P. O'Hare and N.R. Jennings, 1996.

16. R. G Smith. The contract net protocol: High level communication and control in a distributed problem solver. *IEEE Trans. on Computer*, 29(12), 1980.

17. G. Wiederhold. The architecture of future information systems. Stanford University Computer Science Dept., 1989.

18. W. Wu and D. M. Dilts. Integrating diverse cim data bases: The role of natural language interface. *IEEE Trans. on Syst., Man and Cyb.*, 22(6):1331–1347, 1992.

A reactive logical agent*

Carlo Meghini

Consiglio Nazionale delle Ricerche,
Istituto di Elaborazione della Informazione,
Via S. Maria 46, I-56123 Pisa, Italy,
E-mail: meghini@iei.pi.cnr.it
Phone: +39 50 593405
Fax: +39 50 554342

Abstract. A system for developing and executing reactive, autonomous, rule-based agents is presented. The rules consist of sentences of a temporal logic connecting the present and past history of the system to its future states, and are interpreted at run time. The design and the implementation of the system are illustrated, along with some experimental performance measures derived in a real-time setting, where the agent has been put at work. These measures show that, even is such severely constrained context, the system can efficiently handle agents embodying up to a few hundreds rules.

Keywords: Reactive logic-based autonomous information agents, distributed systems.

1 Introduction

The considerable amount of research and development spent on deductive databases and rule-based systems demonstrates that declarative programming is a desirable paradigm for the construction of applications for information systems. In this study, we address the problem of applying declarative programming to distributed information systems, by presenting the design and implementation of autonomous reactive agents, acting as specialized executives in a network of cooperating systems. In particular, this paper describes a system, the Automatic Event Raising System (AERS), which allows to develop applications running against information systems, in a declarative, rule-based fashion.

The interaction between AERS and the information system, as well as the rest of the environment, is based on *events:* AERS receives events to which it reacts by outputting other events. The reaction is determined by the rules, which are statements of a temporal logic connecting the present and past history of the system to its future state. The core of the system is an interpreter of the

---

* This work has been partially supported by the European Commission, in the context of the ESPRIT Project IMIS (Integrated information Management for Industrial control Systems, n. 6548).

rules which decides what rules to apply at any given time instant and enforces the effects of the selected rules. The syntactical structure of the rules is designed to guarantee efficient execution. Each AERS application can be seen as an autonomous agent devoted to a limited number of tasks, which it carries out by re-acting to events.

After discussing related work in the next section, an overview of AERS is presented in Section 3. Section 4 introduces syntax and semantics of the rule language, whose usage in a case study is sketched in Section 5. The feasibility of AERS is then substantiated by the performance measures presented in Section 6, while Section 7 discusses optimizations aiming at enhancing such performance.

2 Relation to similar work

AERS is an execution machine for a subset of the temporal logic TRIO [4], which has been implemented in order to check the satisfiability, the consistency and the completeness of a specification. This implementation was not usable, as AERS requires the computation of the *truth* of a TRIO sentence in a specific state. Technically, what AERS does is called model-checking on a linear sequence of states.

The idea of specifying agent-based systems in terms of a temporal logic is central also to the system METATEM [3], a programming language centered around a temporal logic, developed for specifications of agents running in a concurrent environment. However, two important differences exist with AERS. First, the language of METATEM is much richer than that of AERS, as it includes a full-fledged first-order syntax and five temporal operators for future-time, and five for the past-time. Second, the reasoning mechanism of METATEM [2] is based on (an approximation of) validity, in the style of systems such as PROLOG. In trading-off expressiveness for efficiency, METATEM chooses to retain a great expressiveness and accepts to pay for it in terms of the efficiency and the completeness of its inferential apparatus.

Finally, a more powerful approach to the development of reactive rational agents is presented in [5], where meta-logic tools are employed to express knowledge about the basic operations of a reactive agent. This approach can be seen as a generalization of our own, which has been conceived with a definite commitment to efficiency.

3 Overview of the system

As illustrated by Figure 1, AERS[2] views time as a linear sequence of *configurations,* having a beginning, the 0-th configuration, and extending indefinitely in the future. A *cycle* is the passage from one configuration to the next one in time. A configuration consists of the following components:

---

[2] A more detailed account of AERS is presented in [6].

- the *Service Queue*, the set of event occurrences currently being processed;
- the *State*, an assignment to a set of variables, called state variables;
- the *History*, a sequence of past service queues, each relative to a past time instant and called an *History record*. The history record relative to the instant i contains the event occurrences that were active at i.

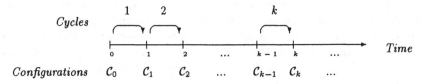

Fig. 1. Time, configurations and cycles.

In addition, AERS includes two more components:

- the *Waiting Queue*, a queue were the event occurrences received from the external world are accumulated to be considered in the next cycle;
- the *programme*, a sequence of rules that specify the behaviour of the system.

When the k-th cycle ($k \geq 1$) begins, the Service Queue is empty, the History contains the service queues of the previous $(k-1)$ cycles, and the Waiting Queue contains the event occurrences that have been received during the operation of the $(k-1)$-th cycle.

During the k-th cycle the system makes the following steps (see Figure 2):

1. it moves the Waiting Queue onto the Service Queue, so making active the event occurrences accumulated during the operation of the $(k-1)$-th cycle;
2. it checks the antecedent of each rule against its configuration. For each antecedent satisfied, in a way to be described later, the associated consequent will be executed. This will generate:
   - new event occurrences which are sent to the external world and to the Waiting Queue to be considered in the next cycle;
   - a new State.
3. it adds the occurrences of the Service Queue to the History as the last record, and empties the Queue.

The $(k+1)$-th cycle will find in the Waiting Queue the event occurrences that have arrived from outside during the execution of the k-th cycle and those that have been generated in the k-th cycle as a result of the execution of step 2.

The dynamics of the AERS is completely specified by giving the initial configuration $\mathcal{C}_0$, which consists of: an empty service queue, an initial state and an empty history.

The length of each cycle ranges in between (a) the minimum amount of time needed to test all the rules of the programme for an estimated maximum of input events per cycle, and (b) the maximum amount of time within which two events can be considered as simultaneous. The former parameter is typically

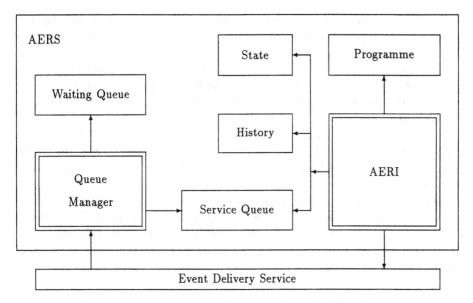

Fig. 2. Architecture of the Automatic Event Raising System

quantitative, and is discussed in a critical setting in Section 5; the latter is more of a qualitative nature, and depends on the semantics of the application.

Figure 2 presents the architecture of AERS, in terms of threads (double-framed boxes), data structures (single-framed boxes) and the access relations between these two (arrows). AERS runs on a Sun SPARC Station 5 with 32M RAM, under the Solaris 2.4 operating system. It consists of three basic threads: the main thread (not shown in Figure 2), the Queue Manager and the interpreter of the rules (AERI).

Input and output AERS interacts with the external world through events, carried by messages which are sent and received via an event delivery service. In the current implementation, the role of the event delivery service is played by the global event manager (GEM [8]), which provides a communication facility based on sockets and the TCP/IP protocol. However, AERS is made independent from any specific delivery service by the thread EDSI (Event Delivery Service Interface, not shown in Figure 2), which acts as an interface between the delivery service and the rest of the system.

The Queue Manager The Queue Manager runs in parallel with the other threads of the system and realizes the step 1 of the cycle operations previously given. Its basic role is to receive events coming from the external world and accumulate them in the Waiting Queue. Upon receiving an occurrence of a particular event, the *end_of_cycle* event, the Queue Manager transfers the Waiting Queue into the Service Queue and re-enters the receiving loop.

The rule Interpreter The Interpreter checks the antecedent of each rule against the current configuration, and, for each antecedent found to be true, executes the operations specified in the associated consequent.

After processing all the rules in the programme, the Interpreter invokes a thread that archives the Service Queue in the History, thus sanctioning the end of the operations of the current cycle. This thread, called the History Indexer, is described in Section 6.

The performance of AERS mostly depend on the efficiency of the rule checking. It is well known that the complexity of a truth evaluator such as the AERS Interpreter increases with the expressiveness of the adopted rule language. In particular, the richer in operators and the more general in syntactical structure is the rule language, the harder is the task of the Interpreter. The rule language, presented in the next section, has been designed keeping in mind this trade-off. From the evidence gathered so far, it turns out that the rule language is expressive enough to allow the coding of realistic applications, while attaining a satisfactory performance.

4 The rule language

An AER programme consists of three main sections: the event, the state variables and the rule declaration section.

In an event declaration section, the programmer defines the event types that will be referenced in rules, giving for each type the list of parameters. The type of a parameter, as well as of any other value that can appear in an AER programme, can be either basic, that is one of: integer, real, string, or it can be an array of basic type elements.

State variables are local value holders, used to maintain a model of the external world. They can be queried and updated only through rules.

Rules can be either *simple* or have a case structure, in which case they are named *rule_blocks*. All non-state variables occurring in a rule are understood to be existentially quantified.

4.1 Simple rules

A simple rule is an expression of the form:

$$[!]\ Predicate \rightarrow Actions$$

to be read as: "when *Predicate* becomes true then perform *Actions*." *Predicate* is a DNF sentence whose basic constituents may specify conditions on: the occurrence of events either in the present (*event literals*) or in the past time (*event clauses*); on time (*temporal atoms*); or on variables (*variable atoms*). On the right hand side of the rule, any number of two kinds of actions can be specified: the raising of an event occurrence or an assignment to a state variable.

A simple rule is optionally preceded by an exclamation mark. Rules without exclamation mark are interpreted exhaustively, that is, *all* the variable bindings (see below) are sought which make true the antecedent of the rule; for each such binding, the consequent of the rule is executed. When the exclamation mark is used, the rule is interpreted in a non-exhaustive way: only the *first* binding which makes *predicate* true is considered. By execution of an action, the raising of an event or the modification of a state variable value is meant, as explained below.

Event literals Conditions on event occurrences are expressed via predicate symbols corresponding to event types. For instance, for an event type describing the opening of a valve, having as parameters the area and the number of the valve, and the operator performing the operation, the rule language provides the 3-place predicate symbol *Open_valve* having one term for event parameter. An event literal has the form:

$$[\textbf{not}]\ P(t_1, \ldots, t_n),$$

where P is a predicate symbol and $t_1, \ldots, t_n$ are *terms*, that is expressions denoting a simple value which can be built out of constants, variables and function symbols. For example, following the usual notation for constant symbols and variables, *Open_valve(x,y,o)* is a literal which is true in the configuration fragment shown in Table 1 for two variable bindings, namely $(x = 1, y = 1)$ and $(x = 1, y = 2)$. A positive event literal is called an *event atom*.

Area	Valve	Operator
1	1	o
2	1	p
1	2	o

Table 1. Occurrences of the *Open_valve* event.

Event clauses The specification of conditions on occurrences of events is done by using the temporal operator *Past* as follows:

$$[\textbf{not}]\ Past(\alpha,\ t)$$

where α is an event literal and t a temporal period. For example:

$$Past(\textbf{not}\ Open\_valve(3,10,"DCM"),\ \textbf{at}\ 5)$$

is true if and only if $Open\_valve(3, 10, "DCM")$ was false 5 cycles ago, i.e. if there was no active occurrence of the event **Open_valve** with the displayed parameters 5 cycles ago. The above clause can be understood as an abbreviation of the formula of the TRIO logic:

$$Past(\alpha, t) \wedge t = 5.$$

For the specification of past time periods, the language provides three 2-placed predicate symbols (**at**, **before**, and **after**) and the 3-placed predicate symbol **in-between**, which can be understood as a convenient abbreviation of mutually consistent **before** and **after** predicates on the same time variable. A time distance is a non-negative integer.

Variable atoms A variable atom states a simple condition on a variable occurring in an event literal, and is of the form $v \, \omega \, \pi$ where v is the variable in question, π is a term, and ω is one of the standard 2-placed arithmetical comparison operators. For instance, in:

$$Open\_valve(x, 10, "DAM") \wedge x \neq 2$$

the second conjunct is an event variable atom that requires that the valve mentioned in the preceding event atom be different from 2. Of course, event variable atoms may be much more complicate than this one, depending on the form of the terms that occur in them. Since state variables can be arrays, state variable atoms may have a variable as index, or the special operator "$*$", e.g. "$v[*]$" denotes all the elements of the array v.

Temporal atoms Temporal atoms are simple conditions on the current time (denoted by the variable **now**) expressed by the same temporal operators used in event clauses. Examples of temporal atoms are:

now at $01.10.1993{:}10{:}00{:}00$ and
now in-between $01.10.1993{:}00{:}00{:}00$ $02.10.1993{:}00{:}00{:}00$.

The truth of a temporal atom is established by considering the temporal variable **now** as a state variable whose value is obtained by the system at the beginning of each cycle. Then, in checking a temporal atom specifying that the current time should be inside a temporal interval $[t_1, t_2]$ (with the possibility that $t_1 = t_2$) the system checks that $[t_1, t_2]$ overlaps with the interval $[\mathbf{now}, \mathbf{now} + c]$, where c is the length of the cycle. This amounts to check that the interval specified in the clause *spans* the current cycle, so that the clause can be considered to be true during the current cycle.

4.2   Rule blocks

A rule block is a sort of case structure, having the form:

$$
\begin{aligned}
[!] \; predicate \; c_1 &\rightarrow a_1 \\
c_2 &\rightarrow a_2 \\
&\cdots \\
[c_n] &\rightarrow a_n .
\end{aligned}
$$

predicate is said to be the block antecedent, each c_i is said to be the case antecedent, while a_i is the corresponding list of actions, with the additional requirement that the variables that occur in each case antecedent must be a subset of those occurring in the block antecedent.

The block antecedent expresses a general condition which, when met by the current system configuration with a certain variable binding, causes the evaluation of the case antecedent c_1. If c_1 is true, the action sequence a_1 is executed and the evaluation of the other cases is omitted by looking for the next binding the satisfies the predicate (unless the "!" is used, in which case the evaluation of the rule block stops). Otherwise, the second case is evaluated in the same way, and so on, up to the completion of the case structure. This behaviour is captured by the following sequence of rules:

$$predicate \text{ and } \quad c_1 \; \rightarrow a_1$$
$$predicate \text{ and } \quad \neg c_1 \text{ and } \quad c_2 \rightarrow a_2$$
$$...$$
$$predicate \text{ and } \neg c_1 \text{ and } \quad ... \quad \text{ and } \neg c_{n-1} \text{ and } c_n \rightarrow a_n$$

of which the rule block has to be considered as an abbreviation. Optionally, the rule block is concluded by a *catch*, which is simply a case with an empty antecedent and captures the rule:

$$predicate \text{ and } \neg c_1 \text{ and } ... \text{ and } \neg c_n \rightarrow a.$$

Rule blocks give a considerable gain in expressiveness and in efficiency. As far as the former is concerned, a rule block provides a sort of modularization mechanism, allowing to group in a single unit the rules that handle similar cases. As far as the latter is concerned, each binding of the variables in the predicate is computed only once, and used in performing at most n tests, whereas in the equivalent rule sequence all these bindings are computed *and* used n times.

For space reasons, we omit the specification of the formal semantics of AER programmes.

5   A case study

As an example of the use of AERS, a programme to handle the well-known case of the dining philosophers (see, for instance, [9]) has been developed. This section shows a couple of the rules of the programme[3] and reports the results of experiments that have been conducted on it.

In the dining philosophers table, there are a number of positions, each consisting of a seat, a dish and a fork. Philosophers come to table to dine, but can eat only if they hold a fork in each hand. This requirement may cause a philoso-

---

[3] For space reason, it is not possible to present the whole case study in detail; the interested reader can find it in [7].

pher to starve because her forks are never simultaneously available, or it may cause deadlock, when *all* philosophers starve. In order to represent the dinner, AER uses several state variables, among which the following two arrays:

Pos[i] records who is sitting at position i. It holds −1 if the seat at position i is free (initial value) or k if that seat is occupied by philosopher k.

Phil[i] records the state of the philosopher sitting at position i. In particular, it holds the value THINK if the philosopher has no forks and has made no fork request.

The following rule block handles the acceptance of philosophers at the table. Informally, a philosopher x submitting a request (AskSit) to sit at position y is not accepted if she is already sitting (case 1, that is if for some i Pos[i]=x) or she requests an occupied seat (case 2, if Pos[y]$\geq$ 0). Otherwise (case 3), she is accepted at the table by accordingly modifying the state variables Pos[y] and Phil[y], and by outputting an instance of Sit which acknowledges the successful completion of the request.

AskSit(x y): Pos[i]=x $\longrightarrow$ YouAlreadySit(x);
           Pos[y]$\geq$0 $\longrightarrow$ DontSit(x);
           $\longrightarrow$ Pos[y]=x, Phil[y]=THINK, Sit(x y).

The next rule is a simple rule enforcing a time out. If a philosopher has been accepted at the table no earlier than DIV_TO cycles ago (first event clause in the rule antecedent) and, in the meantime, she has not requested any fork (second and third clauses), a notification is output, to signal that she should start the dinner.

Past(Sit(x y), at DIV_TO) and not Past(AskPickFork(L y), in-between DIV_TO 0) and not Past(AskPickFork(R y), in-between DIV_TO 0) $\longrightarrow$ PleaseStartDinner(y).

Overall, the programme for the dining philosophers consists of 13 simple rules and 9 rule blocks, 3 of which have 2 cases, 4 have 5 cases and 2 have 10 cases. Running the programme on 5 philosophers, for at least 32 cycles with different, the observed average time needed for the evaluation of rules is well below 100 milliseconds.

6 Optimizations

In this section two techniques are presented which optimize the operation of the Interpreter. Only the first one is implemented in the current version of the system.

6.1 The History Indexer

The History Indexer (HI) is a thread of the AERS process whose main task is to file the current Service Queue into the History. The HI runs in parallel with the Interpreter and the Queue Manager and performs two basic operations: filtering and indexing.

The filtering process consists in discarding from the Service Queue to be filed the occurrences of the events which are known to be never accessed in the future. There are two kinds of such occurrences. First, those of the events that are referenced by no event clause. Second, those which do not match with any event clause. In fact, there is one case in which it can statically be determined whether an occurrence will ever match an event clause. This happens when *all* the event clauses referencing the same event have a constant value in correspondence of the same parameter. If an occurrence does not match any of these parameters, then it will never satisfy an event clause.

By reducing the size of the History, the filtering produces a save in space and access time. An additional speed up mechanism is given by the indexing, which is performed after filtering and consists in the construction of an History Index record corresponding to the Service Queue which is being handled. An index record is a sequence of pairs (event_id, position) which record, for each event present in the Service Queue, the id of the event and the position at which its occurrences can be found. When checking a positive event clause, the History Index guides the Interpreter to look only in potentially relevant History records; when checking a negative event clause, an access to the History Index may solve the entire problem, as the absence of occurrences is sufficient to this end.

6.2   Rule pre-selection

Rule pre-selection is a technique aiming at saving work to the rule Interpreter by avoiding it the checking of rules which are guaranteed not to be fired. The key concept to this end is that of *applicability* of rules. A simple rule is applicable, at a certain cycle, if for at least one disjunct of the rule antecedent, all the events occurring in event atoms have a non-empty set of occurrences in the Service Queue. A disjunct satisfying this condition is called a *critical* disjunct (CD). For instance, the rule:

```
[StartEating(x) and Phil[x]≠ EAT and Past(MayEat(x), in-between ECS_TO 0)] or
[StartEating(x) and Phil[x]≠ EAT and Past(PleaseEat(x), in-between FAST_TO 0)]
     → Phil[x]=EAT, GoodEnjoy(x).
```

is applicable if there is at least one occurrence of the **StartEating** event in the Service Queue, in which case both the disjuncts of its antecedent are critical. A rule block is applicable at a certain cycle if both its antecedent and at least one case antecedent contain a CD.

It is easy to verify that, for each cycle, a rule is executed if it is applicable at that cycle. Consequently, the Interpreter could retain correctness, while greatly gaining in efficiency, by only checking applicable rules. Happily, applicable rules can be computed by the Queue Manager in a dynamic, incremental way, using a very efficient algorithm based on that presented in [1] to compute the closure of a set of attributes under a given set of functional dependencies. The algorithm takes as input the Waiting Queue and returns the list of the CDs to be used by the Interpreter in the next cycle, and has complexity $O(o \cdot d)$, where a is the number of events in the Waiting Queue and d is the number of disjuncts in the AER programme.

7 Conclusions

AERS is an attempt to import declarative programming in the world of reactive agents. It propose to use temporal logic for the specification of applications, rather than for just the design and verification phases of the system life-cycle. We believe that AERS demonstrates the success of this attempt. Despite the prototypical nature of the system, it has been implemented on top of state-of-the-art technology and integrated with an advanced communication facility such as GEM. The performance of AERS is encouraging, and there is still room for optimization.

References

1. C. Beeri and P.A. Bernstein. Computational problems related to the design of normal forms relational schemas. *ACM Trans. on Database Systems*, 4(1):30–59, 1979.
2. M. Fischer. Representing and executing agent-based systems. In *Proceedings of the ECAI Workshop on Agent Theories, Architectures and Languages*, Amsterdam, Netherlands, 1994.
3. M. Fischer. A survey of concurrent METATEM–the language and its applications. In *Proceedings of ICTL, First International Conference on Temporal Logic*, Bonn, Germany, 1994.
4. Carlo Ghezzi, Dino Mandrioli, and Angelo Morzenti. Trio: A logic language for executable specifications of real-time systems. *Journal of Systems and Software*, 12:107–123, 1990.
5. R. A. Kowalski. Using metalogic to reconcile reactive with rational agents. In K. KApt and F. Turini, editors, *Meta-Logics and Logic Programming*. The MIT Press, 1995.
6. Carlo Meghini and Fausto Rabitti. The automatic event raising system. Technical report, ESPRIT III Project n. 6548–IMIS, Deliverable Spe-2.5, January 1995.
7. Carlo Meghini, Fausto Rabitti, and Ilaria Campanari. Automatic event raising at work. Technical report, ESPRIT III Project n. 6548, March 1994.
8. S. Spence, H. Evans, and M. Atkinson. The design of GEM. Submitted for publication.
9. Andrew S. Tanenbaum. *Operating Systems Design and Implementation*. Prentice Hall, Englewood Cliffs, NJ, 1987.

Neural Fuzzy Agents for Database Search

Sanya Mitaim and Bart Kosko
Signal and Image Processing Institute
Department of Electrical Engineering—Systems
University of Southern California
Los Angeles, California 90089-2564

Abstract

A neural fuzzy system can help learn an agent profile of a user. The fuzzy system uses if-then rules to store and compress the agent's knowledge of the user's likes and dislikes. A neural system uses training data to form and tune the rules. The profile is a preference map or a bumpy utility surface over the space of search objects. Rules define fuzzy patches that cover the bumps as learning unfolds and as the fuzzy agent system gives a finer approximation of the profile. The agent system searches for preferred objects with the learned profile and a new fuzzy measure of similarity. We derive a new supervised learning law that tunes this matching measure with new sample data. Then we test the fuzzy agent profile system on object spaces of flowers and sunsets and test the fuzzy agent matching system on an object space of sunset images.

1   Profile Learning and Object Matching

An intelligent agent can act as a smart database filter [6, 10]. It can search a database or search a space of objects on the behalf of its user. The agent can find and retrieve objects that the user likes. Or the agent can find and then ignore or delete objects that the user does not like. Or it can perform some mix of both. The agent acts as a filter because it maps a set of objects to one or more of its subsets. The agent is smart to the degree that it can quickly and accurately learn the user's tastes or object profile and use that profile map to search for and rank preferred objects as in Figure 1.

Agent search depends on set structure in a still deeper way. The search system itself may have many parts to its design and may perform many functions in many digital venues. But at some abstract level the agent partitions the object space into two fuzzy sets or multivalued sets with blurred borders. The agent partitions the space into the fuzzy set of objects that it assumes the users likes and the complement fuzzy set of objects that it assumes the user does not like. Then the agent can rank some or all of the objects in the preferred set and pick some of the extremal objects as its output set.

The agent must have a profile of its user so that it can group and rank objects. It must somehow learn what patterns of objects the user likes or dislikes and to what degree he likes or dislikes them. This profile is some form of the user's preference map. The user may state part of this map in ordinal terms: "I like these red flowers more than those blue flowers. I like the large purple flowers

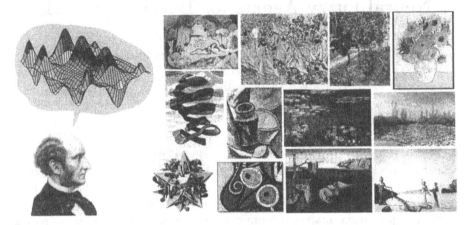

Fig. 1. A neural fuzzy agent learns a user's utility surface as the user samples a database. The 12 bumps or extrema on the preference map show how much the user (or the agent who acts on the user's behalf) likes or dislikes the 12 paintings.

about the same as I like the small red-white flowers." The objects may be fuzzy patterns or fuzzy clusters in some feature space. Microeconomic theory ensures that under certain technical conditions these complete ordinal rankings define a numerical utility function unique up to a linear transformation [3]. So we can in theory replace the ordinal claim "I like object A at least as much as I like object B" with some cardinal relation $u(A) \geq u(B)$ and vice versa. The utility function $u : \mathcal{O} \to R$ converts the ordinal preference map into a numerical utility surface in some object space $\mathcal{O}$ of low or high dimension. The user likes the surface's peak objects and dislikes its valley objects.

This paper uses neural fuzzy systems to learn the user's profile or utility surface as a set of adaptive fuzzy if-then rules. The rules compress the profile into modular units. They allow the profile to grow from a first set of sample data or question-answer queries and allow it to change shape as the agent samples more preference data. These fuzzy systems are universal approximators [7] even though they suffer from exponential rule explosion in high dimension [9]. Their first set of rules give a quick but rough approximation of the user's profile. Each rule defines a fuzzy patch or subset of the object space (or product object space). Mean-square optimal rules cover the extrema or bumps [8, 9] of the profile surface and other rule patches quickly fill in between these bumps as learning unfolds. The utility profiles grow finer as the user states more numerical ranks for test objects or pattern clusters.

The paper also combines neural learning and fuzzy set theory to search for preferred objects. We cast this problem as one of fuzzy similarity matching and define a new measure for the task and show how supervised learning updates this measure. The user gives the system matching degrees in the unit interval for a test space of sunset images. Supervised gradient descent tunes the measure and defines a similarity surface over the sunset object space. Future systems can combine the "smart" techniques of fuzzy profile learning with fuzzy object matching to aid in the agent search process.

2 Neural Fuzzy Function Approximation: Patch the Bumps

A fuzzy system $F : R^n \rightarrow R^p$ covers the graph of an approximand f with m fuzzy rule patches of the form $A_j \times B_j \subset X \times Y = R^n \times R^p$ or of the word form "IF $X = A_j$ THEN $Y = B_j$." The if-part fuzzy sets $A_j \subset R^n$ and then-part fuzzy sets $B_j \subset R^p$ have set functions $a_j : R^n \rightarrow [0,1]$ and $b_j : R^p \rightarrow [0,1]$. The system can use the joint set function a_j or some factored form such as $a_j(x) = a_j^1(x_1) \cdots a_j^n(x_n)$ or $a_j(x) = \min(a_j^1(x_1), \ldots, a_j^n(x_n))$ or any other conjunctive form for input vector $x = (x_1, \ldots, x_n) \in R^n$.

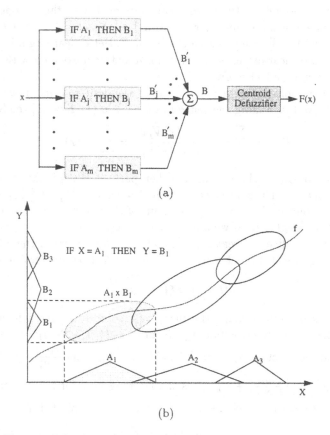

(a)

(b)

Fig. 2. (a) The parallel structure of the additive fuzzy system. Each input $x \in R^n$ fires each fuzzy rule to some degree to give a convex sum as the output: $F(x) = \text{Centroid}(\sum_{j=1}^m w_j a_j(x) B_j)$. (b) Fuzzy rules define patches in the input-output space and cover the graph of the approximand f. This leads to exponential rule explosion in high dimensions. Optimal lone rules cover the extrema of the approximand.

An additive fuzzy system [7] sums the "fired" then-part sets B'_j :

$$B(x) = \sum_{j=1}^{m} w_j B'_j = \sum_{j=1}^{m} w_j a_j(x) B_j. \tag{1}$$

Figure 2a shows the parallel fire-and-sum structure of the standard additive model (SAM). These systems can uniformly approximate any continuous (or bounded measurable) function f on a compact domain [7].

Figure 2b shows how three rule patches can cover part of the graph of a scalar function $f : R \to R$. The patch cover shows that all fuzzy systems $F : R^n \to R^p$ suffer from *rule explosion* in high dimensions. A fuzzy system F needs on the order of k^{n+p-1} rules to cover the graph and thus to approximate a vector function $f : R^n \to R^p$. Optimal rules can help deal with the exponential rule explosion. Lone or local mean-squared optimal rule patches cover the extrema of the approximand f [8]. They "patch the bumps". Better learning schemes move rule patches to or near extrema and then fill in between extrema with extra rule patches if the rule budget allows.

The scaling choice $B'_j = a_j(x)B_j$ gives a *standard additive model* or SAM. Appendix shows that taking the centroid of $B(x)$ in (1) gives [9] the SAM ratio

$$F(x) = \frac{\sum_{j=1}^{m} w_j a_j(x) V_j c_j}{\sum_{j=1}^{m} w_j a_j(x) V_j} = \sum_{j=1}^{m} p_j(x) c_j. \tag{2}$$

V_j is the finite positive volume or area of then-part set B_j. c_j is the centroid of B_j or its center of mass. The convex weights $p_j(x) = (w_j a_j(x) V_j)/(\sum_{i=1}^{m} w_i a_i(x) V_i)$ give the SAM output $F(x)$ as a convex sum of then-part set centroids. We can ignore the rule weights w_j if we put $w_1 = \cdots = w_m > 0$.

Supervised gradient descent can tune all the parameters in the SAM model (2) [9, 11]. A gradient descent learning law for a SAM parameter ξ has the form

$$\xi(t+1) = \xi(t) - \mu_t \frac{\partial E}{\partial \xi} \tag{3}$$

Learning laws move and shape the fuzzy rule patches to give a finer approximation in terms of the error function $E(x) = \frac{1}{2}(f(x) - F(x))^2 = \frac{1}{2}\varepsilon(x)^2$. The product sinc set function $a_j(x) = \prod_{i=1}^{n} a_j^i(x_i) = \prod_{i=1}^{n} \sin(\frac{x_i - m_j^i}{d_j^i})/(\frac{x_i - m_j^i}{d_j^i})$ and chain rule $\frac{\partial E}{\partial \xi_j^k} = \frac{\partial E}{\partial F} \frac{\partial F}{\partial a_j} \frac{\partial a_j}{\partial a_j^k} \frac{\partial a_j^k}{\partial \xi_j^k}$ gives the learning laws for all of parameters of SAM with constant rule weights $w_1 = \cdots = w_m > 0$ as in [9, 11]

$$m_j^k(t+1) = m_j^k(t) + \mu_t \, \varepsilon(x) \frac{p_j(x)}{a_j^k(x)} \frac{c_j - F(x)}{x_k - m_j^k} \left(a_j^k(x) - \cos(\frac{x_k - m_j^k}{d_j^k})\right) \tag{4}$$

$$d_j^k(t+1) = d_j^k(t) + \mu_t \, \varepsilon(x) \frac{p_j(x)}{a_j^k(x)} \frac{c_j - F(x)}{d_j^k} \left(a_j^k(x) - \cos(\frac{x_k - m_j^k}{d_j^k})\right) \tag{5}$$

$$c_j(t+1) = c_j(t) + \mu_t \, \varepsilon(x) \, p_j(x) \tag{6}$$

$$V_j(t+1) = V_j(t) + \mu_t \, \varepsilon(x) \left[c_j - F(x)\right] \frac{p_j(x)}{V_j}. \tag{7}$$

3 Sunset and Flower Profile Learning

We can define user preference maps on an image space of sunsets or flowers. Each person has her own likes or dislikes and defines her own fuzzy pattern of object clusters. This is the reason we tested our system on these complex images.

Recent works on object recognition [17] and content based image retrieval system [12] have shown that features can define the "look" of the images. Examples of these features include colors, shapes, and textures. Research in machine vision seeks a set of invariant features that can discriminate all images into smaller clusters [1, 2, 12, 13, 17].

We used a multi-dimensional histogram of an image as features for our fuzzy agent prototype on image spaces of sunsets and flowers. The color histogram has many advantages. It is easy to compute and is translation and rotation invariant [17]. Researchers [12, 17] got good results from their image recognition and image database retrieval systems using color histograms. But the histogram technique ignores the spatial correlation of pixels in images and many researchers suggest other local features [1]. We also use the image dispersion σ_{ij} [14] as an addition feature to compute the histogram of images:

$$\sigma_{ij} = \frac{1}{W^2} \left[\sum_{m=-w}^{w} \sum_{n=-w}^{w} [x(i+m, j+n) - \bar{x}(i+m, j+n)]^2 \right]^{1/2} \quad (8)$$

where $W = 2w + 1$ and $\bar{x}(i, j) = \frac{1}{W^2} \sum_{m=-w}^{w} \sum_{n=-w}^{w} x(i+m, j+n)$ is a sample mean in the $W \times W$ window centered at pixel location (i, j).

For each image we obtain its 4-D normalized histogram. The first 3 components are hue (h), saturation (s), and intensity (v) in the HSI color space [14]. The other component is the standard deviation (σ) of the intensity component. We view this normalized 4-D histogram as an input discrete probability density function to our fuzzy system and represent it in the mathematical form

$$T(h, s, v, \sigma) = \sum_{i=1}^{N_h} \sum_{j=1}^{N_s} \sum_{k=1}^{N_v} \sum_{l=1}^{N_\sigma} t_{i,j,k,l} \, \delta(h - \bar{h}_i) \delta(s - \bar{s}_j) \delta(v - \bar{v}_k) \delta(\sigma - \bar{\sigma}_l) \quad (9)$$

where N_h, N_s, N_v, and N_σ are number of bins on axes of hue, saturation, intensity, and variances. So the total number of histogram bins is $N = N_h \times N_s \times N_v \times N_\sigma$. $\bar{h}_i$ is the bin center of the ith hue and likewise for $\bar{s}_j, \bar{v}_k$, and $\bar{\sigma}_l$. $t_{i,j,k,l}$ is a normalized frequency of occurrence of the feature vector $(\bar{h}_i, \bar{s}_j, \bar{v}_k, \bar{\sigma}_l)$. This histogram T is the input to the fuzzy system. Appendix and [9] show that this gives us a generalized SAM ratio (2) as a set-SAM [9]:

$$F(T) = \frac{\sum_{j=1}^{m} w_j \, a_j(T) \, V_j \, c_j}{\sum_{j=1}^{m} w_j \, a_j(T) \, V_j} \quad (10)$$

where

$$a_q(T) = \int_X a_q(h, s, v, \sigma) \, T(h, s, v, \sigma) \, dh \, ds \, dv \, d\sigma$$

$$= \sum_{i=1}^{N_h} \sum_{j=1}^{N_s} \sum_{k=1}^{N_v} \sum_{l=1}^{N_\sigma} t_{i,j,k,l}\, a_j(\bar{h}_i, \bar{s}_j, \bar{v}_k, \bar{\sigma}_l) \tag{11}$$

defines the correlation of a fuzzy set function $a_q : X \subset R^4 \to [0,1]$ with a 4-D histogram of an image T.

We tested the fuzzy agents with 88 flowers images and 42 sunsets images. We assigned subjective impression values to all images as numbers from 0 to 10. The value 10 stands for "It is very beautiful–I love it" and 0 stands for "I really hate it". The histogram bins are 8:4:4:4 for $h : s : v : \sigma$ and so are the fuzzy sets. There are total of 512 bins and 512 fuzzy rules. We initialized the fuzzy agent so that it would be "indifferent" to all images (a score of 5) and trained it with supervised gradient-descent learning. The initial maximum absolute error was 5 and the mean absolute error was at 2.45. After 40,000 epochs the fuzzy agent converged to our preference map and gave a score close to ours. This held for almost all test images. The maximum absolute error was 0.96 and the mean absolute error was 0.18. This error stemmed from too few features. More features would improve the system's accuracy but at the expense of greater rule complexity.

We used a histogram in our prototype because it is easy to compute. It also captured the relative amount of colors and textures in the image that affect much of human perception. The fuzzy agent can use other inputs from image database. This might include features such as shapes [1, 12, 13], textures [12, 13], wavelet transforms [2, 18], or other statistical measures [13]. This feature selection depends on the agent's database needs.

4 Fuzzy Equality for Object Matching

A fuzzy system can assist in database search. The fuzzy equality measure [9] between two fuzzy sets can define the similarity between objects. The equality measure $E(A, B)$ measures the degree that a fuzzy set A equals a fuzzy set B. Suppose fuzzy sets A and B are nonempty. Then $E(A, B) \in [0, 1]$, $E(A, A) = 1$, and $E(A, \emptyset) = 0$ for the empty set $\emptyset$. A fuzzy system maps histograms of two input images with its if-then rules to the output fuzzy sets A and B. Then the equality measure gives a value near 1 if two histograms "look alike" and gives a value near 0 if they do not. [9] defines a equality measure from the *counting* or *cardinality* [9] function c of a fuzzy set as

$$E(A, B) = \mathrm{Degree}(A = B) = \frac{c(A \cap B)}{c(A \cup B)} \tag{12}$$

where $c(A) = \sum_{i=1}^{N} a_i$ or $c(A) = \int_{R^n} a(x)\, dx$ for integrable fuzzy set function $a : X \to [0, 1]$, $a \cap b(x) = \min(a(x), b(x))$, and $a \cup b(x) = \max(a(x), b(x))$. Then supervised gradient descent learning tunes the parameters of A and B to match a user's perception of similar images as in Figure 3.

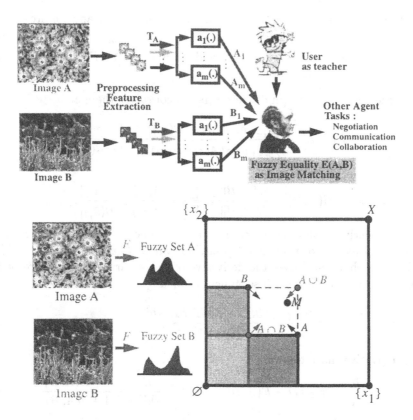

Fig. 3. Supervised learning tunes the fuzzy equality measure $E(A, B)$ in a fuzzy cube to better approximate the user's perception of similar images.

5 Fuzzy Image Matching

We use the same features as in the previous section to match images. Let the histograms of two images be T_A and T_B. Again we consider these two N-bin histograms as discrete probability density functions on the domain vector $(\bar{x}_1, \ldots, \bar{x}_N)$ and there are total m rule patches for a fuzzy system. Then we obtain two m-D vectors of set values $(A_1, \ldots, A_m)$ and $(B_1, \ldots, B_m)$ from T_A and T_B as

$$A_j = a_j(T_A) = \sum_{i=1}^{N} T_A(\bar{x}_i) \, a_j(\bar{x}_i) \tag{13}$$

$$\text{and} \quad B_j = a_j(T_B) = \sum_{i=1}^{N} T_B(\bar{x}_i) \, a_j(\bar{x}_i). \tag{14}$$

So the output fuzzy sets A and B from the histograms T_A and T_B are

$$A(\bar{x}_i) = \sum_{j=1}^{m} A_j \, a_j(\bar{x}_i) \quad \text{and} \quad B(\bar{x}_i) = \sum_{j=1}^{m} B_j \, a_j(\bar{x}_i). \qquad (15)$$

Then the fuzzy equality (in discrete version) computes the match

$$E(A, B) = \frac{\sum_{i=1}^{N} \min(A(\bar{x}_i), B(\bar{x}_i))}{\sum_{i=1}^{N} \max(A(\bar{x}_i), B(\bar{x}_i))} = \frac{1 - \bar{d}(A, B)}{1 + \bar{d}(A, B)} \qquad (16)$$

where

$$\bar{d}(A, B) = \frac{\|A - B\|}{\|A + B\|} = \frac{\sum_{i=1}^{N} |A(\bar{x}_i) - B(\bar{x}_i)|}{\sum_{i=1}^{N} |A(\bar{x}_i) + B(\bar{x}_i)|}. \qquad (17)$$

We next derive a supervised learning law to tune the parameters of the set function. Square error for a desired matching value D has the form $SE = \frac{1}{2}(D - E)^2$. Then chain rule gives the derivative of the squared error with respect to the kth parameter of the jth set function m_j^k as

$$\frac{\partial SE}{\partial m_j^k} = \frac{\partial SE}{\partial E} \frac{\partial E}{\partial \bar{d}} \frac{\partial \bar{d}}{\partial m_j^k} \qquad (18)$$

The derivatives have the form

$$\frac{\partial SE}{\partial E} = -(D - E(A, B)) \quad \text{and} \quad \frac{\partial E}{\partial \bar{d}} = -\frac{1 + E(A, B)}{1 + \bar{d}(A, B)} \qquad (19)$$

$$\frac{\partial \bar{d}}{\partial m_j^k} = \frac{1}{\|A + B\|} \left(\frac{\partial}{\partial m_j^k} \|A - B\| - \bar{d}(A, B) \frac{\partial}{\partial m_j^k} \|A + B\| \right) \qquad (20)$$

where

$$\frac{\partial}{\partial m_j^k} \|A - B\| = [a_j(T_A) - a_j(T_B)] \sum_{l=1}^{N} \text{sign}(A(\bar{x}_l) - B(\bar{x}_l)) \frac{\partial a_l(\bar{x}_l)}{\partial m_j^k}$$

$$+ \left[\frac{\partial a_j(T_A)}{\partial m_j^k} - \frac{\partial a_j(T_A)}{\partial m_j^k} \right] \sum_{l=1}^{N} \text{sign}(A(\bar{x}_l) - B(\bar{x}_l)) \, a_j(\bar{x}_l) \qquad (21)$$

$$\frac{\partial}{\partial m_j^k} \|A + B\| = [a_j(T_A) + a_j(T_B)] \sum_{l=1}^{N} \frac{\partial a_l(\bar{x}_l)}{\partial m_j^k}$$

$$+ \left[\frac{\partial a_j(T_A)}{\partial m_j^k} + \frac{\partial a_j(T_A)}{\partial m_j^k} \right] \sum_{l=1}^{N} a_j(\bar{x}_l) \qquad (22)$$

since $a(x) \geq 0$ for all $x \in X$. The condition $a_j(T_A) = \sum_{i=1}^{N} t_i \, a_j(\bar{x}_i)$ from (11) gives

$$\frac{\partial a_j}{\partial m_j^k}(T_A) = \sum_{i=1}^{N} t_i \frac{\partial a_j}{\partial m_j^k}(\bar{x}_i). \qquad (23)$$

So we can move or reshape the fuzzy sets to approximate desired matching values. Figure 3 shows a block diagram of a fuzzy agent for image matching. The simulation used a 4-D version of the 1-D Laplace set function $a_j^k(x_k) = \exp\{-|\frac{x_k - m_j^k}{d_j^k}|\}$ in (23). The partial derivatives of the Laplace set function $a_j(x) = a_j^1(x_1) \cdots a_j^n(x_n)$ with respect to its parameters m_j^k and d_j^k are

$$\frac{\partial a_j}{\partial m_j^k} = \text{sign}(x_k - m_j^k) \frac{1}{|d_j^k|} a_j(x) \tag{24}$$

$$\text{and} \quad \frac{\partial a_j}{\partial d_j^k} = \text{sign}(d_j^k) \frac{|x_k - m_j^k|}{(d_j^k)^2} a_j(x). \tag{25}$$

We trained the fuzzy matching system on a space of sunset images with the histogram intersection in [17]

$$S(H, I) = \frac{\sum_{i=1}^{N} \min(H_i, I_i)}{\sum_{i=1}^{N} H_i}. \tag{26}$$

The fuzzy system gave only a rough approximation of the histogram intersection.

6 Conclusions

Neural fuzzy systems can assist agents in many ways. We have shown how these adaptive function approximators can both help learn a user's preference map and help choose preferred objects cast as features of low dimension. Other neural fuzzy systems can more fully combine these two fuzzy tasks to aid in agent database search. Future research in this direction will depend in turn on advances in pattern recognition and machine vision. Neural fuzzy systems might also assist agents when agents bargain [15] or cooperate with other agents [4]. Then your agent may try to learn the other user's profile as well as learning your own profile.

Agents could also help neural fuzzy systems approximate functions from training samples. Today most neural fuzzy systems work with just one fuzzy system and one supervised or unsupervised learning law. Rule explosion in high dimensions may force the user to replace the lone fuzzy system with several smaller systems. Agents can help combine these fuzzy systems [9] if they pick and change the weights or rankings of each system based on sample data or domain knowledge. Agents can also pick which learning law to use or which set of parameters to use as the system tunes its rules on line. Still more complex hybrids can use nested agents within multi-system function approximators and use the approximators to help higher-level agents learn profiles and search databases and perhaps perform other agent tasks.

The fuzzy agent also needs to improve how it acquires knowledge [16]. The agent should not ask the user too many questions. The agent needs to learn the user's profile fast enough before it tires the user. Researchers have long searched for techniques that can lessen the number of numerical questions the system must ask the user [16]. The bootstrap and other statistical methods [5] may offer more efficient ways for an adaptive agent to sample its user and its environment.

References

1. T. Caelli and D. Reye, "On the Classification of Image Regions by Colour, Texture and Shape," *Pattern Recognition*, vol. 26, no. 4, pp. 461–470, 1993.
2. S. F. Chang and J. R. Smith, "Extracting Multi-Dimensional Signal Features for Content-Based Visual Query," in *SPIE Symposium on Visual Communications and Signal Processing*, May 1995.
3. G. Debreu, "Representation of a Preference Ordering by a Numerical Function," in *Mathematical Economics: Twenty Papers of Gerard Debreu*, chapter 6, pp. 105–110. Cambridge University Press, 1983.
4. M. Dorigo, V. Maniezzo, and A. Colorni, "Ant System: Optimization by a Colony of Cooperating Agents," *IEEE Transactions on Systems, Man, and Cybernetics-Part B: Cybernetics*, vol. 26, no. 1, pp. 29–41, February 1996.
5. B. Efron and R. J. Tibshirani, *An Introduction to the Bootstrap*, Chapman & Hall, 1993.
6. W. I. Grosky, "Multimedia Information Systems," *IEEE Multimedia*, vol. 1, no. 1, pp. 12–24, Spring 1994.
7. B. Kosko, "Fuzzy Systems as Universal Approximators," *IEEE Transactions on Computers*, vol. 43, no. 11, pp. 1329–33, November 1994.
8. B. Kosko, "Optimal Fuzzy Rules Cover Extrema," *International Journal of Intelligent Systems*, vol. 10, no. 2, pp. 249–255, February 1995.
9. B. Kosko, *Fuzzy Engineering*, Prentice Hall, 1996.
10. P. Maes, "Agents that Reduce Work and Information Overload," *Communications of the ACM*, vol. 37, no. 7, pp. 31–40, July 1994.
11. S. Mitaim and B. Kosko, "What is the Best Shape for a Fuzzy Set in Function Approximation?," in *Proceedings of the Fifth IEEE International Conference on Fuzzy Systems (FUZZ-96)*, New Orleans, September 1996, vol. 2, pp. 1237–1243.
12. W. Niblack et al., "The QBIC Project: Querying Images by Content Using Color, Texture, and Shape," Research Report RJ 9203 (81511), IBM, February 1993.
13. A. Penland, R. W. Picard, and S. Sclaroff, "Photobook: Tools for Content-Based Manipulation of Image Databases," in *SPIE: Storage and Retrieval for Image and Video Database II*, February 1994, vol. 2185, pp. 34–47.
14. W. K. Pratt, *Digital Image Processing*, Wiley Interscience, second edition, 1991.
15. J. S. Rosenschein and G. Zlotkin, "Consenting Agents: Designing Conventions for Automated Negotiation," *AI Magazine*, vol. 15, no. 3, pp. 29–46, Fall 1994.
16. E. Santos Jr. and D. O. Banks, "Acquiring Consistent Knowledge," Technical Report AFIT/EN/TR96-01, Air Force Institute of Technology, January 1996.
17. M. J. Swain and D. H. Ballard, "Color Indexing," *International Journal of Computer Vision*, vol. 7, no. 1, pp. 11–32, 1991.
18. M. Vetterli and J. Kovačević, *Wavelets and Subband Coding*, Prentice Hall, 1995.

Appendix. The Standard Additive Model (SAM) Theorem

SAM Theorem. Suppose the fuzzy system $F : R^n \to R^p$ is a standard additive model: $F(x) = \text{Centroid}(B(x)) = \text{Centroid}(\sum_{j=1}^{m} w_j a_j(x) B_j)$ for if-part joint set function $a_j : R^n \to [0, 1]$, rule weights $w_j \geq 0$, and then-part fuzzy set $B_j \subset R^p$. Then $F(x)$ is a convex sum of the m then-part set centroids:

$$F(x) = \frac{\sum\limits_{j=1}^{m} w_j a_j(x) V_j c_j}{\sum\limits_{j=1}^{m} w_j a_j(x) V_j} = \sum\limits_{j=1}^{m} p_j(x) c_j. \tag{27}$$

The convex coefficients or discrete probability weights $p_1(x), \ldots, p_m(x)$ depend on the input x through

$$p_j(x) = \frac{w_j a_j(x) V_j}{\sum\limits_{i=1}^{m} w_i a_i(x) V_i}. \tag{28}$$

V_j is the finite positive volume (or area if $p = 1$) and c_j is the centroid of then-part set B_j:

$$V_j = \int_{R^p} b_j(y_1, \ldots, y_p)\, dy_1 \cdots dy_p > 0, \tag{29}$$

$$c_j = \frac{\int_{R^p} y b_j(y_1, \ldots, y_p)\, dy_1 \cdots dy_p}{\int_{R^p} b_j(y_1, \ldots, y_p)\, dy_1 \cdots dy_p}. \tag{30}$$

Proof. There is no loss of generality to prove the theorem for the scalar-output case $p = 1$ when $F : R^n \to R^p$. This simplifies the notation. We need but replace the scalar integrals over R with the p-multiple or volume integrals over R^p in the proof to prove the general case. The scalar case $p = 1$ gives (29) and (30) as

$$V_j = \int_{-\infty}^{\infty} b_j(y)\, dy \tag{31}$$

$$c_j = \frac{\int_{-\infty}^{\infty} y\, b_j(y)\, dy}{\int_{-\infty}^{\infty} b_j(y)\, dy}. \tag{32}$$

Then the theorem follows by expanding the centroid of B and invoking the SAM assumption $F(x) = \text{Centroid}(B(x)) = \text{Centroid}(\sum\limits_{j=1}^{m} w_j a_j(x) B_j)$ to rearrange terms:

$$F(x) = \text{Centroid}(B(x)) \tag{33}$$

$$= \frac{\displaystyle\int_{-\infty}^{\infty} y\, b(y)\, dy}{\displaystyle\int_{-\infty}^{\infty} b(y)\, dy} \tag{34}$$

$$= \frac{\displaystyle\int_{-\infty}^{\infty} y \sum_{j=1}^{m} w_j\, b'_j(y)\, dy}{\displaystyle\int_{-\infty}^{\infty} \sum_{j=1}^{m} w_j\, b'_j(y)\, dy} \tag{35}$$

$$= \frac{\displaystyle\int_{-\infty}^{\infty} y \sum_{j=1}^{m} w_j\, a_j(x)\, b_j(y)\, dy}{\displaystyle\int_{-\infty}^{\infty} \sum_{j=1}^{m} w_j\, a_j(x)\, b_j(y)\, dy} \tag{36}$$

$$= \frac{\displaystyle\sum_{j=1}^{m} w_j\, a_j(x) \int_{-\infty}^{\infty} y\, b_j(y)\, dy}{\displaystyle\sum_{j=1}^{m} w_j\, a_j(x) \int_{-\infty}^{\infty} b_j(y)\, dy} \tag{37}$$

$$= \frac{\displaystyle\sum_{j=1}^{m} w_j\, a_j(x)\, V_j\, \frac{\displaystyle\int_{-\infty}^{\infty} y\, b_j(y)\, dy}{V_j}}{\displaystyle\sum_{j=1}^{m} w_j\, a_j(x)\, V_j} \tag{38}$$

$$= \frac{\displaystyle\sum_{j=1}^{m} w_j\, a_j(x)\, V_j\, c_j}{\displaystyle\sum_{j=1}^{m} w_j\, a_j(x)\, V_j} \qquad \square \tag{39}$$

'Learning' Based Filtering of Text Information Using Simple Interest Profiles

Elmar Haneke

University of Bonn – Department of Computer Science III
Römerstraße 164, 55117 Bonn, Germany
e-mail: haneke@cs.bonn.edu

Abstract. The rapid growth of public information systems, e.g. UseNet or World-Wide-Web, increases the need for tools filtering the information. A significant problem in many information filtering agents is that the user is forced to define his interests explicitly. This task is unacceptable for most users. Approaches which automatically generate interest profiles suffer from the disadvantage that the profiles are very complex. Therefore, a *review* is not practicable for the user.

A new information filtering agent, NewsSIEVE, with automatically generated simple profiles solves this problem by complex evolutionary optimization procedures processing the user's feedback. Due to the size and structure of the interest profiles generated by NewsSIEVE, a review is much easier than it would be for most other learning filtering agents. Using simple profiles reaches a significant performance. A small amount of classified data is sufficient to double the percentage of interesting messages.

1 Introduction

The rapid increase of information in public systems like UseNet or World-Wide-Web makes filtering agents selecting information of interest increasingly more important. A single individual can handle a small part of the available information only.

A facility incorporated in many news reading programs is to select messages by a *killfile*. A killfile is a list of names and key-words. A message is discarded if the sender is included in the list or one of the key-words is found in the subject-line. This filtering is based on interests exactly indicated by the user.

To avoid the need for an explicit specification of the interests *learning* filtering agents were designed: The user starts reading unfiltered messages and marks interesting or unimportant texts, respectively. From this feedback the agent automatically generates an interest profile. Currently, such filtering agents are using techniques like neural networks, vector spaces, and case-based reasoning [8]. The disadvantage of these approaches is that the generated interest profiles are very complex and therefore *a review is not practicable for the user*. To increase the acceptance of a filtering agent the considerable prerequisite is that on the one hand the use of the filtering agent requires a low additional work only and that on the other hand the implemented mechanism can be reviewed easily.

To reach a wide acceptance for filtering agents the project 'NewsSIEVE' (selecting interesting messages with verifiable estimations) demonstrates a new access to comply with the users demands. The user must be able to review the interest profile easily.

To reach a comprehensible interest profile NewsSIEVE on the one hand extends the vector space approach to a rule system which allows scorings for groups of words. On the other hand an evolutionary optimization procedure is used to find the most important rules. Therefore, the interest profile in NewsSIEVE consists of a small set of rules only which can be reviewed with acceptable overhead.

Comparing the performance of different filtering agents often suffers from the small amount of feedback data used for evaluating the agent. In contrast, NewsSIEVE is available to the public to collect the data required for the quantitative analysis of the filtering procedure.

NewsSIEVE reaches a good performance with small interest profiles. The number of words occurring in the rule system is smaller than the number of classified messages.

2 Related Work

2.1 Information Retrieval and Filtering

The research field of information retrieval has a long tradition which has its origin in the management of library catalogues. In information retrieval, interesting information usually is searched by evaluating a query. Techniques have been developed to allow the user to start with a simple query which is improved in the second step by the user's feedback [11].

Learning information filters may be described as a retrieval system in which the primary query has a low specificity. But, by interpreting the user's preferences via feedback the information becomes increasingly specific. A lot of techniques known from machine learning and information retrieval are used for information filtering: neural networks ([4] or [7]), rule systems [9], vector-spaces [6], case-based reasoning [8] as well as hybrid approaches using several methods simultaneously. These techniques all suffer from the disadvantage that the interest profile formed from the feedback is very complex. Therefore, a review of the learned similarities is not practicable for the user. He has to rely on the ability of the filter to provide a qualified selection.

To avoid this disadvantage in NewsSIEVE the vector-space approach is extended to a rule-system and an evolutionary optimization procedure is used to find a compact description of the user's interests.

2.2 Intelligent Agents

The research field of *intelligent agents* deals with computer software which does its work predominantly independent from the user. Intelligent agents can be used to search for information or to signal new interesting data. In both applications the agents are based on the same techniques as conventional information retrieval systems. For the search in distributed systems as the World-Wide-Web *mobile agents* are added as a new approach: In order to search for the information a program is sent to the system in which the information is expected to be found and the result of the search is returned.

For filtering UseNet messages, the use of a mobile agent is not useful because all information is available on a single local server. For this reason NewsSIEVE is designed as a *static agent* which evaluates the incoming messages according to the user's interests. The message filter waits for the user asking for new messages.

2.3 Evolutionary Optimization

The principle of the *evolutionary optimization* was developed simultaneously in the United States [3] and in Germany [10] in the middle of the 60ies. In both approaches, a set of solution candidates is alternately extended and reduced by *mutation, recombination*, and *selection*. For evolutionary optimization, the scoring function only has to satisfy very basic requirements. Therefore, the procedure can be used to solve a wide range of optimization problems. But, usually no meaningful lower-bound for the quality of the solution can be determined.

Many variations of evolutionary optimization have been developed. The main differences concern the layout of the three basic steps. Further developments concern the control of the search for new solution candidates [1] and the procedure for multi-dimensional scoring functions [5].

In NewsSIEVE evolutionary optimization is used to construct the rules describing the user's interests.

3 Architecture of the NewsSIEVE Filtering Agent

3.1 Design Goals

The most essential qualities of a filtering system are the *performance* and the *comprehensibility* of the choice mechanism. The comprehensibility of the choice mechanism can hardly be judged objectively because the subjective opinion is substantial. One criterion for the comprehensibility is the size and complexity of the description of the field of interest.

Therefore, NewsSIEVE was designed to use a simple set of rules and to work out a limited list of items for processing the messages.

3.2 Performance Criteria

Performance measures: How effectively can the filter distinguish between interesting and uninteresting messages. In order to score *selecting filters* two measurements from the assessment of information retrieval systems, can be used:
- *Precision* (Percentage of interesting objects in the output)
- *Recall* (Percentage of interesting objects found)

For a *scoring filter*, the definition of precision and recall can be used, if the filter is reduced to a selecting filter. The meaning of the results depends on the reduction. A possible reduction arises from the assumption that the filter is used to reduce the message volume by a constant percentage. With this assumption the first part of the ordered result can be considered as the output set.

3.3 Data Objects

A filtering system for text information must be able to handle information in natural language. A procedure which seems to be reasonable at first glance, is a language analysis of the documents – if the filter understands the content of the text, a very good result can be expected. The disadvantage of this procedure is that the analysis mechanisms are very complex. Therefore, the language analysis probably will not lead to a simple choice mechanism.

To get a simple choice mechanism in NewsSIEVE the documents are reduced to their words. As the frequency of a word in the text is related to its importance NewsSIEVE additionally evaluates the frequency of each word. Reducing the texts to their words is a common technique in information retrieval [11]. More complex mechanisms do not absolutely promise a superior filtering performance but they probably will not result in simple choice mechanisms.

3.4 Feedback from the User

In an interactive system feedback can be carried out explicitly or by implication (e.g. the time of displaying a message). Both feedback manners can be used in a filtering agent.

The evaluation of the feedback indicated by implication is problematic because the user's behaviour must be interpreted correctly. An above-average long displayed text may have different reasons:

- The user is interested in the text and therefore reads it exactly. The longer time of display in this case indicates a positive feedback.
- The user needs a lot of time to notice that the text is not interesting because the text has a high similarity with an interesting text. The interpretation as a positive feedback is not completely wrong.
- The user was interested in the message but, his interest was satisfied by the presented information. Therefore, a negative feedback would be carried out.
- The user was interrupted while reading the text. For this reason the reading seems to take a lot of time. This problem can be cleared only by an extensive observation of the user which certainly notices what the user is actually doing.
- In a network like the Internet it is possible that the reading process is delayed by a short network failure.

As a consequence of these problems NewsSIEVE does not process feedback indicated by implication.

Explicit feedback can be obtained as a value or as a grouping. In a graphic user interface a value can be entered with a sliding regulator. The operation for the user is as easy as a grouping. The actual precision of the scoring is possibly smaller than the precision defined by the range of values: Presumably no exact value is indicated at 100 possible settings. Small differences are probably coincidental.

For using a grouping as feedback the number of groups must be determined. NewsSIEVE offers three possible scorings to keep the operation simple: *positive*, *negative*, and *unscored*. The messages of the last group are not evaluated.

3.5 Modelling User Interests

In NewsSIEVE user interests are modelled using a rule system which is a refinement of the vector retrieval technique.

Vector retrieval, a standard procedure of information retrieval, works with the text data base as a vector space where every dimension corresponds to a word [11]. Searching query and texts are regarded as vectors. In the query vector, a score is assigned to every word. This score indicates the importance of the word for the desired subject area. The vectors for the texts are calculated from the frequencies of words. The retrieval process consists of the comparison of the query vector with all vectors saved in the data base. Usually the scalar product is calculated on the vectors scaled to length 1. The documents are displayed sorted by scores.

This retrieval procedure can be used as a scoring filter [6]: The vectors of the documents with feedback are summed to a query vector. The output of the filter is calculated by searching the new messages with this vector. Evaluating many training examples, the sum vector will contain many values different from 0. Therefore, the review of the interest profile becomes more complicated.

An advantage of this procedure is that message filters based on vector retrieval can be implemented very simply. A decisive disadvantage of the procedure is that the occurrence of a word is judged in isolation. The context has no influence on the calculation.

The description of the field of interest becomes substantially more precise if a score can be assigned to the occurrence of a group of words instead of single words. This change is not complicating the review of interest profiles. Small groups of words are as easy to review as single words.

To carry out this improvement in NewsSIEVE vectors are refined to a rule system. A rule assigns a score to a group of words. Missing words can also be interesting for the meaning of other words. Therefore, the absence can also be used in the rules of NewsSIEVE. The total score of a text arises from the sum of all scores assigned. The following example demonstrates the structure of the rules:

```
filtering agent ⇒ 1.5
filtering coffee ⇒ -2
agent !secret ⇒ 1
```

The first rule scores messages containing both 'filtering' and 'agent' with '1.5'. The second rule assigns the score '-2' to messages containing both 'filtering' and 'coffee'. The third rule assigns the score '1' to messages containing 'agent' in which 'secret' is not found.

In addition to the simple structure a description of the field of interest with as few rules as possible must be found to make the filtering easily comprehensible.

3.6 Consideration of Changes in the User Interests

User interests will change during the long-term use of the filtering agent. A comparison of current feedback with older feedback can detect changes. This comparison will probably result only in vague statements. Therefore, this attempt is not used in NewsSIEVE.

The filter must be able to react on new interests without an exact notification of the changes. New interests are taken into account by implication if later feedback is more emphasized in the calculation than older feedback. Therefore, the importance of training examples is reduced in an exponential decay. For the calculation a decay period of a week is used. The consideration of training examples with a very low importance is neglected. All examples with a value of less than 1% of the value of the latest feedback are excluded from the calculation.

3.7 Technical Realization

NewsSIEVE is created as a multi-user system with a central server. The server scores the messages and evaluates the user's feedback. The users communicate with the server using standardized programs (WWW-Browser, Telnet, Java). This architecture brings the following advantages to a single-user system on a local computer:

- The overall required work load is reduced by the centralization of the scoring, because a large part of work can be done for several users together at the same time.
- The users do not have to install any special software on the local computer. NewsSIEVE uses the usually available programs.
- Updates of the software can be done on the server without informing the users. They always work with the current software version.
- The centralization is able to incorporate feedback of all users. In decentralized systems a communication between the users would be necessary. At the moment the facility of *collaborative filtering* is not used in NewsSIEVE.
- The agent is available for all users using any computer in the Internet.

The server transfers only articles which the user actually reads. Therefore, the amount of data transmitted is small and does not outweigh the advantages. In case of area covering usage, servers in the local area of the user should be used.

When the filtering agent is operating on a central server, data security becomes an important aspect. NewsSIEVE controls the access by using a password. The server even can be used with anonymous access without storing the identity of the users.

NewsSIEVE is publicly accessible at the URL 'http://jod.informatik.uni-bonn.de: 8080/'. The user interface mainly uses HTML forms. To simplify the reading and judging of messages, a JAVA-applet is used. Some of the available JAVA implementations still have serious bugs at the moment. Therefore, the messages can also be read by using a telnet connection.

In addition to the basic functions like logon and group selection, NewsSIEVE offers the possibility to display the scoring rules calculated from the feedback and to store own rules for the scoring. The user indicates, for which period the stored rules should not be replaced by rules generated automatically.

4 Generation of Interest Profiles

The calculation of the scoring rules used as an interest profile is done by an evolutionary algorithm. Calculation procedures of this class start with a coincidental construction of solution candidates. The set of solution candidates is alternately processed by selection and mutation. The best solution candidates are selected during the selection phase. New solution candidates are constructed from the existing candidates by randomized operations during the mutation phase. This is carried out by changing single candidates or by combining two candidates. The goal of the calculation is to construct a small rule system which correctly classifies the training examples.

4.1 Scoring the Quality of Solution Candidates

For scoring the quality of solution candidates the scores assigned to training examples are limited to the interval $[-1, +1]$. Ideally the score of 'negative' texts is -1 and of 'positive' $+1$. The quality of the rule system can be scored by the difference of the actual score to the respective ideal, s_i is the score of the training example i:

$$score = \sum_{i\ positive} |1 - s_i| + \sum_{i\ negative} |-1 - s_i|$$

Since the scores s_i are limited to interval $[-1, +1]$ we can simplify $|1 - s_i|$ to $1 - s_i$ and $|-1 - s_i|$ to $1 + s_i$.

The result of the calculation only depends on the difference of the scores of the solution candidates. Therefore, the constant summands ($+1$ and -1) can be removed. Better solution candidates should get larger values than worse solutions. Therefore, the signs of the summands should be changed. In summary the following scoring formula results:

$$score = \sum_{i\ positive} s_i - \sum_{i\ negative} s_i$$

The score of an ideal solution candidate is equal to the number of training examples. Alternatively other nonlinear scorings can be used. The formula fulfils the intended purpose and facilitates an exact calculation of the optimal rule weights (see below).

As mentioned above later training examples are more emphasized than older one. This is carried out by assigning weights to the training examples. For calculating the scoring of the rule system the score of each training example is multiplied with it's weight. The score of an ideal solution is equal to the sum of the weights of all training examples. This results in the following scoring formula, s_i and w_i are the scoring and the weight assigned to training example i:

$$score = \sum_{i \ positive} s_i * w_i - \sum_{i \ negative} s_i * w_i$$

4.2 Scoring the Size of Solution Candidates

The calculated rule system should well describe the training examples and simultane-ously be as small as possible. By this the user can easily review the result. To receive small, good solution candidates during the optimization, the following fact can be used: *The probability to construct small, good rule systems by combining two solution candidates increases, if more rule groups with a high quality-density are available.* The quality-density of a rule system is the quotient of the quality-scoring defined above and the size of the rule system. Rule groups with a high quality-density contain criteria which are well suitable for the recognition of relevant texts. The absolute score of the rule group is low because the meaning is not sufficient without additional details. This can be balanced by the combination with other rule groups. Therefore, the goal to construct small solutions can be augmented by selecting such solutions also where the quality score is high in proportion to the size (*density*).

To achieve the minimization of the rule system size at the end of the calculation a scoring must be used which combines quality and size of the solution candidates. The quality density is unsuitable for this purpose. The percentage increase of the quality-score is minimal at the end of the calculation and therefore, the change of the size is dominant. If the distance to the ideal score is used instead of the reached score, this disadvantage is outweighed. The percentage change of the distance becomes larger at the end of the calculation. Since better solutions are scored with smaller values in both scorings, the product is calculated. During the selection phase, solution candidates with a small combination of the size and the difference to the ideal quality-score, are selected for the calculation (*differencescore*).

4.3 Optimization of Rule Weights

The first attempts to calculate the rule weights as a part of the evolutionary procedure did not end with sufficiently useful results. Since a practicable procedure is available with guaranteed optimal solution, the calculation of the rule weights as a part of the evolutionary procedure was not further examined.

The score of the rule system proved to be a linear combination of the rule weights: The score of a single training example is the sum of the weights of all rules with true conditions. This condition does not depend on the rule weights. The score of the rule system is a weighted sum of the scores of all training examples.

The score of a training example is restricted to the interval $[-1, +1]$. Since the score is a weighted sum of the rule weights, this restrictions is a linear constraint.

Therefore, the calculation of the optimal rule weights is a linear program. The Simplex algorithm is used to get the optimal values. In the Simplex matrix most values are equal to 0. 0-values are generated if a rule is not true for a training example. This fact is used for a technical acceleration of the calculation.

Rule weights are optimized for every solution candidate constructed during the calculation. Old weights cannot be taken for the construction of a new rule system. The scoring calculated with the old weights sometimes differs considerably from the optimal score and the new optimal weights have a significant difference to the old weights.

4.4 Optimization of the Rule System

The evolutionary calculation procedure used for the calculation of the rule system is similar to a genetic optimization. Mutation and combination operations are often defined with binary strings for this optimization method. In contrast to the binary strings in NewsSIEVE the definition of the operations is done with the structure of the scoring rules. A selection is executed after the mutation phase. The best candidates are selected according to the three scorings (*'score'*, *'density'*, and *'differencescore'*). The following operations are executed at random in the mutation phase:

AddRule: Adds a further rule which contains a single word.
DeleteRule: Deletes a rule.
SplitRules: Randomized removal of the half rule system.
CombineRules: Two rules are combined to a new one. The combination
               is carried out by calculating the union set of the words in
               both rules. As an option taken at random the words in one
               of the rules are negated.

In addition to the mutation taken at random, all new solution candidates are divided into a good and a bad half with the rule weights. This influences the optimization to find smaller solution candidates.

In the first step of the combination of two rule systems the common rules of both rule systems are taken. The remaining rules are taken, deleted, or combined in pairs at random. The combination is carried out in analogy to the mutation operation *CombineRules*. A rule from each of the two rule sets is used for the combination.

With the mutation operations mentioned above an arbitrary rule system can be constructed. This does not depend on the initial rule set constructed at random. The operations *AddRule*, *DeleteRule*, and *CombineRules* are sufficient for the construction. Therefore, the mutations are suitable for the optimization procedure. This is confirmed by the practical results. All alternatives have equal probabilities at the decisions in the change operations.

5 First Results

In opposite to other research groups which are evaluating the agent with very small examples constructed by the authors (e.g. 33 messages in average [9]), NewsSIEVE is evaluated by using data from the 'real world' application. In comparison to other projects more data is available at the moment, but it is still not sufficient for an exact measurement of the performance.

The first results can be summarized as follows: The rule systems judge very exactly the training examples from which they were calculated. The scoring reaches nearly the ideal value. The filtering of testing data not used for the calculation reaches a significant concentration of interesting messages at the beginning of the sorted output list.

To measure the performance, the following calculation was done off-line on the feedback data. All messages have been judged by the user either as 'interesting' or as 'uninteresting':

1. The messages are taken at random into two sets: The training-set and the test-set.
2. The training-set is used to create the rules.
3. The messages in the test-set are scored according to the rules created from the training-set.
4. To get the values shown in figure 1 the messages are ordered by score.
5. The ordered messages are processed in ten intervals of equal size. For each interval, the number of interesting and uninteresting messages is counted.

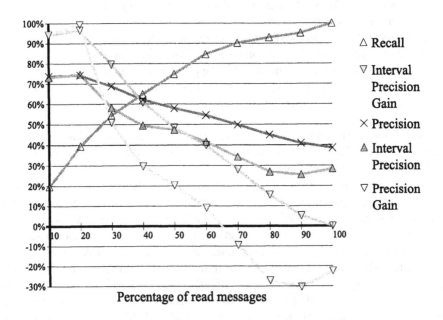

Fig. 1. Results of the filtering procedure

Figure 1 contains the following values calculated from the counting:

- *Recall*: $\dfrac{|interesting_{read}|}{|interesting_{total}|}$

- *Precision*: $\dfrac{|interesting_{read}|}{|read|}$

- *interval Precision*: $\dfrac{|interesting_{interval}|}{|interval|}$

- *Precision Gain*: $\dfrac{precision}{percentage\ of\ interesting\ messages}$

- *Interval Precision Gain*: $\dfrac{interval\ precision}{percentage\ of\ interesting\ messages}$

The values are averaged over 30 calculations on three different feedback sets. The average size of the test-sets is about 59 messages.

The calculation gives the following results: Reading the top part of the output list doubles the percentage of interesting messages in comparison to unfiltered messages. Half of the interesting texts are read with only 27% of the total. By reading 50% of all messages 75% of all interesting ones are reached. Reading 65% of all messages is more interesting than reading unsorted news – at this point, 88% of all interesting messages are found.

The size of the rules generated from the feedback data is about 58 words in average. Most rules assign a scoring to a small set of no more than two or three words. Due to the small size and the simple structure of the rule sets comparing the generated interest profile with his own field of interest is practicable for the user. The review is much easier than it would be for most other learning filtering agents.

6 Future Work

6.1 Incorporating Additional Information

The further research will investigate the use of additional information from the unscored texts. At the moment only statistical information about the word frequency is used from all texts. These details are used for the calculation of the document vectors: A word is important for the content if it has a frequency above the average.

A starting-point for the improvement in the calculation is the consideration that the filter has to distinguish not only between interesting and uninteresting training examples, but also between interesting and *unscored texts* of the searched groups. This idea can be translated into action by adding unscored texts to the training examples.

Since the number of unscored texts is usually substantially greater than the number of training examples, it is not sensible to include all unscored texts in the calculation. If only a random sample of the unscored texts is included in the calculation, the expected positive effect is reduced considerably. A significant improvement of the results will be reached by a suitable choice or a summary of unscored texts.

With a summary procedure, the processing of the training examples can possibly also be improved: The evaluation of combinations of several similar training examples might facilitate better results than the evaluation of single texts.

6.2 Possibility of Interventions for the User

The possibility of interventions and control for the user in NewsSIEVE actually is limited to displaying and replacing the created scoring rules. A further possibility of intervention is the additional post-processing of the training examples: If the user can change the scoring of the training examples, he can correct training examples no longer valid if the field of interest changes. The adaptation of the filtering agent to the new interests is significantly accelerated. Without a change of the field of interest, an additional correction of the training examples can be meaningful. An uniform scoring can be reached if the training examples are classified simultaneously.

7 Conclusions

The main goal of the NewsSIEVE project is to provide a learning filtering agent which allows the user a review of the interest profile generated from the feedback. Due to the size and structure of the profiles generated by NewsSIEVE, a review is much easier than it would be for most other learning filtering agents.

Using simple profiles for filtering reaches a significant performance. It is not really necessary to use complex interest profiles to do the filtering job. The performance reached with the rules generated from 60 classified messages demonstrates that a small amount of classified data is sufficient to reach a significant performance. Reading the first part of the filtered messages doubles the percentage of interesting ones.

References

1. Battiti, R. and Tecchiolli, G. The reactive tabu search. In: *ORSA Journal on Computing* Vol. 6, No. 2, pp. 126-140, 1994.
2. Hoffmeister, F. and Bäck, T. Genetic algorithms and evolution strategies: Similarities and differences. Technical Report No. SYS-1/92, University of Dortmund, 1992.
3. Holland, J. H. Adaptation in natural and artificial systems. The University of Michigan Press, Ann Arbor, 1975.
4. Jennings, A and Higuchi, H. A personal news service based on a user model neural network. In: *IE-ICE Transactions on Information and Systems*, 1992.
5. Kursawe, F. A variant of evolution strategies for vector optimization. In: *Parallel Problem Solving from Nature – Proceedings of the 1st Workshop PPSN*, Lecture Notes in Computer Science, Vol. 496, pp. 193-197, Springer-Verlag, Berlin, 1991.
6. Lang, K. NewsWeeder: Learning to filter netnews. In: *Proceedings of the 1995 Machine Learning Conference*, Morgan Kaufmann, Lake Tahoe, 1995.
7. McElligott, M. and Sorensen, H. An evolutionary connectionist approach to personal information filtering. In: *Proceedings of the Fourth Irish Neural Network Conference*, Dublin, 1994.
8. Mock, K. J. Intelligent information filtering via hybrid techniques: Hill climbing, case-based reasoning, index patterns and genetic algorithms. Thesis, University of California, Davis, 1996.
9. Payne, T. R. Learning email filtering rules with magi, a mail agent interface. MSc Thesis, Department of Computing Science, University of Aberdeen, 1994.
10. Rechenberg, I. Evolutionsstrategie: Optimierung technischer Systeme nach Prinzipien der biologischen Evolution. Formmann-Holzboog, Stuttgart, 1973.
11. Rijsbergen, C.J. Information retrieval. Butterworths, London, 1979.
12. Wooldridge, M. and Jennings, N. R. Intelligent agents: Theory and practice. In *The Knowledge Engeneering Review*, Vol. 10 No. 2, pp. 115-152, 1995.

An Organized Society of Autonomous Knowledge Discovery Agents

Ning Zhong[1], Yoshitsugu Kakemoto[2] and Setsuo Ohsuga[3]

[1] Dept. of Computer Science and Sys. Eng., Yamaguchi University
[2] Graduate School of Engineering, The University of Tokyo
[3] Dept. of Information and Computer Science, Waseda University

Abstract. We have been developing a methodology and system for autonomous knowledge discovery and data mining from global information sources. The key issue is how to increase both *autonomy* and *versatility* of our discovery system. Our methodology is to create an organized society of autonomous knowledge discovery agents. This means (1) to develop many kinds of knowledge discovery and data mining agents (KDD agents in short) for different objects; (2) to use the KDD agents in multiple learning phases in a distributed cooperative mode; (3) to manage the society of the KDD agents by multiple meta-control levels. Based on this methodology, a multi-strategy and cooperative discovery system, which can be imagined as a *softbot* and is named GLS (Global Learning Scheme), has being developing by us. This paper briefly describes our methodology and the framework of our GLS system.

1 Introduction

Generally speaking, *discovery* is a thinking process of human being for forming the hypothesis from the observed facts and testing/verifying it when he/she meets with surprised facts. In other words, *discovery* is a kind of un-supervised (human or machine) learning for acquiring knowledge. Although the means of scientific discovery can be divided into two types: theory-driven and data-driven, data-driven discovery is more one in the history of science and technology [30]. In particular, the number and size of available databases in many fields are growing so fast that there will never be enough human experts to analyze all data in databases and to discover conceptual knowledge from them. Hence, systems with the capability of automatic knowledge discovery from databases will play an increasingly important role [15].

We have been developing a methodology and system for autonomous knowledge discovery and data mining from global information sources. The key issue is how to increase both *autonomy* and *versatility* of our discovery system. Our methodology is to create an organized society of autonomous knowledge discovery agents. This means

- to develop many kinds of knowledge discovery and data mining agents (KDD agents in short) for different objects;

- to use the KDD agents in multiple learning phases in a distributed cooperative mode;
- to manage the society of the KDD agents by multiple meta-control levels.

The methodology is based on the viewpoint of "the society of mind" developed by Marvin Minsky [8]. That is, the society of autonomous knowledge discovery agents is made of many smaller components which are called *agents*. Each agent by itself can only do some simple thing. Yet when we join these agents in an *organized* society, this leads to implement more complex discovery tasks.

Based on this methodology, a multi-strategy and cooperative discovery system, which can be imagined as a *softbot* and is named GLS (Global Learning Scheme), has being developing by us [18, 21, 24]. This paper briefly describes our methodology and the framework of our GLS system. It includes to outline the architecture of the GLS system, to describe several kinds of KDD agents that have been developed or have been developing, to discuss how to plan and organize the discovery processes, how to manage the KDD agents, and our future work.

2   The Architecture of the GLS System

Fig.1 shows the architecture of the GLS system. We can see that GLS is divided into three levels: two meta control levels and an object level. By means of the top level, a discovery process can be planned and organized by communicating with a user or learning from environment according to different discovery objects. Based on the discovery process planned and organized, the KDD agents are dynamically generated by a meta agent. Furthermore, the KDD agents can be used in a distributed cooperative mode and are managed by a meta agent. On the other hand, in the object level, the KDD agents are divided into three groups, that is, three learning phases: *pre-processing, knowledge elicitation,* and *refinement and management.* Generally speaking, since uncertainty, incompleteness and dynamics of data in databases, the discovered knowledge is only the hypothesis and the hypothesis must be managed and refined. The multiple learning phases that are controlled by the meta levels serves the discovery process based on the repetitive process of incipient hypothesis generation/evaluation and management/refinement as shown in Fig.2.

3   The KDD Agents

The agents in our sense are not static but dynamic, i.e., they are dynamically generated and composed of Intelligent Mail Box. And their IDs are composed of names of workstation and agent. An agent can try to solve a discovery task or a sub-task, or something that serves this task but necessary to another agent's solving of the task. It can interact with other agents to help solve the task. In the rest of this section, we will describe the main KDD agents that have been developed or have been developing by us.

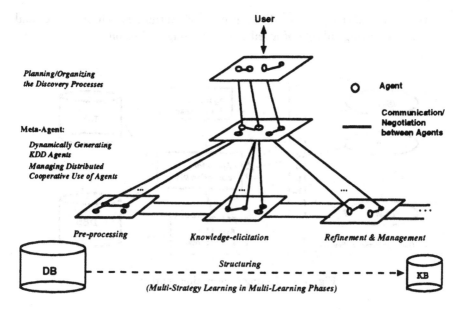

Fig. 1. The architecture of the GLS system

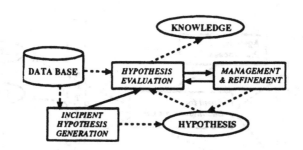

Fig. 2. The process of knowledge discovery from databases

3.1 The Agents for Pre-processing

In pre-processing, several kinds of agents are needed for data collection, data cleaning, data selection and decomposition.

First, some agent is used for collecting information from global information sources, as shown in Fig.3, and the agent can be cooperatively used with other agents for discretization of continuous values and conceptual abstraction. As a result of the collection, a large database (or more databases) can be generated dynamically.

Second, a large database can be decomposed into several local information sources as shown in Fig.4. Like the process for collecting information from global information sources, the agent for decomposing a database can be cooperatively used with some other agents for discretization of continuous values, conceptual abstraction, selecting subsets of attributes, sampling and so on.

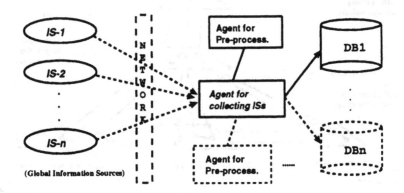

Fig. 3. Collecting information sources

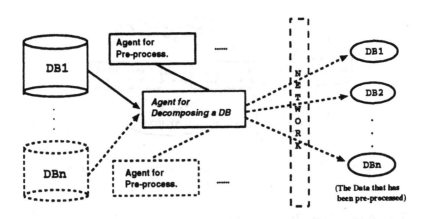

Fig. 4. Decomposing a database

Here, we briefly describe several kinds of agents for forming scopes/clusters, which have been developed as a step of pre-processing of a discovery process, as examples.

When a database is very large and complex, the possibility of which knowledge (e.x. the functional relationship) is discovered from all data in this database is very little and it is also time-consuming. But if some attribute(s), in which the data were divided into scopes, are used as conditions or criteria that knowledge should meet, then knowledge with conditions may be discovered as fast as possible; Or a database is decomposed into several clusters (i.e., sub-databases), then the methods for searching knowledge can be respectively performed for every cluster in parallel. However, we cannot wish that a method for forming scopes/clusters is good for all applications since the complexity of databases and the diversification of discovery tasks. Hence, GLS provides the following agents for selectivity:

- *Attribute oriented clustering using background knowledge (CBK)*. Attribute oriented clustering is a kind of operation for abstracting the data in an attribute. A result of the operation is that scopes are formed. Furthermore, the formed scopes can be used as the qualitative values for further clustering other attributes [20]. CBK is a method of clustering by using background knowledge. That is, background knowledge is used for conceptual abstraction (generalization) and/or the quantization of continuous values.
- *Quantization by the division of ranges (QDR)*. Unlike CBK, QDR is an automated method for clustering numeric attribute, in which scopes/clusters are formed by an algorithm based on a criterion of classification [20].
- *Forming scopes/clusters by nominal or symbolic attributes (FSN)*. That is, nominal or symbolic attributes are used for forming scopes/clusters. In comparison with the related methods, the most novel feature of FSN is that it can decide, by automatic search and statistics, which nominal or symbolic attributes can be used for forming scopes/clusters [23].
- *Stepwise Chow test (SCT)*. SCT is used for clustering time-series data. That is, scopes/clusters are formed by an algorithm based on a criterion called Chow-Test that was introduced by Chow to distinguish whether a structure change occurred in sample data or not [1]. SCT can discover automatically the structure changes in time-series data, cluster time-series data by discovering structure changes, and analyze/delete automatically unstable data in the area of continuous structure changes [23].

3.2 The Agents for Knowledge Elicitation

Currently, three kinds of agents, named KOSI (Knowledge Oriented Statistic Inference), DBI (Decomposition Based Induction) and GDTG (Generalizations Distribution Tables Based Generalization), can be used for eliciting knowledge such as *structural characteristics, concept clusters* and *if-then rules* (see Fig.5) from the local information sources that have been pre-processed.

KOSI pays attention to the functional relationships between any two attributes for discovering *structural characteristics* from databases [23]. *Structural characteristics* are a kind of important regularity hidden in databases, which are denoted by regression models for describing three kinds of functional relationships: the *exact, strong* and *weak* ones according to which method in KOSI was successfully used for discovering them and their errors. In a sense, KOSI can be regarded as an extension of BACON and its several successors for processing the data with more uncertainty [4]. The key point of this extension is to enhance the capability of processing uncertainty systematically by extending the heuristic

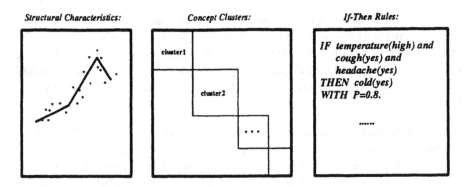

Fig. 5. Three kinds of typical knowledge

search and the search control, as well as combining them with some statistical methods.

KOSI supports qualitative/quantitative discovery and the search is divided into three types for providing a systematic manner of finding functional relationships. Two types of searches are used in *attribute calculation* which is a kind of operation in which new attribute is generated as a function of the existing attributes. They use respectively different type of heuristics (we call *heuristics-type-1* and *heuristics-type-2*) and are the basic searches in KOSI. Where, *heuristics-type-1* is mainly used for finding the *exact* functional relation which is almost always holds for the collected data; *heuristics-type-2* is mainly used for finding the *strong* functional relation which holds qualitatively for the collected data. Third type is the search based on regression analysis. It is mainly used for further evaluating/selecting the best functional relationships from the results of attribute calculation, and/or finding the *weak* functional relation which presents the structure hidden in the collected data. Furthermore, a model-base and meta/domain knowledge are used for controlling the multi-search. Finally, the selected functional relationships are denoted by regression models as the structural characteristics discovered, so that they can be easily managed and refined in the next learning phase.

DBI pays attention to the dependency relationships between any two attributes for discovering *concept clusters* from databases [20]. DBI is based on the concept of Simon and Ando's near-complete decomposability that has been most explicitly used in economic theory as a technique to study and evaluate the dynamics of systems of great size and complexity [16]. This technique is based on the idea that in many large systems all variables can somehow be clustered into a small number of groups. This idea is of course quite general, and has, at least indirectly, been productive in disciplines other than economics. As the theoretical basis of DBI, we transformed the concept of Simon and Ando's near-complete decomposability into the one of near decomposability of databases. A key feature of DBI is the formation of concept clusters or sub-databases through analysis and deletion of noisy data in decomposing a database. That is, the decomposition of databases is also a kind of aggregation and abstraction, and some minor factors (or noise) are neglected in decomposing. As the result of decomposing a database, concept clusters or sub-databases are formed, and they are used as background information for further learning in the next learning phase.

GDTG pays attention to the probabilistic distribution relationships between attribute values and their generalizations for discovering *if-then rules* with *strengths* from databases [28]. The central idea is to substitute *Generalizations Distribution Tables (GDT)* for the "version space" defined by Mitchell [9] as a hypothesis search space for generalization, in which the probabilistic relationships between concepts and instances over discrete domains are represented. Thus, not only the uncertainty of a rule including the prediction of possible instances can be explicitly represented in the strength of the rule, but also noisy data and missing data can be handled effectively, and biases for search control can be selected. Furthermore, the Generalizations Distribution Tables are represented by connectionist networks for rule discovery in a parallel-distributed cooperative mode [29]. This approach basically belongs to incremental, bottom-up fashion like "version space", but it also has some advantages belonging to top-down fashion.

3.3 The Agents for Refinement and Management

The refinement and management for the discovered knowledge are the important functions in a discovery system. *Refinement* means acquiring a more accurate knowledge (hypothesis) from a coarse knowledge (hypothesis) according to data change and/or the domain knowledge; *Management* includes representing a or more discovered knowledge (hypotheses) in a knowledge-base, recording the time and history of the evolution process of the discovered knowledge and the relationship among them according to the results of refinement, as well as selecting a suitable knowledge for use. Furthermore, we consider that the capabilities for management and refinement can be divided into the following two main aspects:

- Managing and refining the discovered knowledge (hypotheses) according to data change. That is, how to manage and refine the discovered knowledge (hypotheses) when the data in a database were updated (added/deleted);
- Managing and refining the discovered knowledge (hypotheses) for acquiring the more high-level knowledge. That is, how to acquire the more high-level knowledge from several knowledge (hypotheses) discovered from a database.

Currently, two kinds of agents, named IIBR (Inheritance Inference Based Refinement) and HML (HML (Hierarchical Model Learning), have been developed for processing the first aspect stated above. The second aspect involves other some agents that is being developed.

By means of IIBR, the structural characteristics denoted by regression models, which are discovered from a database by KOSI, can be represented by Multi-Layer Logic formulae and the sets of data for showing their errors in a knowledge-base, and can be easily managed and refined [22, 25]. IIBR is based on inheritance inference and error analysis, as well as meta reasoning and multiple worlds/levels of KAUS and the capability of expansion of Multi-Layer Logic [12, 11]. IIBR can find matches to models for similar situations to those under study, to give a starting model for analysis. A good starting model can save a user much time, and effective inference can also save storage space by eliminating the need to save similar models. Main functions of IIBR are (1) The method of the model representation is used to represent the discovered structural characteristics (regression models) in a knowledge-base for management and refinement easily; (2) Inheritance relationship among regression models can be evaluated quantitatively; (3) A family of regression models is managed by a rule chain and an inheritance graph of regression models; (4) Meta reasoning is cooperatively used with quantitative evaluation in refinement for acquiring the best regression model; (5) A regression model that should be used can be selected from a family of regression models. And the discrimination models can be generated dynamically to select the regression model that should be used when a database is divided into several clusters.

On the other hand, by means of HML, concept clusters, which are discovered from a database by DBI, can be represented by the Multi-Layer Logic formulae with hierarchical models in a knowledge-base, and can be easily managed/refined [19, 27]. HML is based on the model representation of Multi-Layer Logic with the hierarchical structure [11]. A key feature of HML is the quantitative evaluation for selecting the best representation of the Multi-Layer Logic formula by using cooperatively a criterion based on information theory (entropy) and domain knowledge. Main functions of HML are (1) Hierarchical modeling for concept clusters discovered from databases. That is, concept clusters discovered from databases are added to a knowledge-base as *classification knowledge with hierarchical models*; (2) Automatic selection of quantifiers in the prefix of the Multi-Layer Logic formula that is used for representing the *classification knowledge*; (3) Automatic selection and refinement of hierarchical models. That is, the best hierarchical model is selected by evaluating the information of Multi-Layer Logic when more hierarchical models were generated along with data change (e.g., add, delete or update data) in databases; (4) Domain knowledge can be cooperatively used with quantitative evaluation in refinement for acquiring the more refined hierarchical model; (5) More hierarchical models generated along with data change in databases can be managed by using the set chains of hierarchical models and an inheritance graph of hierarchical models. These set chains and the inheritance graph are managed by a meta knowledge level.

4   Meta Control Levels

Our system is not merely a collection of the KDD agents stated above and all the rest that will be developed if necessary. For the KDD agents would not work at all unless those agents were linked to one another by a suitable graph of interconnections. As a result of linking the graph, a discovery process is organized dynamically. In other words, we need to use meta control levels, as shown in

Fig.1, for solving some meta-level problems and controlling the meta or object level. The main roles of a meta control level are to generate dynamically the KDD agents, allocating resources, adaptive self-configuration of steps in a discovery process, managing interaction/communication among agents in use, synthesizing part-results of discovery and so on. Furthermore, the meta-level is controlled by a meta-meta-level which is used for planning and organizing dynamically the discovery processes and controlling this process as the coordinator.

4.1 Planning of the Discovery Processes

Planning for organizing dynamically the discovery processes is a key component to increase both autonomy and versatility of our system. Typically, a discovery process is the one in which there are more discovery steps performed in succession by using the KDD agents as stated in Section 2.1 in a distributed cooperative mode. The KDD agents can be represented by a graph of discovery goals/subgoals, and a plan describes a way to arrive at a goal state from a given initial state. Unlike classical planning methods, there is not the sharp distinction of planning and execution phases in our system.

Since the discovery process is basically a multi-step process, and the KDD agents have been divided into three groups based on three learning phases, the planning can be done in a multi-step mode (see Fig.6). For example, in the pre-processing phase, we can first plan how to decompose a database into several information sources by using cooperatively some KDD agents. And then based on the result of the sub-plan, we do next sub-plan, that is, how to allocate system resources to the decomposed local information sources, and what kinds of the KDD agents are used for searching hypotheses from the sources and so on. On the other hand, in many cases, agents' plan may be either conflicting or ambiguous because of incompatible states, incompatible orders of activities, or incompatible use of resources. Therefore, we need to use a kind of probabilistic planning and to solve conflicts by a particular agent (coordinator) or through negotiation. Furthermore, since the discovery processes that are organized are essentially a *repetitive* process as shown in Fig.2, this implies that revising a plan and re-planning are necessary [5].

4.2 Managing the KDD Agents

Managing the KDD agents (see Fig.7) includes to generate dynamically the KDD agents in a or more workstations according to the result of planning and orga- nizing a discovery process, and manage interaction and communication among agents.

There are two main jobs for the management. The first job is the decompo- sition and allocation of discovery task. We use a method called *Partial Global Planning* (PGP) developed by Durfee and Lesser for this purpose [2]. PGP is designed to have a flexible approach to coordination that does not assume any particular distribution of subproblems. Nodes coordinate in response to current situation, each node can represent and reason about the actions and interactions

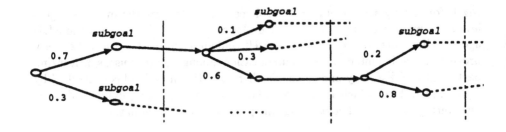

Fig. 6. Planning and organization of the discovery processes

of groups of nodes and how they effect local activities. These representations specify how different parts of the network plan to achieve more global goals. A partial global plan is a general structure for representing coordinated activities in terms of goals, actions, interactions and relationships. The PGP maintains a solution-activity map which represents what the nodes are doing, including the major plan steps the nodes are concurrently taking, their costs and expected results.

The second job is to allocate resources for the KDD agents. Allocating resources to the KDD agents is basically a scheduling task that synchronizes activities to avoid and resolve conflicts. The schedule is built in a cooperative fashion through local computation and communication. We will use a scheduling algorithm, called *self-coordinated local scheduling* designed by Zhang [17], in our system.

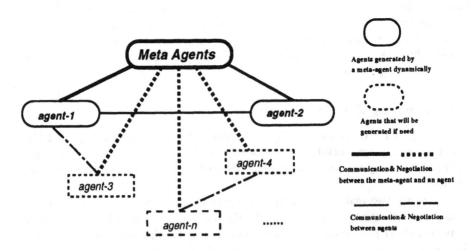

Fig. 7. Managing the KDD agents

5 Intelligent User Interface

An interface between users and the organized society of autonomous knowledge discovery agents is needed for combining autonomous discovery and interactive discovery.

Currently, the GLS system mainly involves autonomous discovery that considers the formal value of information (i.e., the intrinsic value). However, it is necessary to consider the semantic value of information when we would like to construct *laws of science* from *laws of nature*, *new theory* from the *discovered knowledge* [10, 30]. What is called the *semantic value* of information is to consider the intention of the user and/or use a large amount of the background knowledge in the discovery processes. For this, we need to develop both a large-scale background knowledge-base and an intelligent user interface for our system.

6 Concluding Remarks

We presented a methodology for increasing both *autonomy* and *versatility* of a discovery system, and the framework of our GLS discovery system based on this methodology. In comparison, GLS is mostly similar to INLEN in related systems [7]. In INLEN, a database, a knowledge-base and several existing methods of machine learning are integrated as several operators. These operators can generate diverse kinds of knowledge about the properties and regularities existing in the data. INLEN was implemented as a toolkit like GLS. However, GLS can organize dynamically the discovery processes performed in either the centralized or distributed cooperative mode. Moreover, the refinement for knowledge is one of important capabilities of GLS that was not developed in INLEN.

Since the GLS discovery system to be finished by us is very large and complex, however, we have only finished several parts of the system and have undertaken to extend it for creating a more integrated, organized society of autonomous knowledge discovery agents. That is, the work that we are doing takes but one step toward a multi-strategy and cooperative discovery system.

References

1. Chow, G.C. 1960. Tests of Equality Between Sets of Coefficients in Two Linear Regressions. *Econometrica*, 28(3).
2. Durfee,E.H. and Lesser,V.R. 1989. *Negotiating Task Decomposition and Allocation using Partial Global Planning*. Distributed Artificial Intelligence Vol.2.
3. Fayyad,U.M., Piatetsky-Shapiro,G et al (eds.) 1996. *Advances in Knowledge Discovery and Data Mining*. AAAI/MIT Press.
4. Langley, P. & Zytkow, J.M. 1989. Data-Driven Approaches to Empirical Discovery. *Artificial Intelligence*, 40(1-3):283-312.
5. Liu, C. and Conradi, R. 1993. Automatic Replanning of Task Networks for Process Evolution in EPOS. Proc. the 4th European Software Engineering Conference (ESEC'93), LNCS 717, Springer Verlag, pp.437-450.
6. Matheus, C.J., Chan, P.K. & Piatetsky-Shapiro, G. 1993. Systems for Knowledge Discovery in Databases. *IEEE Trans. Knowl. Data Eng.*, 5(6):904-913.
7. Michalski, R.S. et al. 1992. Mining for Knowledge in Databases: The INLEN Architecture, Initial Implementation and First Results. *J. of Intell. Infor. Sys.*, KAP, 1(1):85-113.

8. Minsky,M. 1986 *The Society of Mind*, Simon and Schuster, New York.
9. T.M. Mitchell. Generalization as Search. *Artificial Intelligence*, Vol.18 (1982) 203-226.
10. Ohsuga, S. 1970. On the Value of Information and Decision Making. *Information Processing in Japan*, Vol.10, pp.97-108.
11. Ohsuga, S. & Yamauchi, H. 1985. Multi-Layer Logic - A Predicate Logic Including Data Structure as Knowledge Representation Language. *New Generation Computing*, 3(4):403-439.
12. Ohsuga, S. 1990. Framework of Knowledge Based Systems. *Knowl. Based Sys.*, 3(4):204-214.
13. Ohsuga, S. 1995. A Way of Designing Knowledge Based Systems. *Knowledge Based Systems*, 8(4):211-222.
14. Ohsuga, S. Symbol Processing by Non-Symbol Processor. *Proc. 4th Pacific Rim Int. Conf. on Artificial Intelligence (PRICAI'96)* (1996).
15. Piatetsky-Shapiro, G. & Frawley, W.J. (eds.). 1991. *Knowledge Discovery in Databases*. AAAI/MIT Press.
16. Simon, H.A. & Ando, A. 1961. Aggregation of Variables in Dynamic Systems. *Econometrica*, 29:111-138.
17. Zhang,X. 1996. Co-scheduling Parallel Workloads across Networks of Workstations, invited talk at Yamaguchi Univ. Japan, June 1996.
18. Zhong, N. & Ohsuga, S. 1992. GLS - A Methodology for Discovering Knowledge from Databases. *Proc. 13th Int. CODATA Conf. entitled "New Data Challenges in Our Information Age"*, A20-A30.
19. Zhong, N. & Ohsuga, S. 1993. HML - An Approach for Managing/Refining Knowledge Discovered from Databases. *Proc. 5th IEEE Int. Conf. on Tools with Artif. Intell. (TAI'93)*, 418-426.
20. Zhong, N. & Ohsuga, S. 1994a. Discovering Concept Clusters by Decomposing Databases. *Data & Knowl. Eng.*, Elsevier Science Publishers, 12(2):223-244.
21. Zhong, N. & Ohsuga, S. 1994b. The GLS Discovery System: Its Goal, Architecture and Current Results. *Proc. 8th Inter. Symp. on Methodologies for Intell. Sys. (ISMIS'94)*. LNAI 869, Springer, 233-244.
22. Zhong, N. & Ohsuga, S. 1994c. IIBR - A System for Managing/Refining Structural Characteristics Discovered from Databases. *Proc. 6th IEEE Int. Conf. on Tools with Artif. Intell. (TAI'94)*, 468-475.
23. Zhong, N. & Ohsuga, S. 1995a. KOSI - An Integrated System for Discovering Functional Relations from Databases. *J. of Intell. Infor. Sys.*, KAP, 5(1):20-50.
24. Zhong,N. and Ohsuga,S. 1995b. "Toward A Multi-Strategy and Cooperative Discovery System", *Proc First Inter. Conf. on Knowledge Discovery and Data Mining (KDD-95)*, AAAI Press, 337-342.
25. Zhong,N. and Ohsuga,S. 1996a. "System for Managing and Refining Structural Characteristics Discovered from Databases", *Knowledge Based Systems*, Elsevier Science Publishers, 9(4):267-279.
26. Zhong,N. and Ohsuga,S. 1996b. "A Multi-Step Process for Discovering, Managing and Refining Strong Functional Relations Hidden in Databases", *Proc. 9th Inter. Symp. on Methodologies for Intell. Sys. (ISMIS'96)*. LNAI 1079, Springer, 501-510.
27. Zhong,N. and Ohsuga,S. 1996c. "A Hierarchical Model Learning Approach for Refining and Managing Concept Clusters Discovered from Databases", *Data & Knowl. Eng.*, Elsevier Science Publishers, 20(2): 227-252.
28. Zhong,N. and Ohsuga,S. 1996d. "Using Generalizations Distribution Tables as a Hypothesis Search Space for Generalization", *Proc. 4th Int. W. on Rough Sets, Fuzzy Sets, and Machine Discovery (RSFD'96)* (in press).
29. Zhong,N. and Ohsuga,S. 1996e. "Representing Generalizations Distribution Tables by Connectionist Networks for Evolutionary Rule Discovery", *Proc. 1996 Asian Fuzzy Systems Symposium* edited in the invited session on *Rough Sets and Data Mining* (in press).
30. Zytkow, J.M. 1993. Introduction: Cognitive Autonomy in Machine Discovery. *Machine Learning*, KAP, 12(1-3):7-16.

Cooperative Information Agents and Communication

E. Verharen

Infolab, Tilburg University
POBox 90153, 5000 LE Tilburg, The Netherlands
tel. +31 13 4662767, fax. +31 13 4663069, email: E.M.Verharen@kub.nl

F. Dignum

Faculty of Mathematics & Computer Science
Eindhoven University of Technology
POBox 513, 5600 MB Eindhoven, The Netherlands
tel. +31 40 2473705, fax. +31 40 2463992, email: dignum@win.tue.nl

Abstract

Research in Information Systems has switched its focus from data to communication. Communication between different autonomous ISs requires a certain amount of intelligence of each system. The system should be able to know which queries it can/may handle and also be able to negotiate about the information that it will give. In short, these systems evolve into what is called Cooperative Information Agents (CIA). We describe an architecture for these CIAs in which the relations of a CIA with other CIAs are handled on two levels. The messages themselves are handled by the communication manager. The communication manager can also negotiate a contract with other CIAs. The contracts (which may include communication or transaction protocols) between agents are handled by the contract manager of the CIA responsible for the contract. The messages between the agents are modeled using speech act theory which provides for a rich and flexible communication. In addition, we describe a lexicon in which the conceptual meaning of the terms of communication can be defined. Together, these levels provide an integrated and rich semantics for the communication between CIAs. These can be interorganizational, as in EDI applications, or intraorganizational, as in Workflow Management.

1 Introduction

Traditionally an information system (IS) was considered as one central database and a set of users accessing the database through application programs or directly via an SQL interface. Today, databases are connected to each other and have to be accessible using electronic networks and EDI, while still maintaining their autonomy. Complete integration of the various resources might not be possible for technical or organizational reasons, hence the growing reliance on interaction between systems. This led to the paradigm of cooperative information systems (CIS) introduced in [15]. Furthermore, for systems to be able to cooperate with others they must have an intelligent interface that can cope with all types of requests and eventualities. In this light CISs become active in several ways. A CIS actively maintains its information; it can communicate with other systems and reason about the information that it contains. It might decide to search for information that it needs by inquiring for it from other CISs if it knows that it does not contain the information itself, preferably in ways it negotiates with (and lays down in contracts with) those other systems. It can respond more intelligently to messages explaining why a request does not have an answer, or propose alternatives. And it can negotiate about which requests it is willing to respond to and which requests will have no effect. For this purpose the CIS should contain a task module that plans the tasks the CIS has to fulfill. We refer to an autonomous CIS with tasks and contracts as a *Cooperative Information Agent* (CIA). This term was also used by Klusch in [10] and in the title of this workshop.

In our view the CIA approach has consequences for what is called database semantics and knowledge representation. The traditional focus on logic and algebra to describe the semantics of database or knowledge base content needs to be widened to include the semantics of the communication. Since interfaces often have to reconcile different conflicting viewpoints, and have to be established by different, autonomous, parties, and because they are therefore more difficult to adapt, there is an increasing need for standards, such as reference ontologies. In [10] this problem is tackled by introducing Local Information Models (LIM) for each CIA. These are linguistic based descriptions of the content of the data or knowledge base that is maintained by the CIA. In a way these LIMs are the database interfaces through which the other CIAs can approach the database. In our approach we place much more emphasis on the communication and negotiation between CIAs that takes place in occasional contacts. Because the abilities of the CIA to communicate and negotiate take an important place we claim that the influence of *linguistics* for these systems should go beyond that of a natural language interface.

In this paper, we introduce a (conceptual) architecture for CIAs, that integrates much of our previous work ([4, 5, 22, 25]), that we hope to use as a basis for future implementation. Although it does not play a big role in this paper, the linguistic theory of Functional Grammar [7], including its theory of the Lexicon, plays a crucial role in the organization of the information towards the other CIAs. One could say that the LIMs of our CIAs are based on this theory. We use the theory of speech acts as developed by Searle [19, 20] and Habermas [9] to describe the communication itself.

Because a CIA must be able to reason about its tasks and the information that it possesses we think it is crucial that there is an underlying formal theory in which the agents can be described (including the communication). We have described this theory in a multi-modal logic (see e.g. [6]). In this paper, because of space limitations, we only indicate how the communication part can be formally described in this logic.

The structure of this paper is as follows: in section 2, our framework of a CIA is presented. In section 3 we describe the task manager which is the central unit of the CIA in more detail. In section 4 we describe the function of the Lexicon for communication and the role of Functional Grammar. Section 5 takes a closer look at the communication components of a CIA, i.e. the communication manager and contracts. Because of space limitations we only briefly hint on the formal specification technique. Section 6 compares our perspective with other agent approaches, and section 7 gives some conclusions and areas for further research.

2 CIA Framework

In figure 1 we show the (global) architecture of a CIA as we use it. Although it shares similarities with other agent architectures described in the literature (e.g., the general architecture of a social agent in [26], the TAEMS architecture [27], see also [28]) we feel that both the structure and working of the components, based on our communication-oriented approach, is distinct. In the rest of this section we will give a short overview of the most important features of the components in this architecture.

An *agent* is typically a piece of software that has certain capabilities, actions that it can perform, and certain tasks and responsibilities (delegated to it by a human agent). The actions can be database actions such as updates, or communicative, such as providing some piece of information, or sending a message to another agent. Each agent has an *agenda* containing the actions to be performed by the agent, instantly or at some designated time. We view a CIA as a kind of normative system, in which the coordination of activities is governed by making commitments, described by obligations and authorizations of the communicating agents. In such a system the agenda consists of the *obligations* of the agent. An obligation is the result of a commitment to perform a certain act and authorizations restrain or allow the commitment to and operation of an act (including doing other communicative acts). We assume that the agenda is not fixed but can be manipulated by the agent. The agent can add new obligations to the agenda (typically done on the request of another agent) and can reason about them. Obligations can be the result of the (sub)task of the agent, but can also follow from the contract (see section 5). Items can be removed from the agenda by performing actions or by violating the obligation. In the latter case usually some compensatory action has to be performed.

The principle engine of an agent is its *task manager*. It maintains the tasks an agent (can) perform(s). That is, it plans and schedules the tasks, it maintains the agenda and it handles failures of tasks. The pro-active behavior of a CIA is determined by the tasks the CIA gets at its inception. New tasks can arise from the interactions with other agents. On the lowest level the agent performs *actions* and *transactions*. Actions can be performed by the agent itself without interaction with other agents. Transactions are actions that involve the interaction with other agents. The transactions are stored in a transaction database (not shown in figure 1). The basic building blocks of transactions are the messages which will be described in section 5. The tasks and the task manager are described in the next section.

Transactions are used in a *contract* describing the communication behavior between two agents concerning some business relation and process. The contract also specifies what should happen in case of violation of one of the obligations, or cancellation by one of the agents, possibly leading to other obligations described by another transaction in the contract, and triggering a "contingency" plan, describing what should happen in order to get the subtask fulfilled. Both agents have direct access to the contracts between them. The *contract manager* monitors the contracts that a CIA is involved in and decides what steps to take when a contract is breached. Contracts and contract managers are more fully described in section 5.

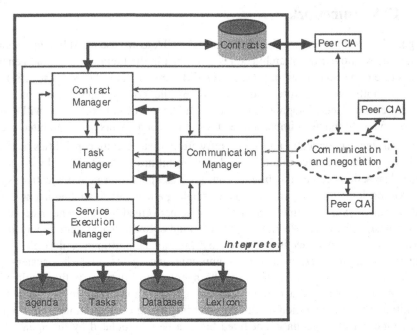

figure 1. CIA Architecture

The *communication manager* handles all external communication of a CIA. We do not assume that the CIAs follow a fixed communication protocol. Therefore we need a rich communication language in which also the intent of each message is clear. This is achieved by basing the messages on the theory of speech acts (Searle [19]). Using speech acts we can model existing protocols that are often used, e.g., the Contract Net Protocol. However, the CIA can also react when other agents do not follow the same protocol. The communication manager draws heavily on the *Lexicon* for the definition of the terms that are used in the communication with other CIAs.

The Lexicon is the system that stores and manages the terminology of a certain domain. It describes the information of the discourse including the message types, and corresponds to the Conceptual Model describing the static and dynamic structure of the Universe of Discourse. The population of this model (possibly including inference rules) is stored in the database. We will say more about the lexicon in section 4.

The last functional component is the *service manager*, that manages the services a CIA can give to other CIAs. I.e., it checks whether the other agents are authorized to request the service and if the service is available. It may also handle simple exceptions within the services (usually when the service can be restarted). It maintains a database with information about services the CIA can provide itself and also services provided by other CIAs. In this way it assists the task manager in the execution of tasks that the CIA cannot perform itself but has to ask from others. We do not describe the service manager in this paper as it is of little importance for the communication of CIAs.

The only component not mentioned so far is the actual database or knowledge base that is maintained by the CIA. We do not make any presupposition about the format of the database. It can be a relational, object oriented, or deductive database, just a flat file or anything else containing information. It is possible to use the theory of Functional Grammar to describe the information as is shown in [24]. It gives a uniform representation for the information, the lexicon and the communication.

3 Tasks and the Task Manager

3.1 Tasks

A *task* is a meaningful unit of work assigned to an agent. Performing the task often involves initiating communication transactions (This can be seen as (1) in fig. 3). However, the task's specification and updates thereof do concern the agent in question only, whereas changes in the possible transactions (involving other agents) can only be made by consent of those agents. For that reason, we make a distinction between task and contract, where the contract corresponds to the agreements between agents and the task draws on this potential for fulfilling an agent's goal.

Tasks are typically described in some task language (e.g. TasL [13]). It allows the specification of tasks and subtasks, alternatives and temporal constraints. Especially when tasks involve the initiation of transactions they are prone to many types of failures, including traditional ones like system and network failures, and possible deadlocks caused by concurrent processes ([12]). More interesting a failure occurs when a transaction (as one subtask) is initiated that does not commit (e.g., request info) ((2) in fig. 3), but also when the transaction does commit first, and the resulting deontic state is violated later (e.g., the company does not deliver), or because of cancellation ('cancel' in fig. 3), whereby the other party undoes an achieved effect. These features of transactions directly influence the task specification. For a CIA, it is important that tasks are not embedded in application code, but made explicit so that the Reasoner can use them in scheduling or rescheduling the work. Rescheduling is necessary when a subtask fails or a planned subtask becomes superfluous.

3.2 The Task Manager

The execution model of the Task Manager will be as follows: when a task is called or a goal is established, the Task Manager devises a plan to fulfill the goal or perform the task. The plan consists of a number of subtasks with precedence relations and alternatives. The subtasks are put on the agenda in the right order. The task manager then tries to perform all subtasks, backtracking when a task fails or an exception occurs. To keep the task specification simple, we give the designer the opportunity to specify a contingency plan separately (see below) (triggered by (4)).

Our execution model enforces a "structured approach" in the task specification. We do not allow for arbitrary abort or commit dependencies between subtasks over the boundaries of the parent tasks. This modularity is enforced to keep the specification transparent and maintainable. In [6] a first attempt in implementing tasks is made by giving preferences to goals. This gives us the opportunity to reason over preference relations on (sub)tasks and how they influence each other.

A notorious problem with contingencies is that later (dependent) subtasks may already have completed, but their result have become obsolete. Whether they have to be retried or not depends on what kinds of results they have produced. Therefore a separate contingency plan can be specified, consisting of a set of *results* (such as supplier list, ticket-reservation) that have an internal object structure (not specified here) and come about by certain subtasks and can become invalidated by other subtasks. When this occurs, a task can be triggered to repair the damage. This task can make use of the fact that all the essential results obtained so far (and not invalidated) are explicit. E.g., if a hotel-reservation is dependent on an airline-reservation, and the flight is canceled; the contingency plan can try to repair the damage by trying another airline. Only if that fails the hotel-reservation has to be canceled (independently, there can be a sanction on the party canceling, as specified in the contract).

4   Lexicon

In this section we discuss the Lexicon as the place to store (linguistically) specified organization knowledge. It stores and manages the terminology of a certain domain, i.e., it explicitly represents the *mutual* understanding about a concept of all agents involved. This can be used in the initial phase (negotiation) of setting up the contract. It also has a 'private' part that contains the agent's knowledge about the domain.

In [23] a linguistic approach is presented in which the lexical definition as well as the lexical structures are based on linguistic primitives. The Lexicon defines the possible predicate frames describing the domain. That is, structural information, in particular the taxonomic relation, designating subsumption or subtyping, but also semantic sets and pre- and postconditions for dynamic predicates; and conceptual information (predicate schemata, i.e. 'stereotypes', including essential but not necessary characteristics of a concept), specified in Functional Grammar (FG).

Note that lexical definitions should not be considered as exhaustive characterizations of a concept. A definition is made relative to a certain context. Within the context, the definitions must differentiate different concepts, and provide a *basis* for mutual understanding.

Following linguistic theory, the concepts are organized in a taxonomy and around prototypes. The higher levels of this taxonomy form a basic ontology, including primitive concepts like "entity", "event", "state". In the case of complex concepts, such as actions, the lexical entry includes a frame containing the roles of the participants, such as "agent", "recipient". The definition of a concept is in principle simply the (natural language) dictionary entry. However, the definition can be parsed and stored internally in a linguistic representation formalism like FG, which allows formal treatment. Moreover, lexical research has shown that definitions typically make use of a small array of basic structures, such as the "isa", "partof" relation and "purpose". This allows for even more formalization and hence computational processing, while the definition can still be expressed in natural language.

Following are a few examples of lexicon definitions. The italicized noun phrase indicates a taxonomic link to a superconcept:

car: a closed *road vehicle* on more than three wheels driven by a motor engine
model(car): the *name* of a registered car design
registration no(car): a *string* of 6 alphanumeric characters uniquely identifying a car

The following example defines the action **sell** as a transfer action with three semantic roles (ag stands for agent and rec for recipient). The incondition says that the action includes a payment action of the recipient.

```
sell(ag X:human)(P:thing)(rec Y:human)
isa transfer
pre = own(ag X)(P), price(P) = D
post = own(ag Y)(P)
inc = pay(ag Y)(D)(rec X)
```

In circumscribing the terminology for a particular application domain, the knowledge engineer might draw on available terminologies for the generic domain. Such generic terminologies might draw in turn on more general dictionaries. We assume that the CIAs can draw their own lexicon from this hierarchy of lexicons. When more ontologies, ISO standards and domain lexicons become available, it is possible for negotiating CIAs to set up a mutual understanding by making a reference to such a given set of concepts. It could also use a bilingual (certified) Lexicon that translates Dutch business concepts to French, for example. It should be clear to which definitions both CIAs commit themselves .

5   Communication and Contracts

In general we can distinguish four phases of communication. The first phase is the inquiry and negotiation about the terms of the contract. In this phase authorizations can be established on the basis of which some actions can be performed in the following phases.

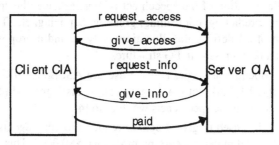

figure 2. Communication in a (prototypical) information gathering procedure

In figure 2 this corresponds to the requesting and sending of access rights. The access rights authorize the client to request some information on some specified conditions. In most of the literature about interactions between autonomous systems this negotiation phase gets most attention. In [18] protocols are given according to which the negotiation should be performed. Many theories from game theory are used to secure an optimal outcome of the negotiations and coalition forming (see e.g. [10]). In this architecture we abstract away from the considerations (utility functions) that determine the behavior of each CIA. Each CIA can use a different criteria to enter a cooperation. We only describe the effects of the messages that the agents send during the negotiation. In this way we can describe exactly which are the obligations and authorizations under the contract resulting from the negotiations.

The second phase consists of the acceptance of the contract, i.e. the authorizations and obligations that follow from it. In the example this is included in the request which implies an acceptance of the conditions of the access rights.

The third phase is the fulfillment of the contract, i.e. following a protocol according to the terms agreed upon in the contract. In the example this corresponds to the actual information request, information delivery and payment sequence. What makes our CIAs different from most other cooperating is that also in this phase the CIAs are autonomous. They can at any moment decide not to honor the contract they agreed upon. Of course this will have repercussions, but a CIA might decide they are less damaging to it than following the contract. So, even though a CIA agreed upon disclosing some information to another agent it might decide later to withhold some of it because the information is too secret.

The last phase is the satisfaction phase, which has no specific messages in the model. This is perhaps because satisfaction is often implicit, and only dissatisfaction leads to communicative acts, such as appeals to warrant.

5.1 Communication Modeling

To describe the semantics of communication processes, we need to specify the meaning of the *information* and *communication* aspects of the messages. The specification of the structure of the *message* is based on the theory of speech acts as developed by Searle ([19]). Illocutionary logic ([20]) is a logical formalization of the theory and is used to formally describe the message structure itself, that is, the types and effects of the messages. The illocution (=illocutionary force) of a speech act indicates what the intention of the speech act is. For instance, the speaker might be asserting, denying, predicting, confirming, greeting, baptizing, etc. The illocution of the message first of all defines the illocutionary type, and a propositional context (both of which can be expressed in FG structures).

The basic illocutionary types that we use are ASSERT, DIRECT, COMMIT and DECLARE ([1, 19, 20]), but many more can be distinguished (cf. [2, 3]). For a motivation of the set of basic speech acts we refer to [4].

The DIRECT is used to give orders or requests to other agents. E.g. "give me all information about all managers earning more than $80.000". This type of message can result in an obligation for the receiving agent to deliver the information. The obligation only arises if there is some basis of authorization for the request (or order). The authorization can be given explicitly beforehand in a negotiation phase or it can follow from a hierarchical relationship between the agents (one is the 'boss' of the other). Important is that the effect of the message depends on the relationship between the agents. The effect of a DIRECT message is at most an obligation. The receiving agent can still autonomously decide to fulfill the obligation or not.

The COMMIT is used to create obligations for oneself. If a request is made by another agent which has no authorization then an agent can honor the request by committing itself to the action. E.g. "I will give all information about all managers earning more than $80.000 and less than $200.000".

The ASSERT is used to inform another agent about a (believe about a) fact, e.g. "the salary of Carl Boss is $90.000". It is, of course, up to the receiving agent to determine whether it believes this fact as well. Again if prior to this message the sending agent has got some authority to base the speech act on then the receiving agent might have to believe the fact.

The last illocution is the DECLARE. This type of message is the only one that can actually create new (abstract) facts. E.g. "I give you access rights to the employee database". The effect of this message is that the receiving agent now has some new rights, of course only if the message is based on some authority. As can be seen from the example, this type of message can be used to explicitly give authorizations to other agents. It is therefore an essential message type for the negotiation phase while it hardly occurs in the other phases of the communication.

We argue that with the above basic illocution types all types of primitive messages that are used in other protocols, like e.g. Contract Net, can be described. We have shown this for some common message types such as OFFER, COUNTEROFFER and ACCEPT in [14].

It is a characteristic of messages that they seldom stand on their own. For example, a request is typically followed by an acknowledgment, commitment or refuse message. Therefore messages can be organized in transactions. This is done on basis of the effect of one message and the preconditions of the next message. In this way protocols can be build for sequences of messages that appear often. However, the communication is not limited to protocols that are predefined.

5.2 Dynamic Deontic Logic

Because the messages have effects for other agents and the agents must be able to reason about these effects it is very important that the messages and their effects are formally described. For the semantics of communication models, we have made use of Dynamic Deontic Logic ([11, 25]). The fundamental reason for the use of deontic concepts in communication modeling is that coordination of behavior always requires some form of mutual commitment. If an agent does not execute an action it has committed itself to, this causes a violation of the commitment. Because the action should be executed in the future, it cannot be guaranteed, so the interpretation "it will happen in all future courses of events" is too strong, but the interpretation "it will happen in some course of events" is too weak. Interpreting "α is obligatory" as: "not doing α violates a commitment" we get a more precise meaning of what it is that something is on an agent's agenda. Violations do not cause logical inconsistency, but can be the trigger for sanctions or repair actions.

The Deontic Dynamic Logic is combined with illocutionary logic to obtain a full logical framework in which the communicative behavior of a CIA can be specified. At this place we only give a brief description of the different types of messages and their effects in this logic. For a full description of the formal semantic models and language we refer to [4, 5, 25].

The main component of the following formulas is every time of the form $[\alpha]\varphi$, which means that after the performance of the action α the formula φ holds.

The COMMIT is described with the following formula:

$$[\text{COMMIT}(i,k,\alpha)][\text{DECL}(k,P_{ik}(\alpha(i)))]O_{ik}\alpha$$

which means that after agent "i" commits itself towards agent "k" to perform "α" and agent "k" declared that agent "i" is permitted to perform "α" then agent "i" has the obligation towards "k" to actually perform "α".

The effect of a DIRECT depends on the authorization of the speaker:

$$\text{auth}(i,\text{DIR}(i,k,\alpha)) \rightarrow [\text{DIR}(i,k,\alpha)]O_{ki}\alpha$$

which means that if agent "i" is authorized then after it orders agent "k" to perform "α" agent "k" has the obligation towards "I" to perform "α".

$$[\text{DIR}(i,k,\alpha)]K_k \text{ INT}_i\alpha(k)$$

If agent "i" is not authorized the only effect of the order is that agent "k" knows that agent "i" intents him to perform "α".

The effect of a DECLARE also depends on the authorization of the speaker:

$$\text{auth}(i,\text{DECL}(i,f)) \rightarrow [\text{DECL}(i,f)]f$$

If agent "i" is authorized then the declaration of the fact "f" actually creates that fact.

$$\varphi \rightarrow [\text{DECL}(i,f)]\text{Pref}_i(f \mid \varphi)$$

If agent "i" is not authorized the effect of the declaration of fact "f" under the circumstances φ is only that agent "i" prefers the fact "f" to hold in the circumstances that φ hold.

Finally the effects of the ASSERT are described as follows in logic:

$$[\text{ASS}(i,k,f)]K_k B_i f$$

If agent "i" asserts the fact "f" to agent "k" then afterwards agent "k" knows that agent "i' believes fact "f".

$$\text{auth}(i,\text{ASS}(i,k,f)) \rightarrow [\text{ASS}(i,k,f)]B_k f$$

If agent "i" asserts the fact "f" to agent "k" with authorization then afterwards agent "k" also believes fact "f".

With the above formulas we can infer the exact effects of each message in a protocol. Both in the case when a certain message is expected (and thus usually

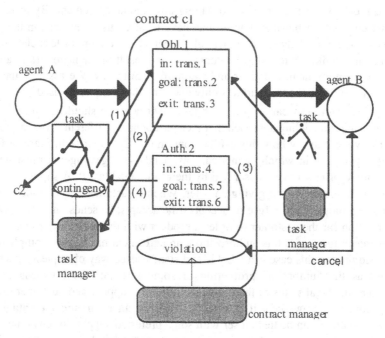

figure 3. Contracts and Tasks

authorized) as well as when it is unexpected. It is also possible to calculate the precise effects of the complete communication protocol that is used. This makes it easier to react to breakdowns in the communication.

5.3 Contracts

The agreements about the interactions between the CIAs are described in the contracts. In figure 3 we give an overview of the relation between the contract and the tasks of the CIAs involved in the contract.

In our framework, contracts conceptually specify obligations between different parties about services provided to each other. If a particular service is not being fulfilled, it is possible to reason over this violation and take a remedial action without forcing the whole task to abort ((3) in fig. 3). A contract describes the authorized communication behavior among providers and receivers of services. If the provider does not adhere to the obligation, in the case of a CIA, it is the job of the Contract Manager to impose the violation policies. It would complicate the task specifications and lower the reusability if this communication is included in the task. As stated before the Task Manager should only be responsible for ensuring that a task is brought to its goal, not how violation of commitments are dealt with. In this way, the process is more flexibly responsive to failures.

From a technical point of view, a contract is nothing but a protocol binding different parties to their commitments by explicitly specifying the type of services agreed upon, the obligations and the failure recovery methods. From an organizational point of view, a contract between interoperable systems involving different organizations also has the purpose of laying down some agreement. By grounding it in other contracts or business law, it may have legal status. Contracts, in the general sense of agreements between commercial partners, can be more or less elaborate. For instance, in Goldkuhl's model [8] a contract is the result of the negotiation, and boils down to a commitment to deliver and a commitment to pay. We assume that such a contract is set up by the two partners only once and then frequently used.

Since contracts can be more or less elaborate, we should require from the communication modeling approach that it can account for different levels of contracts. We briefly want to say how this can be done in our CIA approach. Starting from an empty cyberspace in which agents can just send messages, agents must have the possibility to offer services (described by their individual tasks). A supplier agent can then provide the service of giving an offer. When a customer agent requests for this service, the supplier can refuse or accept. If he accepts, he sends an offer, that is, an authorization for the customer to order a product with the obligation to pay for it. If the customer agent uses this authorization, an agreement has been accomplished. All that is required in this case is a reliable and standardized way of requesting a service, as well as the "umbrella" protection of some international business law that guarantees the legal status of the obligations of both supplier and customer described in the contract. Nowadays it is often considered an economic advantage when business relations can be tied closer with some preferred supplier or customer. In that case, the two parties want more agreements beforehand, for example about a guaranteed delivery time. Such a contract has to be set up. This can be supported by another service of the agent that offers contracts (that can be provided by the organization) rather than specific products. If the customer accepts the offer, a mutually agreed contract is accomplished.

6   Comparison with Other Agent Frameworks

Above we introduced an agent-oriented framework for CIAs. Agent theories and architectures have gained much interest lately, both from the software engineering and AI discipline. Although there is no consensus in the AI community about precisely which combination of information attitudes (like knowledge and belief) and pro-attitudes (like desire, intention, commitment, choice) are best suited to characterize agents, a number of approaches have gained much support.

Perhaps the best known agent theory is Rao and Georgeff's BDI framework ([16]). They developed a logical framework on three primitive modalities: Belief, Desires and Intention. And although in other work ([17]) they consider the potential for adding (social) plans to their formalism, the BDI framework considers agents in isolation; it ignores the communicative aspects that are central in our approach.

Another influential approach is the one taken by Shoham ([21]) in which he uses the mentalistic notions knowledge, belief, intention, and obligation to characterize an agent. He also describes a new agent-oriented programming paradigm based on this notion of agents. The CIA framework takes a similar stance to agent characterization in which obligations play a central role. In [22] we described how we can use this paradigm to experiment with an implementation of the CIA framework.

The architecture that probably resembles ours most closely is the one used in the ADEPT system ([14]). They also specify services and contracts. However, the communication protocols that the agents can use are more limited than ours. Also they do not have a specific component dealing with ontologies. An agent must keep so-called acquaintance models for all agents that it communicates with to determine the terminology that it can use.

In [10], Klusch describes an architecture of CIAs that do have a specific component that deals with common ontologies etc. He specifies a Local Information Model for each agent through which other agents can see the information that the agent contains. The CIA's defined there, however, lack an explicit communication component. The communication protocols are fixed. They do give more explicit details about the ways optimal contracts (coalitions) can be formed. However, once a contract is established the CIA's cannot violate the contract anymore, thus loosing some of their autonomy.

7 Concluding Remarks

In this paper, we have described an architecture for Cooperative Information Agents. Contracts were presented as a way of modularizing the normative specifications. Both the negotiation phase to establish the contract as well as the contract itself can be modeled using our formalism. Contracts are specified by using interoperable transactions, together with deontic constraints and rules for appropriate action when violated. The use of a rich communication language makes it possible to specify very flexible interactions between agents. By using contracts, which establish obligations and authorizations between agents it is possible to minimize the communication that is needed in standard situations.

In the lexicon we can describe the ontology used by the agent. Although we did not describe it in this paper, the agreement of the agents about the meaning of the terms that are used in the communication is of prime importance. This can be supported by using standard lexicons for general terms and related domain lexicons for specific domain knowledge.

We have sorted out the complex concept of 'compensation' into two more focused notions: compensation of the other party, as specified in the contract, and compensation, or contingency handling, of the task. For contingency handling, we propose a separate specification part that monitors the results obtained and invalidated so far. Although exception handling is a complex issue and will remain so, the least we can do is try to manage the complexity. This is the most important but modest goal of the task/contract distinction. We also consider it an advantage that task management can be turned into a local issue, rather than a concern of the (global) multidatabase. In this way the global control is kept to a minimum, which makes the specification and implementation more flexible.

Our main short-term goal is to build a prototype implementation of CIAs based on the architecture that we sketched in this paper and test our ideas in practice. We are currently working on an implementation using Java as implementation platform.

8 References

1. Austin J.L., *How to do things with words*, Clarendon Press, Oxford, 1962.

2. Balmer T. and W. Brennenstuhl *Speech Act Classification: A Study in the Lexical Analysis of English Speech Activity Verbs*, Springer-Verlag, Berlin, 1981.

3. Chang M.K. and C.C. Woo, "A Speech Act Based Negotiation Protocol: Design, Implementation and Test Use", *ACM Transactions on Information Systems (TOIS)*, vol.12, no.4, pp. 360-382, 1994.

4. Dignum F. and H. Weigand, "Communication and Deontic Logic", *Information Systems, Correctness and Reusability*, R. Wieringa and R. Feenstra (eds.), World Scientific, Singapore, pp. 242-260, 1995.

5. Dignum F. and H. Weigand, "Modeling Communication between Cooperative Systems", *Proc. of CAISE'95*, J. Iivari et. al. (eds.) (LNCS-932), Springer-Verlag, Berlin, pp. 140-153, 1995.

6. Dignum F. and B. van Linder, "Modeling Rational Agents in a Dynamic Environment: Putting Humpty Dumpty Together Again", *Proc. of the 2nd workshop of the ModelAge Project*, J.L. Fiadeiro and P.-Y. Schobbens (eds.), Sesimbra, Portugal, pp. 81-92, 1996.

7. Dik S.C., *Functional Grammar*, North-Holland, Amsterdam, 1978.

8. Goldkuhl G., "Information as Action and Communication", *The Infological Equation, Essays in honor of B. Langefors*, B. Dahlbohm (ed.), Gothenburg Studies in Information Systems, Gothenburg Univ., 1995.

9. Habermas J., *The Theory of Communicative Action: Reason and the Rationalization of Society, Volume One*, Beacon Press, Boston, 1984.

10. Klusch M. and Shehory O., "Coalition Formation Among Rational Information Agents", W. vd Velde and J. Perram (eds), Proc. MAAMAW-96, LNAI-1038, Springer-Verlag, p. 204-217, 1996.

11. Meyer J.-J.Ch., "A different approach to deontic logic: deontic logic viewed as a variant of dynamic logic", *Notre Dame Journal of Formal Logic* 29(1), pp. 109-136, 1988.

12. Ngu A., R.A. Meersman and H. Weigand, "Specification and verification of communication for interoperable transactions", *Int.l. Journal of Intelligent and Cooperative Information Systems* 3(1), pp.47-65, 1994.

13. Nodine M.H., N. Nakos and S. Zdonik, "Specifying Flexible Tasks in a Multidatabase", *ACM SIGOIS Bulletin* 16 (1), p. 13-17, 1994.

14. Norman T., Jennings N., Faratin P. and Mamdani E., "Designing and Implementing a Multi-Agent Architecture for business process management" J. Mueller, M. Wooldridge and N. Jennings (eds.) Intelligent Agents III - Proceedings ATAL-96, p.149-162, 1996.

15. Papazoglou M. et.al. "An organizational framework for intelligent cooperative IS", IJICIS-1(1), 1992.

16. Rao A.S. and M.P. Georgeff, "Modeling rational agents within a BDI-architecture", *Proc. of Knowledge Representation and Reasoning (KR&R-91)*, R. Fikes and E. Sandewall (eds.), Morgan Kaufmann Publishers, San Mateo, pp. 473-484, 1991.

17. Rao A.S. and M.P. Georgeff, "Social plans: preliminary report", *Proc. of Decentralized AI 3 - MAAMAW-91*, E. Werner and Y. Demazeau (eds.), Elsevier Science Publishers, Amsterdam, 1992.

18. Rosenschein J. and Zlotkin G., "Rules of Encounter", MIT Press, 1994.

19. Searle J.R., *Speech Acts*, Cambridge University Press, 1969.

20. Searle J.R. and D. Vanderveken, *Foundations of illocutionary logic*, Cambridge University Press, 1985.

21. Shoham Y., "Agent-oriented programming", *Artificial Intelligence* 60, pp. 51-92, 1993.

22. Verharen E., H. Weigand, and O. De Troyer, "Agent-oriented information system design", *Working Papers. of ISCORE'94*, R. Wieringa and R. Feenstra, (eds), Vrije Universiteit Report IR-357, Amsterdam, pp. 378-392, 1994.

23. Weigand H., *Linguistically Motivated Principles of Knowledge Based Systems*, Foris, Dordrecht, 1990.

24. Weigand H., "Assessing Functional Grammar for Knowledge Representation", *Data and Knowledge Engineering* 8 (1992), pp. 191-203, 1992.

25. Weigand H., E. Verharen, and F. Dignum, "Integrated Semantics for Information and Communication Systems", *Proc. of IFIP DS-6* , R. Meersman, L. Mark (eds), Stone-Mountain, Georgia, IFIP, 1995.

26. Moulin B. and B. Chaib-draa, "An overview of distributed artificial intelligence", in: *Foundations of distributed artificial intelligence*, G. O'Hare and N. Jennings (eds.), John Wiley and Sons Inc., New York, pp. 3-55, 1996.

27. Decker K. and V. Lesser, "Task environment centerd design of organizations", AAAI Spring Symp. on Computational Organization Design, Stanford, 1994.

28. Special issue on Intelligent Agents, IEEE Expert, december, 1996.

Achieving Efficient Cooperation in a Multi-Agent System: the Twin-Base Modeling

Wen Cao, Cheng-Gang Bian, Gunnar Hartvigsen

Department of Computer Science
Institute of Mathematical and Physical Sciences
University of Tromsø, N-9037 Tromsø, Norway
Email: cao@cs.uit.no, bian@stud.cs.uit.no, gunnar@cs.uit.no

Abstract. The *Virtual Secretary* 2 project (*ViSe2*) focuses on the construction of a multi-agent cooperation system. As a research vehicle, we have chosen to build intelligent agents that perform secretarial tasks for their users either by themselves or via cooperation. An individual *ViSe2* agent has limited knowledge and problem-solving capabilities. To act better for its user, the agent interacts with other peers to solve problems. In this sense, an agent's ability to reason about the other agents' activities and thus find the peer becomes a key issue. In this paper, we propose a *twin-base* (*cooperator-base* ⊎ *task-base*) modeling for efficient cooperation in a small agent group. The *cooperator-base* collects stable information of the others and acts as an auxiliary base to the *task-base*. The *task-base* provides direct mappings between tasks and relevant expert agents that can perform such tasks. A *capability revision* process is proposed for keeping the mapping information consistent. With such *twin-base* modeling, when an agent receives a task that is beyond its capabilities, the agent can directly retrieve the best qualified peer from its *task-base*, and ask the peer to perform the task. To test the validation of the *twin-base* modeling, we have implemented a prototype of *ViSe2* multi-agent cooperation system. The experimental results show that the system achieves the anticipated functionality: an individual agent performs the user's task by either retrieving results from its local knowledge base system, or consulting peer agents to take over the job. More precisely, to verify our intuition that the *twin-base* modeling achieves efficient cooperation, we compare the performance of our model with other cooperation approaches, i.e., the *contract net protocol* [2], the *assisted coordination* approach [4], and the *acquaintance model* approach [14, 7]. Results received so far indicate that our method achieves the most efficient cooperation with high on-line performance.

1 Introduction

As information explodes, no genius can remember everything and solve every problem, instead, a cooperative *team-work* becomes attractive and popular. As such, people's problem-solving capabilities not only rely on their knowledge, experience and hard work, but also depend on their abilities to efficiently seek assistance from relevant experts. This phenomenon in human society has motivated us to study the cooperation manner in the *Virtual Secretary*[1] multi-agent system (*ViSe2*). The *ViSe2* is an intelligent agent that can assist its user in major secretarial work. Each agent has limited knowledge and problem-solving capabilities. When facing a task beyond an agent's capabilities, the agent can consult a peer and ask it to take over the job. In this sense, the agent's ability to reason about the others' activities and find the peer becomes a key issue. The goal of this paper is to figure out a way for agents to attain such abilities in a most efficient manner – to achieve efficient cooperation in a small agent group.

So, the problem is: how to reason about the other agents' activities and select the best set of peers in a decentralized multi-agent system? The most straightforward way is through communication. In the *contract net protocol* [2], when an agent needs help from the others in the group, it broadcasts a *task-announcement* message. The other agents evaluate their resources and submit bids to the *original agent*. The original agent then evaluates these bids and assigns the task to the most suitable one. The *contract net protocol* is appropriate in a decentralized control regime where the agent does not know in advance the other agents' information. With the generality of the broadcast, this approach becomes inefficient in many cases. To eliminate this broadcasting communication, an *assisted coordination* approach [4] is proposed. In this approach, there is a central *manager agent* that monitors the overview picture of the group, any agent wishing to locate peers sends a message to the manager agent and receives the address of the peer agent. Lashkari's collaborative framework [9], Genesereth and Ketchpel's federated system [4] are two examples of this approach. In the collaborative framework, *bulletin board agent* plays the role of the manager agent, while in the federated system, the *facilitator agent* takes the similar role. The *assisted coordination* approach can be applied to a large agent group with multi-managers. In addition, the implementation is simple since only the manager agent contains the necessary code for cooperation [4]. The *assisted coordination* approach eliminates the broadcasting cost, but communication is needed to locate a peer agent. Communication in a distributed system is generally much slow than the computation [12], therefore, to achieve efficient cooperation, it is better to allow each agent to monitor the activities of the others and figure out the peer agents by itself instead of through communication. Wittig and Jennings suggest an *acquaintance model* to capture the meta-level information of cooperative agents [14, 7]. In their agent architecture, there are a *self* model that represents the information of the agent itself, and *acquaintance models* that specify data of other agents sharing similar interests or capabilities. To locate peer agents, the agent evaluates acquaintance's activities and selects the best qualified agents for

---

[1] *Virtual Secretary* is an on-going project at the University of Tromsø, and partly supported by the Research Council of Norway (Grant no. 112577/431) [5]. This project includes two phases: the first phase focuses on user-model-based software agents for information filtering and process migration based on mobile computing network; the second phase concentrates on multi-agent cooperation in a distributed system, which is called *ViSe2* in this paper.

cooperation. This approach decreases the communication overhead, while it increases local computation required to maintain the *acquaintance model* [14]. To decrease such maintenance work and on-line evaluation cost, we propose a *twin-base (cooperator-base ⊎ task-base)* approach for efficient cooperation in a small agent group. The *cooperator-base* collects stable information of the others and acts as an auxiliary base to the *task-base*. The *task-base* provides direct mappings between tasks and relevant expert agents that can perform such tasks. A *capability revision* process is proposed for keeping the mapping information consistent. With such *twin-base* modeling, at run time, when an agent receives a goal that is beyond its capabilities, the agent can directly retrieve the best qualified peer from its *task-base*, and ask the peer to perform the task. To test the validation of the *twin-base* modeling, we have implemented a prototype of *ViSe2* multi-agent cooperation system, and compared the system performance of our model with other cooperation approaches, i.e., the *contract net protocol* [2], the *assisted coordination* approach [4], and the *acquaintance model* approach [14, 7]. Experimental results received so far indicate that the *twin-base* modeling achieves most efficient cooperation with high on-line performance and low maintenance cost.

The remainder of the paper is organized as follows: first we describe the *ViSe2* multi-agent cooperation system and develop a *twin-base* approach for efficient cooperation in a small agent group. Then we present *ViSe2* system architecture to fulfill the *twin-base* cooperation approach. Finally we illustrate the implementation and experimental results to validate the *twin-base* cooperation approach.

2   The ViSe2 Multi-Agent Cooperation System

In a *ViSe2* multi-agent system, there is a small number of agents connected via a reliable network. Each agent is related to one user and provides expert services in some application domains. Agents are organized into a cooperative group for the purpose of knowledge sharing. They are willing to help each other: each one provides some of its capabilities to the others, and benefits the others' services as well. An agent in the group can withdraw or provide new services to the other agents dynamically. Furthermore, an agent could enter or leave the cooperative group dynamically. There is a special agent in the group called *cooperation trader*, which is responsible for agent registering and address trading.

In the cooperative group, when an agent receives a task under its problem-solving capabilities, it invokes a goal-driven search in its local knowledge-base to retrieve the user-wanted information; if the task is beyond the agent's problem-solving capabilities, the agent figures out a peer, and forwards the task to the peer agent for cooperative problem-solving. Generally speaking, in the *ViSe2* multi-agent environment, cooperation is necessary in the following cases [1]:

1. An agent has no idea of how to handle a task. It could ask for assistance from those agents who are experts in the field, or who have experienced the same kind of problem before. Cooperation in this area considers that agents share the problem-solving capabilities and results. In this sense, it falls into *result sharing*.

2. An agent lacks some information to complete a task. It should ask those agents who own the information for help. Cooperation in this area could be called *information sharing*.

3. An agent only has the ability to perform one fraction of a large task. Therefore, several agents have to work together to fulfill the job. Cooperation in this domain is called *task sharing* and agents cooperate with one another to play a joint action.

To sum up, in a user-agent interaction, a user gives a high-level request of *what to do* and leaves the details of *how to do* to the agent. The agent can satisfy the request alone if its local knowledge-base provides enough information, otherwise, the agent should find out the peers and ask them to take over the job. In this sense, the problem of locating peers has become a critical issue in achieving efficient cooperation.

3 Twin-Base Modeling for Efficient Cooperation

A key question for cooperation is: how to efficiently locate the peer in a cooperative group? The *contract net protocol* [2] generalizes a blind inquiry broadcasting and therefore makes the peer locating process quite costly. The *assisted coordination* approach [4] still need much communication to locate peer agents. The *acquaintance model* approach [14, 7] decreases the communication overhead, while it increases the local computation to maintain the *acquaintance models*. With this consideration, we propose a *twin-base* (*cooperator-base* $\uplus$ *task-base*) approach that allows an agent to monitor the activities of other agents, and locate the peer agent directly from its *task-base*. To capture the other agents' information for cooperation yields three questions:

1. What kind of information do agents need for cooperation?
2. How to model this information for efficient cooperation?
3. How to maintain this information in a changing environment?

3.1 Information Contained in the Cooperation

The purpose of cooperation is to allow agents to share knowledge with each other. To satisfy the knowledge sharing, first of all, an agent must figure out a peer agent to consult. Therefore, we let each agent collect and monitor the *capabilities* of the others and use the captured information to locate a peer agent. An agent's capabilities are actually the goals in its knowledge-base with abstract descriptions. Second, in a distributed environment, each agent defines its local information model: data structure and data query. So if an agent wants to ask assistance from a peer agent, it should know in advance the schema information of the peer agent, and thus invokes operations in a meaningful format. The schema information is *meta-data* of *capability*. Finally, we need domain *state* to record auxiliary information for peer locating. It includes *address*, *statistics* and *trust* attributes. The *address* is recorded in the form of *Name.IP_Address.Port*.

The *statistics* contains the number of rules an agent possesses. It is used to indicate the agent's problem-solving power. The *trust* records an agent's preference to peer agents. A peer agent's *trust* value is updated dynamically by user's feedback preference. Both *statistics* and *trust* values help an agent to choose *who is the best peer*. The agent would like to contact those peer agents with high *trust* value and good *statistics* record.

To summarize, our agent modeling focuses on the following domains:

capability deals with an agent's problem-solving abilities. It is used to locate a peer agent in the cooperation.

meta-data describes an agent information schema. It is used to translate the information among different agents.

state contains an agent's *address*, *statistics* and *trust*. It is an auxiliary domain for peer locating.

3.2   Twin-Base: Cooperator-Base ⊎ Task-Base

In a general *acquaintance model* approach, at run time, when an agent receives a goal that is beyond its capabilities, it evaluates the other agents' capabilities and skills with the help of its *acquaintance models*, recognizes those peer agents that have the capabilities to achieve the goal, figures out the most qualified peer, and contacts it for help. In fact, for a particular task, the evaluating and reasoning process will give a relatively *stable* result of *who can help me* over a period of time. Thus, if we let agents do the evaluation and reasoning work before they accept tasks from users, then system response time can be decreased and system on-line performance will be increased. The *twin-base* modeling came from this *pre-evaluation* idea.

The *twin-base* consists of *cooperator-base* and *task-base*. The *task-base* employs the *pre-evaluation* idea. It provides direct mappings between tasks and the relevant expert agents that can carry out the tasks. In the *task-base*, each tuple is related to one task and recorded as follows:

task_distribution(Task_Description, Agent, Dependence).

The *Task-Description* states the goal that the *Agent* can perform. It is enhanced from the *capability* domain. If the goal should be further divided into sub-goals, then domain *Dependence* specifies those sub-goals and their related agents. If more than one agents can achieve the same goal, tuples containing these agents are sorted in the *task-base* based on the agents' priorities evaluated as follows:

Rule 1 Self-solving has the highest priority. If the host agent can carry out the task, then the agent has the highest priority. There are two reasons for us to employ this rule. Firstly, to ask assistance from the others will increase the communication overhead, and thus reduce the system performance. Secondly, for security reasons, the agent should trust itself more than anyone else.

Rule 2 Non-host agents are sorted corresponding to their *state* information. It is better to choose the agents with high *trust* value and good *statistics* record.

The *cooperator-base* collects stable information of the other agents and acts as an auxiliary base to the *task-base*. The *cooperator-base* is built on (1) *state* information (2) *meta-data* of other agents' *capability* discussed in the Sect. 3.1.

The *task-base* plays the main role in an on-line cooperation process. Receiving a task that is beyond its problem-solving capabilities, an agent can compare the received task with those *task-descriptions* in its *task-base*, select the first matched tuple, and consult the retrieved peer agent for help. In this sense, an agent can directly retrieve the best qualified peer with the help of its *task-base*, while leaving those evaluation and reasoning work in the agent's free time.

The *twin-base* modeling is different from other approaches in the sense that it allows agents to perform reasoning work before they accept tasks from their users. As such, the system on-line performance will be increased and the repeated reasoning processes can be avoided. With this respect, we argue that the *twin-base* modeling improves the efficiency of cooperation. In addition, the *twin-base* modeling is easy for maintenance, and thus the local computation time is acceptable.

3.3 Capability Revision Process

The *task-base* provides direct mappings between tasks and the related agents that can perform such tasks. As stated in the Sect. 2, information in the *task-base* is changed frequently: agents' capabilities are dynamically changed; agents enter or leave the cooperative group dynamically. So, even if the *task-base* provides a clear information snapshot of a group at one time, it does not mean that it can provide the consistent mapping information at all times. In order to allow the *task-base* to keep the most updated information, we have developed a *capability revision* process to monitor the information changing. The *capability revision* process is invoked as a result of meta-level information exchange.

Let an agent set $\mathcal{A} = \{A_1, A_2, \ldots, A_n\}$, and a task set $\mathcal{T} = \{T_1, T_2, \ldots, T_m\}$. As stated in the Sect. 3.2, the *task-base* is recorded in the following tuple:

$$\langle \text{Task\_Description, Agent, Dependence} \rangle$$

More precisely, for an agent A_i ($A_i \in \mathcal{A}$) performs a task T_j ($T_j \in \mathcal{T}$), the tuple is shown as follows:

1. $\langle T_j, A_i, \emptyset \rangle$, represents that the agent A_i individually performs the task T_j.
2. $\langle T_j, A_i, \bigcup_{k=1}^{m'} \langle T_{j_k}, A_{j_k} \rangle \rangle$, states that the agent A_i is a coordinator of the joint task T_j, which can be divided into m' subtasks T_{j_k} performed by corresponding agents A_{j_k}.

To maintain the *task-base* most updated, the following *capability revision* processes are defined:

Revision 1. *Detecting an agent A_i leaves the group, then*

1. $\forall\, T_j \in \mathcal{T}$, tuples $\langle T_j, A_i, \emptyset \rangle$ *should be deleted.*

2. $\forall T_j \in \mathcal{T}$, tuples $\langle T_j, A_i, \bigcup_{k=1}^{m'} \langle T_{j_k}, A_{j_k} \rangle \rangle$ should be deleted.

3. $\forall T_j \in \mathcal{T}$ and $\forall A_j \in \mathcal{A}$, if $\exists A_i \in \{A_{j_1}, A_{j_2}, \ldots, A_{j_{m'}}\}$, then tuples $\langle T_j, A_j, \bigcup_{k=1}^{m'} \langle T_{j_k}, A_{j_k} \rangle \rangle$ should be deleted.

Detecting an agent A_i leaves the group, then all tasks performed by this agent are not available any more, and all joint-tasks that their sub-tasks are dependent on the agent are not available as well. It is easy to detect these inconsistent tuples. Any tuples that the second domain matched A_i are inconsistent. In addition, any tuples with third domain containing A_i are inconsistent as well.

Revision 2. *Detecting a task T_j is not available now, then*

1. $\forall A_i \in \mathcal{A}$, tuples $\langle T_j, A_i, \emptyset \rangle$ should be deleted.

2. $\forall A_i \in \mathcal{A}$ and $\forall T_i \in \mathcal{T}$, if $\exists T_j \in \{T_{i_1}, T_{i_2}, \ldots, T_{i_{m'}}\}$, then tuples $\langle T_i, A_i, \bigcup_{k=1}^{m'} \langle T_{i_k}, A_{i_k} \rangle \rangle$ should be deleted.

In like manner, detecting one task T_j is not available, then all tuples including the task should be deleted. Additionally, all tuples containing T_j as a sub-task should also be deleted.

Revision 3. *Detecting a new agent A_i enters into the group with capabilities $\{T_1, T_2, \ldots, T_{m'}\}$, then*

1. Tuples $\{\langle T_j, A_i, \emptyset \rangle \mid j = 1, 2, \ldots, m'\}$ are added into the task-base, where an agent A_i individually performs the task T_j.

If there are m agents ($\{A_1, A_2, \ldots, A_m\}$) that can perform the same task T_j, then a *priority_evaluation* process is invoked to sort these agents based on *statistics* record and *trust* value, and those tuples $\{\langle T_j, A_i, \emptyset \rangle \mid i = 1, 2, \ldots, m\}$ are stored in the *task-base* in the order of their priorities.

Revision 4. *Detecting an existing agent A_i learns new capability T_j, then*

1. a tuple $\langle T_j, A_i, \emptyset \rangle$ is added into task-base, if the task T_j is not a joint action.

2. a tuple $\langle T_j, A_i, \bigcup_{k=1}^{m'} \langle T_{j_k}, A_{j_k} \rangle \rangle$ is added into the task-base, if the task T_j is a joint action.

Obviously, with the *capability revision* process, it is very convenient to manipulate information changing, and the maintenance work is proceeded off-line.

4 System Architecture

Based on the *twin-base* modeling in a small agent group, a *ViSe2* agent is constructed in following functional components (Fig. 1):

User Interface This module offers an interface between a user and a *ViSe2* agent. The user gives a high-level request of *what to do* through the interface.

Communication Interface This module offers an interface among different agents. It consists of a set of message rules and procedures driven by the *Agent Brain* process for sending and receiving messages over the network.

Agent Brain This is the central module of an agent. The *Agent Brain* keeps listening to the communication channel. While an incoming message is detected, a *message evaluation* procedure is proceeded to analyze the type of message and invoke the related operations, e.g., call the *Problem-Solver* module to perform the task, invoke the *Cooperation* module to figure out the peer agent or revise the *task-base*.

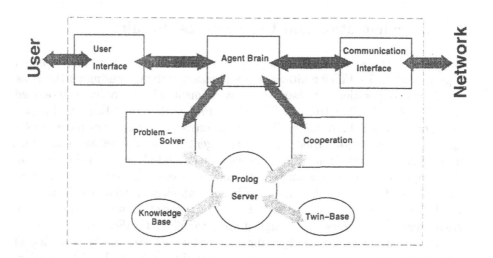

Fig. 1. The ViSe2 Multi-Agent System Architecture.

Problem-Solver Accepting a task definition from the *Agent Brain*, the *Problem-Solver* invokes a goal-driven search in its local knowledge-base to retrieve the information that the user wants or other agents require.

Knowledge-Base An agent is a specialist in some application domains. The *Knowledge-Base* consists of this domain level information.

Cooperation This module is responsible for peer locating with the help of its *Twin-Base*. Additionally, it will revise its *task-base* as a result of meta-level information exchange.

Twin-Base This module consists of *cooperator-base* and *task-base*. It includes all the necessary information for agent cooperation.

Prolog Server It is an inference engine. The *Prolog Server*, together with the *Problem-Solver* and *Knowledge-Base* constitute a local knowledge base system that is responsible for performing tasks. While the *Prolog Server*, together with the *Cooperation* module and *Twin-Base* make up a cooperative system for locating peer agents.

Essentially, the *Agent Brain* detects two kinds of messages in the problem-solving scenarios:

1. task specifications from its user or other agents in the group.
2. change of the meta-level information from the other agents in the group.

Thus, an individual agent works in two states:

1. to perform user's task by either retrieving a result from its local knowledge base system, or consulting the peer agent to take over the job.
2. to revise its cooperation information by invoking *capability revision* process.

5 Implementation and Experimental Results

Based on the *twin-base* modeling and system architecture, we have implemented a prototype of the *ViSe2* multi-agent cooperation system, focusing on the issue of efficient cooperation in a distributed environment. The prototype is developed with *Tcl/Tk* [11], *TclX* [10], *Tix* [3] and *BinProlog* [13] on HP-Unix, and partly based on the work of *IDEAS* [8]. The system consists of two separate parts: *ViSe2* agent(s) and *cooperation trader*. The *ViSe2* agent can be installed and started up in a distributed environment. It can work either stand-alone or via cooperation. The cooperation could be arranged only while the *cooperation trader* is on service. An individual *ViSe2* agent is an expert in some application domains. To test the validation of our prototype, we have built four types of knowledge-base: *album*, *travel*, *wine* and *clothing*, and assigned them to different *ViSe2* agents.

The experimental results show that our system achieves the functionality of what we expected: an individual agent performs the user's task by either retrieving a result from its local knowledge base, or consulting the peer agent to take over the job; in addition, as a result of interaction of meta-level information, agents perform *capability revision* process to maintain the *task-base* consistent. More precisely, to verify our intuition that the *twin-base* modeling achieves efficient cooperation, we compare the system performance of our model with other cooperation approaches discussed in the Sect. 1. The performance is measured by mean response time, which is defined as the interval between a user's request submission and the beginning of the corresponding response from the system [6]. Individual agent's Prolog encoding knowledge is between 300 – 800 lines. The experimental results are illustrated in Fig. 2, five lines, from bottom to top, represent the mean response time of agents' local query, remote query with *twin-base* modeling, remote query simulating *acquaintance model* approach [14, 7], remote query simulating *assisted coordination* approach [4] and remote query simulating *contract net protocol* [2].

The local query achieves the best performance provided that the problem domain is under an agent's capabilities. While an agent receives a task that is beyond its problem-solving capabilities, it consults a remote peer to take over the task. To locate the peer, in the *twin-base* modeling approach, at run time, the agent can directly retrieve the peer agent from its *task-base*. For a remote query

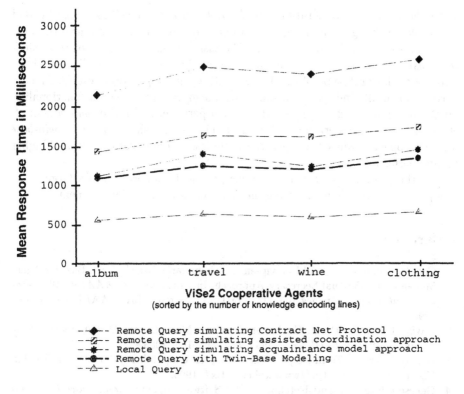

Fig. 2. The Mean Response Time of Cooperative Agents.

simulating *acquaintance model* approach, the agent evaluates the acquaintance's capabilities and selects the best qualified peer to perform the task. In this case, it takes an agent on-line time to *evaluate_who* and *select_best*. Therefore, it takes more time than the *twin-base* modeling does. In a remote query simulating *assisted coordination* approach, during a cooperation process, the agent should first consult the *manager agent* to get the address of a peer agent and then send the request to the peer agent, and asks it to take over the job. This approach is less efficient than *acquaintance model* since it includes communication overhead. The fifth line represents remote query simulating *contract net protocol*. This method generalizes broadcast communication, and therefore is less efficient than other approaches.

Different approaches have unlike advantages in their applications. As we have seen, the *twin-base* modeling achieves most efficient cooperation in the *ViSe2* multi-agent application.

6   Concluding Remarks

In this paper, we have developed a *twin-base* approach for efficient cooperation in a small agent group. The *twin-base* is composed of *cooperator-base* and *task-base*.

With the *twin-base* cooperation model, while an agent receives a goal beyond its problem-solving capabilities, it can query the *task-base* to retrieve the best peer and ask it to take over the task. The *task-base* is updated through *capability revision* process. To test the validation of the *twin-base* modeling, we have implemented a prototype of the *ViSe2* multi-agent cooperation system. The experimental results indicate that our system achieves the expected functionality. Furthermore, we briefly compare the system performance of the *twin-base* modeling with other cooperation approaches. The results show that the *twin-base* modeling benefits efficient cooperation from less communication cost and higher on-line performance.

For the future, some other issues, e.g., efficient cooperation in a large agent group, security problems, learning mechanisms, are under development.

References

1. Cao, W., Bian, C. G., and Hartvigsen, G.: Cooperator-Base [+] Task-Base for Agent Modeling: the Virtual Secretary Approach. In *Proceedings of AAAI-96 Workshop on Agent Modeling*, pages 105–111, Portland, Oregon, USA. AAAI Press, August 1996.
2. Davis, R. and Smith, R. G.: Negotiation as a Metaphor for Distributed Problem Solving. *Artificial Intelligence* 20(1): pages 63–109, 1983.
3. Expert Interface Technologies: Tix – Programming Library for the Tk Toolkit, Version 4.0. URL: http://www.xpi.com/tix/. 1995.
4. Genesereth, M. R. and Ketchpel, S. P.: Software Agents. *Communication of the ACM* 37(7): pages 48–53, 1994.
5. Hartvigsen, G., Johansen, S., Helme, A., Widding, R. A., Bellika, G., Cao, W.: The Virtual Secretary Architecture for Secure Software Agents. In *Proceedings of the First International Conference on the practical Application of Intelligent Agents and Multi-Agent Technology (PAAM'96)*, pages 843–851, London, U.K. The Practical Application Company Ltd, April 1996.
6. Jain, R.: The Art of Computer Systems Performance Analysis. John Wiley and Sons, 1991.
7. Jennings, N.: Cooperation in Industrial Multi-agent Systems. World Scientific, 1994.
8. Klusch, M., Scheew, O. and Grossmann, B.: Interactive Development Environment for Agent System. URL: ftp://ftp.informatik.uni-kiel.de/pub/kiel/ideas, Christian-Albrechts University of Kiel, Germany, 1995.
9. Lashkari, Y., Metral, M. and Maes, P.: Collaborative Interface Agents. In *Proceedings of the Twelfth National Conference on Artificial Intelligence*. AAAI Press, 1994.
10. Lehenbauer, K. and Diekhans, M.: Extended Tcl (TclX), Version 7.4a. URL: ftp://ftp.cs.berkeley.edu:/ucb/tcl/. NeoSoft Company, 1995.
11. Ousterhout, J.: The Tcl and Tk Toolkit, Tcl Version 7.4, Tk Version 4.0. URL: http://www.sunlabs.com/research/tcl, The University of California at Berkeley, 1995.
12. Smith, R.G. and Davis, R.: Frameworks for Cooperation in Distributed Problem Solving. *IEEE Transaction on Systems, Man and Cybernetics* 11(1): pages 61–70, 1981.

13. Tarau, P.: BinProlog 4.00 Software and BinProlog 4.00 User Guide. URL: ftp://clement.info.umoncton.ca/pub/BinProlog, 1995.
14. Wittig, T.: ARCHON – an architecture for multi-agent systems. Ellis Horwood, 1992.

Approaching Interoperability for Heterogenous Multiagent Systems Using High Order Agencies*

Wilfred C. Jamison

Department of Computer and Information Science
Syracuse University, Syracuse, NY 13244
wcjamiso@cat.syr.edu

Abstract. Research activities in multiagent systems (MAS) continue to gain momentum. Implemented systems are also becoming more visible. The problem, however, is that these systems can operate only in their own environment and utilize their own knowledge bases. A framework design is developed whereby heterogenous multiagent systems can interoperate through an environment that enables their respective agents to engage in a collaborative problem solving, consult each other and share knowledge bases. This setup could potentially create a very powerful agency system that can handle more difficult problems and deliver better solutions at a shorter time. The framework is designed to work with new and existing MAS. Our high order agency approach also does not introduce unreasonable complexities in developing new MAS. This paper presents a high-level description of the framework design.

KEYWORDS: Multiagent system, Agent Collaboration, Interoperability

---

* A joint project with IBM Intelligent Agent Center of Competence. Visit http://www.raleigh.ibm.com/iag/iaghome.html

1 Introduction

We are interested in a system of *heterogenous agents*[2] that are involved in a collaborative work. Our framework aims at integrating a number of MAS without introducing drastic changes in their design and implementation.

While most frameworks are agent-centric, the ACACIA[3] framework is composed of *high order agencies*. The notion of high order agency encapsulates the rendering of agency functions by a conglomerate of mostly diverse agents. Thus, a basic organizational structure and a unified set of interfaces are formed. We describe the ACACIA framework and illustrate our concept of agency collaboration. Although we maintain a macro level discussion, we also include some of the highlights in our runtime design.

2 Motivation

While agents and agent systems are being developed by individual groups, our motivation is to create an infrastructure for inter-agent collaboration among these groups. Different agent designs are based on different principles where each has its strong points. With cross-agent interactions, a bigger agency is created from which we expect to gain the benefits derived from the synergy of these strong points. Furthermore, knowledge sharing produces more "intelligent" agents by enabling them to absorb and learn from the various knowledge sources. Indeed, this "learning by sharing" maximizes the worth of these sources. The diversity and breadth of the resultant knowledge base also gives us higher confidence in our solutions. From a practical point of view, this greatly reduces redundant knowledge engineering, expands the total workforce and increases the degree of parallelism. As a result, we expect for improvements in performance despite all the communications overhead incurred. Another point is that heterogeneity in general offers more flexibilities to the agent developers. Equally important is the support that it contributes to the modern user's perception and expectation of open computing.

---

[2] Agents developed from different frameworks and possibly for different platforms.

[3] Agency Collaboration Architecture for Cooperating Intelligent Agents

3 The ACACIA Framework

A well-known approach to this type of interoperability problem is to introduce a common layer underneath the heterogenous systems. Protocols for low level communication are established and runtime system supports are implemented. While this has been adapted in many systems[4], we approach the problem instead by providing an environment *above* the MAS. The first approach introduces more complexities when building a new MAS. More sadly, existing MAS are not benifited unless they are re-engineered and recoded. The ACACIA framework caters to both new and existing MAS without introducing unreasonable complexities on the part of the agent builders.

3.1 The Agency Structure

The most common human notion of an *agency* involves the organized representation of an actor by an agent in pursuit of its needed services. From another viewpoint, an agency is an agent management structure achieved by pooling expert agents together as a group. Yet another is the marketing perspective where expertise are hired, rendered and compensated.

A software agent is the most basic form of agency and which is, in fact, the subject of most research. In our case, we use the notions mentioned above as our metaphor for structuring and organizing agents. By incorporating management routines, a group of agents form a high order agency which can be treated as a single entity with a formal set of services gathered from each member agent.

An ACACIA agency has two subgroups: the *management* group and the *workgroup*. The former is responsible for all external and internal agency affairs. It is composed of an *agency manager* who represents the agency in all of its planning activities, a *backup manager* who supports the agency manager and takes over when necessary, a *secretary* who is responsible for maintaining information for the agency, and an *adaptor* that handles all communications between the the two subgroups. Meanwhile, the latter group is comprised of expert agents whose sole task is to perform the actual problem solving. The union of their exper-

---

[4] CORBA is an example.

tise reflects the agency's overall capabilities. These are registered in a repository maintained by the secretary called the *agency directory*.

Fig. 1 is a logical picture of the architecture. The arrows depict the lines of communications. There are two types of agencies: the ACACIA defined *system agencies* and a number of *transient agencies*[5] that dynamically join and leave the system at runtime. A minimal ACACIA system is comprised of all the system agencies and at least one transient agency.

An expert agent can be a member of only one workgroup and may be involved in one project at a time. A *project* is the execution of a solution plan by one or more workgroups. As long as there is no commitment to any project, an agent may decide to leave its workgroup anytime. Within an agency, the management and the workgroup interface with each other through the adaptor agent who renders a two-way message translation service. To be able to do this, the adaptor has to know the interfaces or API of its workgroup.

Meanwhile, the system agencies consist of the *Surrogate Client Agency* (SCA), *Central Information Agency* (CIA), *Postal Agency* (PA), and *Management Resource Agency* (MRA). The SCA is composed of agents called *surrogate clients* who serve as the interface to the user clients. The CIA is the agency that keeps all central information. In addition, a group of agents are assigned to manage and maintain the *global directory*, the *collaboration protocol repository*, and the *global blackboard*. The PA provides communication services to all of the agencies. Finally, the MRA is the agency where management services can be sought. This is where the manager, secretary and adaptor agents are pooled. Whenever a new agency joins, its management group is formed from the MRA.

3.2 The ACNET

An existing MAS is mapped to a workgroup. This means that at the workgroup level, we maintain the MAS's current configuration. We then virtually connect the heterogenous workgroups together through our framework to form a MAS network called the *ACACIA network* (ACNET). The physical network may be

---

[5] In our context, the use of transient agencies and *agencies* are interchangeable.

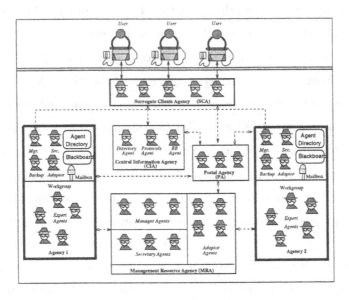

Fig. 1. Logical View of the ACACIA Framework

composed of one or more heterogenous machine platforms where each can host any number of agents and MAS.

Each workgroup is paired with only one management group. The management group can be placed anywhere in the ACNET. However, its best location is within or near the vicinity of its workgroup's host machine. We use KQML which is based on the notion of performatives [8] for communication. All management agents speak KQML and therefore every adaptor translates its workgroup's language to KQML and vice versa. We classify adaptors based on the language they translate. The ACACIA system libraries provide different implementations of each type of adaptors. In the future, we will also provide facilities for users to create user-defined translation rules. Finally, the workgroup operates exactly in the same way as a stand-alone MAS with the adaptor viewed as just another MAS client.

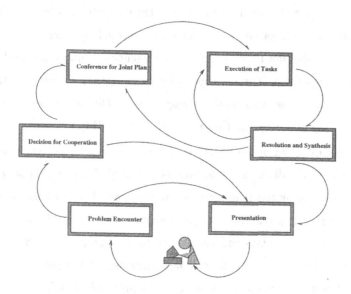

Fig. 2. Problem Solving Paradigm

3.3 Cooperative Problem Solving

The bottomline of all these efforts is *cooperative problem solving*. Our paradigm [6] for problem solving is summarized in Fig. 2. The whole idea is to form a coalition of high order agencies when no single agency can work on a problem alone. The brief descriptions below should give a clear working scenario of the whole paradigm.

Problem Encounter. A problem specification is presented to the system through one of the surrogate clients (Refer to Fig. 1 again). At the design level, each high order agency has its representative surrogate client who interfaces between the client and the management using ACACIA's mail messaging subsystem. The surrogate also takes care of all *user presentation* issues. The problem specification is written in a *Common Problem Specification Language* which standardizes many of the problem description concerns known in DAI such as *ontologies* or common domain vocabularies, and service types and names.

Decision for Cooperation. The agency secretary notifies the agency manager of any job request mail. The latter evaluates the problem by looking at

---

[6] We assume that there is no user interaction while problem solving is in progress.

the requirements and match them against their capabilities and availabilities. If the evaluation is negative, it is referred to selected agencies by multicasting a *request-for-evaluation* mail. The receiving agencies evaluate the problem and return their appraisals. The manager selects one agency to carry on the problem from among those with positive responses [7]. This procedure may also be implemented by adapting the *Contract Net* protocol [14].

Conferencing for a Joint Plan. In the previous stage, when no agency can be selected a call for a conference is initiated. It is at this stage that a joint plan is made by the managers. There are a number of methods that were proposed for planning [12]. In most joint planning activities, the problem is decomposed into several tasks and distributed to the agents. A number of method exists [5] [3] [14] [1]. Our framework welcomes any of the planning strategies available although we adapt the Contract Net protocol by default.

A coordination plan may also be laid out. Alternatively, this stage can be executed by the users or programmers who present the plan to the system. When a plan cannot be formulated, the surrogate client is informed immediately about the failure.

Execution of Tasks. Each agency manager submits his task plans to his adaptor. Aside from the list of tasks, the plan includes other information such as points of synchronization, data sources, constraints and others. The task plan is written in a proprietary language embedded in a KQML message. The adaptor submits the plan to the group in its expected format. From there. the workgroup performs its internal planning and proceeds with its execution. ACACIA is a tightly committed system. Each agent is bound to fulfill its part and terminates only when it is accomplished or when the current conditions make its achievement impossible or when a termination is decided by the group.

Resolution and Synthesis. At any point during the computation, the requesting agency can mail all the working agencies to rendezvous and present a report. Each one shall present all tasks accomplished and any other reports such as *starvation* based on TIME-OUTS, non-functional and dead agents, inavailability of data, *etc*. From these, decision has to be made as to whether the

---

[7] The selection policy used can be arbitrarily chosen by the designer or implementor.

computation may proceed or not. The users can also be given the report and override the decision.

Presentation. Successful or not, the final result is given back to the requesting agency who later sends the result to the requesting surrogate client. Finally, the surrogate client gives the result back to the user client.

3.4 Cooperation By Communication

We regard communication as the primary way of achieving cooperative work. Our scheme for relaying requests, inquiry and information is based mainly on mailboxes. There exists a system agency called the *Postal Agency* that takes care of this functionality. A set of agents called the *postmen* deliver and collect from all agencies. A successful mail delivery does not guarantee an immediate attention from the receiver so we include an optional instruction to inform the agency secretary immediately about the new mail.

Cooperation within the workgroup is abstracted by the MAS internal processing. ACACIA's main concern is on inter-agency and management-workgroup cooperation. The former is implemented by a *distributed blackboard system* [11] [6] with each agency maintaining its local blackboard. A global blackboard is a mirror image of the union of all local blackboards. All information, coming to and leaving from the agency, are received and written into the blackboard by the secretary. On the other hand, the adaptor bridges these information between the workgroup and the secretary. A write operation triggers the secretary to send new information to the affected agencies. Figure 3 summarizes our description.

3.5 Communication Patterns

An approach taken is the idea of *communication[8] patterns* in which we assert that some classes of problem solving procedures follow the same patterns of agent communications. By identifying these classes, we can define some coordination protocols and store them in a repository. We call this collection of protocols the *Collaboration Protocols*. As a simple example, some problems may follow a simple

---

[8] Here, the use of communication is synonymous to our notion of coordination.

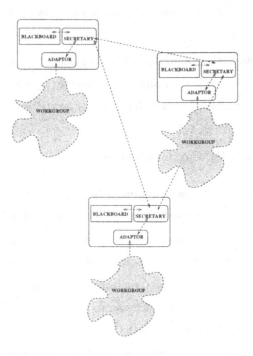

Fig. 3. Communication lines for Inter-agency Cooperation

master-slaves communication pattern where one agency multicasts to a set of agencies. These agencies perform some processing and return their responses to the master agency who waits until all responses are received. The master then performs more computations based on these and sends a message to a subset of the original set, usually to only one agency. A *bidding problem* may satisfy this where the slave agencies take the bidder's role. Another problem could be *redundant programming* in which the slave agencies are given the same problem by the master but solve it differently. The master agency collects all final results, compare them, make some actions or decisions and send further messages. Here, we see that the coordination requirements for both problems are the same. The difference lies only on the message contents being passed.

The class of a given problem may be provided, typically by the user, and therefore the appropriate protocol pattern can be retrieved. Note that a problem may be using one or more patterns from the repository. The overall approach improves system performance especially that the collaboration protocols can be fine tuned anytime.

4 Runtime Environment

Each workgroup has its own specific runtime environment which is independent of the ACACIA runtime. The runtime environment of an ACACIA system consists of one ACNET. One of the machines in the network is a central host where the server kernel is installed by an administrator. Each ACACIA system is given a system ID[9]. The server kernel manages and oversees all other nodes in the ACNET. The global data and system agents are also found in the central host. The global data are mirror images of all local data. They are maintained for system related purposes such as system recovery, versioning, tracing, consistency check and others. Meanwhile, the *Collaboration Protocol* repository is maintained solely by authorized users. A separate module is written for this functionality. To connect a MAS to an ACNET, an ACACIA client kernel has to be loaded in the same machine as the MAS. This kernel takes care of the many local administrative and system functions including the low-level communication routines. The client kernel binds to a server kernel which can be specified by the user or can be randomly chosen by the client kernel after having probed for existing server kernels. One or more client kernels may reside in one machine in the same way that multiple MAS can co-exist. All MAS that are connected to the same ACACIA system are managed by the same client kernel[10].

The management group is implemented by a multithreaded module where most of the system agents are implemented as active objects [4]. The adaptor object communicates with its corresponding workgroup by behaving like a client to the MAS. The secretary agent holds the local blackboard and the local directory as part of its knowledge base. The mailboxes are first class objects with a complete set of interfaces. They are also held by the secretary. See Figure 4. Whenever the data in the central host are updated, these agents are informed and their copies are refreshed.

---

[9] This equates to the host name plus a user-defined name.

[10] At the moment, we do not allow a MAS to connect to several ACACIA systems.

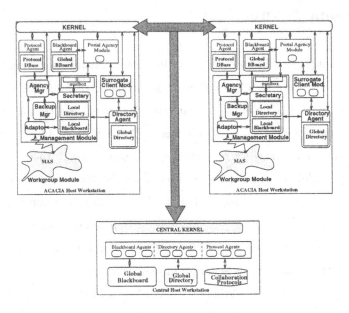

Fig. 4. ACACIA's Runtime Environment

Each agency has another module that contains the active object implementation of the surrogate clients. They interface with user clients in the workstation where they are located using a simple dialog windowing system. Similarly, the postal agency module implements the *postmen*. These postmen are assigned to specific transient agencies where they are responsible for dropping and collecting mail. They pass around the mail among themselves until the target postmen are reached. They consult the directory agent to determine the addresses of the agencies.

Joining the system can be initiated asynchronously by a client kernel. Once the kernel is loaded, a surrogate client is created who later binds the client kernel to a server kernel using one of the two methods already mentioned. Then a runtime is created which includes connecting the management module to the joining MAS and updating the global directories. Leaving the system is done simply by discarding the entry from all directories and destroying the local runtime of the MAS.

5 Conclusion

We know the benefits derived from an interoperable multiagent system and so we developed the ACACIA framework. This framework rests upon the idea of high order agencies to provide an infrastructure for agent collaboration. By incorporating the management metaphor, multiagent systems become agencies that can be glued together by the managing agents and by using KQML as the common language. Interoperability is realized and collaboration becomes possible. We also discussed briefly on the runtime system design. The most important contribution of this research is the interoperability approach that originates from above. The *nesting effect* enables existing MAS to join the framework freely. Furthermore, the design avoids the introduction of complex procedures for future agent builders.

References

1. Bond, Alan H. and Gasser, Les,(editors) "An
   Analysis of Problems and Research in DAI", *Readings in Distributed Artificial Intelligence*, Morgan Kauffman Pub. Inc., San Mateo, California, 1988.

2. Byrne, Ciara and Edwards, Peter, "Building Agent-Based Systems", Department of Computer Science, Univ. of Aberdeen, King's College, ABERDEEN, Scotland, UK. *AUCS/TR9405*.

3. Cammarata, Stephanie, McArthur, David and Steeb, Randall, "Strategies of Cooperation in Distributed Problem Solving", *Readings in Distributed Artificial Intelligence*, Alan H. Bond and Les Gasser (editor), Morgan Kauffman Pub. Inc., San Mateo, California, 1988.

4. Cardozo, E., Sichman, J.S., Demazeau, Y., "Using Active Object Model to Implement Multi-Agent Systems", *Proc. of the 5th IEEE Int. Conf. on Tools with Artificial Intelligence*, 1993, Boston, USA.

5. Davis, Randall and Smith, Reid G., "Negotiation as a Metaphor for Distributed Problem Solving", *Readings in Distributed Artificial Intelligence*, Alan H. Bond and Les Gasser (editor), Morgan Kauffman Pub. Inc., San Mateo, California, 1988.

6. Durfee, Edmund H., Lesser, Victor R. and Corkill, Daniel D., "Cooperation Through Communication in Distributed Problem Solving Network", *Dis-*

tributed Artificial Intelligence, Michael N. Huhns (editor), Pitman Publishing, London. 1987.

7. Finin, Tim, Fritzon, Rich and McKay, Don, "A Language and Protocol to Support Intelligent Agent Interoperability", *Proceedings of the CE and CALS Washington '92 Conference*, June 1992.

8. Finin, T., Weber, J., Fritzon, R., McGuire, J., Shapiro, S., Beck, C., "Draft Specification of KQML Agent Communication Language", *http://www.cs.umbc.edu/kqml/*, June, 1993.

9. Franklin, Stan and Graesser, Art, "Is it an Agent or just a Program? A Taxonomy for Autonomous Agents", *http://www.msci.memphis/franklin*, March 5, 1996.

10. Gamma, E., Helm, R., Johnson, R. and Vlissides, J., **Design Patterns, Elements of Reusable Object-Oriented Software**, Addison-Wesley Pub. Co., 1995.

11. Hayes-Roth, Barbara, "A Blackboard Architecture for Control", *Readings in Distributed Artificial Intelligence*, Alan H. Bond and Les Gasser (editor), Morgan Kauffman Pub. Inc., San Mateo, California, 1988.

12. Katz, Matthew J. and Rosenschein, Jeffrey S., "Plans for Multiple Agents", *Distributed Artificial Intelligence Vol. II*, Les Gasser and Michael N. Huhns (editor), Pitman Publishing, London. 1989.

13. Rosenschein, Jeffrey and Zotkin, Gilad, **Rules of Encounter, Designing Conventions for Automated Negotiation among Computers**, The MIT Press, Cambridge, Mass., 1994.

14. Smith, Reid G. and Davis, Randall, "Frameworks for Cooperation in Distributed Problem Solving", *Readings in Distributed Artificial Intelligence*, Alan H. Bond and Les Gasser (editor), Morgan Kauffman Pub. Inc., San Mateo, California, 1988.

15. Sycara, Katia P., "Multiagent Compromise via Negotiation", *Distributed Artificial Intelligence Vol. II*, Les Gasser and Michael N. Huhns (editor), Pitman Publishing, London. 1989.

16. Wooldridge, Michael and Jennings, Nicholas R., "Agent Theories, Architectures and Languages: A Survey", in Wooldridge and Jennings Eds., **Intelligent Agent**, Berlin:Springer-Verlag, 1-22.

Ascription of Intensional Ontologies in Anthropological Descriptions of Multi-Agent Systems

Rafael H. Bordini[1], John A. Campbell[1], and Renata Vieira[2]

[1] Computer Science Department
University College London
E-mail: {R.Bordini, jac}@cs.ucl.ac.uk
[2] Centre for Cognitive Science
University of Edinburgh
E-mail: renata@cogsci.ed.ac.uk

Abstract. This paper introduces a new way of describing ontologies used in Multi-Agent Systems (MAS) which is intended as a means to allow interoperability of MAS. It is inspired by a pragmatic theory of intensionality worked out as part of an anthropological approach to agent migration. An agent observing an unfamiliar society of agents can ascribe such an ontology to that MAS by interviewing those agents, somewhat in the way a social-anthropologist does in fieldwork practice. We present this new form of ontology which is based on the concept of subjective intensionality, concentrating particularly on individual terms. We also discuss how an agent can ascribe this sort of ontology to a society it does not know. Moreover, we formalise some of these ideas using a framework for formalisation of agent theories, based on the Z formal specification language. Further, we compare our proposal to other current approaches to ontology. We conclude by stating our expectations from this work concerning the foundational aspects of interaction among disparate agencies.

1 Introduction

We have been dealing for some time with what we have called *migration of agents* [4–6,9]. The basic idea is that certain individual agents should be able to interact in societies of agents which were designed using different paradigms or theories of agents, or which had different histories of autonomous evolution.

Some agents should be able to produce anthropologically-based formal descriptions of the cultures present in all kinds of MAS, which could then be used by migrating agents in their processes of adaptation. Such formal descriptions must include several aspects of a society (see [4]); in the current paper we concentrate particularly on the ontological description of terms from the communication language of the society being described. For this particular problem, we propose here the use of a pragmatic theory of intensionality [26]. In this paper we present our approach using Luck and d'Inverno's [19] formal framework for specification of agent theories.

One possible application of the ideas to be presented in this paper is inter-operation of systems [14,27]. These ideas are particularly relevant if the systems do not employ similar definitions for the terms used to communicate and represent knowledge. Our approach can be seen as a step towards the solution to the problem of ontological mismatch among information agents. By information agents we mean both mediators to databases [17,28,27] or agents for gathering information in the Internet [10] acting as a MAS.

We shall provide the necessary background for both parts of our studies (the anthropological and the semantic/pragmatic sides) in Section 2. Section 3 presents our approach to the problems introduced above and a formalisation of our concept of ontology. We then discuss our approach in Section 4 and compare it with one other way of treating the same problem, while Section 5 considers the relevance and consequences of the present work.

2 Background

This section has two parts, giving the necessary background for the two studies that we have worked out together to build the ideas in this paper.

2.1 Anthropologically-Based Migration

We have introduced the idea of using anthropological fieldwork with unexplored communities as a source of inspiration for solutions to the problem we have been investigating, namely the migration of agents among disparate societies. We propose the use of Cognitive Anthropology [25] as a theoretical foundation for the search for such inspirations. Basically, the intention of the cognitive approach to social anthropology is to discover the "organizing principles underlying behaviour" in unexplored societies (in other words, "how different peoples organize and use their cultures" [25]) and to rely on fairly formal methods for specifying theories for each particular culture.

The general idea of providing formal models of each culture is particularly interesting for our counterpart work on computational societies. Not only should an *anthropologist agent*, ideally, be able to generate a formal description of an *artificial culture*, but also a *migrant agent* could use it in its process of adaptation to that particular target society. Giving formal *cultural descriptions* of agent communities resembles somewhat the work on a framework for formalising agent theories by d'Inverno and Luck [11,19], which we use here to formalise our own theories. However, by drawing lessons from Social Anthropology, one can further comprehend the full richness of all the aspects that may characterise an artificial culture (and consequently formalise them); above all, we can progress toward a point where agents will be able to deal with these formal descriptions themselves.

Besides providing these initial thoughts on a suitable theoretical foundation for our project, we claim that research methods in anthropology [2] can provide useful techniques for an agent's adaptation to a strange society. Accordingly, we have investigated some techniques currently used by anthropologists in fieldwork practice and discussed how they could be used in the computational counterpart situation. We have presented some tactics that a migrant agent can exploit and some social features which can be handy in such a process of agent adaptation. One of these features, based on the idea that the existence of key informants is of fundamental importance in ethnographic work, is to provide target societies with *informant agents*, to which we shall allude later in this paper. They are key agents in the society, and they must have some specific characteristics (e.g., understand the information needed by the anthropologist agent, have the intention to give or try to get such information, etc.). For this particular work, the chosen informant agents should be able to give accurate information about the terms being described by the anthropologist agent.

We have argued in [3] that our complete project provides a new way of viewing interoperation of MAS. We have compared it to the KQML approach to interoperability [14], and we shall do the same, regarding particularly the ontological aspect, in Section 4.1.

2.2 Subjective Intensionality

This section briefly describes the idea of intensionality in meaning. Our approach is motivated by the notion of mental states of language users. The account is based mainly on the language users' acceptance relation with sentences, as we see in the subsections below. The material presented here is concerned with the meaning of individual terms. The definitions in this section are presented in detail elsewhere [26]. They are based on the work of R.Martin [22].

Roughly speaking, the *intension* of an expression is what is known about it in order to identify the object/entity to which it refers. We can say that intension is related to notions of mental entities, properties, relations, and concepts, while *extension* is related to objective entities (objects, structures). Furthermore, the notion of intensionality to be raised here is a subjective one; *subjective intensions* are particular to an individual language user in a given time with respect to a language expression. Since these are notions intrinsic to the users of the language, they are called pragmatical intensions.

Subjective intensions are associated with the intuitive notion of "connotation" of a term or name. Connotation should be understood as the set of those properties which are associated with the term in the mind of an individual. The properties are associated with the term in such a way that they are normally borne in mind when the individual uses that term. Also, *quasi-intensions* are linguistic reductions of the mental entities relative to intensions. Therefore, the terminology "subjective quasi-intension" emphasises that the theory deals with virtual classes of expressions related with time and particular users of the language; that is, a linguistic reduction of the cognitive notion of connotation.

One interesting feature of this approach is that the classical philosophical problem concerning the accessibility to mental entities is circumvented by the formalisation of "quasi-mental entities". Moreover, this escaping of mentalism still conserves the strength of intensional notions, including their subjective nature. The point is that we have a notion inspired by mental states, which reflects mental states, but we avoid the problem that mental states are not observable.

We now present some definitions that we use later in Section 3. In order to define subjective quasi-intensions, the acceptance relation between agents and expressions is introduced. The definition, originally described in [22], follows.

Definition 1 (Acceptance Relation). Acceptance is an empirical relation, observed by an experimenter who asks questions by means of a set of sentences which represent a logical theory. Whenever an agent answers affirmatively to one of these sentences we say that the agent accepts the sentence at that time.

Given this notion of acceptance, it is now possible to define subjective quasi-intension of individual constants.

Definition 2 (Subjective Quasi-Intension). The notion of subjective quasi-intension for an individual constant concerns the sentences which refer to that constant and which are accepted by a given language user.

This definition is based on syntax; that is, subjective quasi-intensions are classes of expressions rather than classes of what the expressions designate. This is important to prevent the intractable problem of checking the truth of the definitions in the state of affairs in the world; it is sufficient to find out the knowledge about the things that the agents use to communicate.

Besides subjective intension, which concerns a single agent and a single instant of time, other notions relative to subjective intensions are considered below.

Definition 3 (Intersubjective Quasi-Intension). Intersubjective quasi-intensions are relative to groups of language users at a certain time. An intersubjective quasi-intension is the equivalent class of all the subjective quasi-intensions of a certain group of users.

Intertemporal quasi-intensions are relative to a user at all times. *Objective quasi-intensions* can also be defined on the basis of acceptance. They are at the same time the intertemporal and intersubjective quasi-intension of expressions, that is, a class whose members are members of subjective intensions of all users at all times. They are said to be an essential property, as they are universally accepted (in a specific community).

The understanding of a concept can be defined as the situation in which the subjective intension of a term relative to an agent is the same as the intersubjective intension of all agents, some expert group or a specialist.

3 Ascribing Ontologies

3.1 The Anthropologist Agent Interview for Ontology Construction

We have seen in Section 2.2 that, based on quasi-intensions, a definition for an expression can be given by a set of properties that are accepted by a group of agents as being related to the expression. This is the key point for allowing an anthropologist agent to ascribe an ontological description to a community of agents; it can do so by interviewing the group of informant agents that it takes from that particular community. Terms that have a unanimous definition among the informant agents should be registered in the construction of an ontology for that community.

It is important to note that the anthropologist agent itself needs a theory (i.e., a set of attributes for each term) to interview the informant agents. The sentences in this theory will be submitted to the informant agents in order to check whether they accept the sentences or not. We have argued in [4] that an anthropologist agent can use its past experience with other communities in its current fieldwork with an unfamiliar society. This idea also applies for the problem of creating the set of sentences to be used in the interview. The initial theory for a term to be tested with the informant agent can be taken from previous experiences with other communities or from the definition of that term for the anthropologist agent itself.

In case of completely unknown terms, a more elaborate interview will have to take place. The anthropologist agent should then ask the informant agents to tell of all sentences they have associated with that term in their knowledge representation, instead of just asking them to confirm or deny an initial theory. However, one cannot expect that all informant agents in all societies are able to participate in this sort of more complex interview. Once the anthropologist agent has an initial theory obtained from at least one informant agent, it can proceed with the interview as described before.

The activity of an anthropologist agent ascribing ontologies to communities of agents resembles the multidisciplinary subject of ethnography of communication (see, e.g., [16]), and is its computational counterpart.

3.2 A New Kind of Ontology

We here take "ontology" to mean very much the same as proposed by Gruber [15], i.e. the definition of a set of representational terms[1] (stated as a logical theory). However, we recall that the theory of intensionality presented here deals only with individual terms. We believe that the major contribution of this approach to ontology description in relation to others is not so much on the representational aspect but that this particular theory allows us to provide agents with mechanisms for dealing with ontologies themselves.

We provide the following definition for our conception of ontology.

Definition 4 (Intensional Ontology of Terms). An Intensional Ontology of Terms is a set of terms where each one is associated with the minimal set of predicates which is necessary and sufficient to distinguish (unequivocally) each term from every other term in the universe of discourse of a communicating society.

---

[1] In this particular context, the representational terms are those used in the communication language of a MAS.

In this approach, the definition of a term is a set of predicates that are considered to hold for that term. It is important to appreciate that not all predicates that hold for the term are needed for an ontological description of it (this is the difference between knowledge representation and commitment to ontological conventions [15]). Furthermore, if a taxonomy for the predicates is available, this should be reflected in the minimal set of predicates: it should include only the most general ones.

3.3 Formalisation of Intensional Ontologies

In this section we formalise the sort of ontology that we are dealing with in this work, which we have called *Intensional Ontology*. We use the framework for formalisation of agent theories specifically, which was elaborated by Luck and d'Inverno [11,19–21] based on the Z formal specification language [24]. We assume some familiarity both with the framework and with Z notation.

We begin by introducing the following basic types:

$$[Term, Sent, TimeInterval]$$

and we also use the following abbreviation for the type *Pred*:

$$Pred == Term \rightarrow Sent$$

where *TimeInterval* is taken to be the set of time intervals in the usual sense. *Term* is the set of individual constants of the communication language used by the agents in the target society. *Pred* is the set of predicative constants of the agent's language. Note that a predicate when applied to a term is a sentence (*Sent*) of the agents' language, instead of its truth value. We consider here only this sort of sentences. The use of logical connectives within this quasi-intensional approach is given in [26].

We now present the definition of an *InformantAgent* which is built on the definition of *AutonomousAgent* which is part of Luck and d'Inverno's framework (see, e.g., [11]).

```
┌─ InformantAgent ─────────────────────────────────────
│ AutonomousAgent
│ asked_sentences : ℙ Sent
│ ti : TimeInterval
│ accepts _ : ℙ(Sent × TimeInterval)
│ subjective_quasi_intension : (Term × TimeInterval) → ℙ Pred
├──────────────────────────────────────────────────────
│ ∀ s : Sent • accepts(s, ti) ⇒ s ∈ asked_sentences
│ ∀ t : Term • subjective_quasi_intension(t, ti) =
│         {p : Pred | accepts(p(t), ti)}
└──────────────────────────────────────────────────────
```

A *InformantAgent* keeps in *asked_sentences* the set of sentences that the anthropologist agent asks at time *ti*. The predicate *accepts* refers to the acceptance relation explained in the previous section. Informant agents may accept or reject sentences. In the schema we require that an accepted sentence is among the asked ones. The predicate *accepts* is not fully defined here because it would demand a complete formalisation of the epistemological behaviour of the agent, which is not the intention of this paper. Furthermore, it may be defined according to different conceptions of acceptance. Finally, the *subjective_quasi_intention* of an *InformantAgent* regarding a term t at time ti is given as the set of all predicates that the agent accepts for that term at the given time.

We have defined so far the state space of an *InformantAgent*. Next, we present one of the operations that the anthropologist agent does in a target society. It is specified in the schema *Interview* which alters the state of an informant agent (this is the meaning of the declaration $\Delta InformantAgent$).

Interview
$\Delta InformantAgent$
$asked\_sentences? : \mathbb{P}_1\ Sent$
$ti? : TimeInterval$

$asked\_sentences' = asked\_sentences?$
$ti' = ti?$

In this Z schema the set *asked_sentences* is given as input, i.e., it is a variable which represents the set of sentences (*Sent*) asked by an anthropologist agent when ascribing an ontology to a community of agents. How an anthropologist agent conceive this set of sentences to be asked was mentioned in Section 3.1, but its formalisation is out of the scope of this paper. The time interval (ti) at which the ontology is ascribed is also an input. The inputs in that schema change the state of the informant agent by changing the *asked_sentences* and ti variables, thus changing the sentences the agent accept and its subjective quasi-intensions, through the invariants in the schema *InformantAgent*. This gives the idea that the behaviour of an informant agent changes through time and according to the logical theory under investigation by the anthropologist agent.

We can now present the specification of what a society to which an anthropologist agent will ascribe an intensional ontology is like.

TargetSociety
$as : \mathbb{P}_1(AutonomousAgent \cup InformantAgent)$
$intensional\_ontology\_of\_terms : Term \nrightarrow \mathbb{P}_1\ Pred$

With this schema, we mean that a target society being observed by an anthropologist agent has a non empty set of agents. Some of these agents may be informant agents and others are ordinary agents. The ontology to be created by the anthropologist agent is also accessible in a target society. It is a function that maps terms to the sets of properties that characterises them. The initial value for the variables in the schema above is given next.

```
┌─ InitialTargetSociety ─────────────────────────────────────────
│ TargetSociety
│ ─────────────────────────────────────
│ intensional_ontology_of_terms = {}
└─────────────────────────────────────────────────────────────────
```

We now present the schema for the operation *AscribeIntensionalDescription-OfTerms*, which represents the action of an anthropologist agent ascribing an intensional ontology of terms to a certain community of agents. This operation changes the state of a society by augmenting its *intensional_ontology_of_terms*, thus the need for the declaration Δ *TargetSociety*. The input *ias* is a non-empty set of Informant Agents which are chosen by the anthropologist agent among the agents in the community at a given time (*ti*), as mentioned in Section 3.1.

```
┌─ AscribeIntensionalDescriptionOfTerms ─────────────────────────
│ $\Delta$ TargetSociety
│ ias? : $\mathbb{P}_1$ InformantAgent
│ ti? : TimeInterval
│ intersubjective_quasi_intension :
│         ($\mathbb{P}$ InformantAgent × Term × TimeInterval) → $\mathbb{P}$ Pred
│ ───────────────────────────────────────────────────────────────
│ ias? ⊆ as
│ ∀ t : Term; i : InformantAgent | i ∈ ias? •
│           intersubjective_quasi_intension(ias?, t, ti?) =
│                   {p : Pred | i.accepts(p(t), ti?)}
│ ∀ t : Term | intersubjective_quasi_intension(ias?, t, ti?) ≠ {} •
│       intensional_ontology_of_terms' =
│           intensional_ontology_of_terms ∪
│               {t ↦ intersubjective_quasi_intension(ias?, t, ti?)}
│ as' = as
└─────────────────────────────────────────────────────────────────
```

The *intersubjective_quasi_intension* of a term (*t*) is the set of predicates accepted by all informant agents (*ias*) at a certain time (*ti*) for that term. The ontological description of terms for that community at a certain time is given by a partial function *intensional_ontology_of_terms* which maps a term (*t*) to the *intersubjective_quasi_intension* of the informant agents (*ias*) for that term at the given time (*ti*) [2]. When the intersubjective quasi-intension is an empty set, the anthropologist agent cannot ascribe a definition to that term. Recall that by the signature of *intensional_ontology_of_terms* (i.e., a partial function) we assure that a term is not defined more than once in the ontology and we express that not all terms used by the agents need to be in the ontological description at one time. Finally, we state that the set of agents (*as*) of the target society is not changed by the ontological ascription, as one would expect.

We emphasise that as we use the intersubjective quasi-intension of the terms being defined, they might not be valid *ad infinitum*. Thus, the anthropologist

---

[2] Note that in the present formalisation we do not constrain the ontological description of a term to a minimal set as discussed in Definition 4.

agent may need to review the ontology it has ascribed to a particular society from time to time, as autonomous evolution within societies takes place or the anthropologist agent alters its set of informant agents. One can refer to this as *evolutional ontology*, since we intend the agents to change them evolutionally. However, based on the concept of objective quasi-intentions (see Section 2.2), some subset of the ontology may form an immutable part of it, composed of the terms universally accepted in that community.

Finally, we remark that this sort of modular formalisation and the availability of the specification of some general agent notions provided by the framework allowed a clear specification of our ideas on ascription of ontologies for MAS. Also, as Luck and d'Inverno claim [11], the framework can be used directly in the implementation of simulations of the agent theories formalised, which is obviously an advantage for further developments of the present work.

4 Discussion

4.1 A New Approach to Interoperability

In [3] we have devoted a section (called *"Contributions to the Critique of KQML"*) to comparing our approach to interoperability and the KQML approach (see the work on the Agent Communication Language by the Knowledge Sharing Effort [14][3]). We agreed with Cohen and Levesque's critique that KQML needs further semantic clarification [7], but we have further expanded it in the light of our ideas on interoperability. In this section we shall deal particularly with the ontological aspects; one can refer to our cited text for a complete discussion.

There is a point that we have introduced in our conception of MAS that makes things rather complicated. The fact that agents may be able to change their languages and culture (as in the example of human evolution) may cause some difficulties with the formal descriptions that agents are supposed to have available when migrating, as they may not be up to date. That is the reason why we proposed the existence of *anthropologist agents* which should ideally be able to generate formal descriptions of languages (ethnography of communication) and cultures, just as social anthropologists do.

Consequently, we believe that it is not desirable for MAS designers to try or expect to specify ontologies completely (as in the KQML approach) but agents should be able to modify their own ontologies, due to evolution, and use these formal descriptions of ontologies (which are just part of cultural descriptions) when migrating. For this sort of complex MAS, it is not sufficient to have an ontology which was specified by the designer of the MAS at the beginning of its history. That is why it is necessary that the anthropologist agent should be able to ascribe ontologies to MAS. We have outlined a theory of intensionality that

---

[3] We give further references to that work in [3]. One can also find several papers on that approach at URL http://www.cs.umbc.edu/.

can support the creation of ontological descriptions by interviewing informant agents, which is also supported by our ideas on anthropologist agents.

We agree that the KQML approach may turn out to be very useful for work on particular kinds of MAS (e.g. the information agents in [10]). However, due to the variety of cognitive and social issues involved in migration between different cultures, we think our approach is more suitable for the sort of MAS influenced by deep theories of social sciences that can be used by researchers in "human" disciplines akin to DAI for simulation of complex social phenomena, as claimed by Conte and Castelfranchi [8].

4.2 The Context of the Project

To make use of the anthropological scheme we have outlined elsewhere, an anthropologist agent must first be in possession of information relevant to the modelling of the MAS. This is of two kinds: sentences expressing properties of MAS that are usually or often true, and data recorded in observations of the target MAS. The anthropologist's sentences are either exact translations of sentences of the former type (offered for approval or denial) or sentences expressing suggested correlations between items of data (e.g. "X causes Y") or opinions about significance of items (e.g. "X is very important/peculiar to your society"). Bernard [2] gives many examples of good anthropological fieldwork behaviour that can be reduced to such forms.

Common to both kinds of sentence, and also for the questions the anthropologist agent has to ask the informant agents to be able to ascribe an ontological description to the community, is the need for a suitable "pidgin" vocabulary for terms that may not mean the same to the anthropologist agent and the MAS, or may not even make sense inside the world of the MAS. The simple terms and categories of Conceptual Dependency Theory [23], which is already well known in AI, have the right level for this job. It is desirable for any design of agents intended for use in a community of agents to include some such "pidgin" feature if the community is to accept new agents during its lifetime.

We are using this approach in the problem of adaptation of a foreign agent to the collective behaviour of a team of players of the British ball game of cricket [4]. Although even the surface features of the game are quite complicated, the framework is sufficient to express the exchanges between the foreign agent, which behaves like an anthropologist, and the cricket MAS.

5 Conclusion

We have presented a new way of specifying ontologies used in societies of agents based on a theory of intensionality, which goes perfectly together with our anthropological approach to migration of agents that aims at allowing interactions among agents of disparate communities. In particular, ontological commitment is fundamental for cooperation of information agents [17,10]. We have argued its likely superiority to the KQML approach to ontology regarding a particular sort of MAS which is founded on complex aspects of social and cognitive sciences [8]. It is also important from the point of view of believable agents [1], regarding adaptation capabilities.

Providing agents that can learn to interact with different communities not only allows interoperation of disparate Multi-Agent Systems (MAS) without the need of standardisation on models and languages of agents but also brings to light several issues of interest in the disciplines that form the foundations of MAS. At least one such discipline is potentially important in the adaptation process associated with the immigration of a foreign agent, but is not generally recognised as such, namely Social Anthropology. We suggest that it should be among the disciplines of interest to MAS if we are to consider the proposed way of promoting interoperation of MAS.

This paper mentions several fields of social sciences which have been so far neglected as correlates to DAI (e.g., social anthropology, ethnolinguistics). Besides, it is interesting to note that the theories present in both works used in this paper (on the anthropological and semantic/pragmatic sides) follow philosophical principles which are familiar to the Positivist school. It is currently argued that such theories are dead for social sciences because they fail to comply with the intrinsic "human" aspects of the problems involved. However, it seems we have still to discover their potential contributions to the computational counterpart problems in DAI, where the formal aspect is essential. Thus, peripherally, this paper suggests that it is helpful to make further investigation of fairly old work on social science as sources of inspiration for open problems in DAI [13,12]. However, we do agree with Gasser [12], as we stated in [4], that the latest theories in social sciences provide the basic principles underlying the appropriate conception of DAI as an inherently social one.

Finally, we stress that what we have presented here is one of the steps to be taken toward a whole cultural description which is to be used when an agent needs to adapt to a community that is not the one for which it was originally designed.

Acknowledgements

We would like to acknowledge the great help from Mark d'Inverno and Michael Luck who commented on an earlier version of this paper, specially on the Z specifications. We thank Antônio Carlos da Rocha Costa and Rosa Maria Viccari for their valuable contributions to both the work on migration of agents and on subjective intensionality when they were first conceived. We are also grateful to the Brazilian agencies CAPES and CNPq for the grants to, respectively, Rafael Heitor Bordini and Renata Vieira.

References

1. Joseph Bates. The role of emotion in believable agents. *Communications of the ACM*, 37(7):122–125, July 1994. Special Issue on Intelligent Agents.

2. Harvey Russell Bernard. *Research Methods in Anthropology: Qualitative and Quantitative Approaches.* Sage Publications, Thousand Oaks, California, second edition, 1994.

3. Rafael H. Bordini and John A. Campbell. Anthropologically-based migration: a new approach to interoperability. Research Note UCL-CS [RN/95/79], Department of Computer Science, UCL, London, 1995. Draft. URL: http://www.cs.ucl.ac.uk/staff/R.Bordini.

4. Rafael H. Bordini and John A. Campbell. Towards an anthropological approach to agent adaptation. In *Proceedings of the First International Workshop on Decentralized Intelligent and Multi-Agent Systems (DIMAS'95)*, pages p. II/74 – II/83. Dom Wydawnictwa Naukowych, Krakow, November 1995. UCL-CS [RN/95/78]. URL: http://www.cs.ucl.ac.uk/staff/R.Bordini.

5. Rafael Heitor Bordini. Suporte lingüístico para migração de agentes. Master's thesis, CPGCC da UFRGS, October 1994.

6. Rafael Heitor Bordini, Antônio Carlos da Rocha Costa, Jomi Fred Hübner, and Rosa Maria Viccari. Linguistic support for agent migration. In Lesser [18]. Extended Abstract.

7. Philip R. Cohen and Hector J. Levesque. Communicative actions for artificial agents. In Lesser [18].

8. Rosaria Conte and Cristiano Castelfranchi. *Cognitive and Social Action.* UCL Press, London, 1995. 215p.

9. Antônio Carlos da Rocha Costa, Jomi Fred Hübner, and Rafael Heitor Bordini. On entering an open society. In *XI Brazilian Symposium on Artificial Intelligence*, Fortaleza, October 1994. Brazilian Computing Society.

10. Keith Decker, Anandeep Pannu, Katia Sycara, and Mike Williamson. Designing behaviors for information agents. In *To appear in the Proceedings of the First International Conference on Autonomous Agents (AGENTS-97)*, February 1997. URL: http://www.cs.cmu.edu/ softagents/publications.html.

11. Mark d'Inverno and Michael Luck. A formal view of social dependece networks. In *Proceedgins of the First Australian Workshop on Distributed Artificial Intelligence, in conjunction with the Eighth Australian Joint Conference on Artificial Intelligence (AI'95)*, 1995.

12. Les Gasser. Social conceptions of knowledge and action: DAI foundations and open system semantics. *Artificial Intelligence*, 47(1–3):107–138, January 1991.

13. Les Gasser and Michael N. Huhns. Themes in distributed artificial intelligence research. In Les Gasser and Michael N. Huhns, editors, *Distributed Artificial Intelligence*, volume II. Pitman / Morgan Kaufmann, London, 1989. Research Notes in Artificial Intelligence.

14. Michael R. Genesereth and Steven P. Ketchpel. Software agents. *Communications of the ACM*, 37(7):48–53, July 1994. Special Issue on Intelligent Agents. URL: http://logic.stanford.edu/sharing/papers/.

15. Thomas R. Gruber. Toward principles for the design of ontologies used for knowledge sharing. In Nicola Guarino and Roberto Poli, editors, *Formal Ontology in Conceptual Analysis and Knowledge Representation.* Kluwer Academic Publishers, 1993. URL: http://www-ksl.stanford.edu/knowledge-sharing/papers/.

16. Dell Hymes. *Foundations in Sociolinguistics: An Ethnographic Approach.* Tavistock Publications, London, 1977.

17. Matthias Klusch and Onn Shehory. Coalition formation among rational information agents. In W. van der Velder and John Perram, editors, *Proceedings of the Seventh Workshop on Modelling Autonomous Agents in a Multi-Agent World (MAAMAW'96). Lecture Notes in Artificial Intelligence*, volume

1038, pages 204–217, London, 1996. Springer Verlag. LNAI Series. URL: http://falbala.informatik.uni-kiel.de/inf/Kandzia/index-us.html.

18. Victor Lesser, editor. *First International Conference on Multiagent Systems (IC-MAS'95)*, Menlo Park, June 1995. AAAI Press / MIT Press.

19. Michael Luck and Mark d'Inverno. A formal framework for agency and autonomy. In Lesser [18].

20. Michael Luck and Mark d'Inverno. Formalising the contract net as a goal-directed system. In Walter Van de Velde and John Perram, editors, *Agents Breaking Away: Proceedings of the Seventh European Workshop on Modelling Autonomous Agents in a Multi-Agent World*, number 1038 in Lecture Notes in Artificial Intelligence, pages 72–85. Springer-Verlag, Eindhoven, January 1996.

21. Michael Luck, Nathan Griffiths, and Mark d'Inverno. From agent theory to agent construction: A case study. In *Pre-Proceedings of the Third International Workshop on Agent Theories, Architectures and Languages (ATAL-96)*, Budapest, Hungary, August 1996.

22. Richard M. Martin. *Toward a Systematic Pragmatics*. North-Holland, Amsterdam, 1959.

23. Roger C. Schank and Robert P. Abelson. *Scripts, Plans, Goals and Understanding: An Inquiry into Human Knowledge Structures*. The Artificial Intelligence Series. Lawrence Erlbaum Associates Inc., Hillsdale, New Jersey, 1977.

24. J. M. Spivey. *The Z Notation: A Reference Manual*. International Series in Computer Science. Prentice Hall, Hemel Hempstead, second edition, 1992.

25. Stephen A. Tyler, editor. *Cognitive Anthropology*. Holt, Rinehart and Winston Inc., New York, 1969.

26. Renata Vieira and Antônio Carlos da Rocha Costa. The acceptance relation and the specification of communicating agents. In *First International Conference on Intelligent and Cooperative Information Systems – Special Track in Issues on Cooperating Heterogeneous Intelligent Agents*, Rotterdam, 1993. IEEE.

27. Gio Wiederhold. Interoperation, mediation, and ontologies. In *Proceedings of the International Symposium on Fifth Generation Computer Systems (FGCSOB94), Workshop on Heterogeneous Cooperative Knowledge-Bases*, volume W3, pages 33–48, Tokyo, Japan, December 1994. ICOT. URL: http://db.stanford.edu/pub/gio/gio-papers.html.

28. Gio Wiederhold and Michael Genesereth. The basis for mediation. In *Proceedings of COOPIS'96 Conference*, pages 138–155, Vienna, Austria, May 1995. To appear in IEEE Expert, 1997. Available from {coopis@cs.toronto.edu}. URL: http://db.stanford.edu/pub/gio/gio-papers.html.

Interoperability of Distributed and Heterogeneous Systems Based on Software Agent-Oriented Frameworks

Zakaria Maamar and Bernard Moulin

{maamar,moulin}@ift.ulaval.ca
Computer Science Department and Research Center on Geomatics
Laval University
Ste-Foy, QC G1K 7P4, Canada

Abstract. The paper introduces the concept of software agent-oriented frameworks for the design and the development of interoperable environments. Interoperability is a process that allows cooperative interactions between several systems. These latter are distributed on networks and can present incompatibilities in different ways (material, software, terminology). As a solution, we suggest to develop multiagent systems that will enable heterogeneous systems to interact efficiently. These systems are composed of software agents integrated in a framework architecture. Our research is applied to the SIGAL project[1] which aims at developing an interoperable environment for georeference libraries. A georeference library is a metadatabase describing several geodocumentary resources available in an organization. Most organizations developed their georeference libraries without considering a real standardization with other partners in the field. Therefore, we intend to set up software agent-oriented frameworks that will support georeference library interoperability by providing users with services that will free them from worrying about information distribution and terminological disparities.

1 Introduction

The huge development of information and communication technologies provides a growing number of services offered to the public and companies, those services being usually used independently from each other. However, combining several services in order to answer users' needs is a much more complex operation, especially when these services are distributed and heterogeneous. It is, therefore, necessary to solve *interoperability problems* for the systems offering those services on networks.

---

[1] SIGAL stands for "Système d'Information Géographique et Agent Logiciel" (Software Agent and Geographic Information Systems). It is a project jointly undertaken by the Computer Science Department and the Research Center on Geomatics at Laval University.

There exist a number of studies in the field of system interoperability, in particular those conducted by the Object Management Group (OMG) [12], that aims at adapting Object-Oriented technology (OO) to distributed contexts. OMG's objective is to set up distributed systems offering services that can be called for in a transparent way (in regard to their individual characteristics). These systems adopt a dynamic and OO client/server architecture with the possibility for a client machine to become a server, and *vice versa*. To create such systems, the suggested approach is based on the creation of *object-oriented frameworks* [13]. These frameworks must be given the capacity to provide users with services in a way which is independent from distribution and heterogeneity constraints applying on these services. However, there exist only few *design methods* that can orient designers when developing object-oriented frameworks and monitoring their evolution, especially when they have to be distributed on communication networks. Therefore, our work aims at providing such a method.

In addition, because of the increasing complexity of using services on the network, it is urgent to *assist users* in performing various kinds of operations. Current use of network services requires from the user to locate adequate services, to adapt to their interfaces, and to understand their structural and terminological characteristics. In this paper, as a possible solution, we suggest to involve several specialized components called *software agents* [1,2,9] that will perform these different operations on behalf of users. However, given the complexity of exploiting services in distributed and heterogeneous environments, we suggest to gather these agents in *teams*. Depending on the context in which they evolve, these teams have to cooperate, negotiate and coordinate their actions and, possibly, solve various conflicts.

Teams of software agents can be thought of as multiagent systems. For designing such systems, we rely on different studies on cooperation, coordination, negotiation and conflict resolution conducted in the field of *Distributed Artificial Intelligence* (DAI) [10]. Based on these DAI techniques, we propose to specify distributed systems, using frameworks composed of software agents, which expands the classical view of frameworks composed of distributed objects [13]. In this paper, we present the main concepts needed for designing so-called *software agent-oriented frameworks*. Each framework is composed of one or several teams of agents that are able to achieve services offered by the framework and invoked by users. Software agents teams can be set up in a unique framework or in several frameworks, which leads to the creation of an interoperable multiframework environment.

Our research on software agent-oriented frameworks is applied to the *SIGAL project*, in which we aim at developping an interoperable environment for *georeference libraries*. A georeference library is a base of data describing several geodocumentary resources (maps, air or satellite photos, etc.) available in an organization. While the exploitation of only one georeference library seems simple, it is a very complex task to work concurrently with several georeference libraries in order to answer user's needs. Indeed, each georeference library is characterized by its own informational content, by its own vocabulary used in the metadata descriptions, by its own presentation formats, and by its own exploitation functions. All these differentiating elements would need that a user adapt to each georeference library requirements and understand their different information and structural characteristics; which is an impossible task. In order to help users in doing these tasks, we aim at developping an interoperable environment of georeference libraries. Such an interoperable environment will provide users with services that will not require knowledge of the individual characteristics of the interconnected georeference libraries.

The paper is organized as follows. Section 1 proposes guidelines to deal with the interoperability problem, based on a number of techniques borrowed from DAI and object-oriented technology. Section 2 presents the basic notions of software agent-oriented frameworks. Section 3 describes the architectural characteristics of SIGAL environment and how this latter operates. Section 4 summarizes the main points brought out by our research study.

2   A Software Agent-Oriented Framework

Software agents are autonomous entities having the following abilities: assist users in the accomplishment of their tasks, collaborate with each other to jointly solve different problems, and answer users' needs [9]. In this section, we present the main characteristics of a software agent-oriented framework and its operation mode.

A *software agent-oriented framework* (Fig. 1) offers a set of *services* that can be requested either by users or by other frameworks.

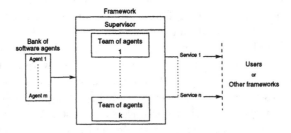

Fig. 1. Representation of the software agent-oriented framework concept

A framework is an environment composed of one or several *teams of software agents*. The services provided by a framework are achieved by different agent teams set up by the framework which selects the relevant agents in a *bank of software agents*. This bank contains several agents having different functionalities which are specific to the application to be developed and of the characteristics of the information systems to be interconnected. In the SIGAL project, our application aims at developing an interoperable environment of georeference libraries which involves three types of frameworks (server, client, local-source). Those frameworks are composed of different kinds of agents which play specific roles (see Section 3.1). For instance, the local-source framework integrates the following agents: Coordinator, Interaction and Knowledge agents (see Section 3.4 for more details).

Teams of agents are composed of several software agents and are structured in different ways according to their responsabilities in the framework. A team is characterized by a set of roles that agents must fulfill according to their capabilities. A role is identified by a list of parameters: role name, goals to achieve, and offered and required services. Considering these parameters a framework selects appropriate agents from the bank of software agents.

In a team of agents, we particularly distinguish the *team supervisor's* role, which coordinates team's activities (coordination tasks, evaluation of agent activities, resolution of internal conflicts). The supervisor agent interacts with the framework's supervisor in order to inform it about the local situation.

Services provided by a framework fulfill specific user's needs such as information search and/or browsing, request formulation, etc. When a service is invoked by a user, the framework's supervisor agent activates a scripting procedure, called *realization scenario*, which specifies the characteristics and the interaction protocols of the agent teams that will perform the various operations required to carry out the service. According to that realization scenario, the framework supervisor creates teams composed of agents that will play the roles specified by the scenario. At their own levels, team supervisor agents activate realization scenarios in order to coordinate the activities of their software agents. A realization scenario is a generalization of the notion of scenario [3] which is used in object-oriented methods such as FUSION [4] and OMT [15] in order to specify the allowed interactions between various kinds of components: frameworks, agent teams and software agents.

A realization scenario is composed of the following elements: software agents types and roles played in the scenario, scheduling sequences indicating in which order agents should perform their plans, the list of internal and/or external information resources which provide knowledge required by the agents to achieve their operations, and an evaluation procedure used to monitor the various agents' operations. For instance, in the SIGAL environment, a data request directed to a georeference library is defined by an *access scenario* (Fig. 2) which involves two Interaction-Agents, each respectively belonging to a client framework and to a local-source framework. The client framework's Interaction-Agent has the knowledge structures needed to transform user's request into a data request expressed in a form compatible with the data manipulation language of the georeference library. The local-source's Interaction-Agent processes the data request and activates the access plan which queries the georeference library. Then, it transmits the answer to the client framework's Interaction-Agent.

If a framework cannot carry out a service on its own, it can require complementary services from other frameworks. For example, in the SIGAL environment, a request such as "Give me the list of geodocuments describing zone X and produced after January 1996" requires a search across all the interconnected

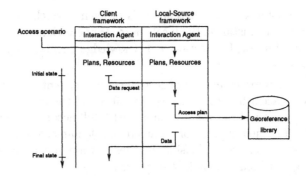

Fig. 2. Representation of a realization scenario example

georeference libraries. A cooperation scenario is invoked by the framework which receives the user's request. Such a scenario provides the framework supervisor with plans to create the relevant agent teams and monitor their activities in order to deliver the answer to the user (Fig. 3).

Fig. 3. Cooperative interaction of several frameworks

3 Presentation of the SIGAL Environment

3.1 SIGAL's Architecture

Before elaborating the SIGAL environment, we studied several issues such as the distribution of georeference libraries, their access rights, communication support channels (local and/or wide-area networks) and similar studies in the field of traditional information-systems interoperability [6,8,16,14]. All these studies agree on the following objectives:

- Maintain the autonomy and independence of the systems to be integrated in an interoperable environment. To this end, associate to the systems *facilitator agents* [5,6] or *information agents* [16] which allow the systems to interact despite their disparities (material, software, terminological).
- Reduce the informational disparities of the various interconnected systems by introducing *mediator agents* [6,17] or a *metadatabase* [8] that translate the local-system knowledge into a common knowledge which is understood by all the systems.

– Introduce *interface/task agents* [16] or *global query systems* [8] in order to help users satisfy their needs without worrying about the distribution and disparities of the information provided by the interconnected systems.

Based on these considerations, we proposed an interoperable architecture for the SIGAL environment (Fig. 4). It is characterized by the use of a *client/server* approach, by the introduction of the technique of *mirror sites*, by the proposition of three types of frameworks (server, client, local-source), and finally by the creation of client frameworks by the server frameworks, whenever it is necessary.

By analogy to information agents of [16], the *local-source frameworks* maintain the autonomy and the independence of the georeference libraries in the interoperable environment. Therefore, local-source frameworks interface the georeference libraries with communication networks and process the data requests sent by the client frameworks.

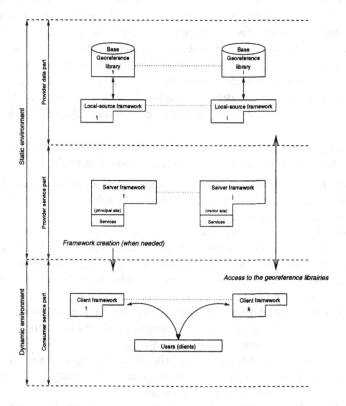

Fig. 4. Multiframework architecture of the SIGAL environment

The server framework is the backbone of the SIGAL environment, since it monitors all the operations needed to support the services offered to the users and to other frameworks. In order to avoid *overloading* the server framework, we suggest to duplicate it on *mirror sites*. In highly distributed environments, the techniques of mirror servers is used to orient users toward less loaded servers. However, in such an architecture, it is important to maintain the coherence of the information duplicated on the server frameworks and consequently to define *reliable update protocols*. In the SIGAL environment, these functions are implemented as a set of services supported by server frameworks: a service to modify the informational content of a georeference library, and a service to connect a new georeference library to the SIGAL environment.

When users need information from several georeference libraries, they invoke relevant services on the server framework. The invocation of such services on the server initiates the creation of a *client framework* generated on the *user's machine*. This client framework is composed of teams of software agents which are needed for fulfilling the service. Hence, the server framework delegates those operations to the client framework and limits its involvement to their monitoring. Once all those operations are executed, the client framework can be either deleted or recorded for further uses. Users would better choose the closest server site in order to reduce waiting delays when the server and client frameworks interact.

Two categories of services are offered by server frameworks : *user services* and *SIGAL services*. A user service fulfills a need that involves several georeference libraries. The user formulates his information request independently from the distribution and heterogeneity constraints of the georeference libraries. SIGAL services support several operations that allow insertion or deletion of a georeference library, as well as the modification of georeference libraries' informational content.

According to the various services to be offered and to SIGAL's architectural characteristics, different types of agents have been identified:

1. *Coordinator-Agent*: it monitors the performance of operations needed to fulfill the various services at a local level (within a framework) and at a global level (between frameworks).
2. *Domain-Agent*: it resolves knowledge disparities by using the common knowledge which is recorded in the Ontology Base. This agent is located in the framework server and is comparable to mediator agent as defined in [17].
3. *Help-Agent*: it presents to users the services which are offered by server frameworks. It is located in server frameworks.
4. *Interaction-Agent*: it mediates interactions between either teams or frameworks, monitoring the exchange of informational and structural components required by the frameworks and their agents.
5. *Interface-Agent*: by analogy to [16], the Interface-Agent assists users in formulating their needs using the knowledge and vocabulary of the application domain. It is located in client frameworks
6. *Knowledge-Agent*: it knows the protocols through which a georeference library accepts requests and provides back informations. This agent also monitors changes occurring in the georeference library during local knowledge updates. The Knowledge-Agent is similar to information agents of [16].
7. *Learning-Agent*: by analogy to [11], it provides new knowledge to the agents of the framework, thanks to internal and external interactions with other SIGAL components.

8. *Resolution-Agent*: it processes user's requests. Therefore, the resolution process may require a decomposition of the request into sub-requests which are sent to the relevant georeference libraries. The Resolution-Agent is similar to task agents of [16].

9. *Scenario-Agent*: it manages the realization scenarios that specify the procedures needed to carry out user services and SIGAL services.

In the following sub-sections, we describe the architectures of the server, client, and local-source frameworks.

3.2 A Server Framework

A *server framework* (Fig. 5) is responsible for carrying out services required by users, or necessary to maintain SIGAL's architecture.

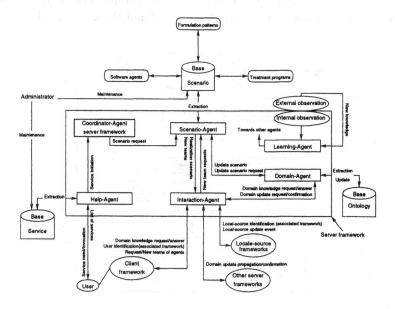

Fig. 5. Server framework's internal architecture

A server framework gathers a team of several agents: *Coordinator, Help, Scenario, Interaction, Domain* and *Learning* agents. Moreover, this team has access to three informational resources; the *Service, Scenario* and *Ontology* Bases. The Service Base is accessible through the Help-Agent and contains a list of user and SIGAL services offered by the server framework. The Scenario Base is accessible through the Scenario-Agent and contains the realization scenarios available to the teams. The Scenario Base contains several components: (1) formulation patterns that are used to help a user to specify his needs according to the vocabulary and the knowledge contained in the ontology base (see Section 3.5 for more details), (2) the characteristics of agent roles needed to carry out the scenarios, and (3) the procedures used to build the plans that are executed by the agents during the scenario. The Ontology Base provides a detailed description of knowledge contained in each georeference library. This Base is similar to that proposed in [8].

In a server framework, the Coordinator-Agent acts as a global supervisor of realization scenarios initiated by this framework: it monitors the progress of the agent teams executing these scenarios. The Interaction-Agent allows the server framework to interact with client frameworks, local-source frameworks and other server frameworks (mirror sites and/or principal). Finally, Learning-Agent aquires new knowledge and transfers it to the agents of this framework.

3.3 A Client Framework

The *client framework* is created by the server framework which has been accessed by the user who required a given service. A client framework (Fig. 6) is set up *temporarily* on the user's computer in order to fulfill the user's need.

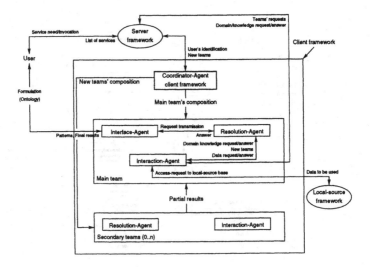

Fig. 6. Client framework's internal architecture

A client framework is composed of a *Coordinator-Agent* and of one or several agent teams according to the number of georeference libraries necessary to process the user's request. The Coordinator-Agent of the client framework is created by the server framework. Then this agent creates the *main agent team* and assigns it the activities prescribed in the realization scenario that identifies the invoked service. When required the Coordinator-Agent also creates secondary teams.

The main team is composed of three agents (Interface, Resolution and Interaction) and is responsible for processing the user's request as well as identifying which georeference libraries must be accessed. According to the number of georeference libraries needed, the main team asks the server framework for additional agents. One or several *secondary teams* are created and gather each an Interaction agent and a Resolution agent. The main team is the teams allowed to communicate with the server framework. Each team (main or secondary) interacts with a specific local-source framework of the georeference library in order to solve the sub-problem that has been assigned to it by the Resolution-Agent of the main team.

3.4 A Local-Source Framework

Each *Local-source framework* (Fig. 7) interfaces a georeference to the SIGAL environment. It is assigned to a specific server framework in order to keep it informed about the changes occurring in the informational content of the georeference library. When such a change occurs, the Domain-Agent of the server framework updates its *Ontology Base*, and these updates are propagated to the other servers. This mechanism preserves the *coherence* of the various copies of the Ontology Base through the network. All update operations are specified by *update scenarios*. A local-source framework also processes the *data requests* directed to its associated georeference library.

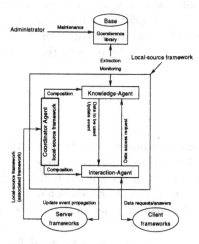

Fig. 7. Local-source framework's internal architecture

The local-source framework is composed of three agents (Coordinator, Interaction and Knowledge). The *Coordinator-Agent* sets the other agents and monitors the operations performed in the local-source framework. The *Knowledge-Agent* interacts with the georeference library in order to get the data requested by the *Resolution-Agents* of different teams. These data are transmitted by the *Interaction-Agent*. This agent allows the local-source framework to interact with server and client frameworks.

3.5 Reducing ontological disparities

Dealing with the *knowledge disparities* of existing systems is an outstanding problem that has to be solved when developing an interoperable environment. Indeed, each system is part of an organization that has its own needs, a specific terminology and original procedures. In order to enable these systems to inter-operate, we have not only to conceive a material and a communication software infrastructure, but also to harmonize the terminology used in the representation of the exchanged knowledge. We must build a common ontology [7]. In the SIGAL project, the ontology available in the *Ontology Base* is an exhaustive description of knowledge structures manipulated by each georeference library.

By establishing a common ontology for the application domain, we offer a common terminological basis for the various interconnected systems, hence reducing for users the risks of getting inconsistent information. In SIGAL's case, ontological disparities exist at different levels. First, being generally developed in an independent way, georeference libraries present disparities in the vocabulary used to describe their data (different ontologies), which makes it difficult for users to consult several georeference libraries simultaneously. Second, current georeference libraries do not help users when formulating their requests. Moreover, a user has to express his needs according to his own vocabulary and to his own comprehension of the domain. Unfortunately, a user is not always able to get the information he is searching for, because georeference libraries cannot adapt to these terminological differences (disparity user-ontology/georeference library-ontology). In SIGAL, the agent teams of the client, server and local-source frameworks cooperate in order to solve the problems resulting from *ontological disparities*.

4 Conclusion

In this paper, we presented the major characteristics of a software agent-oriented framework and its application to the SIGAL project. A framework is made up of teams of software agents, that are able to fulfill services offered to users by frameworks. These agent teams can be set up in a unique framework or in several frameworks leading to the creation of an interoperable multiframework environment.

In SIGAL project, we identified three kinds of frameworks (server, client, local-source). They are the basic components of an interoperable environment for georeference libraries.

We are currently developping a prototype that implements the SIGAL architecture. We use an "Orbeline software[2]" called VisiBroker, which is used to define the behavior of the client and server components. The frameworks and agent teams are built on top of the Orbeline. This is what helps them to manage the SIGAL distributed operations.

---

[2] An Orbeline is a software that respects the conventions defined by the OMG for developing an object-oriented distributed environment.

Acknowledgments

This research is supported by the National Sciences and Engineering Research Council of Canada and by the Research Center on Geomatics of Laval University. The authors thank G. Babin and Y. Bédard for fruitful discussions on several issues presented in this paper.

References

1. Special issue on intelligent services. *Communication of the ACM*, 37(7), 1994.
2. Special issue on intelligent internet services. *IEEE Expert*, 10(4), 1995.
3. J.M. Carroll. *Scenario-Based Design*. Wiley, 1995.
4. D. Coleman, P. Arnold, S. Bodoff, C. Dollin, F. Gilchrist, F. Hayes, and P. Jeremaes. *Object-Oriented Development The Fusion Method*. Prentice Hall, 1994.
5. M.R. Genesereth. An agent-based approach to software interoperability. In *Proceedings of the DARPA Sotware Technology Conference*, 1992.
6. M.R. Genesereth and A.P. Ketchpel. Software agents. *Communication of the ACM*, 37(7):48–53, July 1994.
7. T.R. Gruber. Toward principles for the design of ontologies used for knowledge sharing. Technical report, Knowledge Systems Laboratory, KSL 93 − 04, Stanford University, Stanford, California 94305, August 23, 1993.
8. C. Hsu. *Enterprise Integration and Modeling − the Metadatabase Approach*. Kluwer Academic Publisher, Boston, Mass., USA, 1996.
9. S.-N. Hyacinth. Software agents: An overview. *Knowledge Engineering Review*, 11(3):1–40, Sept 1996.
10. B. Moulin and B. Chaib-Draa. An overview of distributed artificial intelligence. In *Foundations of Distributed Artificial Intelligence*, pages 3–55. G.M.P. O'Hare and N.R. Jennings editors, 1996.
11. A. Namatame and Y. Tsukamoto. Learning agents for cooperating hyperinformation systems. In *Proceedings of the International Conference on Intelligent Cooperative Information Systems*, pages 124–133, May 12–14, 1993.
12. OMG. Object Management Group. http://www.omg.org/, 1996.
13. R. Orfali, D. Harkey, and J. Edwards. *The Essential Distributed Objects Survival Guide*. John Wiley & Sons, 1996.
14. M.P. Papazoglou, Laufmann S.C., and T.K. Sellis. An organizational framework for cooperating intelligent information systems. *International Journal of Intelligent and Cooperative Information Systems*, 1(1):169–202, 1992.
15. G. Rumbaugh, J. Blaha, W. Premelani, F. Eddy, and W. Lorensen. *Object-Oriented Modeling and Design*. Prentice Hall, 1991.
16. K. Sycara, K. Decker, A. Pannu, M. Williamson, and D. Zeng. Distributed intelligent agents. In *IEEE Expert*, July 1996. http://www.cs.cmu.edu/, (submitted).
17. G. Wiederhold. The architecture of future information systems. Stanford University Computer Science Dept., 1989.

An Architecture for Transparent Access to Semantically Heterogeneous Information Sources

Christine Reck *, Birgitta König-Ries

Institut für Programmstrukturen und Datenorganisation
Fakultät für Informatik, Universität Karlsruhe, D-76128 Karlsruhe
[reck|koenig]@ira.uka.de

Abstract. We propose an agent architecture that provides transparent access to a set of distributed, heterogeneous, and autonomous information sources. Our objectives are twofold: First, we want to support quick development of mediators by automatically deriving mediator specifications which are subsequently fed to a mediator generator. Second, we wish to supply the user with a relatively simple model of the information provided in the system so that he can formulate queries without being aware of the existing information sources or service providers and their locations. The system then uses its knowledge about available information sources to generate appropriate query execution plans.

1 Introduction

In recent years, the number of information sources offered on the net has grown tremendously. Support for access to these information sources has mostly taken the form of browsing and search tools. However, the responsibility of finding the right information sources, phrasing queries against them, and interpreting the responses still lies with the user. In view of the wide variety of available information sources, each with its own particular data model, query mechanism, and semantics, this may present a challenging task.

We propose an agent architecture which provides transparent access to such heterogeneous and autonomous information sources and which is primarily based on the concept of mediation [21]. The focus of our work is twofold: We wish to support the quick development of mediators by automatically deriving their specifications, which are subsequently fed to a mediator generator, and we see a need for the automatic generation of query evaluation plans for user queries phrased against a simple model of the available information.

The remainder of this paper is organized as follows: In Section 2 an overview of the architecture is given. Afterwards, the problems we focus on are explained in more detail. Section 3 introduces our concept for the generation of mediators. Section 4 deals with the generation of query execution plans. Finally, in Section 5 we draw some conclusions and describe future work. Related work will be covered in the respective sections.

* Supported in part by a DFG postgraduate fellowship (Graduiertenkolleg) at Fakultät für Informatik, University of Karlsruhe

2 The Architecture

Overview. Figure 1 gives an overview of the agent architecture we propose, showing details of those components we are particularly interested in. The components depicted as ovals or circles are agents: autonomous, cooperative entities capable of making inferences based on their knowledge.

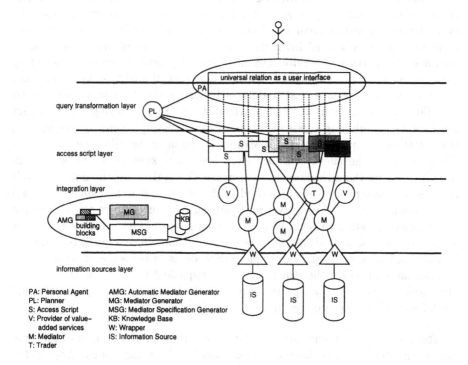

Fig. 1. Overview of the layered architecture

There are four layers, which we now describe.

The *information sources layer* includes autonomous *information sources (IS)* and *wrappers (W)*. The IS are allowed to be heterogeneous with respect to data formats, transport protocols, internal structure (e.g., RDBMS, OODBMS, WWW servers, file systems), and, most importantly, semantics. IS are connected to the system through wrappers. Some aspects of heterogeneity can be resolved at the wrapper level, e.g., conversion to global data formats or transport protocols. Furthermore, wrappers store meta-information about their IS.

In the *integration layer* we have different *service providers* (SP): *mediators (M)*, *traders (T)*, and *providers of value-added services (V)*. Mediators are employed to overcome semantic heterogeneity. Additionally, they are able to integrate and refine information. Sometimes, no appropriate mediator for a particular task may exist. In this case, one must be generated by the *automatic mediator generator* (see Section 3). Traders can be thought of as "yellow pages" for services available in the system. Every service provider registers its services with a trader. Finally, there are providers of value-added services. These are not essential to integration, but otherwise useful, e.g., collecting the cheapest offer for particular goods or services, enhanced directory services, etc.

In the *access script layer* we have *access scripts*, which encapsulate knowledge about and basic interactions with the service providers in the integration layer. Their raison d'etre is that retrieving information directly from service providers is somewhat like assembly language programming: one needs to worry about the exact service providers involved, their locations and interfaces, etc. Moreover, there are certain standard interaction patterns, such as asking a trader for a provider of a particular service, obtain offers for goods or services, presenting data to the user, etc., which are routine and best thought of as a unit. Access scripts are programs that handle such basic tasks. In a way they can be thought of as instructions of an abstract machine. "Programming" this abstract machine, i.e., combining access scripts into sequences implementing user queries, is the task of the query evaluation planner in the layer described next.

The purpose of the *query transformation layer* is to support a simple user interface based on the *universal relation model*. The entirety of the data available from the access script layer is presented to the user as if it were a single universal relation (which is, of course, never materialized). The user poses queries against this universal relation with the help of a personal agent (PA), which is created as soon as the user signals his intent to query the system. Once a query is complete, it is the task of a *query evaluation planner* to devise a sequence of access script invocations that will gather the information requested (cf. Section 4).

Our work focuses on two aspects of this architecture: mediator generation and the translation of user queries into access script sequences.

Related work. A number of architectures allowing integration of information from heterogeneous information sources has been developed. Approaches from the databases community range from tightly integrated federated systems to loosely integrated multidatabase systems (see [2, 6]). The former do not scale easily to large networks, and the latter forego transparency because the user needs to know which subsystem to query. Thus, neither of them seems suitable in our setting, although they provide very useful techniques, e.g., for schema integration. Recently, the problem has been addressed using techniques from distributed systems. One major development is CORBA, the Common Object Request Broker Architecture [12]. This architecture offers transparent access to objects across networks, overcoming the technical heterogeneity of the underlying systems. It does not deal with semantic heterogeneity. We use CORBA as a platform for our implementation. Other important approaches stem from the research in distributed AI. Some of the main contributions are made as part of I[3] [22], the ARPA-sponsored Intelligent Integration of Information program. I[3] includes a generic system architecture designed to present an initial categorization of the principal "services" that can be used to support the intelligent integration of highly heterogeneous information sources. Our work can be interpreted as a concrete instantiation of this generic architecture.

3 Generation of Mediator Specifications

In this section we focus on the integration layer of the architecture described above. In a large network of heterogeneous information sources, mediators are needed to combine and semantically integrate data from different sources (cf. [21]). This task typically entails conversion between data models, schemas, ontologies, etc., and also the aggregation or refinement of data. Currently, mediators are designed and constructed individually. Mediator generators (see "Related Work" below), are available to aid the translation from a formal specification of a mediator to executable code. The specifications must nevertheless be drafted by hand. In large, rapidly evolving networks of information sources, it is not possible to foresee every mediator needed. Thus, it should be possible to generate mediators "on the fly", e.g., when a new IS joins the system. In this case, manual specification of individual mediators is not feasible. Instead, one must look for techniques to automatically – or at least semi-automatically – derive mediator specifications from descriptions of the information sources they are supposed to integrate. In the following we discuss the design of a mediator specification generator (MSG) which attempts to derive mediator specifications from source metadata automatically. It should be noted that this design is still in an early stage: whereas some of the concepts presented in this section (such as the metamodel of information models and a library of mediation methods) are fairly specific and in part already implemented, others are more suggestive in nature and represent directions we want to explore. In the following subsections we will review related work (Section 3.1), introduce information models (Section 3.2), discuss the inputs the MSG uses (Section 3.3), and describe the invocation of the MSG (Section 3.4).

3.1 Related Work

Mediator specification generation builds on mediator generation. Current approaches (e.g., [9, 13, 23]) do not support the user in finding a specification, but rather concentrate on the building of the mediator once the specification is given. In contrast, we try to provide means to find a specification, which can then be fed to an existing mediator generator.

Another important branch of work we rely heavily on is schema integration. Here, quite a number of different and more or less automated approaches exist (cf. [1, 4] for an overview) Our goal is to identify suitable existing methods that can be combined by the MSG in order to find appropriate mappings.

3.2 Information Models

On an abstract level, mediators can be characterized as mappings from data expressed according to one or more *input information models* to data expressed according to an *output information model*, and of queries against the output information model to queries against the input information model. An information model (IM) in our sense is a particular way of representing real-world concepts as data. For example, the fact that the rental car with the registration number KA-GH 123 is a BMW and costs 300 German marks per day may in one IM be represented as a tuple ⟨KA-GH 123, BMW, 300⟩ of the relation CAR(NUMBER, MAKE, PRICE). In another IM there is a "KA-GH 123" object with a "make" attribute that points to the BMW object and a "price-group" object that points to a price-group class, etc. The notion of "information model" is of necessity somewhat vague, because the notion of "real-world concept" is, but there are manifest aspects such as the data model, the schema, integrity constraints, properties at the instance level (e.g., statistics about distributions of values) and so on, that can be captured in the system. Thus, in the context of our system, the term information model refers to a combination of a data model, a schema, and other parameters describing the semantics of a particular source. IMs are represented as instances of IM schemas, which in turn are instances of a single IM meta schema. The reason for having multiple IM schemas is that the structure of an IM varies greatly with the data model used in that IM. Thus, there are IM schemas for relational IM, o-o IM, graph-structured IM, etc.

As an example, consider the relation CAR(NUMBER,MAKE,PRICE) about rental cars again. A description of its IM may look like this:

```
CAR in Relation                         PRICE
    hasAttributes:                          domain: integer;
        NUMBER                              average: 300;
            domain: string;                 min: 100;
            avg_length: 9;                  unit: dollar/day;
            percentage_numeric: 33;     hasProperties:
            percentage_alpha:   45;         key: NUMBER;
        MAKE                                foreignkey: MAKE;
            domain: string;                 numberoftuples: 250;
            avg_length: 6;
            percentage_alpha: 98;
```

In our system, we have two classes of IMs: those of the external IS, and those of internal system components, e.g., other mediators.

The IM of the sources is stored in the wrappers. Whenever a new source is added to the system, the administrator (DBA) has to make available in the wrapper a description of the IM of the source by "filling in" the appropriate IM schema. The information needed to do so can be extracted automatically from the IS, thus minimizing the effort when adding a source to the system. An important aspect here is, that no mapping of terms to a common ontology is required, i.e. the terms of the underlying information source are used. However, if such a mapping is known, it can be accommodated in the IM, and might ease the generation of mediators.

Obviously, it facilitates the cooperation and coordination of internal components (e.g., SP, access scripts, etc.), if their IMs are similar. Thus, we assume a unique system wide data model and a unique system wide annotated ontology. However, different components may differ in their schema, i.e. use different parts of the ontology and combine them differently. Thus, we do not require a global schema. Obviously, we need a rich data model to capture the information in the schemas of the IMs. Additionally, we need the possibility to add meta-models, e.g., our meta-model of IMs. In our implementation, we use ConceptBase (CB)[5] and its data model Telos. CB is a client-server deductive object base system developed primarily for modeling purposes supporting infinite classification hierarchies.

3.3 Information the MSG Uses

To develop specifications, the MSG relies on the following inputs:

Desired input and output information models. Obviously, in order to develop mappings between IMs, the MSG has to know these models. Mediators (and thus the MSG) have to deal with both classes of IMs described above.

Auxiliary information. To retrieve synonyms, semantic subsumptions etc., thesauri, ontologies, dictionaries and other domain-specific knowledge bases should be available.

A library of mediation methods. One important part of our work is to transform existing mediation methods into a library of building blocks that may be combined freely. As a basis, we need at least one building block to overcome each kind of schematic conflict that may arise. The possible kinds of conflict are: (cf. [4]) differences in terminology, in structure and in focus. A complete classification of conflicts and resolution techniques is given in [6]. Equally important are building blocks capable of *detecting* conflicts (using, e.g., [8, 18]). Building blocks offering conversion functions [17], or the definition of generalization, specialization and aggregation hierarchies [9] cover additional aspects.

3.4 Invoking the MSG

There are two occasions on which the MSG may be invoked. The first is when a new information source joins the system. In this case, the source's DBA may invoke the MSG. As input he submits those concepts from the system-wide ontology that relate to his IS. Together with the annotations of these concepts in the system ontology and the system-wide data model, this specifies the desired output IM. The MSG loads the input IM from the wrapper of the new source, may use auxiliary knowledge, and tries to derive an appropriate mediator specification, i.e. a mapping from the input to the output IMs. If the MSG is not able to find a mapping by itself, the DBA who has invoked the MSG is queried for additional input, e.g., he might be asked whether two attributes that seem to be similar can be treated as identical. Finally, when a specification has been derived, it is fed to the mediator generator.

The second situation evolves if a user asks a query not foreseen by the DBAs of the sources concerned. In this case the trader will either find a wrapper for a suitable IS, but will not be able to find an appropriate mediator, or finds one or more mediators offering just part of the functionality required[2] The trader thus invokes the MSG. If the mapping needed is rather simple and can thus be specified automatically (e.g., a user asking for a price in dollar and an IS

---

[2] Assume there exist two mediators: one mapping the IM of Avis, and the other that of Hertz. To answer a user query asking for all cars, a third mediator is needed, integrating answers from the first two.

providing prices in German marks), the appropriate mediator specification is generated on the fly and subsequently fed to a mediator generator as described above. In case this is not possible, the query is answered without the information the new mediator would have made available (i.e. possibly incompletely), and a message indicating the need for mediator generation is sent to the respective source DBAs.

4 Access Scripts and the Universal Relation Interface

4.1 Motivation

In this section, we focus on the access script layer and the query transformation layer of the architecture (cf. Fig. 1). Recall that access scripts may be viewed as instructions of an abstract "net access" machine that must be combined to implement user queries. In the following, we describe the process of "compiling" a user query into an access script sequence.

The access scripts have a number of input parameters and a number of output parameters. The parameters represent concepts of the UoD. The basic idea is to view them as attributes in a relational model so that each access script represents a relational schema with the input and output parameters as its attributes. Note that access scripts differ from relations because one is not able to retrieve the information represented by an access script in an arbitrary way, but rather one has to submit values for the input attributes of the access script in order to obtain values for the output attributes. The set of these relational schemas can be viewed as a database schema modeling the information accessible through the access scripts. To simplify the user view, the user is given a single relation whose schema consists of the union of all attributes (the universal relation) as an interface. Whenever the user queries the universal relation, we need to generate a query evaluation plan.

Example. Consider a travel information system. We assume that there are information sources on various means of transport (airlines, trains, car rental companies, etc.), traders that know the location of these sources, and mediators that perform semantic integration. We moreover assume that we have access scripts to implement the following functions:

- Script S_1: Given a service category, ask a trader for mediators that understand requests in that category (type *Category* $\rightarrow$ *Mediator*).
- Script S_2: Given a mediator and a service category, determine the list of parameters needed in order to obtain a bid (type *Mediator* $\times$ *Category* $\rightarrow$ *Parameters*).
- Script S_3: Given a list of parameters, obtain values for them from the user (type *Parameters* $\rightarrow$ *Values*).
- Script S_4: Given a mediator, a service category, and a list of values for the parameters of that service category, obtain bids (type *Mediator* $\times$ *Category* $\times$ *Values* $\rightarrow$ *Bid*).

Suppose the user wishes to rent a car. He selects the service category "car-rental" and asks for bids b. The system searches for a combination of access scripts that, given values for the *Category* attribute, finds values for the *Bid* attribute and derives the execution plan

S_1("car-rental", m), $S_2(m$, "car-rental", p), $S_3(p, v)$, $S_4(m$, "car-rental", $v, b)$.

When this plan is executed, the following happens. S_1 locates a mediator m providing the "car-rental" service (it is assumed that, through mediation, this service comes with some standard interface). S_2 obtains from m a description p of the parameters of this service. S_3 uses p to build and display a form that the user fills in, providing the specifics v of his request (pickup and return dates, car class, location, etc)., which S_4 then uses to obtain bids from m.

The problem we consider in this section is the generation of such a query evaluation plan. First, we take a more detailed look at the universal relation interface, user queries, and access scripts. Afterwards we show how query evaluation plans are generated.

Due to space limitations, we restrict ourselves to an overview of the results. A detailed description can be found in [16].

4.2 Related Work

Universal relation systems have been treated widely in the literature (see, e. g., [11, 10, 20, 7] for surveys of various aspects and [19] for an introduction). The main question when adopting a universal relation approach is which instance of the universal relation to choose. Instead of classic approaches (like weak instance or representative instance), we choose (like [15]) the *full disjunction* [3]. While [15] materializes the full disjunction by a sequence of outerjoins, we wish to avoid full materialization, and instead use access scripts to gather just the information requested in the user query. The major problem is that access scripts cannot be combined in an arbitrary way, but only in ways prescribed by their distinction between input and output attributes. In [14] a similar problem is studied. There, binding patterns are used to specify so-called query templates that a given source can answer. The semantics of query templates is defined as a conjunction of certain base predicates. Queries are similar to query templates in that they are also specified by predicates with binding patterns and their semantics is again defined as a conjunction of base predicates. The task then is to answer a query using a conjunction of query templates such that the semantics of the query is the same as the semantics of the conjunction of query templates. Our problem differs from their approach in that the semantics of a query is not prespecified, but must be derived from the attributes that it mentions.

4.3 The Model

Attributes. We assume that there is some finite universe **Attr** of attributes that suffice to describe all aspects of the UoD [3]. We require that attributes are

---

[3] There may be different UoDs corresponding to unrelated contexts, in which case the user chooses a context before posing the query.

used consistently by all access scripts, in the sense that occurrences of the same attribute always refer to the same "role" (at the very least, such occurrences should refer to the same fixed domain, which we denote by $dom(A)$). We refer to domain elements as constants.

Access Scripts. An *access script* consists of an *access script type* and an *extension* of that type. Access script types are denoted $S : \mathcal{I} \to \mathcal{O}$ where S is a unique name, and $\mathcal{I}$ and $\mathcal{O}$ are disjoint sets of attributes called input and output attributes of S, respectively. An extension of $S : \mathcal{I} \to \mathcal{O}$ is a relation over $\mathcal{I} \cup \mathcal{O}$ not necessarily finite or single-valued. For example, an access script converting dollars to German marks has an infinite extension, whereas an access script producing a set of tourist attractions for a given city has a multivalued extension.

We refer to the set of access script types as **AS** and assume that **Attr** is the set of attributes mentioned in these types. To have some notion for the extension of each access script type, assume that there is a mapping I that assigns to every access script type an extension of that type.

Universal Relation. We believe that for our work every join-consistent connection of two or more relations should be treated as valid. Therefore, instead of using the classical universal relation models (like weak instances or the representative instance), we use what Galindo-Legaria [3] calls a *full disjunction* [4]. This is defined as follows.

Let $\mathcal{R}$ be a set of relations, and let $\mathcal{A}$ be the union of the schemas of the relations in $\mathcal{R}$. The full disjunction of $\mathcal{R}$, written $FD(\mathcal{R})$, is a relation over schema $\mathcal{A}$. It is obtained by taking all subsets $\mathcal{S} \subseteq \mathcal{R}$, forming for each subset $\mathcal{S}$ the natural join of its members (which may involve forming Cartesian products if the schemas are not connected), padding all tuples so obtained with null values to obtain tuples over $\mathcal{A}$, and collecting the padded tuples into $FD(\mathcal{R})$. Formally:

$$FD(\mathcal{R}) = \bigcup_{\mathcal{S} \subseteq \mathcal{R}} pad_{\mathcal{A}}(\bowtie \mathcal{S}),$$

where $pad_{\mathcal{A}}$ denotes the operation of padding with null values to obtain tuples over $\mathcal{A}$. Note that the full disjunction may contain information which is not "reachable" through the access scripts, because extensions of access script types are only accessible in a way restricted through the access script type, as explained above.

Queries. We consider conjunctive queries over a set of predicates. The syntax of the predicates is as follows. For every attribute set $\{A_1, \ldots, A_n\} \subseteq$ **Attr** an n-ary predicate symbol $P_{\{A_1, \ldots, A_n\}}$ is introduced. A *query predicate* is an expression of the form $P_{\{A_1, \ldots, A_n\}}(e_1, \ldots, e_n)$, where $e_i \in dom(A_i) \cup \mathcal{V}$ for $1 \leq i \leq n$ (where $\mathcal{V}$ is a set of variable symbols). A *query* is a conjunction of query predicates. Queries are conveniently written as tableaux, e.g., the tableau corresponding to

---

[4] Actually, our definition of full disjunction is not quite the same as Galindo-Legaria's, because we allow Cartesian products in a full disjunction, and we do not minimize with respect to tuple subsumption.

query $P_{\{AB\}}(a, x), P_{\{AC\}}(x, c)$ over attribute set $\mathbf{Attr} = \{A, B, C, D\}$ is

A	B	C	D
a	x		
x		c	

In general, the tableau corresponding to a query q is a matrix (a_{ij}) with one column for every attribute in $\mathbf{Attr}$ and one row for every predicate in q. For row i corresponding to query predicate $P_{\{A_1,\ldots,A_n\}}(e_1,\ldots,e_n)$ and column j corresponding to attribute A, the entry a_{ij} is e_k if $A = A_k$ for some $k \in \{1,\ldots,n\}$, and blank otherwise. An *answer* to a query is a valuation, i.e., a mapping from variables to constants, such that for every predicate $P_{\{A_1,\ldots,A_n\}}(e_1,\ldots,e_n)$ in the query, the tuple $(e_1,\ldots,e_n)$ is, after applying the valuation to variables occurring in $e_1,\ldots,e_n$, in the total projection[5] of the extension u of the universal relation onto $\{A_1,\ldots,A_n\}$. The set of all answers to a query q is denoted by $[\![q]\!](u)$.

Access script sequences. A query is evaluated by translating it into a sequence of calls to access scripts and then executing the sequence. A call to an access script is specified by the access script type that is called and the parameters of the call. To make this notion precise, we introduce for every access script type $S : \mathcal{I} \to \mathcal{O}$ in $\mathbf{AS}$ a predicate symbol $S_{\mathcal{I};\mathcal{O}}$ of arity $|\mathcal{I} \cup \mathcal{O}|$ and say that an *access script predicate* is an expression of the form $S_{\{I_1,\ldots,I_m\};\{O_1,\ldots,O_n\}}(e_1,\ldots,e_{m+n})$, where $I_1,\ldots,I_m \in \mathcal{I}$ and $O_1,\ldots,O_n \in \mathcal{O}$ are the input and output attributes of S, respectively. Each argument e_i is either a variable or a constant of the appropriate domain. Arguments $e_1,\ldots,e_m$ are called the *inputs*, arguments $e_{m+1},\ldots,e_{m+n}$ are called the *outputs* of the predicate.

An *access script sequence* is a list of access script predicates. As an access script sequence corresponds to a sequence of calls to access scripts, one must guarantee the sequence to be *executable* in the sense that a variable symbol appearing as an input of some predicate also occurs as an output of an earlier predicate (that is, all inputs are "known" by the time an access script is called).

When executing a sequence s, we obtain valuations for the variables mentioned in the sequence such that for every predicate $S_{\mathcal{I};\mathcal{O}}(e_1,\ldots,e_{m+n})$ occurring in s, the tuple $(e_1,\ldots,e_{m+n})$ is, after replacement of variables with their assigned values, in the extension $I(S)$ of the access script type S. Such a valuation is called an *answer* to s, and the set of all answers is denoted by $[\![s]\!](I)$.

For an access script sequence to be a correct implementation of a query, two conditions must be satisfied in addition to executability. Informally, they can be stated as follows (see [16] for details). Assume that the query is given in tableau form where each row of the tableau corresponds to one query predicate. Then for each access script predicate $S : \mathcal{I} \to \mathcal{O}$ in the sequence, there must exist a row of the tableau such that the arguments of the predicate are the entries of that row in the columns corresponding to $\mathcal{I} \cup \mathcal{O}$. That is, it is not allowed to call an access script with parameters of more than one row. The second condition

---

[5] The total projection $\Pi\!\downarrow_{\mathcal{A}}(r)$ of a relation r onto attribute set $\mathcal{A}$ is defined as the set of those tuples in the ordinary projection of r onto $\mathcal{A}$ that do not contain any null values.

states that each variable is computed somewhere and every constant mentioned in the query is used somewhere (i.e., as parameter of an access script call). If an access script sequence fulfills these conditions w.r.t. some query, we call it *sound* for that query.

One can show that the valuations produced by an access script sequence sound for query q are always answers to q. That is, such an access script sequence does not produce "wrong" answers.

4.4 Generation and Execution of Query Evaluation Plans

The approach to generating query evaluation plans is to view the access scripts as operators with pre- and postconditions and to use a planning algorithm. The planning algorithm produces one or more sound access script sequences.

So far, we use a simple forward chaining algorithm to search for sound access script sequences. The inputs of the algorithm are the set **AS** of access script types and a query q given in tableau form. The output is an access script sequence. Using backtracking, it is possible to generate multiple access script sequences. One can show that the generated access script sequences are sound (see [16] for details).

Execution of an access script sequence involves calling the various access scripts listed in the sequence with proper arguments. We developed an execution model for access script sequences where the variable bindings produced by the access scripts in the sequence are kept in a so-called *blackboard relation*. This is a relation over the variables mentioned in the query which is used to determine the input parameters whenever an access script is invoked, and to store results (valuations for a certain set of variables) when the call to an access script returns.

5 Conclusions and Future Work

In a world where vast quantities of information are provided on the net and the user is in danger of getting lost in a sea of information, it is absolutely essential to provide support for using the "resource" information. In our approach the dynamic generation of query evaluation plans provides a solution for the choice and coordination of information sources, while the dynamic generation of mediators tackles the problem of minimizing human effort when adding new IS.

In the future, we intend to validate these concepts by comprehensive scenarios. An interesting extension to the planner would be to generate a new query evaluation plan based on existing ones and the results produced so far, whenever an error occurs during the execution of the plan.

References

1. C. Batini, M. Lenzerini, and S. B. Navathe. A comparative analysis of methodologies for database schema integration. *ACM Computing Surveys*, 18(4):323–364, 1986.

2. M. W. Bright, A. R. Hurson, and S. H. Pakzad. A Taxonomy and Current Issues in Multidatabase Systems. *IEEE Computer*, 25(3):50–60, 1992.

3. C. A. Galindo-Legaria. Outerjoins as Disjunctions. In *Proc. of ACM SIGMOD*, pages 348–358, Minneapolis, Minnesota, USA, 1994.

4. H. Jamil and P. Johannesson. Semantic interoperability - context, issues and research directions. In *Proc. of the 2. CoopIS*, pages 180–191, Toronto, Canada, 1994.

5. M. Jarke, S. Eherer, R. Gallersdörfer, M. A. Jeusfeld, and M. Staudt. Conceptbase - a deductive object base for meta data management. *Journal on Intelligent Information Systems*, 4(2):167–192, 1995.

6. W. Kim. *Modern Database Systems*. Addison-Wesley, 1995.

7. F. Leymann. A Survey of the Universal Relation Model. *Data&Knowledge Engineering*, 4:305–320, 1989.

8. W. Li and C. Clifton. Semantic integration in heterogeneous databases using neural networks. In *Proc. of the 20th VLDB, Santiago, Chile*, pages 1–12, 1994.

9. L. Liu, C. Pu, and Y. Lee. An Adaptive Approach to Query Mediation across Heterogeneous Information Sources. In *Proc. of the 1. IFCIS CoopIS*, pages 144–156, Brussels, Belgium, 1996.

10. D. Maier, D. Rozenshtein, and D. Warren. Window functions. In P. Kanellakis and F. Preparata, editors, *Advances in Computing Research 3: The Theory of Databases*, pages 213–246. JAI Press, 1986.

11. D. Maier, J. D. Ullman, and M. Y. Vardi. On the Foundations of the Universal Relation Model. *ACM TODS*, 9(2):283–308, 1984.

12. Object Management Group, Inc. (OMG). *The Common Object Request Broker: Architecture and Specification, Version 2.0*, July 1995.

13. Y. Papakonstantinou, H. Garcia-Molina, and J. Ullman. MedMaker: A Mediation System Based on Declarative Specifications. In *Proc. Intl. Conf. on Data Engineering*, pages 132–141, New Orleans, USA, 1996.

14. A. Rajaraman, Y. Sagiv, and J. D. Ullman. Answering Queries Using Templates with Binding Patterns (Extended Abtract). In *Proc. 14th ACM PODS*, pages 105–112, San Jose, California, 1995.

15. A. Rajaraman and J. D. Ullman. Integrating Informations by Outerjoins and Full Disjunctions. In *Proc. 15th ACM PODS*, pages 238–248, Montreal, Canada, 1996.

16. C. Reck and G. Hillebrand. Implementing a Universal Relation Interface Using Access Scripts with Binding Patterns. Technical Report 1996-40, Universität Karlsruhe, November 1996. Available via ftp://ftp.ira.uka.de/pub/uni-karlsruhe/papers/Techreports/1996/1996-40.ps.gz, submitted for publication.

17. A. Rosenthal and E. Sciore. Description, conversion, and planning for semantic interoperability. In *Proc. of DS-6*. IFIP, 1996.

18. W. W. Song, P. Johannesson, and J. A. Bubenko Jr. Semantic similarity relations in schema integration. In *Proc. of ER-92*. Springer, 1992.

19. J. D. Ullman. *Principles of Database and Knowledge-Base Systems*, volume 2. Computer Science Press, 1989.

20. M. Y. Vardi. The Universal-Relation Data Model for Logical Independence. *IEEE Software*, pages 80–85, march 1988.

21. G. Wiederhold. Mediation in the architecture of future information systems. *IEEE Computer*, 25(3):38–48, 1992.

22. G. Wiederhold. *Intelligent Integration of Information*. Kluwer, 1996.

23. G. Zhou, R. Hull, and R. King. Generating data integration mediators that use materialization. *Journal of Intelligent Information Systems*, 6(2/3):111–134, 1996.

Multi-Level Security in Multiagent Systems

Gerd Wagner   gw@inf.fu-berlin.de

Inst.f.Informatik, Univ. Leipzig, Augustusplatz 10-11, 04109 Leipzig, Germany,
Tel+Fax: (+49 30) 834 95 69.

Abstract. Whenever agents deal with confidential information, it is important that they comply with a principled security policy. We show how the database concept of *multi-level security* can be applied to inter-agent communication. This includes the case where an unauthorized agent is misinformed on purpose in order to protect confidential information.

1   Introduction

In certain applications, it is essential to protect confidential information from unauthorized access. While access restrictions in relational databases have to be defined within the database schema, implying that only entire tables (i.e. predicates) can be protected, the concept of *multi-level security (MLS)*[1] allows to protect single rows of a table (i.e. atomic sentences) according to their security classification. The MLS concept is not concerned with lower-level security issues such as authentification, or secure message transport protocols, but only with the definition of secure query answering and secure update in information systems.

We show how multi-level security can be achieved in multi-agent and multi-database systems. This requires that the security restrictions defined in MLS tables have to be taken into consideration in inter-agent communication. We formalize multi-level security on the basis of our theory of vivid knowledge and agent systems introduced in [Wag95, Wag96].

A *vivid agent* is a software-controlled system whose state is represented by a knowledge base, and whose behavior is represented by means of *action* and *reaction rules*. The basic functionality of a vivid agent comprises a knowledge system (including an update and an inference operation), and the capability to represent and perform actions in order to be able to generate and execute plans. Since a vivid agent is 'situated' in an environment with which it has to be able to communicate, it also needs the ability to react in response to perception events, and in response to communication events created by the communication acts of other agents. Reactions may be immediate and independent from the current believe state of the agent but they may also depend on the result of deliberation. In any case, they are triggered by events which are not controlled by the agent.

We do not assume a fixed formal language and a fixed logical system for the knowledge base of an agent. Rather, we believe that it is more appropriate to choose a suitable knowledge system for each agent individually according to its

---

[1] See, e.g., [Lan81, JS91, SWQ94].

domain and its tasks. In simple cases, a relational database-like system (admitting of atomic sentences only) will do the job, while in more involved cases one may need the ability to process, in addition to simple facts, uncertain, temporal or confidential information, or even such advanced capabilities as deductive query answering and abductive reasoning.

While certain agents may have rather limited capabilities, others are quite complex. We call the simplest form of a vivid agent a *reagent*. A reagent does not have explicit goals and intentions but only beliefs about the current state of affairs. It reacts to events in its environment, taking into account what it currently believes. A reagent updates its beliefs and draws inferences from them for answering queries by applying the respective operations of the vivid knowledge system it is based on.

A cooperative knowledge base can be viewed as a reagent, since cooperative query answering can be achieved on the basis of reactive communication protocols defined at design time (without planning for user-defined tasks communicated at run time). A multidatabase (MDB) system, involving inhomogeneous nodes with a global distribution schema, can therefore be conceptualized as a multi-reagent system. Notice that if there were only relational databases in a MDB, there would be no communication, since the semantics of RDBs assumes their completeness, i.e. a standard RDB has never any reason to ask another database for additional information. Communication between databases requires incomplete knowledge.

2 Vivid Knowledge Systems

The knowledge system of a vivid agent is based on three specific languages: L_{KB} is the set of all admissible knowledge bases, L_{Query} is the query language, and L_{Input} is the set of all admissible inputs, i.e. those formulas representing new information a KB may be updated with. While the input language defines what the agent can be told (i.e. what it is able to assimilate into its KB), the query language defines what the agent can be asked. Where L is a set of formulas, L^0 denotes its restriction to closed formulas (sentences). Elements of L^0_{Query}, i.e. closed query formulas, are also called *if-queries*.

Definition 1 (Knowledge System) *An abstract knowledge system[2] K consists of three languages and two operations: a knowledge representation language L_{KB}, a query language L_{Query}, an input language L_{Input}, an inference relation $\vdash$, such that $X \vdash F$ holds if $F \in L^0_{\text{Query}}$ can be inferred from $X \in L_{\text{KB}}$, and an update operation Upd, such that the result of updating $X \in L_{\text{KB}}$ with $F \in L^0_{\text{Input}}$ is the knowledge base $\text{Upd}(X, F)$.*

---

[2] See also [Wag95].

Definition 2 (Answer Operation)   *The answer operation* Ans *is defined for if-queries F by*

$$\text{Ans}(X, F) = \begin{cases} \text{yes} & \text{if } X \vdash F \\ \text{no} & \text{if } X \vdash \neg F \\ \text{unknown} & \text{otherwise} \end{cases}$$

and for query formulas G with free variables $x_1, \ldots, x_n$ by

$$\langle c_1, \ldots, c_n \rangle \in \text{Ans}(X, G(x_1, \ldots, x_n)) \quad \text{if} \quad X \vdash G(c_1, \ldots, c_n)$$

We now present two important examples of knowledge systems: relational databases, and MLS databases.

2.1 Relational Databases

A relational database is a finite set of finite relations (tables) corresponding to a finite set of atomic sentences. For instance, a hospital database may contain facts expressing who is currently a patient and what are their diagnoses, $\Delta_{hosp} = \{Patient, Diagnosis\}$, where

$$\text{Patient} = \begin{array}{|c|} \hline \text{BY} \\ \text{MJ} \\ \text{JB} \\ \hline \end{array} \quad \text{Diagnosis} = \begin{array}{|c c|} \hline \text{BY} & \text{alc} \\ \text{JB} & \text{mal} \\ \hline \end{array}$$

The propositional representation of Δ_{hosp} is

$$X_{hosp} = \{p(BY), p(MJ), p(JB), d(BY, alc), d(JB, mal)\}$$

representing the information that Boris Yeltsin (BY), Michael Jackson (MJ), and James Bond (JB) are currently patients of the hospital, and the diagnosis of BY is alcoholism, and that of JB is malaria. As a kind of natural deduction from positive facts an inference relation $\vdash$ between a relational database X and an if-query is defined in the following way:

$$\begin{align} (a) \quad & X \vdash a \text{ if } a \in X \\ (\neg a) \quad & X \vdash \neg a \text{ if } a \notin X \end{align}$$

Notice the non-monotonicity of $(\neg a)$: negation in relational databases corresponds to *negation-as-failure*. Compound if-queries, involving conjunction and disjunction, are handled in the standard way. Negated compound if-queries are treated by simplification according to the DeMorgan rules and double negation elimination. We obtain, for example, $X_{hosp} \vdash p(MJ) \wedge \neg d(MJ, alc)$. Because of its built-in general Closed-World Assumption, a relational database X answers an if-query F by either yes or no: the answer is yes if $X \vdash F$, and no otherwise. For instance, $\text{Ans}(X_{hosp}, d(BY, mal)) = $ no. Updates are insertions, $\text{Upd}(X, a) := X \cup \{a\}$, and deletions, $\text{Upd}(X, \neg a) := X - \{a\}$, where a is an atom. For a consistent set of literals E, we have $\text{Upd}(X, E) = X \cup E^+ - E^-$, where E^+ contains the positive, and E^- contains the negative literals of E. For instance,

$$\mathsf{Upd}(X_{hosp}, \neg d(JB, mal) \wedge d(JB, yf))$$
$$= \{p(BY), p(MJ), p(JB), d(BY, alc), d(JB, yf)\}$$

describes a possible transaction. The knowledge system of relational databases is denoted by $\boldsymbol{A}$ (for $\boldsymbol{A}$tomic). We also describe a knowledge system by means of its language table:

$$\boldsymbol{A} = \begin{array}{|l|l|} \hline L_{\mathrm{KB}} & 2^{\mathrm{At}} \\ \hline L_{\mathrm{Query}} & L(\neg, \wedge, \vee, \exists, \forall) \\ \hline L_{\mathrm{Ans}}^0 & \{\text{yes, no}\} \\ \hline L_{\mathrm{Input}} & \mathrm{Lit} \\ \hline \end{array}$$

Knowledge systems extending $\boldsymbol{A}$ conservatively are called *vivid*. Positive vivid knowledge systems use a general Closed-World Assumption, whereas general vivid knowledge systems employ specific Closed-World Assumptions (and possibly two kinds of negation). For instance, $\boldsymbol{A}$ can be extended to the general vivid knowledge system of *factbases*, by allowing for literals instead of atoms as information units. Further important examples of positive vivid knowledge systems are temporal, uncertain and MLS databases. All these kinds of knowledge bases can be extended to *deductive knowledge bases* by adding deduction rules of the form $F \leftarrow G$ [Wag95].

2.2 MLS Databases

In *multi-level secure (MLS)* databases,[3] all information items are assigned a security classification, and all database users are assigned a security clearance, both from a partially ordered set of security levels. For instance, the four security levels *unclassified* (0), *confidential* (1), *secret* (2), and *top secret* (3) may be used to classify entries in a MLS table.

As an example, consider the database of a hospital. Depending on the respective person it may be sensitive information to know whether someone is a patient in the hospital. In the case of a politician, such infomation would be publicly available. But not so in the case of a shy pop star, or a secret service agent. The following MLS tables containing the records of patients and their diagnoses form the hospital database X_{hosp}:

$$\mathrm{Patient} = \begin{array}{|ll|} \hline \mathrm{BY} & 0 \\ \mathrm{MJ} & 1 \\ \mathrm{JB} & 3 \\ \hline \end{array} \qquad \mathrm{Diagnosis} = \begin{array}{|lll|} \hline \mathrm{BY} & \mathrm{alc} & 1 \\ \mathrm{JB} & \mathrm{mal} & 3 \\ \hline \end{array}$$

These tables represent the following beliefs at the respective clearance level:

level	beliefs
0	$\{p(BY)\}$
1, 2	$\{p(BY), p(MJ), d(BY, alc)\}$
3	$\{p(BY), p(MJ), p(JB), d(BY, alc), d(JB, mal)\}$

---

[3] See, e.g., [Lan81, JS91, SWQ94].

The basic principle underlying MLS query answering is called *simple security property* and was defined in the Bell-LaPadula model of *mandatory security*, see [Lan81]. It can also be described by the slogan "no read up", i.e. users are only permitted to read from a level dominated by their own. We will formalize this principle below in the definition of secure inference. As opposed to [SWQ94], we think that it should be defined by the logical semantics of MLS databases how lower-level beliefs carry over to higher-level beliefs.

Notice that it is not possible to preserve privacy and maintain security by simply omitting information, like in the reply *'no answer'* to the question *'Is Michael Jackson a patient in this hospital ?'*. The asking reporter could easily infer from this refusal to answer that MJ must be a patient in the hospital. The only way to maintain security is to give a wrong answer, i.e. to misinform the unauthorized asker. The rationality principle of secure inference is the

(Principle of Minimal Misinformation) Askers are only misinformed about an information item if they are not sufficiently authorized with respect to that item.

Assume, for instance, that Boris Yeltsin is in the hospital with an accute alcoholism. When a reporter asks if BY is in the hospital, he receives the answer *yes*. If he then asks whether BY has drunk too much, the secure answer may be *no* or *unknown*.[4] When being asked what BY suffers from, the hospital information system may reply to the reporter that he has a severe influenca (i.e. a *cover story*).

MLS queries are annotated by the clearance level of the asker. Since reporters have clerance level 0 (unclassified), we get

$$\mathsf{Ans}(X_{hosp}, p(MJ)/0) = \mathsf{no}$$

while a doctor of the hospital with clerance level 2 would get the right answer: *'yes, MJ is a patient in this hospital'*,

$$\mathsf{Ans}(X_{hosp}, p(MJ)/2) = \mathsf{yes}$$

Definition 3 (Security Hierarchy)   *A security hierarchy SH is a finite partial order with a greatest element denoted by $\top$.*

In our examples, we will only use the security hierarchy $\{0, 1, 2, 3\}$ introduced above.

Definition 4 (MLS Table)   *A MLS table R over a security hierarchy SH and a relation schema $r(x_1, \ldots, x_n)$ is a finite subset of $D_1 \times \ldots \times D_n \times SH$.*

---

[4] Notice that this choice in misinforming is only available in the case of incomplete predicates allowing for the answer *unknown*.

Definition 5 (MLS Database)   *A MLS database Δ over a schema $\Sigma = \langle\{r_1, \ldots, r_m\}, SH\rangle$ is a finite set of MLS tables $\{R_1, \ldots, R_m\}$ over the security hierarchy SH. Its propositional representation is*

$$X_\Delta = \bigcup_{i=1}^{m} \{r_i(\mathbf{c})/\lambda : \langle \mathbf{c}, \lambda \rangle \in R_i\}$$

It can be decomposed into a set of relational databases $\{\Delta^\lambda \mid \lambda \in SH\}$, such that

$$\Delta^\lambda = \{R_1^\lambda, \ldots, R_m^\lambda\}$$
$$R_i^\lambda = \{\mathbf{c} \mid \langle \mathbf{c}, \kappa \rangle \in R_i \ \& \ \kappa \leq \lambda\}$$

We write X^λ, instead of X_{Δ^λ}, for the propositionl representation of Δ^λ.

It may be useful to be able to ask questions relative to others' viewpoints. For example, the nurse (with clearance level 1) might need to ask, '*If a reporter (with clearance level 0) asks for a list of the current patients, what will be the answer ?*' She would put this as the query:

$$\mathsf{Ans}(X_{hosp}, (\mathsf{B}_0 p(x))/1) = \{BY\}$$

There is no need to allow for nested B operators.

Definition 6 (Secure Inference)   *Let X be a MLS database, $\lambda, \kappa \in SH$, $l \in \mathrm{Lit}$, $F, G \in L(\neg, \wedge, \vee, \exists, \forall, \mathsf{B}_\lambda)$, and $H \in L^0(\neg, \wedge, \vee, \exists, \forall)$.*

$$
\begin{array}{lll}
(l) & X \vdash l/\lambda & :\Longleftrightarrow \ X^\lambda \vdash_A l \\
(\wedge) & X \vdash (F \wedge G)/\lambda & :\Longleftrightarrow \ X \vdash F/\lambda \ \& \ X \vdash G/\lambda \\
(\vee) & X \vdash (F \vee G)/\lambda & :\Longleftrightarrow \ X \vdash F/\lambda \ or \ X \vdash G/\lambda \\
(\exists) & X \vdash (\exists x F(x))/\lambda & :\Longleftrightarrow \ \mathsf{Ans}(X, F(x)/\lambda) \neq \emptyset \\
(\forall) & X \vdash (\forall x F(x))/\lambda & :\Longleftrightarrow \ \mathsf{Ans}(X, \neg F(x)/\lambda) = \emptyset \\
(\mathsf{B}_\kappa) & X \vdash (\mathsf{B}_\kappa H)/\lambda & :\Longleftrightarrow \ \kappa \leq \lambda \ \& \ X^\kappa \vdash_A H
\end{array}
$$

where $\vdash_A$ is inference in $\mathbf{A}$.

In formalizing secure update, we do not follow the Bell-LaPadula model which requires a "no write down" policy (also called '∗-property') where users are only permitted to write to a level that dominates their own. This principle is supposed to prevent users from passing information directly downward through the security hierarchy. It makes only sense, however, in an intelligence context where a highly authorized user may be spy. In a security policy for normal organizations without particular intelligence concerns it seems more reasonable to assume that users in the higher level of the hierarchy can be trusted not to disclose sensitive information to lower levels. This also corresponds more closely to management practice. We will therefore assume the principle of "no write up" preventing users to overwrite information at levels above their own while permitting them to update lower level information either seriously or for the purpose of misinformation.

Inputs to MLS databases are annotated by the clearance level of the information supplier.

Definition 7 (Secure Update) *Let a be an atom, and l a literal.*

$$\mathsf{Upd}(X, (\mathsf{B}_\kappa a)/\lambda) := \begin{cases} X \cup \{a/\kappa\} & \text{if } \kappa \le \lambda \ \& \ X \not\vdash a/\kappa \\ X & \text{otherwise} \end{cases}$$

$$\mathsf{Upd}(X, (\mathsf{B}_\kappa \neg a)/\lambda) := X - \{a/\mu \in X : \mu \le \kappa \le \lambda\}$$

$$\mathsf{Upd}(X, l/\lambda) := \mathsf{Upd}(X, (\mathsf{B}_\lambda l)/\lambda)$$

The knowledge system of MLS databases, denoted by *SA*, is then defined as

$$SA = \begin{array}{|l|l|} \hline L_{\mathrm{KB}} & 2^{\mathrm{At} \times SH} \\ \hline L_{\mathrm{Query}}^0 & L^0(\neg, \wedge, \vee, \exists, \forall, \mathsf{B}_\kappa) \times SH \\ \hline L_{\mathrm{Ans}}^0 & \{\text{yes, no}\} \\ \hline L_{\mathrm{Input}} & \mathrm{Lit} \times SH \cup \mathsf{B}_\kappa \mathrm{Lit} \times SH \\ \hline \end{array}$$

Notice that in MLS databases, it is not possible to protect negative information by providing suitable misinformation. If, for instance, a hospital has to pretend that James Bond is among its patients, i.e. if the negative information $\neg p(JB)$ has to be protected, say at clearance level 3 (top secret), this cannot be achieved by means of simple MLS tables which would have to record negative entries in addition to positve ones. This is possible, however, in *MLS bitables* which are defined in [Wag97].

3 Specification and Execution of Reagents

Simple vivid agents whose mental state comprises only beliefs, and whose behavior is purely reactive, i.e. not based on any form of planning and plan execution, are called *reagents*. A reagent $\mathcal{A} = \langle X, EQ, RR \rangle$, on the basis of a knowledge system K, consists of

1. a knowledge base $X \in L_{\mathrm{KB}}$,
2. an event queue EQ being a list of instantiated event expressions, and
3. a set RR of *reaction rules*, consisting of epistemic and physical reaction and interaction rules which code the reactive and communicative behavior of the agent.

A multi-reagent system is a tuple of reagents: $S = \langle \mathcal{A}_1, \ldots, \mathcal{A}_n \rangle$.

3.1 Operational Semantics of Reaction Rules

Reaction rules encode the behavior of vivid agents in response to perception events created by the agent's perception subsystems, and to communication events created by communication acts of other agents. We distinguish between epistemic, physical and communicative reaction rules. We use L_{PEvt} and L_{CEvt} to denote the perception and communication event languages, and $L_{\mathrm{Evt}} = L_{\mathrm{PEvt}} \cup L_{\mathrm{CEvt}}$. The following table describes the different formats of epistemic, physical and communicative reaction rules:

epistemic	$\textit{Eff} \leftarrow \text{recvMsg}[\varepsilon, S], \textit{Cond}$
physical	$\text{do}(\alpha), \textit{Eff} \leftarrow \text{recvMsg}[\varepsilon, S], \textit{Cond}$
communicative	$\text{sendMsg}[\eta, R], \textit{Eff} \leftarrow \text{recvMsg}[\varepsilon, S], \textit{Cond}$

The event condition $\text{recvMsg}[\varepsilon(U), S]$ is a test whether the event queue of the agent contains a message of the form $\varepsilon(U)$ sent by some perception subsystem of the agent or by another agent identified by S, where $\varepsilon \in L_{\text{Evt}}$ represents a perception or a communication event type, and U is a suitable list of parameters. The epistemic condition $\textit{Cond} \in L_{\text{Query}}$ refers to the current knowledge state, and the epistemic effect $\textit{Eff} \in L_{\text{Input}}$ specifies an update of the current knowledge state.

In a physical reaction, $\text{do}(\alpha(V))$ calls a procedure realizing the action α with parameters V. In a communicative reaction, $\text{sendMsg}[\eta(V), R]$ sends the message $\eta \in L_{\text{CEvt}}$ with parameters V to the receiver R. Both perception and communication events are represented by incoming messages. We identify a communication act with the corresponding communication event which is perceived by the addressee of the communication act.

Reaction rules are triggered by events. The agent interpreter continuously checks the event queue of the agent. If there is a new event message, it is matched with the event condition of all reaction rules, and the epistemic conditions of those rules matching the event are evaluated. If they are satisfiable in the current knowledge base, all free variables in the rules are instantiated accordingly resulting in a set of triggered actions with associated epistemic effects. All these actions are then executed, leading to physical actions and to sending messages to other agents, and their epistemic effects are assimilated into the current knowledge base.

3.2 Defining the Execution of Reagents

The *perception-reaction-cycle* in the execution of reagents consists of the following steps:

repeat
1. Get the next message from the event queue, and check whether it triggers any reaction rules. If it does not, then repeat 1, else continue.

2. For each of the triggered reaction rules, assimilate the epistemic effect of the triggered action into the knowledge base, and if it is
1) a physical action, execute it by calling the associated procedure.
2) a communicative action, execute it by sending the corresponding message to the specified addressee.

The following *cycle* procedure is a Prolog-style meta-logic specification of the reagent execution model.

```
cycle( KB)
← newEvent( Evt),
    findall( ActEff, (reaction(ActEff,Evt,Cond), demo(KB,Cond)), ActEffs),
    perform( ActEffs, KB, KB'),
    cycle( KB').

perform( [], KB, KB).

perform( [Act/Eff | ActEffs], KB, KB')
← execute( Act),
    assimilate( Eff, KB, KB1),
    perform( ActEffs, KB1, KB').

execute( noAct).
execute( do(Act)) ← call( Act).
execute( send(Msg,To)) ← pvm_send( To, 1, Msg).
```

Here, reaction rules are represented as triples $\langle Act/Eff, Evt, Cond \rangle$ in the table *reaction*. A null action *noAct* is used to represent epistemic actions as *noAct/Eff*. An incoming event message *Evt* is popped from the message queue, and subsequently matched with suitable reaction rules. If the precondition *Cond* of a rule matching *Evt* holds in the current knowledge state, expressed by *demo(KB, Cond)*, the epistemic effect *Eff* associated with the action *Act* is assimilated into the knowledge base, the physical or communicative action *Act* is performed by means of appropriate procedure calls,[5] and *cycle* starts over with the updated knowledge base KB'. The *demo* and *assimilate* meta-predicates are formally related to our knowledge system concepts of inference and update:

$$demo(KB, Cond) :\Longleftrightarrow KB \vdash Cond$$
$$assimilate(Eff, KB, KB') :\Longleftrightarrow KB' = \text{Upd}(KB, Eff)$$

4 Secure Inter-Agent Communication

Similar to the KQML model of communication[6], we assume that the following requirements are met by any vivid agent system:

- Agents may interact asynchronously with more than one other agent at the same time.
- Agents are known to one another by their symbolic names, rather than their IP addresses. There may be special agents, called *facilitators*, which provide address information services in order to facilitate communication.
- An agent communicates verbally with other agents: actively by sending, and passively by receiving, typed messages.[7]

---

[5] The above realization of communication acts is based on the built-in *pvm_send* of PVM-Prolog.

[6] See, e.g., [Lab96].

[7] In addition, there may be non-verbal forms of communication, e.g. by means of perception.

- Messages may be sent over network links, or via specific radio links, or, similar to human communication, by means of audio signals. The transport mechanism is not part of the communication model of vivid agents. Certain assumptions about message passing, however, are necessary or useful:
  - When an agent sends a message, it directs that message to a specific addressee.
  - When an agent receives a message, it knows the sender of that message.
  - The order of messages in point-to-point communication is preserved.
  - No message gets lost.
- Message types are defined by a *communication event language* based on speech act theory.
- The arguments of a message (i.e. the 'propositional content' of the corresponding communication act) may affect the mental state of both the sender and the receiver.

Communication in multiagent systems should be based on the *speech act theory* of Austin and Searle [Aus62, Sea69], an informal theory within analytical philosophy of language. The essential insight of speech act theory was that an utterance by a speaker is, in general, not the mere statement of a true or false sentence, but rather an *action* of a specific kind (such as an assertion, a request, a promise, etc.). Therefore, logic alone is not sufficient for a semantic account of verbal communication.

In our model of agents, the semantics of communicative actions is rather determined by

1. a mentalistic model of agents, defining their *mental state*, together with a notion of mental conditions and mental effects of actions,
2. a satisfaction relation between mental states and mental conditions,
3. an operation that assimilates mental effects into a mental state,
4. the assignment of a mental precondition and a mental effect to each action, and
5. associating with each type of communicative action a type of reaction (of the addressee of a communication act).

In this paper, we use the simple model of *reagents*, where the mental state consists only of beliefs (represented in a KB), the mental satisfaction relation and the mental assimilate operation are ⊢ and Upd, and communicative actions are represented by means of reaction rules.

We use a functional predicate

agent(Agent, Clearance),

for recording the clearance levels of all agents known to an agent. Agents without an entry in this table will be assigned clearance level 0 (unclassified) by default. The following definition of secure communication is based on the assumption that all agents involved in the communication are believed to be truthful and competent by their fellow agents, implying that they normally provide correct information.

The basic inter-agent communication functionality consists of three types of communication events: tell, ask, and reply.

4.1 Tell

The piece of information conveyed by a *tell* act is assimilated into the beliefs of the receiver (according to the above definition of secure update).

This is expressed by the following reaction rules:

$$r_1 : F/C \leftarrow \text{recvMsg}[\text{tell}(F), S], \, agent(S, C)$$
$$r_2 : F/0 \leftarrow \text{recvMsg}[\text{tell}(F), S], \, \neg \exists C(agent(S, C))$$

where F is a formula representing an admissible input, i.e. it has either the form of an atom, $r(\mathbf{c})$, or a negated atom, $\neg r(\mathbf{c})$, possibly prefixed by a subscripted belief operator B_λ, and C is the clearance level of the sender S (F, C, and S are logical variables like in Prolog).

4.2 Ask

Since only agents with incomplete information will ask other agents, we may assume that the knowledge system of an asking agent is F, the system of relational factbases, or any conservative extension of it. Agents with knowledge systems such as A, or SA, have complete information, i.e. for any if-query F, they believe either F or $\neg F$. Such agents will be asked for information by other agents, and they will reply to them, but they will never ask themselves.

For practical reasons, each query is associated with an ID, called *query handle*. This ID is used to store queries in the system table *query* until the answers are received, or until they are timed out. Like in KQML, we distinguish between

1. **askif**: asking an if-query,
2. **askone**: asking for one (possibly non-deterministic) answer substitution, like in Prolog, and
3. **askall**: asking for all answer substitutions (i.e. a table), like in SQL.

The reaction rules for handling an ask-if event use the meta-predicate *ifans(IfQuery, Answer)* which holds in the current knowledge state X, whenever $\text{Ans}(X, IfQuery) = Answer$.

$$r_3 : \text{sendMsg}[\text{replyif}(QID, A), S]$$
$$\leftarrow \text{recvMsg}[\text{askif}(QID, F), S], \, agent(S, C) \wedge ifans(F/C, A)$$

$$r_4 \;\; \text{sendMsg}[\text{replyif}(QID, A), S]$$
$$\leftarrow \text{recvMsg}[\text{askif}(QID, F), S], \, \neg \exists C(agent(S, C)) \wedge ifans(F/0, A)$$

where F is a formula representing a relational database if-query, and the answer value A is either **yes** or **no**. The reactions to ask-all and ask-one events are defined in a similar way:

r_5 : sendMsg[replyall(QID, A), S]
 $\leftarrow$ recvMsg[askall(QID, F), S], $agent(S, C) \wedge allans(F/C, A)$

r_6 : sendMsg[replyone(QID, A), S]
 $\leftarrow$ recvMsg[askone(QID, F), S], $agent(S, C) \wedge oneans(F/C, A)$

using the meta-predicates *allans* and *oneans* providing an answer set, resp. a single answer substitution. We have omitted the rules for the case of a sender without an entry in the *agent* table, since they are analogous to the corresponding rule above.

4.3 Reply

Replies to an if-query are processed as follows:

$$r_7 : F \leftarrow \text{recvMsg[replyif}(QID, \text{yes}), S], query(QID, F)$$
$$r_8 : \neg F \leftarrow \text{recvMsg[replyif}(QID, \text{no}), S], query(QID, F)$$

4.4 An Example of Secure Communication

In our final example, we assume three information agents:

1. A software agent d serving as the personal assistant to the doctor in charge of treating MJ and BY. This agent works with a relational database which does not have complete information about diagnoses. Its initial state is $X_d^0 = \{d(BY, alc)\}$.
2. A software agent s serving as the personal assistant to a secretary working in the hospital administration.
3. The hospital MLS database X_{hosp} from above, which reacts to tell and ask events by assimilating new inputs and replying to queries. Its agent name is hdb (hospital database). It uses the security classifications $agent(s,1)$ and $agent(d,2)$.

Case 1: Assume that a reporter asks the secretary (by email) whether MJ is currently a patient in the hospital. The personal assistant of the secretary, although knowing that $p(MJ)$, asks hdb whether the reporter may know that fact by sending the message askif($B_0p(MJ)$), firing at hdb the reaction rule r_3 with the following instantiation (we omit the query ID):

sendMsg[replyif(no), s]
 $\leftarrow$ recvMsg[askif($B_0p(MJ)$), s], $agent(s, 1) \wedge ifans((B_0p(MJ))/1, \text{no})$

since $\text{Ans}(X_{hosp}^0, (B_0p(MJ))/1) = \text{no}$. After receiving this negative answer, s forwards it to the reporter.

Case 2: Assume that the doctor is wondering if BY was diagnosed to have hepatitis by one of her colleagues, and thus sends the message $askif(Q2, d(BY, hep))$ to hdb, recording the query together with its ID $Q2$ as the fact $query(Q2, d(BY, hep))$. This triggers at hdb the rule

sendMsg[replyif$(Q2, no), d]$
$\leftarrow$ recvMsg[askif$(Q2, d(BY, hep)), d]$, $agent(d, 2) \wedge ifans(d(BY, hep))/2, no)$

since $\mathsf{Ans}(X^0_{hosp}, d(BY, hep)/2) = no$. Agent d reacts to the reply by applying the rule r_7:

$\neg d(BY, hep) \leftarrow$ recvMsg[replyif$(Q2, no), hdb]$, $query(Q2, d(BY, hep))$

yielding the update

$$X^1_d = \mathsf{Upd}(X^0_d, \neg d(BY, hep)) = \{d(BY, alc)\}$$

Notice that X_d, as a relational database, is not capable of recording the negative information $\neg d(BY, hep)$, although it would be useful for avoiding further questions (communication overload) in the style of replication. This indicates that we have to extend the concept of relational databases in the frmework of multidatabase systems.

5 Conclusion

We have shown how the concept of multi-level security can be applied in vivid agent systems. For this purpose, we have defined

1. the knowledge system of MLS databases including a formalization of the "no read/write up" security model, and
2. basic inter-agent communication rules which take security classifications into consideration.

A more realistic treatment would have to account for MLS databases with integrity constraints (such as functional dependencies), where 'cover stories' are overridden by attribute values with a higher classification because of the inconsistency created by the violation of functional dependencies. This can be achieved by a straightforward extension of our present model.

Acknowledgment The author is grateful to the referees whose comments and suggestions have helped to improve the paper.

References

[Aus62] J.L Austin. *How to Do Things with Words.* Harvard University Press, Cambridge (MA), 1962.

[JS91] S. Jajodia and R. Sandhu. Toward a multilevel secure relational data model. In *Proc. ACM SIGMOD*, pages 50–59. ACM Press, 1991.

[Lab96] Y. Labrou. *Semantics for an Agent Communication Language.* PhD thesis, University of Maryland Graduate School, 1996.

[Lan81] C.E. Landwehr. Formal models for computer security. *ACM Computing Surveys*, 13(3):247–278, 1981.

[Sea69] J.R. Searle. *Speech Acts.* Cambridge University Press, Cambridge (UK), 1969.

[SWQ94] K. Smith, M. Winslett, and X. Qian. Formal query languages for secure relational databases. *ACM Transactions on Database Systems*, 19(4):626–662, 1994.

[Wag95] G. Wagner. From information systems to knowledge systems. In W. Hesse E.D. Falkenberg and A. Olivé, editors, *Information System Concepts*, pages 179–194, London, 1995. Chapman & Hall.

[Wag96] G. Wagner. A logical and operational model of scalable knowledge- and perception-based agents. In W. Van de Velde and J.W. Perram, editors, *Agents Breaking Away (Proc. of MAAMAW'96)*, pages 26–41. Springer-Verlag, LNAI 1038, 1996.

[Wag97] G. Wagner. Conceptual foundations of artificial agents. Habilitation thesis, Univ. Leipzig, 1997.

Author Index

Springer
and the
environment

At Springer we firmly believe that an
international science publisher has a
special obligation to the environment,
and our corporate policies consistently
reflect this conviction.
We also expect our business partners –
paper mills, printers, packaging
manufacturers, etc. – to commit
themselves to using materials and
production processes that do not harm
the environment. The paper in this
book is made from low- or no-chlorine
pulp and is acid free, in conformance
with international standards for paper
permanency.

 Springer

Lecture Notes in Artificial Intelligence (LNAI)

Lecture Notes in Computer Science